Acton Society Siena Series

Non-Conforming Radicals of Europe

Edited with a Commentary
by Edward Goodman

DUCKWORTH

i

First published in 1983 by
Gerald Duckworth & Co. Ltd
The Old Piano Factory,
43 Gloucester Crescent, London NW1

ISBN 0 7156 1712 5

Typeset by Dorchester Typesetting Group Ltd.,
Trinity Street, Dorchester and
printed in Great Britain by Unwin Brothers Limited,
The Gresham Press, Old Woking, Surrey

ERRATA Page vi

Biographical notes should read:

Robert Oakeshott

Formerly of the *Financial Times*. A leading authority on the Mondragon Co-operatives and a founder of Job Ownership Ltd., where he works.

Major-General A.E. Younger, DSO, OBE

Former Head of the Royal United Services Institute for Defence Studies. Chairman Acton Society Youth Unemployment Committee, 1979.

CONTENTS

Over the past few years, the Acton Society has been discussing in a continuing series of seminars, subjects relating to 'The desirable sizes of political and economic units and the quality of working life'. This book is a selection of some of the papers given, together with a commentary which attempts to examine the philosophy they have in common. The title is explained by the fact that some of the most individualistic of the participants chose to write on topics of their own conscience and concern rather than strictly that chosen for the seminar. The various subjects that arose were set in the wider context of the Acton Society's concern for the reassertion of human values in the utilitarian industrial process.

The Acton Society takes its name from the nineteenth century historian, Lord Acton, who held that the justification of Liberty lay in the realisation of human values.

List of Contributors to the book and their biographies

Professor Philip Abrams
Head of the Department of Sociology and Social Administration, Durham University, from 1971. Born 1933. Died on October 31st, 1981. Author of *John Locke: Two Tracts on Government*; *The Origins of British Sociology* and *Communes, Sociology and Society* (with A. McCulloch).

René Alleau
French medieval scholar. Has specialised in medieval technology and artisan cultures. Scientific Counsellor to the Encyclopedia Universalis (traditional sciences) and to the Larousse Encyclopedia.

Julia Bamford
Lecturer in the Department of Economics, Siena University.

Père Alain Birou
Dominican monk. Runs 'Économie et Humanisme' and has radio programme of social commentary. Co-author of *Pour un autre developpement*.

Professor Tom Burns
Head of the Department of Sociology, Edinburgh University. Author of *The Management of Innovation*, *Industrial Man* and *The BBC – Public Institution and Private World*.

Dr. Margaret Canovan
Department of Politics, University of Keele.

Sira Dermen
Psycho-analyst and philosopher. An authority on Simone Weil and warden of a home for disturbed children.

Roger Garaudy
Academician of both French and Soviet academics. Resigned from the Communist party and puts forward a neo-Catholic view.

Jean Gimpel
Author of *The Medieval Machine*, *The Cathedral Builders* and *Contre l'art et les artistes*. Renowned for his small-scale models of appropriate technology.

Edward Goodman
Founder and Chairman of The Acton Society. Author of *Forms of Public Control and Ownership*, *The Impact of Size*, which deals with small-scale units, and *Liberty and Revolution*. He is a member of the Joseph Rowntree Social Service Trust.

Peter Harper
Formerly with ITG and a lecturer in Tehran. Now head of a commune in Wales.

Dr. Krishan Kumar
Faculty of Social Studies, Keynes College, Kent University. Has been visiting professor at Harvard and Stanford Universities. Senior Research Adviser to The Acton Society.

Norman Macrae
Deputy Editor of *The Economist*.

Albert Meister
Distinguished French sociologist. Head of the Centre d'étude des Mouvements Sociaux. An authority on self-management and decentralised socialism. Died in January 1982 at the age of 53. Author of *L'Afrique peut-elle partir?*, *Le Système Mexicain*, *l'Autogestion en uniforme* and *l'Inflation créative*.

Robert Oakeshott
Formerly of *The Financial Times*, and founder of Sunderlandia and Mondragon. At present runs Job Ownership Ltd.

Major-General A. E. Younger, DSO, OBE
Former Head of the Royal United Services Institute for Defence Studies. Former member of Army Council. Chairman Acton Society Youth Unemployment Committee, 1979.

Foreword

This book arises out of several Acton Society seminars on the subjects of 'The desirable sizes of political and economic units' and 'The quality of working life'. The Acton Society in conjunction with the Acton Society Trust has organised a series of seminars on these subjects and others related to them, in Italy and England, commencing at the Certosa di Pontignano, Siena, in 1977 and continuing until the present day. The seminars were attended by men and women from several European countries – France, Italy, Germany, Sweden, Yugoslavia, Britain – and from the United States. These seminarists were drawn from many walks of life and included a variety of distinguished members of international organisations, journalists and eminent academics as well as regular Acton Society members.

The subjects chosen by the organisers are reflected in three volumes: economics and human values; the role of central organisations and other hierarchies in making small units of organisation successful; and the various forms taken by organisations in attempts to limit corporate and individual liability. The present volume is different. It is a selection of papers with a unifying moral theme, together with an extended introduction which attempts to explain the philosophy they have in common.

The title under which they have been collected comes from a witty remark made to me by the late Professor Albert Meister, during the first seminar at the Certosa di Pontignano, Siena. 'I am not sure why we all get on so well,' he said, 'but I think it is that you have chosen all nonconformists – not in the English way you use the word. But it is true. I think that you have tried to gather some of the most nonconforming radicals in Europe. Is that right? But don't forget that we are also trying to rediscover our Catholic roots whilst we are enjoying ourselves in this monastery. Radical in both senses, is that not so?'.

He was probably right. Some of the most individualistic of the participants chose to write on topics of their own conscience and concern rather than strictly those chosen for the seminar. The various subjects that arose were set in the wider context of the Acton Society's concern for the reassertion of human values in the utilitarian industrial process. No paper is specifically left-wing or right-wing: all are feeling out a position in the future or preparing the ground for one.

E.G.

Acknowledgements

I should like very much especially to acknowledge the assistance of Miss Sally Smith in bringing about this book as well as in helping to edit some of the papers. It has taken a long time and I should not have been able to continue without her encouragement. I also wish gratefully to acknowledge the hard work of Mrs. Jackie Lebe typing. There are a number of other people for whose service I am very grateful: particularly Mr. Simon Carter for his translations, Mrs. Nina Farhi for her criticisms and Dr. Anne Green for translating and editing several of the papers and for reading through my manuscript. Acknowledgements are also due to individual editors of papers. Mrs. Gaenor Amory and Mr. John Moorehead did a lot of work at an early stage in their preparation.

The occasion should not be missed of thanking Professors Franco Romani, Giovanni Coda Nunziante, Marcello de Cecco and Giovanni Grottanelli for their support on numerous occasions at Siena as well as for making the seminars possible. I am particularly indebted to Franco Romani for the countless conversations which suggested the subjects discussed at these seminars. The last to thank is the person responsible for suggesting a great many of the names of those who attended both the seminars at Siena and who I think understood the collective character they should have and how each should fit into each – Mme Monique Stengel of le Centre du Developpement, OECD, Paris.

The Acton Society as a whole is most indebted to the Rector of Siena University for allowing us to use the beautiful Certosa di Pontignano for our meetings in 1977 and 1979.

E.G.

CHAPTER I

A confusion of issues

> We, in the ages lying
> In the buried past of the earth,
> Built in Nineveh with our sighing
> And Babel itself with our mirth,
> And o'erthrew them with prophesying
> To the old of the new world's worth,
> For each age is a dream that is dying,
> Or one that is coming to birth.
>
> O'Shaughnessy[1]

There are a growing number of questions about the nature, working life and conditions of industrial society which thoughtful people recognise will have to be faced before the end of the century by every technologically advanced society. Opinion is divided: divided not along lines of political allegiance or principle, but according to whether the holder be an optimist or a pessimist. Can mankind's powers of adaptation taken together with his values and the flexibility offered by its use of scientific knowledge, find ways through the dangers that beset it?

Judgement may be suspended while a few of the dangers are recited. Then, later, the nature of industrial society in which they occur must be briefly examined; for this is a nature shared by all technologically advanced societies regardless of ideology. It is indeed the characteristic assumptions of industrialism that are of importance, rather than the ideologies of the contemporary world such as communism, socialism or capitalism, for they all, in a variety of ways, share these assumptions. Even at that point an optimistic or pessimistic judgement will not be justified until at least some of the issues of technological determinism have been debated. Can industrial trends be reversed or their course altered? Has not industrial society become a self-perpetuating artifact in which human beings act out their parts as a means of hiding from themselves their own impotence? Can significant changes be brought about simply by change of values or the naming of social goals? Again the issue of ideology is raised – not any particular ideology of the twentieth century; but whether or not the sheer force of ideas has the power to change social tendencies at all.

In spite of this plea for objectivity and withheld judgement, the account of the issues involved, especially when recited in very summary form, will be depressing. This is bound to be so because it is a one-sided account, even more, because it is not set against any philosophy of change which might yield consistent and positive approaches to all these challenges. But there may well be grounds for optimism; for, if each item on the list is a symptom of the same malaise and if that malaise is curable within the terms of a universal diagnosis, then there is no cause to be gloomy about the future of the human race.

Size, populations and nationalism

Three phenomena characteristic of modern industrial society stand out in many of the papers given at the Siena seminars. The first is the increasing importance given to very large units; for example, units such as towns and cities, industrial corporations or departments of state. The second, derived from that, is the concentration of political and economic power. The third is the deterioration in the standards of skill and responsibility required of the average human being during his working life. These were the principal themes of the series of seminars; but at the first seminar the view was pressed that before the main topics were discussed, there were a number of more basic issues which should be ventilated first: the population explosion and food production, energy supply, the using up of irreplaceable resources, technology, growth rates and a number of other topics relating to the Third World specifically.

Many of the most urgent problems to be faced by society in future, it was claimed, would be the result of the rapidly increased rate of growth in the world's populations and their relentless demands, articulated through the needs of many different cultures and national economies on the earth's finite resources. Professor Tom Burns quoted in his paper, *The Moral Economy of the Rat Race*, the bald comparison made by F. Braudel[2] that whereas the world population had doubled in the four hundred years between 1400 and 1800, it now doubles every thirty to forty years. Population statistics are notoriously unreliable as the basis for prediction; nevertheless, this fact does provide a dramatic setting to any discussion about population growth and its political consequences, which most people will agree are immense.

Estimates of the size of the world's future population vary. A rate of increase of 2 per cent per annum would yield a population of six billion at the end of the century; 1 or 3 per cent per annum, approximately eight billion. Therefore, barring disasters on a grand scale, a figure of seven billion might seem, from the broad tendencies then apparent, to be a fair estimate of the people living in the world in the year 2000. In that event, India would probably account for nearly 700 million of these and China 1,000 (ie an American billion) or more. In the same period, if the most recent tendencies are continued, and having regard always to the unreliability of demographic predictions, the population of the industrial West will be no more than, say, 1,000 million. However, it should also be noted that the present fall in the rate of growth of some populations in the highly industrialised parts of the world, contrary to Malthus's theorem, reinforces confidence in policies on a world scale for defeating the most pessimistic of these forecasts.

In this connection there are two significant correlations: the first relates wealthy countries and falling or stable sizes of population, and the other real poverty and very high birth rates. The inevitable conclusion reached by most who attended the first seminar was the need for a better distribution of the wealth and goods produced by the affluent countries. Unfortunately, it seemed neither the means nor the will to do this efficiently exist. It might be said that industtrial capitalism, solely on utilitarian grounds and disregarding the human consequences in terms of such phenomena as alienation, has solved the problems of production. But only in a few places has it matched the volume of production of which it is capable with corresponding machinery for distribution.

Few would underestimate the dangerous implications of a population explosion in the poorest parts of the world, especially in Asia, Africa and South America. It is to these countries, freshly infected by the virus of nationalism, that the wealthy countries of both western and eastern blocs export their easy-to-use, but sophisticated, armaments. In these countries, too, the population growth has been most rapid and the proportion of inhabitants under the age of 21, the greatest. Indeed, it is likely that in Sri Lanka, Bangladesh, Vietnam and Kampuchea[3] and parts of South America the majority of the population are under 25.

South-East Asia, formerly one of the richest rice-growing regions of the world, in the late 1970s had become a disaster area. The political collapse of Kampuchea and the rise to power of the Pol Pot stimulated sections of young people to acts of unbelievable inhumanity against other people with established positions. In Kampuchea[4] it was said that courts martial of young people between the ages of 17 and 19 had tried and executed their parents' contemporaries.

The epidemic of nationalism has spread from Europe across Asia and Africa. Combined with state socialism and one-party government in the form of national socialism, it produced, first in Germany and Russia and then in many other parts of the world, regimes of persecution and terror, which have now become the standard political norm for all tiny groups of ruthless men and women wishing to control nations on their own brutal terms: left- or right-wing extremists, generals or colonels or simply terrorists with no other identity. Besides this crude violence, nationalism is responsible for many other evils that threaten world society. Almost every country is concerned with its balance of payments surpluses and deficits and the other consequences of trade wars. Then there is the enormous cost of defence budgets inflated by modern technology. For example, in the United States at least half the research undertaken in industrial R & D departments, as well as in universities, is done for defence purposes.[5]

Overshadowing all these concerns is the desire of each developed country for an economic growth rate of more than zero. The number of such countries is all the time increasing. Soon only those' with religious or cultural objections will not demand the same material standards as the West. Yet nature has not the resources to satisfy these demands. Only the West with its present advantages can take the lead in adapting the philosophy of industrialism so that, instead of attempting to satisfy unlimited appetites, it tries to meet the more modest aims of providing human beings throughout the world with the limited means needed by them to find balanced expressions of their individual and characteristic 'bests' in the communities in which they live. In a more human world all kinds of appetites, besides those for material things, need satisfying.

Worthy objectives of material development, it can be argued, may be achieved in industrialised countries within a framework of reallocating resources, as well as devising new techniques that are less spendthrift of natural resources: objectives forming part of what Acton might have called the politics of compassion and concern, or of stimulating the abilities of the worst off and least advantaged in society. It is important to see that the productive capacity is available to do this; but to do it efficiently we need to redefine how we spend our incomes and how we use our present resources rather than to go blindly about increasing our gross national products. This is another aspect of the distribution problem neglected by industrial capitalism and is the theme of H. V. Hodson's excellent book:

'A zero growth economy means anything but stagnation. . . . Conventional measures of growth, such as GNP,' he says, 'are like false prospectuses – they conceal unpleasant facts which might disclose what improvident bad husbandmen and negligent trustees we have been. We could use the same quantity of resources of energy and manpower to entirely different effect. First, we have to decide our priorities. When we have got them right, we can reallocate our resources and plan the use of an energy, human as well as carbon-fossilate, and we can draw upon other sources of energy that neither pollute nor are exhaustible.'[6]

Rich North and poor South: the need for a new model of industrialism

Certainly, every society must decide its priorities and not use more of the world's scarce resources than it does at the moment. This means zero growth rates, but how can they be realistically advocated in view of the expected population explosion discussed above and in view of the known poverty of at least two-thirds of the world's population? Surely then, policies must be conceived on a world-wide scale and be based upon realistic assessments of men's all round needs, both as consumers and producers. In their papers, Professors Garaudy and Adler-Karlsson make similar points, but Adler-Karlsson favours a kind of growth moratorium for rich countries, whereas Garaudy, the French and Soviet academician, is opposed to any kind of zero growth rate philosophy because:

> 'There can be no question of stopping expansion when there are billions of people in the Third World and millions in the rich countries without the means of living a truly human life. The direction of growth should be toward the human enrichment of all, not toward augmenting the power and profits of the few. The aim is that expansion should serve needs, and not needs expansion.'[7]

This quotation from a paper written by him in 1977 not merely raises the somewhat conventional question of whether it is possible to slow down the production of luxury goods for the advanced countries and the rich, whilst speeding up the production of essentials for the poor and needy where they live; but also it points to the more basic issues discussed in the Brandt Report of 1980.[8] Is it, indeed, possible for the interests of the fully developed, the developing and the Third World economies to be made compatible without really drastic changes of assumption and attitude? The underlying assumption of all industrial growth has always been the continuing cheap supply of the raw materials it needed. Thus, the present generation of developing countries has turned away from producing food and other domestic goods for local consumption in their own countries to growing crops to pay for the oil and other essential raw materials of the industrialism they are set upon achieving. This dilemma forms part of a vast topic embedded in which are a great many problems, many of which are dealt with in the Brandt Report. Only greater understanding of the South, in human as well as economic terms, through close study and discussion over a lengthy period of time will reveal the complicated fabric of the ramifications of this topic.

Meanwhile, in the context of some of the issues raised by the present series of papers, Western industrial societies would do well to reconsider the model of industrialism which they offer to the rest of the world. Do their economic practices and techniques match their expressed political values? Returning to the size issue for the moment and taking into account the need to economise on the fuels used in transport, it would be reasonable to ask two further questions: whether smaller units of production could not be employed to serve the needs of those living within a radius of distribution conceived on a more human scale than today's mass markets, and whether the methods of production in these more decentralised organisations could not be less impersonal and more demanding of the human powers of skill and adaptation than those used in today's mass production factories?

Energy

If there were one subject discussed during the whole period of the Siena series of seminars from 1977-1981 which yielded more pessimism than any other, it was that of energy, especially, of course, oil. Writing in 1982 and looking back, it may well be legitimate to question whether this pessimism might not have been unduly severe. But it would be ungenerous not to recognise that the alarm and concern generated by the oil crises of 1973 and 1978, together with the voices of the conservation and radical movements generally, began a quite new period in the collective attitude of mankind, certainly in the West if not throughout the world, towards its resources and towards its physical environment.

How inexhaustible are the more conventional forms of energy supply? How expensive in real terms or in comparison with consumer goods and wages are they likely to become? What substitutes exist and what are likely to be developed first in the short term and then in the longer period? How should contemporary policies take account of these perspectives? These were the questions raised both in the papers and in the discussions.

Paul-Marc Henry, formerly president of the Development Centre of the O.E.C.D. and now French Ambassador at Beirut, estimated in his 1977 paper[9] that at the end of the century the cost of electricity world-wide would be four times as great as it was then. This was an optimistic conclusion compared with the forecasts made later at the end of 1979 in respect of oil supplies. Assuming only the 1977-79 rate of consumption and without making any allowances at all for any more countries becoming industrialised than were then industrialised, it was estimated that the then accessible oil reserves of the world would be exhausted within the following 40 years. Such a gloomy prospect lay at the root of many of the papers presented in the Siena series generally. Producers of oil would be forced to move into marginal lands and to drill deeper as well as to exploit remote sources under the sea and the frozen ice caps of the Arctic and Antarctic; the oil shale in Colorado and the tar sands of Alberta would need to be exploited. Other possibilities had to be examined such as processing liquid fuel from coal. But what would the cost of exploiting these sources be? Some idea of the magnitude of the investment that would be forced on producers by the needs of industrial users might be deduced from the fact that oil rigs in the North Sea were costing more than twenty-five times as much as a traditional oil rig in the Middle East or Texas; or that the pipeline from the North-West territories to Quebec had cost 16 billion dollars against an estimate three years earlier of 5 billion.

All these alternative and substitute sources of supply for oil and natural gas continue to be investigated, but the capital needed for research, development and production were so prodigious that they could only be accumulated at the price of severe inroads into consumer spending power, or even larger increases in the rate of inflation. These depressing assertions were reinforced by the fact of world-wide recession, high interest rates, falling living standards and unemployment in industrial countries exceeding 30 million men and women. Nearly all of this was attributed to the oil crises of 1973 and 1978.

Such was the pessimistic picture that continued to build up until the middle or even the end of 1981. By then supply exceeded demand substantially. Many new fields (more accessible than the Alaskan fields or those under the ice caps) had been discovered and prospected, and the number of drill rigs in operation about doubled in the 1977-81 period. Oil was even found on the border between Ulster and Eire! Supply had increased by so much in the first few months of 1982 that practically all development of marginal fields stopped and most expensive research into developing substitutes has been shelved at least until the end of the depression. On the demand side a combination of the recession, heat-conservation measures and switching to cheaper forms of energy was responsible for a fall approaching 15 per cent.

This is the story of the oil market in the period covered by these papers and discussions, which shows that the pessimism of radical opinion – and of the market itself – was not always well-founded. The nonconforming radicals ought, perhaps, to have shown more confidence in the adaptability and resourcefulness of human nature. Nevertheless, they can well claim that a considerable amount of credit for the fall in demand and the conservation and switching to other forms of energy has been due to their collective voice. Moreover, they should emphasise that the crisis is not yet over; the price of oil is still some ten times what it was in 1973, industrial activity world-wide is still in deep recession and the reserves of oil in the known accessible fields is still limited. Demand for oil, without public opinion being constantly reminded of the need to conserve, will almost certainly become undisciplined again and prices are unlikely to be stable unless the search for new fields and research into viable alternative fuels continues.

There is, for instance, the basic zinc chloride battery which can be recharged in a few minutes at home and will power a vehicle for at least 24 hours. This is an energy decision in favour of the decentralised economy – the home or the neighbourhood. But many of the conventional alternative sources of electricity supply unhappily favour centralisation. Nuclear and hydraulic power and coal-fuelled stations are most economical when administered and controlled centrally. This was acknowledged by the summit meeting of Western Heads of Government at Venice in July 1980. But there are still grave risks to take into account, especially in relation to the generation of nuclear power, risks which the North-South Report underlines:

> 'The problems of radiation risk in power production and in the storage and transport of nuclear waste are unsolved.'[10]

There is also the possibility of theft of materials from which nuclear weapons could be made privately by individuals, or clandestinely by nation-states not party to the various nuclear weapon treaties and agreements. Moreover, highly vocal and critical public opinion has still to be taken into account.

Beyond these objections are two more down-to-earth ones. The first is, can the huge amounts of long-term investment in nuclear power systems be afforded on top of a race in sophisticated technologically based armaments costing nearly 500 billion dollars a year? Surely not, especially bearing in mind that nuclear power generation is probably not the ultimate answer that more fundamental research into exhaustible forms of energy will provide. The second objection is political and libertarian. Nuclear power systems could only be economical if centralised. Whoever controlled such a system of national energy supply or a system supplying a number of contiguous states, be they politicians, technologists or an elite of union leaders, would be in a position to hold any given country to ransom. This point is emphasised when account is taken of the political instability of many countries: regimes change overnight and centralised generating systems using a single form of power make the whole of a nation's industry, commerce and domestic life vulnerable to their caprices.

Possibly a more simple example of the need to face the political dilemma posed by an idea to centralise the production of energy arises in Africa. There is enough hydraulic power between the two bends in the Zaire River (previously the Congo) to generate enough electricity for the whole of Africa with still plenty to spare to beam to Europe by satellite; the first generating stations of the complex needed to put this bold concept into effect is already under construction and supplies the copper mines of Zaire.

If such bodies supplying power on an international scale were to come into existence, they should be brought under some form of independent, international, legal control. One of the strongest principles of British nineteenth-century liberalism was that all rights, duties, privileges and offices of every type of organisation, or corporation, can and ought to be defined in laws, or customs of law, which in turn are enforceable through the courts and arm of the law. This lesson has still to be applied to international organisations and institutions, as well as multinational commercial corporations. Another lesson from the British nineteenth-century liberal experience that bears repetition and the search for new applications, is that no matter how effective may be the power of the courts and central law-making bodies, countervailing powers have also to be vested in decentralised, competitive local units of initiative. According to several of the Siena papers this principle applies conspicuously to the need for the development of alternative small-scale energy sources at competitive prices.[11] Of these, solar heating is already playing an important role in America and the Mediterranean; others, such as wind and tidal generation, are yet to be developed so as to be economically used on a local scale. As the Brandt report believes:

'Ultimately, the human community must rely on inexhaustible sources of energy; solar in the broadest sense, which includes biomass, wind and tides; new forms of nuclear energy supplementing hydro-electric and geothermal sources.'[12]

The cost in investment and research would be enormous, indeed formidable, but if two sets of energy choices could possibly be developed – the first provided by hydraulic and, if needs be, some nuclear power under centralised control or on an international scale, and the other provided by a variety of renewable energy sources decentralised and on a local scale – the consequences for our political and personal liberties would be profound. This is one of the insights which Dr. René Alleau revealed:

> 'Where applied technology is concerned, one has to find a solution for every individual case. . . . There is no overall solution. In each case you have to find the right technology – you have to make very thorough local studies: not only technical studies, but also socio-logical and cultural studies, and also studies of mentality – these are extremely important because industries can transform people, and we can't really commit cultural genocides – cultural genocides are being committed where industries are implanted into inhospit-able countries.'[13]

Man and nature

Hitherto, most of our political thinkers have regarded as sacrosanct the maxim that every society, every civilisation, has been characte-rised by the form of its energy power – slave power and the pyramids, the hand mill and water mill gave feudal society what the steam mill gave early industrial society and one can say that the grid system gave monopoly capitalism. But, in future, if these proposals were to be adopted and the investment made to develop them, the relationship would be reversed. A society, down to the level of the local small town and its environment, would be able, given reasonably similar costs, to choose a form of energy power to accord with the values and aspirations of its inhabitants. Garaudy's paper[14] follows through similar lines of thought and sees very much the value of small, decentralised units of energy-production using a variety of methods of generation other than nuclear-, oil- or coal-based. The advantages are both ecological and political, and afford one of the most delightful prospects of a possible future. One can foresee individually designed buildings of necessarily large undertakings built around and in the more densely populated cities, whilst small-scale units of industrial work were carried on in pleasant, small buildings in the countryside, or in neighbourhood economies, powered by the forms of energy most suited to the ecology and other natural features of the locality.

This somewhat idyllic vision is abruptly intruded upon with the question, why not now? Is not this the kind of development which our present-day electricity supply system ought to have made possible? No technological imperative has been responsible for this century following the pattern of industrial development pioneered by the steam mill and the system of railway lines; to the contrary, men, it seems, have deliberately given up the optimistic vision offered by their own thought out co-operation with nature for the sake of their moral and political, as well as their material needs. Gone is the confidence, voiced more firmly by Marx than by any other nineteenth-century prophet, in the power of the alliance between man and physical nature to make continuous progress against necessity and, in doing so, to increase man's knowledge of himself and that of the universe about him. Instead of the decentralisation of society into authentically-sized communities desired by nearly all nineteenth-century humanists, including Marx, the concentration of industrial organisation has been matched by the concentration of populations into faceless conurbations of mass living. It is a strain that human beings probably cannot long stand; in fact this movement into megapolitan cities and suburbs has been compared to the mass swarming of lemmings to the clifftop in search of suicide. Modern industrial society has already created sizes that are becoming intolerable. What of a future in twenty-five years when Yona Friedman[15] suggests that Java will have a population of over 100 millions and when Paul-Marc Henry's[16] prediction for the city of San Paolo works out at a population of 125 million people?

The State does not wither away

Perhaps the most alarming threat posed by the cult of gargantuanism is one that already comes from the swollen organisations themselves: the state, the government, the civil service and the bureaucracies of the typical commercial corporation. One bureaucracy makes alliances with the others; those of industry, state and the unions come in time to interlock. The cybernetic revolution aids it immensely: office work becomes organised in exactly the same way as mass production factory work; the same specialised sub-divisions of detail work repeated day after day. The few decision-makers become more remote from the workers whom they control and even more so from the realities of the market place. In most large organisations there are declining returns to scale and a time seems approaching when rising raw material and transport costs will put their products beyond the bounds of a profitable market anyhow. So prevalent are these trends that the larger the company, the more likely it is eventually to go bankrupt: the steelmakers, the motor car manufacturers, the shipbuilders in the United Kingdom and many state-owned enterprises in Italy; even the great electronic manufacturing giants are vulnerable. The state has insufficient funds to save them all. Norman Macrae[17] believes the era dominated by the big business corporation and by big bureaucracies is coming to an end of its own accord.

In many countries there is, however, little likelihood of the development of such liberal trends as Macrae values. For example, in Soviet Bloc countries, the cult of gargantuanism combined with the potentialities of modern communication networks presents the threat of economic, political and social oppression that no ancient tyrant or Renaissance philosopher could have foreseen. The paper written by Eugen Pusic from the comparative security and sanity of Yugoslavia reflects the perils that affect so many countries all the way from the Adriatic to Mandalay and from the East German border to the Pacific:

> 'Beyond all limits of the law, statute or natural law, beyond ethical rules and even the most elementary humanitarian considerations, the state can degenerate into an organisation that oppresses, tortures, kills people under its power. It began with fascism and nazism which could still be explained, though not always convincingly as a monstrous pathological deformation of the capitalist order in its last phase. When, later, the truth about Stalinism became known, this explanation was no longer possible. More recent news, from the interventionist war in Vietnam to the military dictatorship in Chile, to South Africa, to the information that governments in sixty countries use torture systematically, demonstrated the danger of the concentration of power in the organisation called the state.'[18]

Youth unemployment and technology

Many of the issues raised in the Siena papers, the expressions of which sometimes contradict each other, are brought to a head in the phenomenon of youth unemployment in the West. Many young people leave school without being able to find any work to do at all. Many others may find employment for a short time but spend most of their lives supported more or less by the state. Various writers, notably Professor R. E. Pahl and J. Gershuny, quoted by Krishan Kumar,[19] believe that they are the pioneers of a new section of the economy, which they call either the informal economy or the neighbourhood economy, or even the domestic economy. Sustained by social security benefits, the rest of their needs are satisfied by the exchange of services or by growing their own food, which is stored in a deep freezer. This also provides assets with which to pay neighbours for their services. A more conventional approach regards with dismay the situation of many school-leavers, and of some university-leavers, too. They find little work to do that matches the abilities and enthusiasm which their education has developed. The world they come into is not the world they expected. Here, surely, is one of the causes for the violence of many young people and of the apathy of so many more. Some commentators see the root cause of both violence and unemployment to be those types of new technology responsible for labour-saving machinery requiring no mental or imaginative effort on the part of their operators. According to critics of this type of technology, the more knowledge which tools and machines absorb in production the more the ordinary worker should be enabled himself to possess the fundamental knowledge which lies at the basis of the machine's construction and use. In this way the new technology, they plead, should be used to make workers more fully human rather than the bored, alienated detail workers they tend to become at present. Other commentators would consider these as naïve views and propose that a different philosophy of work should set the technologists about making different tools. Macrae's paper[20] provides examples of the kinds of tools there could be: particularly to be commended are his ideas of all-purpose, robot-like, small machine tools and of telecommuting, by which he means living in, say, Hawaii and telephoning the results of the work done at home into one of the world's centres of business.

The plea is, therefore, that technology should be used to develop tools and machine tools to suit human skills, interests and abilities rather than for more processes in which specialised human labour is inevitably degraded. Provided a man is willing to work, the opportunity should exist for him to find purposeful activity to match at least some of his aspirations. Indeed, technical knowledge is now so advanced that Marx's famous demand for 'the reversal of the object-subject relationship' can be answered positively. The development of machine tools to achieve the reversal of this relationship would affect not only the topics discussed in the last few pages, but also the subject of innovation itself: is such and such an innovation or invention, from a human point of view, desirable or not?

The need is for what elsewhere has been called a human jury[21] – possibly a long period of public and private discussion aimed at reaching a consensus. The nearest analogy is what used to be called 'the nonconformist conscience' which before the 1914-18 war influenced legislation in Britain and, it was claimed, set the tone of decisive moral opinion on important issues.

Hard-headed opponents of this view will ask, 'Once an arrow has been loosed from a bow, is it ever possible to recall it?' The answer is surely for the bowman to pause and consider before he puts the arrow in the bow or aims it.

Archetypal nonconforming radicals

The topics of size, population growth, energy supply, economic expansion, mass production methods, technology, youth unemployment and the desirable shape of a future economy, are the material from which the contributors to this volume draw and in doing so they express their contrasting views of the future: some with their prophecies of doom and others with their utopian sketches of what human life in the third millennium could be. At this point it is opportune to sketch the characteristic concerns of some of the participants who would probably not object to being described as nonconforming radicals.

Meredith Thring puts the doom view on many topics, but his humanism opens plenty of scapeholes for the persevering. His panacea for all ills is more invention and more machinery:

'It is absolutely essential to have a vision of a machine-served utopia, which would give nine billion people a decent life in the next century.'[22]

But might the world population be stabilised at the eight thousand million level, which he foresees at the beginning of the next century? If not, his prophecy is that unless attitudes are altered radically, the tendency will be for it to double every twenty-five years. His remedy is to persuade parents to limit themselves to a two-child family and to give everyone what he calls, 'a decent standard of living and of education'.[23] In order to achieve this the world's food and energy resources would have to be averaged out on a basis of equality. This, his paper suggests, would mean the rich countries reducing their *per capita* energy consumption (food is a form of energy) by the staggering amount of between a half and two-thirds of their present consumption. No one is left doubting Thring's optimistic estimate of human nature – even in the materialistically-minded West!

Few participants at the 1977 Siena Seminar, where this proposal was first made, showed willing to embrace it! On the other hand they possibly did not face up to the gravity of the predictions on which Thring founded it. In more optimistic vein, Adler-Karlsson quotes Roger Revelle of Harvard as an authority, stating that the present technology for corn production used in Iowa would support a world population of 50 to 60 thousand million people, but at the same time he reports the grave concern of the Symposium on Population, Resources and Environment in Stockholm of 1973:

> 'The world is faced with unprecedented problems in the inter-relations of population, resources and environment. Indefinitely continued growth of population and material consumption is impossible in the finite space of this planet.'[24]

Speaking at the same seminar, Yona Friedman[25] was typical of others who objected to standards of the rich countries being applied to the poorer who had entirely different histories and cultures, therefore quite different needs. Michel Peissel,[26] the French explorer, went even further and in reference to population sizes, criticised speakers for accepting the Western philosophy of death with its implied value of continuing human life for as long as possible and therefore shirking death.

The most entertaining pessimist in 1977 who argued his original views with wit and foresight was Jean Gimpel. He wanted everybody to stop worrying about such issues as energy and material resources because all too clearly, he foresaw an economic depression about to hit industrial society. Moreover, it would be of such depth and severity that factories would be closed and roads half empty, so that energy supply would no longer be a problem. Bankruptcies of Third World nations would lead to their defaulting on their debts to the West and the effects would snowball with terrifying consequences; one of these would eventually be the collapse of the world money-economy and another, a second Wall Street crash.

> 'A Wall Street crash might lead to a 30 per cent fall in industrial production in the West. The number of unemployed could quadruple. Deflation would take over from inflation' . . .[27]

And, he reminded his listeners, deflation was a far worse thing than inflation. But there would be a steep fall in oil prices, and the rich Arab countries would lose much of their political power.

> 'A complete breakdown of law and order would not be improbable. It would be a real heyday for terrorists all over the world. . . . countries like Poland, which are already in economic and political difficulties, would revolt.'[28]

Gimpel's other provocative contribution is on the subject of size itself. He likes things big and thinks we should value our great engineering achievements, motorways for example, and measure them against such monuments of the past as the pyramids and temples of Egypt, but he concedes that it would be a remarkable act of foresight to begin planning small units of enterprise now so that men could survive the day of gloom.

Gimpel's gloomy, nevertheless up to the present, fairly accurate forecasts are to some extent reinforced by Friedman,[29] who also thinks there will be a collapse of money markets and believes that we shall soon witness the disintegration of all large organisations dominating the world; they will be replaced by small, self-reliant units. These will prove beneficial, 'provided we do not oppose what (ie the economic crisis) is in any case irreversible'. He was good enough to give heart to his fellow seminarists all drawn from industrial countries saying that, 'Industrialised man will not disappear', but developing nations will stand a better chance than the rich of adapting themselves to the collapse of large organisations on a world scale. Industrialised man will simply lose his pre-eminence,[30] he concluded.

The most gloomy topic of all is, of course, nuclear warfare. There is in everybody's mind the genuine fear that 'the bomb' will go off. A spontaneous discussion on these lines sprang from the initiative of Major-General Tony Younger,[31] who argued that the employment of a nuclear bomb against a civilian population should be made a special crime and that the principle of individual moral responsibility underlying the Nuremberg Trials should be given solemn recognition. It should be laid down clearly and made known to all armed forces throughout the world that whoever participated personally in using a nuclear device directly against a civilian population would be guilty of a war crime against humanity, punishable according to the precedents of the Nuremberg Courts. The person who ultimately presses the button will be as guilty and in the same degree as the person making the decision, or giving the command to do so.

These five participants, Meredith Thring, Gunnar Adler-Karlsson, Jean Gimpel, Yona Friedman and Tony Younger, together with Paul-Marc Henry, Robert Oakeshott and Peter Harper, whose contributions are yet to be mentioned, Roger Garaudy, Eugen Pusic and the late Albert Meister himself are the contributors who typically illustrate Meister's description of nonconforming radicals of Europe. They could be called pessimists, but that would be wrong. Each is a humanist. The point they have in common is that they have a generous way of drawing attention to problems which puts at risk their personal reputations as public figures. They want their prophecies and forecasts of the nature of future events to be proved wrong. They are optimists who use pessimism as a dramatic method to awaken in their fellow human beings an awareness of common peril.

The moral predicaments of industrialism

To find a balance between optimists and pessimists may be the sane approach to these prophecies until one turns again to the papers that raise some of the moral issues presented by the sophisticated phase of growth now reached by industrial societies. Professor Burns's paper[32] has to be commended in this respect. Each phase of the Industrial Revolution, and behind that the rise of the market economy and even earlier entrepreneurial revolution of medieval capitalism[33] has been prepared by previous changes in moral and intellectual assumptions. The trouble of our age is that we have had no moral preparation for the economic and technological changes that have suddenly come upon us. We live off the residue of a mixed moral heritage left behind by other epochs; the residues of Christianity, utilitarianism and the particular kind of liberalism that drew from these two sources and emphasised the values of personality. Of these three, the values of the utilitarians have by far the biggest influence on our policy-making élites. Immensely successful in shaping methods to deal with nineteenth- and early twentieth-century problems of poverty such as the slums and the destitution of the working classes, they are of very little help at this time when in the West the most acute conditions of perceived scarcity have been largely overcome.

Most industrial nations now exist in 'conditions of surplus value above subsistence'.[34] A wide range of choices concerning not only consumer goods, but also lifestyles, prestige services and exclusive hardware, once available only to the wealthy and aristocratic, is now open to a much wider class and income bracket. However, these manifest themselves to the mass of newly privileged not, in fact, as privileges but as dilemmas. Their utilitarian decision-making apparatus has taken them so far in their striving for success but does not equip them now to face these dilemmas. There is a social as well as an individual aspect to consumption in all these higher reaches of the market. People cannot all want the exclusive enjoyment of the same thing without spoiling that enjoyment for each other.[35] Underpinning the market and all the assumptions of economic life are moral causes, what Adam Smith once called moral sentiments,[36] and it is to these that Burns refers, when he says:

> 'Hirsch presented the problem, and left it with us as a moral problem. But this does not mean that it is insoluble in terms which are economically irrational.'[37]

We have to do our moral homework, get the moral economy right and then ' . . . show what rational, practical alternatives exist'.[38]

Many other contributors besides Burns raise different moral issues, notably Garaudy, Thring, Dermen and Meister. These return our attention to the topics already discussed in this chapter. But underneath all of these, is there not really just one single issue? This is industrialism itself. Does not almost any solution to most of the world's problems that any of us can offer rely both upon machines and upon the ethos of industrialism which has produced them? Can we really go back to a simpler life, even if inside us there is a yearning to do so? The reason for these doubts is well expressed in an article by Robert Heilbroner written in a special supplement to the New York Review of Books.

> 'The machine has stamped the modern mind with notions of efficiency that go very deep and will not, I think, lose their force unless future societies shed, not only capitalist, but industrial assumptions.'[39]

What has to be faced is that in whatever direction mankind turns, it has suddenly come up against the limits of its own condition. These may be, probably are, only temporary limits. But for the moment it would seem that if we try to progress in any direction without reflecting and taking stock – trying, as Burns says, to find out how we have reached the paradoxes that we have – we shall be turned back by these limits. This, at least, is clear from the recitation of confused ideas and contradictions which this chapter has already presented.

ENDNOTES

1. From an ode, 'We are the music makers', Athur William Edgar O'Shaughnessy, 1844-81.
2. F. Braudel, *Capitalism and Material Life, 1400-1800* (Trans. M. Kochan) (Fontana, 1974), p. 1, quoted in Professor Tom Burns's paper, 'The Moral Economy of the Rat Race', p. 74 below.
3. United Nations World Population Conference, Stockholm, 1973. For other well-reasoned estimates see G. Adler-Karlsson's paper, 'Technology, Population and Power', *The Future of Industrial Society*, Vol. II.
4. For supporting documents to this account of the situation in Kampuchea see John Barron and Antony Paul, *Murder of a Gentle Land* (Reader's Digest Association, 1977) and François Pauchard, *Cambodia Year Zero* (Penguin, 1978).
5. See for example Gunnar Adler-Karlsson, *op. cit.*
6. H. V. Hudson, *The Diseconomies of Growth* (Pan/Ballantine, 1972), pp. 53, 103-105 and 109.
7. Roger Garaudy, 'Giving Enterprise a Human Face (Créer des Mutants)', p. 93 below.
8. *North-South: A Programme for Survival*, The Report of the Independent Commission on International Development Issues under the Chairmanship of Willy Brandt (Pan World Affairs, 1980).
9. Paul-Marc Henry, Transcript 6A, Siena seminar, 1977. Transcripts may be referred to at the Acton Society, 9 Poland Street, London W1, provided an appointment is made.
10. Brandt Report, *op. cit.* (1980), p. 167.
11. See especially Paul-Marc Henry, 'Industrial and Other Basic Problems shared by Under-Developed Countries', *The Future of Industrial Society*, Vol. II, and Roger Garaudy, p. 93 below.

12. Brandt Report, *op. cit.* (1980), p. 166.
13. René Alleau, Transcript 6A, Siena seminar, 1977.
14. Roger Garaudy, p. 93 below.
15. Yona Friedman, Transcript 11, Siena seminar, 1977.
16. Paul-Marc Henry, Transcript 6A, Siena seminar, 1977.
17. Norman Macrae, 'The Next Stage in Lifestyles', p. 195 below.
18. Eugen Pusic, 'Workers and Government in a Self-Management Economy', *The Future of Industrial Society*, Vol. II.
19. Krishan Kumar, 'Thoughts on the Present Discontents of Britain', p. 260 below.
20. Norman Macrae, p. 195 below.
21. Edward Goodman, *Liberty and Revolution* (Duckworth, 1975), Ch. 14, p. 203.
22. Meredith Thring, Transcript 5, Siena seminar, 1977.
23. Meredith Thring, 'Woe, woe unless!!', *The Future of Industrial Society*, Vol. II.
24. Gunnar Adler Karlsson, *op. cit.*
25. Yona Friedman, Transcript 11, Siena seminar, 1977.
26. Michel Peissel, Transcript 11, Siena seminar, 1977.
27. Jean Gimpel, 'Small Units – A Danger to Civilisation', p. 111 below.
28. Jean Gimpel, ibid.
29. Yona Friedman, 'The Babel Syndrome (Is Big Collapsing Fast?)', *The Future of Industrial Society*, Vol. II.
30. Yona Friedman, *ibid.*
31. Tony Younger, Transcript 9 of the Siena seminar, 1977. See also 'Military Organisation and Leadership as Paradigms for Industry', p. 155 below.
32. Tom Burns, p. 74 below.
33. See also Amintore Fanfani, *Catholicism, Protestantism and Capitalism* (Sheed & Ward, London 1935).
34. The expression is Albert Hirschman's in *Exit, Voice and Loyalty* (Cambridge, Mass., Harvard paperback and London, reprinted 1978). See chapter II below.
35. Fred Hirsch, *Social Limits to Growth* (Routledge & Kegan Paul, 1977).
36. Adam Smith, *The Theory of Moral Sentiments* (1759). See Burns, note 27, p. 74 below.
37. Tom Burns, ibid.
38. Tom Burns, ibid.
39. Robert Heilbroner, 'The Human Prospect', Special supplement to the *New York Review of Books*, 1974.

Outlooks

For there to be radical changes in industrial society it would seem that there must first be a change in social outlook and values. Few are willing to say exactly how this can happen, although all seem to agree that intellectuals guided by a distinctive moral outlook must play a decisive part in it.

The role of intellectuals and other elites with regard to the predominant outlook of a society is not a constant one. When a society is well established the opinions of intellectuals more often than not reinforce popular assumptions, confining themselves to sharpening certain features and clarifying the implications of others. Their critical faculties strengthen the values on which social choices are taken. But when these values cease having the support they once had and fail to display their previous coherence and relevance the situation is different. Then, unless there is to be complete collapse, the role of intellectuals becomes crucial. The entire stock of society's values will need examining and all its major practices and shared expectations will need fresh assessment.

Such an examination will have to go beyond the values and applications of the dominant outlook and enter into those of any section of opinion which, although sharing some of its techniques, is based outside the frontiers of the society itself. An example today would be societies which practise orthodox Marxism, but which have many of the same industrial techniques as western societies and also eventually the same material expectations. Then, if this comparison comes up with no really satisfying answers, other realms will have to be investigated: intellectual, moral and spiritual. An enormous literature to illustrate this latter point already exists; that concerned with industrial alienation comes readily to mind; the philosophies critical of industrial methods and organisation, such as that of Simone Weil, which Sira Dermen's paper[1] discusses and the view put forward by Père Alain Birou in his paper[2]; or, of course, critiques of the values of industrial society itself from various religious points of view – Garaudy's paper[3] is the best example here. The late Philip Abrams' conclusions[4] must also be taken into account. And we shall have to abandon many values and assumptions of western industrial civilisation, especially some that we still accept more or less uncritically.

The point of these comparisons is two-fold: first to find what assumptions are shared by a given society and its ideological opponents using the same techniques or sharing some of its expectations; second, to establish a criterion by which to judge whether or not these particular assumptions are the cause of the crisis of confidence. As a result of pursuing this second purpose, other values emerge which provide wider-ranging hypotheses, and it eventually becomes apparent that it will be necessary to find new ground, an entirely fresh position, from which to make any effective critique of the complexities of existing society and from which the problems of modern societies can readily be seen in new perspective. This new ground, say that of human personality, or the truly human, will include some of the old criteria but also all else that can be seen, valued and related from this new standpoint. It will, in fact, little by little, provide an entirely new outlook combining the claims of both human and physical nature. When fully articulated it will provide the means for approaching all the problems of industrial society and from it a new ranging order of values and sense of direction will emerge.

It may be concluded, therefore, that only when a critique of an existing society in a state of crisis and moral dilemma has been sufficiently widespread, comprehensive and penetrating can the positive features of a more relevant and creative outlook emerge; to the priorities of which, new forms of technology, industry and economics can later respond. This is often an exceedingly difficult task, because the assumptions of an outlook that were once solely intellectual, become in the course of time garbled and later still, little more than defunct platitudes. Nevertheless, their influence on some of the more conventional and ostrich-like sections of public opinion remains strong; rather like the false confidence given to frightened passengers on a sinking ship by the existence of sturdy steel stanchions to which they can grip.

It is helpful to suggest that, in economic terms, the assumptions of an age, the values and propositions in which the overwhelming majority of a population believes with the utmost determination, provide the demand and the new techniques represent the supply. However, on this view, both strongly held social values and techniques together determine structures; so, as Père Alain Birou states, 'Technical progress is directed by its own will'[5] – tools and techniques have social aims built into them. Nevertheless, although they may have once or do now express a value or set of values, not every technique offered by a current technology is invariably taken up. As Professor A. K. Sen has pointed out, cultural and economic reasons, or availability of skills, present the basis for choice of techniques.[6] René Alleau in his paper points to the vast amount of ancient knowledge, especially Greek and Chinese, which has been lost; indeed, the Greeks had thought out a realistic theory of the atom and the basic laws of astronomy. But no civilisation, save Western, appears to have had the practical drive to apply knowledge to the inventing of new techniques for meeting human material needs. Even then a great many techniques, both medieval and modern, have not been taken up. They lie stored away and mostly forgotten on the technological shelf. 'It would be both presumptious and naïve to ignore history', he says,

> ' . . . and to concentrate on attempting to discover something totally new rather than trying rationally to adapt and improve a technique that already exists in an imperfect form. . . . It is very much in the industry's own interest to research the history of a particular process as thoroughly as possible.'[7]

Today, many thoughtful people would like there to be much more general knowledge of the techniques which are available and to be made aware of the fundamental knowledge out of which new technologies favourable to their values could grow. A paper such as Norman Macrae's[8] on lifestyles of the future is very valuable for this reason. Techniques and tendencies are often paramount in influencing social choices simply for the reason that intellectual elites approve of them as the means of giving effect to the tenets of the popular outlook which they themselves have implanted and kept sharpened. But it is easy to over-emphasise the intellectual's role. In setting a tendency and in fundamental attitudes, hindsight shows, it is vital; later, intellectuals may be carried along by its tide more or less as willing passengers. This may be illustrated by reference to some of the stages in the formulation and eventual popularisation of the artificial utilitarian outlook which, although in a weakened form philosophically, still dominates society. It began in the scientific thought of the seventeenth century and in the attempts during the eighteenth century of political theorists to apply the axioms of this thought to society in a general philosophy of utilitarianism. This was followed by the critique of society made by Bentham[9] and his followers. Actions, Bentham claimed, should be judged solely in terms of whether or not their consequences were useful, or produced happiness (the felicific calculus). This rule applied especially to social activities and legislation. He then went on to equate happiness with satisfying appetite or sensation, and struck a chord in the popular imagination when he suggested that the 'scientific means' for measuring usefulness consisted in examining the human sensations, a set of scales as it were, to discover the balance of pleasure over pain, or the reverse, which a proposed course of action would give. Finally, he posited the need for men to create artificiality in order to formulate the precise means of attaining their betterment in various fields.

These assumptions at first only influenced legislators and members of administrative and intellectual elites, but by the middle of the century new industrial wealth and popular education saw to it that they affected much wider classes; also that they were put into much simpler terms. New means of communication guaranteed this, too; nonconformity, evangelism and new fashions of thought, especially from Germany, widened out the range of ideas that the outlook included.[10] Technical forces helped, too. The very success of industrialism made the typical factory an ideal example for illustrating the idea of society as a social artefact in which the legislative system of the country existed to mass-produce whatever the felicific calculus specified, or the appetites and sensations of significant numbers demanded.

This same specification was later to become the justification for central economic planning and for the giant corporation. In all this the word *good*, meaning both an article of use and a moral quality, became conflated in such a way that, thoughtlessly, the concept of the Good became equated with the total satisfaction of appetite and sensation. This mistake was at least understandable at a time when the concept was applied mainly to the needs of the poor, and when the better educated and more privileged were free to allow their own aims. But to think of it in this way at the present time is manifestly no more than a shallow piece of ready-reckoning for a very confused society.

This is where the *trahison de clercs* comes in and also the point at which the passivity of some intellectuals in face of a popular outlook is illustrated. Intellectuals in this century have been divided over the outlook. Until very recently those who made up the majority depended for their status and success upon their ability to interpret the outlook with deliberate precision, using its precepts to elaborate upon every serious subject. Political commentators often give conspicuous examples of this attitude. The other class is made up of those who mostly – although there are doctrinaire exceptions – share one of the views represented by the papers reproduced here. The contention which, explicitly or not, underlies most of the papers in this volume is that this outlook is shared by capitalism and communism, by socialism and democracy alike. These shared assumptions have been more important in determining values and priorities, and in producing what is produced and consumed, than have been the ideological differences which have divided mankind into its doctrinal camps.

None of the intellectuals, social planners, industrialists or trade unionists who accept uncritically the assumptions and values of this outlook appreciate that it was already out of date before 1939 –

probably before the Webbs contributed to the *Haldane Report on the Machinery of Government*[11] in 1918 or Keynes wrote *The End of Laisser Faire*[12] in 1926. Few of them until very recently, and then mostly in the United States, have felt it their business to examine the artificialised assumptions of the industrial economy. On the other hand, they have introduced absurd labels such as left-wing and right-wing, or even conservationist to confuse some issues and to file others away. Thus the popular cults of gargantuanism and of substituting centralised planning for popular market forces have enveloped most formative opinion, whilst other really crucial issues have been ignored. Most conspicuous of these latter issues is whether or not production and consumption rates should continue to grow regardless of other desirable ends and whether in time the developing nations would not have the same right to achieve the same volume of production in order to enjoy the same standards.

Other intellectuals have not accepted these issues as mere fussy doubts. They have seen them as issues which plainly show their civilisation to be at stake; civilisation or possibly even organised human life on earth. Most of these are raised in the papers that follow and show clearly enough that the ideological shape of a given country's regime makes it neither more nor less likely to be affected by them. So far these criticisms have tended to be piecemeal and to lack a common point of view from which coherence can be given. But not so that of Père Birou who, in his open letter to the writer of this introduction, grasps what it is that makes our present crisis unique.

'Like many other thinkers, you have fears and apprehensions about the nature and the scale of the crisis we are going through. Beyond the employment crisis, the energy crisis, the crisis of the Third World, the crisis of both capitalism and socialism, you sense a crisis of mankind and of civilisation. Everything we have considered for the last four centuries as providing the cultural and social foundations of our life is collapsing beneath our feet.'[13]

The moral setting of industrialism

So far no account has been taken of what Marx would regard as the most powerful force in determining an outlook. This is the typical form of motive power or mechanical power, the role of the wind and water mills in bringing about feudal society and of the steam mill in shaping modern industrialism or capitalism. Not only is much of this argument undeniable, but account also has to be taken of the influence of the typical source of power upon the techniques of a society. There are other forces, too, which have been so far ignored, for example the interaction between a typical outlook and the forms of transport in a society, or again assumptions about authority. Thus, managerial theory and the development of sophisticated ideas about democracy have both been influenced by the assumptions of the popular outlook and themselves have significantly influenced the content of the outlook in its subsequent stages. Another significant factor, as the late Philip Abrams' paper shows[14] is the role of expectations and the fact that a society continues to expect to consume goods similar to those which it is consuming at present. The paper that is most appropriate to these themes is 'The Moral Economy of the Rat Race' by Professor Tom Burns.[15] He emphasises in the first place the moral changes in assumption and outlook which had to take place before capitalism could organise itself around the physical equipment made possible in the age of steam and water power. This event, the second industrial revolution, had to happen in Britain and only in Britain because it was here that the necessary changes in moral outlook had been prepared. The old moral principles protecting the dignity, or to use the puritan expression coined by Overton,[16] the 'self propriety' of the individual had been systematically infringed as nowhere else. This resulted not simply in a free market for labour, but also a competitive one: one man had been deliberately set against another. This involved destroying an ancient religious, and cultural attitude, and both preceded and accompanied more fundamental changes, moral and normative, in the then prevailing social outlook. Most importantly, it had to be ridded of concepts of equality which were as old as classical philosophy and Christianity itself; in particular, the belief that all men and women deserved equal respect before God.[17] This had found expression in the philosophy of Hobbes, especially in the *Leviathan* where he stated the medieval conviction that although men differ in skills, qualities and attainments, when all the faculties of body and mind are 'reckoned together the difference between man and man is not so considerable, as that one man can thereupon claim to himself any benefit to which another may not pretend as well as he'.[18] The idea of the just market, the fair of medieval times, was a part of these moral and normative concepts. Its change to the competitive market of industrial society, the open market, was given force by the individual claiming rights not only as a citizen but as an individual *per se* with strengths and distinctive qualities of his own. Enforcing these claims, he neglected his duties as a citizen, owed both to his sovereign and to his fellows in the community. Society gave up valuing the person for his own sake and gradually drifted away from most ideas of the intrinsically good. 'In more personal, and more fundamental terms, the shift might be rendered as one from self-respect to self-esteem.'[19] Objectively, the esteem a person deserved could be measured by his possessions, his more manifest abilities and the other qualities upon which a market price could be put. In summary, he came to be valued because of what he had achieved – the beginning of the rat race and the recognition of inequalities. Achievement as such became the hallmark of status.[20] Jean Gimpel[21] makes a similar point. Before the High Renaissance, the artist was no more and no less esteemed than any other skilled artisan. Afterwards, he was adulated and his value as a person assessed by the worth which society placed on his painting and sculpture. In our own day this tendency has continued to the point that the artist has become the sole preacher in society – the sole arbiter of social values – to whom attention can respectably be paid.

The instrumental view of people and of their abilities was invaluable in the construction of the utilitarian social artefact and the outlook underlying its construction. But as the industrial process developed it acquired its own claims for changes of moral assumptions. For example, the idea of the mass, so necessary for the assembly line, mass-production, mass-marketing and retailing, for scientific management and the opinion pollsters' venerated conclusions, had itself to be sanctified. This entailed yet another change in the values placed upon equality, inequalities and achievement. In modern industrial society these concepts have come to play exactly the reverse of the roles that Burns describes for them in the earlier period. Each head now has to be counted as one, and no one in the crowd, except the managers, may be more outstanding than another. This new attitude begins at school. There can be no gardens for especially bright or early-blossoming pupils. Flower-beds and grass are expected to be cut to more or less similar levels. This is a political prescription which can hardly be practised for long in the real world without, for example, managements of establishments experiencing steeply rising diseconomies of scale.[22] Bright, well-trained people specialising in different disciplines really are needed.

The spirit of capitalism as a prelude to the industrial outlook

It is interesting to look back behind the second industrial revolution to observe the same interaction between changed moral assumptions and new techniques bringing about the birth of capitalism.

The saving and lending of money is not in itself a sufficient description of capitalism. Borrowing and lending are as old as trade itself. More distinctively characteristic of capitalism is the development of specialised tools out of which there has arisen the specialised division of labour. But behind this, and of greater importance, was 'the spirit of capitalism'. This is the view of Senator Amintore Fanfani in a book[23] he wrote as a young man which was discussed by Professor Franco Romani at both 1977 and 1979 Siena seminars. This spirit grew because,

> 'a small, incipient eagerness for gain urged man towards the rationalisation of his productive actions in accordance with purely economic criteria.'[24]

The possibility for this economic rationalisation of self-interest arose in medieval cities as merchants gradually acquired the freedom without legal or moral impediment to employ the wealth they had previously accumulated. Until then there existed legal and moral constraints which the church and aristocratic classes had been united in enforcing: neither usury nor buying and selling for 'a quick profit' was allowed. But when the church and secular aristocracy took sides against each other, laws to these effects were weakened and craftsmen seized the opportunity to borrow money from the merchant classes even if they were obliged to pay morally prohibitive rates of interest. Doing so was worthwhile if it enabled them to improve their economic efficiency. The principal means of their doing this was to buy or devise more specialised and better tools.

> 'Indeed, it is the capitalist spirit that, by eliminating all extra-economic restrictions, favours improvements in tools and appliances, and encourages them by establishing an economic maximum as goal.'[25]

More specialised and effective tools led to more effective and specialised labour power. It led also to the more capable and knowledgeable craftsman, with some savings behind him, employing others. Often, he borrowed from members of his family, some of whom would probably have joined him in what we would now call family companies or partnerships.[26] This whole development Fanfani is at pains to point out happened long, long before Luther or Calvin, or any characteristic protestant work ethic. Essentially capitalism arose – Burns in his paper[27] emphasises this fact, too – when the moral constraints determining the uses to which accumulated wealth could be put were ignored.

The really crucial and dramatic act representative of the spirit of capitalism and the one that marks a definite break in outlook, on which more than four hundred years of subsequent industrialism has depended, was the revolution in mining techniques. Neither the spirit of capitalism nor the development of industry could make any headway until society had adopted a different stance towards the world of physical nature familiar to man. And it was this change of stance which was marked by the systematic exploitation of mines to produce the raw materials for men to transform into things for their use. Before then, man's attitude to nature had been controlled by the Stoic-Christian view expressed, for example, by Cicero in *Concerning the Nature of the Gods*,[28] where the Stoic spokesman, Balbus, replies to the Epicureans and says that the produce of the earth and its animal creatures were designed for man's use rather than for their transformation. Only since the Renaissance has the spiritual basis really existed for man to do unrestrained violence to nature and to take from it whatever he wants in order to transform its resources for his own purposes.[29] Slowly, as this new attitude to nature has grown, so has that combination of destructiveness and creativity which writers such as Schumpeter[30] claim to be typical of the capitalist form of the industrial system. All constraints, save those of economics, have gone.

The change in stance was illustrated by the sculptors and painters of the Renaissance in whose works man became the acknowledged centre of the universe. Michelangelo's David is, of course, the best known work of this kind. However, Leonardo's depiction of Vitruvian Man with outstretched arms traversing both square and circle is a better illustration of the ideal of man which was to dominate the age which we now recognise was to come. In contrast to being a description of his inner spirit it is a reduction of man to physical proportions which join man the artificer to his artefact. Scarcely a century later Hobbes was to express the thought that human society itself was an artefact of man's contrivance; a transformation of the natural into the artificial.

> 'Societies of men are artificially constructed by men . . . Hobbes' problem is to construct a society from a collection of individuals. The device that reduces the many to a unity is to make them a single person – an artificial person.'[31]

The crucial factor in changing fundamentally a social outlook is, therefore, change of stance.

The mill and the growth of the typical firm

The motive power of the second industrial revolution was coal and steam. That of the first which accompanied the birth and growth of the spirit of capitalism was the mill driven either by wind or by water. It harnessed the forces of nature but did no violence to it. The sources of power on which it draws are inexhaustible and almost costless.[32] It was in the wind and water mills that the firm typical of industrial society developed. On the way to its final form there were many stages, some of which provide inspiration for suggestions in the papers that follow, for the more interesting organisation of the working group.

Jean Gimpel describes the extraordinary variety of industry powered by the mill:

> 'It is an astonishing concept to the modern mind that medieval man was surrounded by machines. . . The most common was the mill, converting the power of water or wind into work: grinding corn, crushing olives, fulling cloth, tanning leather, making paper and so on. These were the factories of the Middle Ages. In the towns and villages the citizen could stand on a bridge over a river or canal and observe the different types of water mill: mills built along the banks, others floating midstream or moored to the banks, and, if he cared to look under the bridge, he might find the same machines built between the arches. If he walked upstream he would find the river dammed to provide a sufficient fall of water to drive the mills' machinery.'[33]

The owner of each of these mills hired out to a variety of independent craftsmen and tradesmen the space and the power they needed to follow their crafts and trades. They paid him a rent for these facilities but they bought their own raw materials and made their own arrangements with those who worked with them, or for them, family or non-family. Whatever they made was theirs to keep or sell or to exchange for something else. In time the mills became more powerful in order to drive the new tools described by Fanfani[34] as marking the advent of the spirit of capitalism. Much later the enterprising mill-owner assumed other roles. He might have sold the goods which his tenants made or acted as their wholesaler and then probably came to lend them capital with which to buy their raw materials and to tide them through difficult economic conditions. The crucial change of role came when the mill-owner, instead of simply buying his tenants' products, contracted to buy from them their time. The contract endeavoured to settle how many hours a week they should work and on what conditions they would sell to him what they produced. One can imagine, too, that often he specified the amounts of goods which he expected them to make in that specified period of time. The tenant was fast becoming the employee. Nevertheless, there still did not exist that master-slave relationship which R. H. Coase[35] claimed to be typical of the nature of the firm as such. This relationship was only consummated when the mill-owner assumed yet another role, that of entrepreneur. At this point he paid his worker a wage and organised his working day not so much according to craft rules as formerly but according to the most efficient manner dictated by the principles of the specialised division of labour. The days of the pinhead maker had come and the spirit of craftsmanship was broken. Gone were the incentives and pleasures of independent work and gone the notion of creative freedom achieved through work. Yet, notwithstanding the relatively poor rewards and gruelling conditions of working life which we can understand there must have been, these two ideals remain. They are clearly ideals which many contemporary writers believe have fresh applications.

Social structures and intellectual and popular assumptions

The remaining three stages of the industrial revolution can also be explained in terms of the same mixture of mechanical power, outlook, change of values and technical equipment. In the third, the railways took coal to a variety of smaller workshops all over the country, but especially those in the south making specialised goods. The fourth coincided with the development of electricity as the main form of industrial power, and was reinforced first by the use of telegraph and then by telephone, the motor engine and the lorry. The fifth stage of the industrial revolution has coincided with what is currently called 'the technological revolution'. In each of these periods the artificial utilitarian outlook was itself undergoing rapid changes and took into itself many other assumptions than those needed to maximise economic performance. These assumptions in the twentieth century have provided the common ground of all ideologies. No longer did the economic Ockham's Razor embodied in the spirit of capitalism determine the size and shape of organisations, nor their techniques, nor their ethos. Instead, these were influenced by the coincidence of a great number of causes which were absorbed into the outlook and settled how the new forms of energy, transport and communications should be used.

Two new sets of assumptions were slowly taken into the outlook from as early as, say, 1870 onwards and these strongly altered its character. The first was a growing prejudice against some of the consequences of competition, and a parallel desire for security: the other was a belief in collectivism which at that time began to grip opinion makers. The evangelical movement with its emphasis on standards of Christian fellowship reinforced the more personal prejudices of the first set of assumptions; whereas the second set were supported by continental fashions of thought, such as scientific socialism, planning, economic materialism, sociology and a certain amount of vague mysticism centred around ideas of state and society.

Historically, the desire to limit risk-taking occurred early and was evinced in the Companies Act of 1856, which not only limited the liabilities of the members of companies but also went back on many of the most radical measures of the reform area, for example, those abolishing the privileges of corporations. In addition, the new companies were given powers never enjoyed before by the chartered companies or common law partnership companies. Chief of these was the right of perpetual succession which, in the opinion of S. J. Prais,[36] was responsible for the nineteenth century amalgamation movement and the twentieth century merger cult. Another manifest tendency of the twentieth century, beginning with the reorganisation of prosperous chemical firms into the ICI, has been what is called industrial rationalisation. In deteriorating trade conditions successful and unsuccessful firms alike combine to cut down and reorganise their resources.[37]

In the eyes of Marcello de Cecco [38] the main cause of the cult of size was the amalgamation in the nineteenth century of locally based banks and the eventual transfer of their headquarters to London. Another move in favour of the control and planning of investment from London was the growth of pension funds, insurance companies and other financial institutions. 'Big likes big.' This is a tendency which the collective opinion of financial journalism and the prospect of big profits made out of takeover bids have done much to promote.

Few large organisations would have been possible without the development of the science of administration. This was first practised systematically by second generation utilitarians such as Edwin Chadwick,[39] and later formed the basis of many of the proposals of the Haldane Committee on Government, 1918. Burns[40] rightly points out that no large scale organisation of government or industry would have been possible without the construction of bureaucratic organisations 'in the strictly Weberian sense'.

The concept of bureaucracy came to be cemented into that of mass organisation in the 1914-18 war: the war of mass production and mass slaughter. These concepts at once found systematic expression in Frederick Taylor's philosophy of scientific management,[41] from which emerged the assembly line and the final minute refinements of the division of labour in both factory and office. All work, first only factory work, but later the office and retailing work of all large organisations also was separated into mental and physical; then, both mental and physical, that is to say administrative and management on the one hand, and skilled work and labour on the other, were broken down into their simplest components. Mechanical equipment and computers have been introduced to refine the process even further.

Harry Braverman has shown that this separation is 'the most decisive step in the division of labour'.[42] Man has been robbed of his power to conceptualise, adapt and put into practice his own plan of work. What is perhaps surprising, from one with his Marxist background, is Braverman's view that what he terms 'the degradation of work' was adopted just as wholeheartedly in communist Russia as it was in the USA.[43]

Another weighty influence – and at first a decisive one – in making the organisation of men *en masse* effective was the perfection of the system of command hierarchy on the Russian front in the Second World War which was almost immediately applied to the very largest commercial organisations. Metaphorically, it is the concept of a telecommunications system extending to all levels of a highly structured pyramid. Commands and messages pass down from a tiny high command at the peak through comparatively few officers, or managers, to many millions of soldiers, or workers, at the base.

Some economists have claimed that economic structures nearly always follow military patterns. General A. Younger[44] describes the development of command theories since Napoleon's time, dwelling particularly on the coming into being of the German General Staff: and it is easy to see how such developments have been the basis for the formation of large economic organisations and their management hierarchies. However, Younger then goes on to point to a contemporary development which, if the military analogy is appropriate, gives additional ground for hope to those who believe in the superior efficacy of small units. According to Younger, the basic unit of decision-making and initiative in the contemporary army is a unit of six men commanded by an able corporal. This unit is capable of acting independently, and surviving on its own for long periods even when cut off from its commanding officer or general staff. It is, of course, in a similar way that mountain, jungle and urban guerrilla forces are organised.

Little imagination is required to foresee the availability of efficient small-scale technology prompting the more resourceful members of society to find the means to bring about similar changes in the structure and character of present-day economic and political organisations. Certainly, many of the assumptions of the contemporary artificial utilitarian outlook now need drastic revision, or should be abandoned altogether.

Paradox and ambiguity

People in the West, and many elsewhere attracted by Western ideals, have been disappointed that conditions of greatly increased production – so-called affluence – have not increased the means of fulfilment of the average person: economic organisations, in which most people spend their most active hours of life, have been alien to the aims of satisfying, within their structures and work-methods, personal aspirations and skills. These disappointments, together with recession and political developments the world over, make it likely that for the time being industrial society is within sight of reaching the limits of its further growth; limits which, after a period of adequate social, psychological and, perhaps above all, spiritual renewal, may quite possibly be expanded.

Recognition of the fact that the limits of industrial society are within visible distance of being reached is already prompting rebellions against the assumptions of its prevailing utilitarian industrial outlook. As this movement grows it will probably constitute by far the most powerful pressure for early change of priorities.

Economic growth and technological progress themselves are the causes of the disappointment of expectations built into the present outlook that governs society. At this point reference can be made again to two books mentioned at the end of the last chapter. Both contain paradoxes which can be elaborated to illustrate some of the puzzles contained within the state of bewildered disillusionment that many experience.

The late Fred Hirsch in *Social Limits to Growth*[45] shows that a great many people brought up in the same cultural or materialistic tradition who have reached a level near to the top of their careers, or who have achieved some similar success, want the same prizes and arrive at the same place at the same time to collect them. This 'bunching up' of the successful spoils their sense of achievement and proves that they have found no recognisable distinction at all; they have remained part of a collective with the characteristics of mass demand operating in conditions of equality of satisfaction in the mass. It was not an Olympic event of excellence, as they supposed, but a rat race at the end of which are not prizes but traps.

Albert Hirschman in his Introduction and Doctrinal Background to *Exit, Voice and Loyalty*[46] describes the paradox that occurs on the constantly advancing frontiers between a 'society in a bare subsistence situation' or one with a bare surplus above subsistence, and a 'society with an increasing surplus above subsistence'. The crossing of the line between these two conditions means that society can afford to relax the disciplines, rules and constraints that enabled it to reach this frontier; but (this is the paradox) it cannot both do this and use the surplus for any other ends. Thus the pace of economic progress has to continue. Moreover, although the surplus for society is a significant one, it is not enough to share out between individual citizens. The conclusion would seem to be that inevitable social slackness is paid for by the individual forfeiting what would otherwise be his share of the surplus.

> ' . . . society is, and then again it is not, in a surplus situation: it is producing a surplus, but is not at liberty *not* to produce it or to produce less of it than is possible; in effect, social behavior is as simply and as rigidly prescribed and constrained as it is in a no-surplus, bare subsistence situation.'[47]

Might it be thought that this surplus be available for achieving collective, rather than individual, aspirations? For example, various groups in substantial numbers might combine to achieve ends that have resulted from their common critiques of particular assumptions of the contemporary industrial outlook: they might wish to experiment with what they see as alternatives to the current mode of industrialism; or they might wish to establish conditions to allow individuals to follow some of their own purposes subject only to the laws of the land in which they live and work? No, not according to Hirschman. Man's attitude towards his ability to produce a surplus is ambivalent:

> 'While unwilling to give up progress he hankers after the simple, rigid constraints on behavior that governed him when he, like all other creatures, was totally absorbed by the need to satisfy his most basic drives.'[48]

And an even more emphatic 'No', from the late Philip Abrams, whose paper,[49] is especially relevant to the whole of this discussion. He sees that it is unrealistic, even in conditions of affluence, to suppose that merely wanting to change the values and structures of working organisations will enable individuals, on their own or collectively, to achieve more ideal methods of work and organisation. Defining the appropriate tools and technology intensifies rather than reduces the problem of alienation.

> 'The trouble is that petty bourgeois refugees from advanced industrialism cannot change their values at will or on the strength of a purely theoretical understanding of their predicament. So they use the tools of craft production to intensify their isolation, not to conquer it.'[50]

Whilst society retains the ethos that it has, piecemeal tinkering and well-meaning reforms will not achieve much. In fact:

> 'The tools of collective production, in whatever form they are

developed, seem to be ruthlessly blunted and distorted by the values of possessive individualism.'[51]

But what lies behind this paradox? Men recognise their needs and in order to satisfy them they invent machines and organise production within a framework of values and culture which limits, at least temporarily, the range of their efforts. In time the organisations come to produce surpluses and simultaneously men allow the former rigid disciplines of their efforts to be relaxed; working hours, for example, are shortened and additional machines are invented to do the really gruelling tasks, even fresh labour from marginal lands is introduced to supplement these machines. What goes wrong? Why is it not possible to use at least some of the surplus that continues to be made in order to organise differently the structures and techniques of production so that they match a more closely defined range of human aspirations? The theme runs through many twentieth-century books. Niebuhr's *Moral Men and Immoral Society*,[52] for instance, makes the observation that men as individuals behave morally and often generously, but the same individuals, when acting collectively or as trustees for a social interest, or for society itself, are mean and feel obliged to exclude the moral dimension from their actions. There seems to be no procedure for balancing the outcomes of individual and collective interest. Is there any way of escaping all these absurdities?

Hirschman provides two clues which are positive. The first is that we ought not to examine our aims in isolation from the social and economic constraints which existed when they were first formed. We need the discipline of constraints; even if it is true that some of those that previously existed have been overcome we ought to be able to define what others still bind us. Although many in the West believe the conditions of affluence can be created, it is certainly not a true belief. Necessity cannot be overcome: Western prosperity has only removed it one or two degrees away, pushing it towards other parts of the world and even from one part of our own society to another. In attempting to create conditions of affluence we merely create different forms of necessity: as we shall see in the next chapter, we in fact allow it to be transformed into more subtle forms of oppression. From now on we ought to look at the forces of necessity with more understanding and as a result to formulate clear rules which will act as constraints upon the fulsome liberty which we mistakenly thought we were about to enjoy and which in fact has been turned into something else: not a paradise of freedom, but a pit of psychedelic demons.

'It seems plausible, indeed, that the *rise* of man above the narrowly constrained condition of all other living creatures was frequently sensed, though it can hardly ever have been avowed, as a *fall* . . .

an act of the imagination may well have metamorphosed this condition which he was really yearning for into its exact opposite, the Garden of Eden.'[53]

Hirschman's second clue is provided by his use of progress as the condition of each of the visions of paradise which he describes; one that rises above the paradox involved in a state of surplus and the other the metamorphosis leading to the Garden of Eden. Therefore, progress itself is under suspicion. Here we return to the utilitarian outlook. Progress was wanted. Affluence was wanted. Put crudely, we are all hooked on progress, and we should be hypocrites to deny that at least some of our reasons for getting into this position are sound ones.

Hirschman is right, and so was Heilbroner,[54] quoted above, when he said that notions of efficiency go very deep and will not lose their force unless our society gives up its industrial assumptions.

But what about these industrial assumptions? Suppose that instead of asking whether or not we are addicted to them, we ask how long it is physically or psychologically possible for them to last. How long will it be before many features of industrialism are overtaken by the issues raised in the last chapter? Suppose we accept the conclusions of many of the authors of the papers that follow and agree that sooner, rather than later, the extension of present modes of industrialism to many other parts of the world, together with the greed for fuels and raw materials of the industrial process itself, will bring the world to a crisis the like of which has never been recorded. For one thing this would mean that suddenly all developed countries would become aware that they were as affected by the vicissitudes of natural necessity as the populations of South-East Asia or South America. Suppose all this, what changes are there that we could make in our outlook, its aims and attitudes, that would be practical and realistic and would still enable us to live above subsistence level, but also to do something else of value with our lives besides allowing ourselves to go on being slaves of the industrial machine? That really is the issue that underlies all the others.

Change and necessity

Is there no event in the past, not an imaginary Golden Age but an actual state of existence, to which some helpful comparisons can be made? There is, of course. Our minds naturally go back more than 400 years to the Renaissance and the period described by Fanfani[55] before it when men sharpened their tools and dropped many of the moral assumptions previously constraining them. It was then that mankind altered its stance towards the natural world and towards the universe: the period of the Renaissance when man began to look upon himself as the centre of the universe and gradually built up a new system of moral assumptions which justified his doing violence without limit to nature for the sake of his transforming its materials into things for his own use.[56] It was what happened then that has led up to the present artificial utilitarian outlook of industrialism and to the disasters that some of the contributors to this volume sense lying in the years not too far beyond.

There can, of course, be no going back materially, conventionally or morally; nevertheless, we can learn from previous ages of transition when men gradually assumed different social, moral and aesthetic, political and economic outlooks.[57] We may define three stages:

1. A critique of industrial society: as this critique develops and the assumptions are worked out step by step and put into practice, the shape of the second stage will become increasingly apparent. Could this stage be called 'practical moral preparation' for:
2. A new stance of man towards nature opening up a different way of his knowing nature in relation to himself? This position would also provide him with a more sympathetic understanding of the needs of human nature.
3. Those changes in moral values and assumptions such as Burns describes in his paper, needed to accompany or to pave the way for the introduction of new working methods and forms of organisation?

The crucial stage is the second one. Human life embodies an ambiguity without recognising which no outlook claiming to base itself upon the truly human – the actually human – could be systematically extended into the conditions of social life and production. Man faces nature, uses it, and is part of it. We must understand that both man and nature are in Mary Bosanquet's words:

'involved in the same catastrophe, the whole creation groaning and travailing *together*, together waiting for redemption. The most elementary biologist, the most simple-minded naturalist cannot possibly be unaware that what we see around us is no nearer to being paradise than what we see within us. No one can perceive the splendour and significance of creation who cannot suffer its grief.'[58]

At the present time man is violent to nature on an unprecedented scale, but he is also concerned for it as his natural home. For these reasons thoughtful and creative people are beginning to recognise that humankind must adopt a different stance towards it and that from this technical, economic and social changes will follow.

The starting points for a change in ideas, as discussed in this collection of papers, revolve round a few central themes which may be summarised as Necessity, Technology, Work regarded as purposeful activity and its organisation. Each of these subjects is grounded in one or other aspects of the relationship of necessity and the human world which will be dealt with in the next chapter.

ENDNOTES

1. Sira Dermen, 'Necessity, Oppression and Liberty: Simone Weil's Thoughts on Work', p. 172 below.
2. Père Alain Birou, 'The Productive System as the Agent of Social Change: Work, Structures and Techniques', p. 142 below.
3. Roger Garaudy, 'Giving Enterprise a Human Face', p. 93 below.
4. Philip Abrams, 'Tools versus Values: notes on the possibility of Communal Work', p. 120 below.
5. Père Alain Birou, p. 142 below.
6. A. K. Sen, *Choice of Techniques* (Blackwell, 1975).
7. René Alleau, 'Technical Resources of the History of Invention', p. 115 below.
8. Norman Macrae, 'The Next Stage in Lifestyles', p. 195 below.
9. Jeremy Bentham, *Principles of Morals and Legislation* (1789, revised 1823).
10. See especially the very suggestive essay by F. R. Leavis, *Mill on Bentham and Coleridge* (Chatto & Windus, 1950).
11. Haldane Committee, Ministry of Reconstruction – *Report of the Machinery of Government Committees*, Cmd. 9230 (H.M.S.O. 1918).
12. J. M. Keynes, 'The End of *Laisser Faire*' (1926), *Essays in Persuasion* (Macmillan, 1931).
13. Père Alain Birou, 'Open letter to Edward Goodman', p. 288 below.
14. Philip Abrams, p. 120 below.
15. Tom Burns, 'The Moral Economy of the Rat Race', p. 74 below.
16. Richard Overton, *An Arrow against all Tyrants* (Facsimile published by *The Rota* at the University of Exeter, 1976).
17. Tom Burns, p. 74 below.
18. Thomas Hobbes, *Leviathan* (1651), Part I, Ch. XIII, referred to by Tom Burns, p. 74 below.
19. Tom Burns, ibid.
20. Tom Burns, ibid.
21. Jean Gimpel, *The Cult of Art: Against Art and Artists* (Weidenfeld & Nicholson, 1970), pp. 36-40.
22. Edward Goodman, 'How the Economies of Scale might benefit Small Units of Spontaneous Co-operation' (Acton Society Occasional Paper No. 18, Siena Series, 1977/79).
23. Amintore Fanfani, *Catholicism, Protestantism and Capitalism* (Sheed & Ward, 1935).
24. Amintore Fanfani, *op. cit.* (1935), p. 85.
25. Amintore Fanfani, *op. cit.* (1935), p. 56. This analysis is confirmed by the first list of inventions having been made by the papal librarian, Giovanni Tortelli, in 1449. A more exhaustive list appears in Polidore Vergil *de Inventoribus Rerum*, 1491. Before these dates the concept of invention was strange to the vocabulary.

26. Maria Teresa Guerra Medici, 'Limiting Liability in the Mediterranean and Levantine Ports during the 12th, 13th and 14th centuries', in Tony Orhnial (ed.), *Limited Liability and the Modern Corporation* (Acton Society/Croom Helm, 1982), p. 122.
27. Tom Burns, p. 74 below.
28. Cicero, *Concerning the Nature of the Gods*, quoted by John Passmore, *Man's Responsibility for Nature* (Duckworth, 1974).
29. A view of man's relationship to nature in strong contrast to that expressed in this section is contained in Margaret Canovan's paper, 'Labour, Work and the Public World: Hannah Arendt's 'Human Condition'', p. 183 below. The worker's attitude to nature is masterful and violent (cf. H. Arendt, *The Human Condition*) (Doubleday Anchor Books, 1959), p. 122. 'The element of violation and violence is present in all fabrication and *homo faber*, the creator of the human artifice, has always been a destroyer of nature. The man-made world provides human life with a background against which individual uniqueness can become visible.')
30. J. A. Schumpeter, *Capitalism, Socialism and Democracy* (George Allen & Unwin, 1954).
31. M. M. Goldsmith, *Hobbes' Science of Politics* (Columbia University Press, New York, 1966), p. 138.
32. See Jean Gimpel's catalogue of models, *Models for Rural Development* compiled by Julia Elton and Ali Baghdadi (Acton Society, 1979).
33. Jean Gimpel, *The Medieval Machine* (Gollancz, 1977).
34. Amintore Fanfani, *op. cit.* (1935).
35. R. H. Coase, 'The Nature of the Firm', *Economica*, November 1939.
36. S. J. Prais, *The Evolution of Giant Firms in Britain* (Cambridge University Press, 1976), p. 33.
37. F. R. Lucas, *Industrial Reconstruction and the Control of Competition* (Longmans, Green & Co., 1937).
38. Marcello de Cecco, 'Keynes' analysis of the British Disease', *The Spectator*, 19 June 1976. See also Transcript 23, Siena seminar, 1977.
39. See for example Elie Halévy, *The Growth of Philosophical Radicalism* (Faber & Faber, 1928).
40. Tom Burns, p. 74 below.
41. Frederick W. Taylor, *Scientific Management* (Harper & Brothers, New York, 1947). Also see Harry Braverman, *Labor and Monopoly Capital: the degradation of work in the twentieth century* (Monthly Review Press, London and New York, 1974), Chapter 4.
42. Harry Braverman, *op. cit.* (1974), p. 126.
43. Harry Braverman, *op. cit.* (1974), p. 12.
44. Tony Younger, 'Military Organisation and Leadership as Paradigms for Industry', p. 155 below.
45. Fred Hirsch, *Social Limits to Growth*, (Rontledge & Kegan Paul, 1977). See also *Economy and Society: Studies in Fred Hirsch's Social Limits to Growth*, ed. Adrian Ellis and Krishan Kumar (Tavistock Publications Ltd./Acton Society, forthcoming).
46. Albert O. Hirschman, *Exit, Voice and Loyalty: Responses to Decline in Firms, Organisations and States* (Harvard, 1970), p. 9.
47. Albert O. Hirschman, *op. cit.* (1970), p. 9.
48. Albert O. Hirschman, *op. cit.* (1970), p. 9.
49. Philip Abrams, p. 120 below.
50. Philip Abrams, ibid.
51. Philip Abrams, ibid.
52. R. Niebuhr, *Moral Men and Immoral Society* (Charles Scribner's Sons, New York, 1934).
53. Albert O. Hirschman, *op. cit.* (1970), pp. 9-10.

54. Robert Heilbroner, 'The Human Prospect' (New York Review of Books, 1974). See p. 18 above.
55. Amintore Fanfani, *op. cit.* (1935).
56. This is the appropriate place for me to acknowledge in this respect my especial debt to T. E. Hulme, *Speculations* (Routledge & Kegan Paul, 1960).
57. T. E. Hulme, *op. cit.* (1960).
58. Mary Bosanquet, *Dietrich Bonhoeffer* (Hodder & Stoughton, 1968).

CHAPTER III

The role of necessity in work and social change

The two papers in this volume which have most to contribute to the understanding of necessity are written by Père Alain Birou and Sira Dermen.[1] One describes the thought of Marx in this respect and stattes grounds of a critique. The second discusses the writings of the French philosopher Simone Weil, who died in 1943 at the age of 34. Her thought will be used as a guide to problems raised in earlier chapters and by the papers generally. Margaret Canovan's paper on some aspects of Hannah Arendt's book[2] describes work and necessity from a different angle and introduces some original concepts.

Marx concentrates his ideas about necessity into the development of his doctrines about the productive process and the forces of production. Work, productive work, is the key concept. How can man use mechanical methods of production to gain an abundance with which to satisfy his basic needs? How can mankind as a whole, as a social force, gain control of the means of production so as to end the alienation imposed upon it by capitalist production. Weil faces similar problems but poses them differently. For her, necessity, not always work, is the key concept. It is an essential condition of human life and never to be ignored:

> ' . . . as long as he (man) continues to constitute an infinitesimal fraction of this pitiless universe, the pressure exerted by necessity will never be relaxed for one single moment.'[3]

So work, she believes, is inevitable; it has to be made human and dignified – man's whole response of body and mind to the forces of nature. Its present character is oppressive and degrading; only methodical thought and sensitive organisation can transform it into the means of liberty. This enables Weil to make work a model for men and women's attempts to come to terms with necessity and nature in other areas of their life. So, for her, work is not the sole category of the human encounter with necessity, as it is for Marx. Organisation is another, and no less important, category. So, too, are the human beings' moral responses to their daily, hourly and capricious encounters with what she calls 'the forces of nature'.[4] Unless we can make these responses positively, courageously or inventively, we fail as human beings. This way of thinking provides her with a very strong conception of liberty:

> 'Living man can on no account cease to be hemmed in on all sides
> by an absolutely inflexible necessity; but since he is aa thinking
> creature, he can choose between either blindly submitting to the
> spur with which necessity pricks him on from outside, or else
> adapting himself to the inner representation of it that he forms in
> his own mind; and it is in this that the contrast between servitude
> and liberty lies.'[5]

This altogether wider view of the relationship of necessity, seen as
much more than the challenges of nature and the pressure of
unsatisfied appetites to the many facets of human life, shows up the
narrowness of Marx's absorption with the role of necessity in
determining the productive process and with the division of labour
typical of industrialism. Thus it also helps to throw into relief the
fundamental kinship of Marxian thought about the labouring and
economic processes with that of the artificial utilitarian outlook. For
example, Marx's own interpretation of freedom from necessity is
precise and founded in a widely shared critique of the industrial
society of his own times: in those terms it is realistic and in accordance
with normal utilitarian aspirations. Freedom from necessity will
accompany the 'free association of producers' or as Birou sees it, it
would be the kind of voluntary self-administering division of labour in
which the general will coincides with individual aspirations.[6] This
Marx describes as the state where:

> 'no one has an exclusive sphere of activity, but may perfect himself
> in any area he pleases, society regulates general production and
> creates for me the possibility of doing today something, tomorrow
> something else . . . as is my pleasure.'[7]

In such conditions men and women will at last have freed themselves
from the distressful, humiliating character of work disciplined by
outside forces. No 'blossoming of human power'[8] is possible whilst
dictated by necessity or by other people, capitalists, owning their
tools, machinery and other means of production.

These ideas play an important role in many of the non-Marxist
papers coming out of the Acton Society Series of Seminars devoted to
such ideas as participation, workers' co-operatives and firms of the
future.[9]

It is by exalting work, the determining role of the division of
labour and the forces of production that Marx makes another
abstraction that he shares with the artificial utilitarian outlook: that of
a conception of civil society which is really a case of special pleading.
'Consumption, the end of production, is how society defines itself for

Marx, just as for Hegel it is defined in terms of the State, the end inherent in civil society.'[10]

It is society, whether capitalist or communist, which regulates activity. Society, as organised society, only comes about because of the need to organise work – compulsorily by forces outside the workers' control under capitalism; voluntarily by workers themselves in communes under communism.[11]

Work is, therefore, in Marx's thought, the really essential human category. It is not simply the driving force of human life, it is also more importantly the *raison d'être* of human life in society. This is a view that Birou regards as typical of the Age of Enlightenment:

'An anthropological option where men as subjects of activity, in other words humanity, make themselves and are creators of their own needs: they create, too, their own usefulness, significance and happiness.'[12]

This belief, Birou comments, is due to the 'new process of industrialism'[13] and once again illustrates that the roots of Marxian thought share common ground with the modern industrial utilitarian outlook.

The idea of man making and recreating himself is closely related to Marx's doctrine of Praxis. This has little or nothing to do with necessity but it does entail first reflecting on the essential nature of work regarded as purposive activity, then understanding the effort, mental, physical and sometimes imaginative, needed to be put into it. Man creates his own self-consciousness, which combined with work in this special sense, enables him to know the external world as well as himself; only through it can he have any true objective knowledge or disentangle reality from illusion. To touch or to work upon a thing is to know it and to recognise it. Work in society is fundamental as a mediator between objective and subjective nature.[14]

As well as adapting some of his ideas about Praxis, Weil shares Marx's fundamental view of necessity; but neither his analysis which emerges from it, nor his assertion that it is human consciousness of necessity that determines history and gives it its meaning. She has, according to Sira Dermen's paper far too clear a view of reality to believe that necessity will ever be conquered, or not form the most enduring pressure on human life.[15] The following quotation is a generous tribute to Marx and at the same time defines Weil's point of departure from him:

'Marx's truly great idea is that in human society as well as in nature nothing takes place otherwise than through material transformations.'[16]

' . . . To desire is nothing; we have got to know the material conditions which determine our possibilities of action.'[17]

The tenor of Weil's philosophy is that a degree of social oppression accompanies all men's attempts, primitive or sophisticated, to transform necessity into production or the administration of institutions. The forces of necessity blown onto the world from outside the universe, when internalised in any large organisation, get transformed into oppressive forms and complicated rules, relationships and hierarchies. The individuals working in them are thus protected from the forces of reality but at the expense of being made blind to and ignorant of the economic and technical conditions that surround them. They become something like mechanical puppets in an overall scheme beyond their understanding or control. The libertarian problem is to limit the power of these transformed forces and to make for men the best bargain. In this respect the important question is not who owns the means of production or who controls the organisation, but how the means of production and forms of organisation are adjusted to human needs and aspirations. For example, the typical vast, modern organisation of complex plant and machinery with its remote methods of management, it is true, has freed itself from the primitive forces of nature, but only to take their place 'in crushing frail humanity'.[18] The modern worker in the supermarket or on the motor car assembly line is less free, more regimented and his personal integrity more undermined than the hunters and agricultural workers, or the wheelwright and carpenter of ancient and medieval times. Of course, this point is not one which would be appreciated by a thorough-going Marxist who understood freedom to mean only freedom from necessity, ie the pressure of material needs.

In the early 1930s, at the age of 24, Weil showed that she both comprehended and feared the magnitude of the twentieth-century problem of organisation. Until then, she claimed, there had been two forms of oppression, namely that of slavery or serfdom exercised by the force of arms and that 'of wealth transformed into capital'. Was there not, she asked, the danger of an additional form of oppression growing up by the side of capitalism; 'oppression in the name of management' instead of the benign and long-hoped-for 'association of free producers'.[19] It was to answer this question, as it were, that she gave up for a time her role of teacher and entered the Renault factory as a worker.

The danger which Weil could perceive is, of course, the same danger which Jo Grimond identifies in his pamphlet *Bureaucracy*[20] and also to which Pusic refers when he writes in his paper of 'the overwhelming power of the machinery of government'.[21] What makes the latter paper especially interesting is that it is written by an adherent of the ruling self-managing socialist movement in Yugoslavia which has tried to put into practice Marx's ideal of an association of free producers, retaining a realistic role for the state yet with a degree of healthy mistrust of it. The ideal put forward is 'the replacement of power and society by an alternative set of relationships and institutions' more favourable to genuine equality of people.[22] Although Pusic condemns a society without the expression of some conflicting interests as 'a tedious utopia', he believes that the current prescription for achieving this ideal is a combination of the rule of law and improved legal regulations 'while simultaneously developing alternative methods'.[23]

Weil has three escape routes from the tyranny imposed by the bureaucracy, and from the remoteness, impersonality and complexity of modern organisation. The first she shares with Pusic – the rule of law and good legal regulations making for improved conditions. The second is to establish the norms for what the right kind of free organisation should be: the ideally free organisation, she describes as one that 'would never be sufficiently vast as to pass outside the range of a human mind'.[24] That is to say it should be suffiiciently small and well co-ordinated to enable every worker to understand the role of his own work and its precise relationship to what his colleagues are doing. This would entail their shariing imaginatively in each others' projects; for the ideally free worker is one who forms a preliminary judgement in his mind of the end he sets himself and then is able to carry through methodically 'the sequence of means suitable for the attaining this end'.[25]

This criterion of ideally free activity recalls the picture of Marx's dud architect who was superior to the most perfect of bees because he first formed a blueprint of his intentions – that is of the house he was going to build – before organising craftsmen to carry it out.[26] For both Marx and Weil in this context it is a human ideal to form mental blueprints and to be subsequently in control of all the movements needed to attain the end set by them: this requires, of course, the right kind of tools and machinery, and in a preliminary way it would be apt to call these 'Weilian tools and machines'; Marx does not follow through his ideal of human labour to the logical conclusion that tools and machines should be made so as to overcome the ddetested division of labour and give back to the worker, in appropriate contemporary forms, his birthright of skill.

Weil's third escape route is, therefore, through the right kind of tools; tools shaped to the tasks they have to perform and the all-round requirements of those using them – ' . . . the less tools are made as extensions of the workers' limbs, the less the vagaries of the mind will interfere'.[27] The ideal is for them to express her very positive concept of liberty.

If these conditions can be met, and Weil is is no doubt that they are realistic, work can be not just satisfying but 'the supremely valuable experience'[28]: indeed it is that very encounter with necessity of which we have lost sight because of mass production machinery and complex modern forms of organisation.

Application of Weilian thought

To what extent do the papers and discussions resulting from the Siena series of seminars give any hope of Weil's conditions being met?

The obvious paper to mention first is Macrae's 'The Next Stage in Lifestyles'. He even starts with Weil's assumption that work can be made free, satisfying and enjoyable. First get rid of the petrifying control of decaying organisations – not simply in industry, but in the social services and many other forms of government and commerce. ' . . . bureaucracy within the organisation will ultimately bring down the big corporations.'[29] Next, discover the size of units where individuals do work healthily, happily and efficiently (overcrowding at work is a cause of illness: see his example of sickness among nurses in hospitals of over 100 beds).[30] Then set about the kind of administrative or management structure needed to co-ordinate all these small organisations. Almost certainly, contracting and sub-contracting by an efficient stem body will be the answer: perhaps this stem body may be the old county council or the depopulated, giant-sized commercial firm's former head office. The final stage will be the conception and making of the tools, the investment projects needed to make all this work. Macrae is sure that it can be done quickly:

> ' . . . one of the few things that computerised planning should be able to do is to cut sharply the time between the design of a new product and its coming off the production line.'[31]

One of Macrae's two most exciting ideas is telecommuting, already described above.[32] The equipment, mostly ssmall-scale electronic, will exist for workers to do their work where they like best to live (it may be next to an opera house, a golf course, or the beach of a South Sea island) and for them to 'telecommute' from it orally and visually to a headquarters somewhere in a dull city centre in another part of the world. The other is for teams of contractors and sub-contractors, working in time chosen by themselves (flexitime) in any part of the world. And again designs will be promptly woorked out and turned into small tools and machines to suit their requirements precisely.

These and more proposals show that Macrae sees that the human use of the computer can design the forms of organisation and contract, the effective tools and techniques that could make even some of Weil's ideal forms of liberty seem out of date.

Pusic's and Garaudy's papers certainly display Weil's concerns. Garaudy shares Macrae's enthusiasm for the idea of contract and believes that it can constitute a link between liberty and coherence. Even closer to Weil's own thought is his endorsement of the proposition that 'genuine decentralisation implies that small units have access to their own means of information. . . '[33] They would have control over the designs of the computers they use and not be dependent on 'the mirage of so-called organisations held together by giant computers.'[34] They should have enough decision-making powers to constitute an effective feedback to their base which would cover their views on internal organisation, techniques of work and ' . . . re-evaluation of the needs of the social environment within which the enterprise is operating.'[35]

And for knowing the sheer joy of simply doing something purposeful with one's time, of using mind and body well, balanced sometimes by just loafing around, simple reflecting, Peter Harper's paper, 'Stay Alive with Style'[36] is to be most strongly recommended. Simone Weil would have approved.

Many of Harper's ideas for Weilian types of work that could be carried out in his relaxed style of commune are appropriate to the third tier of the three-tier economy which is described in the next chapter.

Giving enterprise a human face

Weil's utopia is one made up of ideal-sized organisations reflecting the relationship of its members' thoughts to their actions. In contrast, Marx's utopia might seem to be a machine-served association of free producers. Starting with the belief that man is essentially a tool-user and an efficiency-maximising productive agent, Marx is obliged to recognise that it is an historical fact that machines have taken the place of tools which were once responsive to the user's characteristic ways of doing things. Therefore he makes no prescription in his ideal world for the free producers to get back what would have seemed to be their birthright: there is no provision in his utopia for revolutionary changes in the design of machines to take on the sensitivity to human skill that the tool allowed formerly. Thus, alienation and estrangement are inevitable accompaniments, which he diagnoses with penetrating insight in the *Grundrisse*:

> ' . . . the means of labour passes through different metamorphoses, whose culmination is the machine, or rather, an automatic system of machinery . . . set in motion by an automaton, a moving power that moves itself; this automaton consisting of numerous mechanical and intellectual organs, so that the workers themselves are cast merely as its conscious linkages. . . . Its distinguishing characteristic is not in the least, as with the means of labour, to transmit the worker's activity to the object; this activity . . . merely transmits the machine's work . . . on to the raw material. . . . Not as with the instrument, which the worker animates and makes into his organ with his skill and strength, and whose handling therefore depends on his virtuosity. Rather, it is the machine which possesses skill and strength in place of the worker . . . with a soul of its own in the mechanical laws acting through it.'[37]

Completely mechanised work efficiently operated through the minute division of labour separates man's mind and hands. A timely example might be the automation of the printing process, or computer-controlled operations. The adding machine provides a simpler illustration of the disassociation of mind from function. Mechanised or repetitive industrial work fragments and negates what man – even as a child at school – essentially is. It makes him become, as it were, an automative limb detached from his former pre-industrial self or from his personality regarded as a whole. Also it mocks him: this is Marx's perceptive analogy of estrangement. At the end of each day it confronts him with a mass of identical goods, whereas before he would have seen many fewer articles, but each slightly different and embodying the worker's characteristic skills and aspirations; his mistakes, too. 'As labour constitutes the human being, the reality of the historical division of labour is, in the eyes of Marx, a scandal.'[38] From this Marx believed there would spontaneously follow the material conditions of production needed to overcome necessity. These forces of production would be the outcome of the negotiations with nature by free men: yet at the same time that outcome would be historically determined. These momentous events were both the meaning of human history and the creative factors determining man's social being – the socialised man.[39]

When Marx wrote *Capital* the concept of the socialised man[40] was at the pinnacle of his priorities. Closely associated with it was that of socialising the means of production. At the end of his life and later, at the time of Lenin, his adherents seem to believe that socialism could only be achieved through collectivisation. In time, the major priorities of Marxist thought became subordinated to a narrow ideology of economic planning centred upon a system of what is now prosaically called public ownership or nationalisation. The sense of anti-climax produced by these outcomes in practice is echoed by Roger Garaudy in his paper: 'Nationalisation,' he points out, 'is not a socialist measure . . . '[41] It is no more than an *ad hoc* device for trying to inject some principles of democracy into industries that have become monopolies. Economic structures do not determine content: 'State capitalism does not diminish the alienation of the worker.'[42]

Garaudy's sense of disappointment was shared by the late Harry Braverman, whose book, *Labor and Monopoly Capital*[43] won acclaim from Marxist and non-Marxist thinkers. He claimed that it was the labour process of industrialism that was wrong and that Soviet socialisation had not made it any more human than it had been before the revolution. In fact it had been made worse. Pressures were upon Lenin after the Revolution to show that Communism was at least as efficient, as productive, as capitalism. Therefore he found himself turning to the United States not only for mechanised tools but also for its techniques of scientific management for use in Soviet industry:

> 'In this situation, the respect and even admiration of Marxists for the scientific technology, the production system, and the organised and regularized labor processes of developed capitalism was if anything heightened. . . . We need only recall that Lenin himself repeatedly urged the study of Frederick W. Taylor's *Scientific Management*.'[44]

Braverman goes on to comment that 'the critique of the capitalist mode of production, originally the most trenchant weapon of Marxism, gradually lost its cutting edge'.[45] When it came to be put into practice, even after a proletarian revolution, 'Marxism became weakest at the very point where it had originally been strongest'.[46]

Birou points to an even more conspicuous defect of mature Marxism in its approach to technology and the techniques which then and now dominate all industrial societies:

> ' . . . Marx did not get to grips with the heart of capitalism, that is the capitalisation by privileged groups, of their scientific knowledge and technical power.'[47]

Had this fact been recognised in the formative years by followers of Marx, then the use of various bureaucratic techniques in Russia would surely have been detected before the communist state had become the oppressive superstructure that it is now recognised to be.

Producers' co-operatives and self-management

Many non-Marxist reformers fall into the same intellectual trap as the Soviet leaders at the time of the Russian revolution, that is of assuming that by transferring the ownership of the means of production to a particular or general collective, all other problems – especially those of social oppression, alienation and estrangement – will be solved or banished. For example, Albert Meister suggests that proponents of autogestion often believe that management by ballot box devices will give the worker the feelings of identity he needs in order to overcome his sense of alienation and estrangement.[48] In reality the alienation is largely caused by the machines and estrangement is rooted in the scale of the organisation and its vast heap of produced material piled up against the tiny figures of the men who have pulled the levers.

Besides Pusic's paper on aspects of workers' management in Yugoslavia and Robert Oakeshott's on the Mondragon Co-operatives in Northern Spain[49] there is a full and detailed Acton Society Occasional Paper on the different types of co-operatives in Italy, written by the authority, Robi Ronza.[50]

The aim of autogestion and workers' co-operatives in general is most effectively grasped if Garaudy's golden rule for participation is given priority.[51] This is for decisions to be discussed and shared between the workers and taken by them at the place, or at the level, where the problem is experienced. This rule, he stresses, should apply just as much to the organisation of hospitals and universities, or of local politics, as it does to business enterprises. Manifestly, it is a rule which not only makes a reality of participation but also sets a limit to the size of organisation. For, as Weil shows, it is only in units of a limited size that the work process and its methodical pursuit can be conceptualised; and it is only in such a unit that each worker's voice can be heard and made effective in all decisions taken. Felix FitzRoy emphasises these points and insists that it is conceded by everybody interested in the subject of workers' participation, that they may be achieved in a variety of ways. Flexibility to meet the circumstances of each situation is essential:

> 'This gives the participatory model of economic organisation additional flexibility and relevance compared to more dogmatic "radical" doctrines which are still touted as panaceas for all and any of current social and economic ills.'[52]

FitzRoy's plea for flexibility introduces two other lessons to be learned from successful producers' co-operatives. The first is that the political and cultural setting of a co-operative matter very much. The character of the Mondragon Co-operative and of the different co-operatives in Italy would be different if they had not grown up at a time when their members were identified with minority political and cultural movements; Basque nationalism in the one case and a variety of political and catholic associations in the other. The second lesson concerns the importance of the bank used by the co-operative: it should be local or regional and its funds should come from the area in which it is situated. Moreover, it ought to be thoroughly involved in the successful outcome of the co-operative's plans, know every detail of them and be able to advise with the utmost competence.

It is unlikely, however, that the aims of the world-wide self-management or autogestion movement will remain confined to sharing in the making of important decisions and participating in profits. Even those applied economists whose main concern is the efficiency of private enterprise, are beginning to acknowledge that many of the conditions which sociologists associate with alienation and estrangement impose rising costs on economic organisations independently of who owns them. The problem *par excellence* facing advocates of self-management who wish to overcome alienation in all its aspects is, according to Garaudy, ' . . . to give everyone at every economic, political and cultural level the possibility of being a creative and responsible person . . . '[53] This possibility includes the power to initiate change in the structure and methods of the working organisation. Alienation, it is to be concluded, is a social rather than exclusively economic phenomenon. Nevertheless, it seems to have its roots in working methods and forms of organisation. Simply changing ownership – be it socialist or private enterprise, producers' co-operative or other form of worker-participation – will not be enough.

Work, labour and public life

In contrast to the importance given to the concept of work by writers of papers on workers' co-operatives and other forms of participation, is the description and critique by Margaret Canovan of some of the views expressed in Hannah Arendt's *The Human Condition*.[54] Arendt divides human activity into the categories of Labour, Work and Public Life; of these by far the most important is the last. Opposing definitions of true liberty such as Weil's, she claims that it is an illusion, as well as dangerous, to put forward the aim of individual fulfilment through either labour or work as the ideal of liberty. To do this takes the attention of men and women away from the really important possibilities of human life – above all '*the vita activa*', life in the public realm as practised in classical Greece. Arendt's conception of necessity is also at variance with the views of both Marx and Weil who underline the crucial importance to human life of 'the forces of necessity' and describe, although differently, the ways in which they have been transformed into instruments of social oppression. Instead Arendt understands by necessity what most people mean when they refer to 'the necessities of life' or to 'things necessary to maintain the processes of human life'. In her terms it is the role of labour, not work, to minister to necessity in these senses; whereas work is satisfying to its doers and is entered into with the same methodical, self-conscious intention that Weil ascribes to the activities of ideal liberty.

Labour is of its nature slavish, and the labourer is himself a virtual slave to nature, obeying its processes or endlessly keeping at bay its encroachments on civilised life. She sees no pleasure, merit or intrinsic satisfaction in, for example, the farmer's rich variety of skills, or his powers of improvisation in response to the minutia of each season's challenges, different every year. The efforts of labour are judged by its results which are no sooner produced than are consumed. This drudgery, although essential, is to be seen as no more than the futile toil of staying alive. It is done simply to earn a living, or 'to raise the standard of living' and thus to achieve 'the greater happiness of the greatest numbers'. A paradigm example of the labourer's outlook and illustrating his utilitarian values, is the contemporary ideal of 'production for consumption' attained through the mass manufacturing process. Occupations which were previously creative and enjoyed the status of work are now devalued as soon as they enter the realms of mass machinery and mass marketing. Its commodities are intentionally designed to be consumed quickly in use and to become out of date or fashion.

These characteristics of the labouring process point to the contrast of some of the qualities that distinguish work itself. First and foremost work is a freely chosen activity resulting in durable products that embody some of the aspirations and characteristics, even if only in a limited way, of those who have poured out their intentions and skills upon them. Every man, she suggests, is capable of starting something new and each has his own perspective.

'Work creates something new out there in the world as a visible testimony to the human effort and thought that has gone into it, and, taken together the products of work create a specifically human world with a permanence of its own. . . '[55]

But neither case for freedom through originality, that leading to novelty or that to a specifically human world can be taken too far. In practice work does not give the mass of individuals the freedom to carry out their unique ideas; if freedom were indeed to mean that, very few people could possibly be free at the same time; because each man's projects would inevitably interfere with another's. Work is by no means the distinctive activity of human life. Neither work, nor any other activity with a clear purpose arising out of the individual's encounter with necessity, could be for Arendt as it is for Weil, the supremely valuable experience of human life. It is freedom itself which is valuable and this for Arendt means simply being able to enter the public arena – *the vita activa* – and to move there with one's contemporaries, all engaged in the same essentially messy and unpredictable business of action with one another. Such a life of free speech and action cannot be expected to leave any definite result or to achieve any goal: instead, it is simply an end, worthwhile in itself. The value of work ultimately is that it provides a lasting setting for the *vita activa*, the realm where each man 'can show his uniqueness and strive to leave the memory of his deeds behind him'.[56] Here, then, is that community of equals where the actions initiated by single agents are achieved by the many against the durable background of 'a specifically human world'. It is this which contrasts with what Arendt sees as 'the futility of mortal life and the fleeting character of human time',[57] characteristic of the activity of *animal laborans*. Here, too, one suspects, are hints to some aspects of the fullness of life and of human relationships which Père Birou sees to be missing from the accounts given by Marx of communist society.[58]

Canovan presents her own critique of the severity of Arendt's distinctions and of the strictures on some of our own contemporary goals that they imply. Notably, she detects a certain contradiction in the exemplary praise given to the individual workers' significant contributions 'to making a durable common world',[59] and the labourers' contribution in maintaining it whilst also making philosophical capital out of the commonplace that, 'creation implies destruction. The new product of work is realised at the expense of the material that was there before'.[60] Arendt sees the world of nature as something to be mastered by men, 'although,' Canovan argues, 'a more conservationist attitude . . . seems to be demanded by her own theory'.[61] If the human world is to be at the same time both a stable and a fitting place for creativity – political activity then, as stressed in some of the last chapters, the inevitable separation between man and nature cannot be pressed to the point of endless hostile exploitation. Somewhere, reconciliation, balance and co-operation has to be found.

Before attempting to reach a general conclusion, it will be well to establish some of the points emerging from the more important papers discussed in this chapter. They are:

1. Weilian liberty is easier to approach if there is a deliberate attempt in formulating the project, to work out a consensus between the participants about the end product of their plans, and also about the means of attaining it. This may mean that particular aspirations may have to be modified in a disciplined way; but it also means a limit to the size of the participating unit. The sharing of purpose has to be explicit. Any number of working groups thus constituted may work side by side so as to constitute a single firm making an elaborate product; provided not only that all its activities can be kept within the range of the mind of each single worker, but also provided that a co-ordinating function is recognised and those exercising it are respected and their powers acknowledged.

2. Going out into the public realm to work can be viewed as a step in the direction of the *vita activa*. Workers' participation and discussion of policy issues would surely be an example of this; measures to promote the conservation of scarce resources and to avoid pollution on a significant scale would be others. A different kind of activity congenial to the idea of the *vita activa* would be the highly articulate exchange of opinions on a wide range of subjects typical of workers engaged on repetitive processes, especially the women in assembling shops.

3. For workers' involvement to be effectively enjoyed, there would need to be vested in them property rights, or fractions of property rights, corresponding to their functions. Moreover, in order that these rights should work harmoniously together towards freely resolved ends, there would need to be some qualification of individual property rights. Such constitutional changes might meet some of the objections in Abrams' paper to the roles of benevolent bourgeois initiators of some contemporary producers' co-operatives.

4. In order that workers, labourers and other functionaries should enjoy their roles in anything like the ways sketched in the papers discussed in this chapter, considerable attention should be addressed to the problems of making public those features of the information and financial economies which at present give large-scale organisations such enormous advantages. This suggestion, too, might meet some of Abrams' misgivings.

5. But the more fundamental point made by Birou remains valid. If social and economic, or come to that political, institutions are built on materialistic assumptions and constantly judged on them, the results will be materialistic.[62] If a fuller human life is wished for, if emphasis is wished to be placed on family life, affections and a

wider range of relationships embracing the community, then a set of assumptions based on these values must begin to alter the whole social outlook.

A more general conclusion to be reached is the need to give the constituent parts of the public realm a practicable, realisable meaning, institutions or concepts with concrete counterparts. It is not simply a life of free men whose deeds will live after them that is needed; possibly something a little less heroic. If less attention could be paid to economic reckoning and organisation, and more to the relationships and values needed for all individuals to live robust, full, human lives, that would be a start. Thought, speech and action would inevitably follow. In Anglo-Saxon and Germanic countries the family as a viable organisation with power and initiatives is a concept which industrialism and commercialism have either emasculated, or very nearly destroyed; so, too, the community as a separate realm where individuals irrespective of wealth and achievement may be valued as personalities. In Mediterranean countries this has not happened. Family and community count for more than state or large organisations of power. This is especially true of Italy where many of the papers in this volume were first delivered.

ENDNOTES

1. Père Alain Birou, 'The Productive System as the Agent of Social Change: Work, Structures and Techniques', p. 142 below.
   Sira Dermen, 'Necessity, Oppression and Liberty: Simone Weil's Thoughts on Work', p. 172 below.
2. Margaret Canovan, 'Labour, Work and the Public World: Hannah Arendt's "Human Condition" ', p. 182 below.
3. Simone Weil, *Oppression and Liberty* (Routledge & Kegan Paul, 1958), p. 84, quoted by Sira Dermen, p. 172 below.
4. Simone Weil, *op. cit.* (1958).
5. Simone Weil, *op. cit* (1958), p. 86.
6. Père Alain Birou, p. 142 below.
7. Karl Marx, *German Ideology* (Milhau, 1846), p. 107, quoted by Birou, p. 142 below.
8. See Père Alain Birou, p. 142 below.
9. See Acton Society Occasional Papers, Siena Series, 1977-79, a list of which is included on p. 299 of this volume.
10. Père Alain Birou, p. 142 below.
11. See Marx's *Grundrisse* (Pelican, 1973), *passim*.
12. Père Alain Birou, p. 142 below.
13. Père Alain Birou, ibid.
14. H. B. Acton, *Illusions of an Epoch* (Cohen & West, 1955), p. 35 *et seq.*
15. Sira Dermen, p. 172 below.
16. Simone Weil, *op. cit.* (1958), p. 45.
17. Simone Weil, *op. cit.* (1958), p. 45, quoted by Dermen, p. 172 below.
18. Simone Weil, *op. cit.* (1958), p. 79.

19. Simone Weil, *Revolution Proletarienne* (Paris, 1933), quoted by Dermen, p. 172 below.
20. Jo Grimond, *Bureaucracy* (Unservile State Group/Liberal Publications Department, 1977); also Martin Albrow, *Bureaucracy* (Macmillan, 1970), pp. 37-49, especially pp. 43-45.
21. Eugen Pusic, 'Workers and Government in a Self-Management Economy', *The Future of Industrial Society*, Vol. II.
22. Eugen Pusic, *ibid.*
23. Eugen Pusic, *ibid.*
24. Simone Weil, *op. cit.* (1958), p. 99.
25. Simone Weil, *op. cit.* (1958), p. 85, for Dermen's perception see p. 172 below.
26. Marx, ed. Engels, *Capital* (Swan Sonnenschein, Lowrey & Co., 1887), Vol. I, ch. VII, p. 157.
27. Sira Dermen, p. 172 below.
28. Sira Dermen, ibid.
29. Norman Macrae, 'The Next Stage in Lifestyles', p. 195 below.
30. Norman Macrae, p. 195 below.
31. Norman Macrae, ibid.
32. Chapter I, p. 1 above.
33. Roger Garaudy, 'Giving Enterprise a Human Face (Créer des Mutants)', p. 93 below.
34. Roger Garaudy, ibid.
35. Roger Garaudy, ibid.
36. Peter Harper, 'Stay Alive with Style', p. 207 below.
37. Marx, *Grundrisse*, pp. 692 and 693.
38. Père Alain Birou, p. 142.
39. Père Alain Birou, ibid.
40. Marx, *Capital*, Vol. I, ch. 14. The whole of chapter 14 is revelant here.
41. Roger Garaudy, p. 93 below.
42. Roger Garaudy, ibid.
43. Harry Braverman, *Labor and Monopoly Capital: The Degradation of Work in the Twentieth Century* (Monthly Review Press, 1974).
44. Harry Braverman, *op. cit.* (1974), pp. 11-12.
45. Harry Braverman, *op. cit.* (1974), p. 13.
46. Harry Braverman, *op. cit.* (1974), p. 13.
47. Père Alain Birou, p. 142 below.
48. Albert Meister, 'L'Autogestion: Aspects nouveaux de la Participation', p. 235 below.
49. Eugen Pusic, *op. cit.*, and Robert Oakeshott, 'The Group of Mondragon Co-operatives', p. 218 below.
50. Robi Ronza, 'The Italian Co-operative Movement and the Possible Role of Co-operation in the Framework of an Economy at the Service of Man', *The Future of Industrial Society*, Vol. II.
51. Roger Garaudy, p. 93 below.
52. Felix FitzRoy, 'Alienation, Freedom and Economic Organisation', *The Future of Industrial Society*, Vol. II.
53. Roger Garaudy, p. 93 below.
54. Hannah Arendt, *The Human Condition* (University of Chicago Press, 1958 and Doubleday Anchor Books, 1959).
55. Margaret Canovan, p. 183.
56. Margaret Canovan, ibid.
57. Hannah Arendt, *op. cit.*, p. 10, quoted by Margaret Canovan, ibid.
58. Père Alain Birou, p. 142 below.
59. Margaret Canovan, p. 183 below.
60. Hannah Arendt, *op. cit.*, p. 122, quoted by Margaret Canovan, ibid.
61. Margaret Canovan, ibid.
62. Père Alain Birou, 'Open letter to Edward Goodman', p. 288 below.

CHAPTER IV

A radical vision

One possible conception of an enjoyable life of action emerging from the last chapter is one which allows the individual to move freely between all three spheres categorised by Arendt – labour, work and active life in the community or society. When adequately conceived, each can balance the other and the three together provide opportunities for a full human life. The monotony and apparent futility of some forms of labour may be welcome as a respite from intense thought or mentally exhausting creative work; the debate of wide public issues may distract from problems of work or economic worries. Similarly, many of the satisfactions that Arendt associates with creative work can also be found in spells of skilled physical work, when the individual has control as he does in, say, agriculture, over the formulation and execution of the project in which he is engaged.

How is this kind of reconciliation between the different categories of activity to be achieved so that no one need feel imprisoned in any one of the three spheres? The answer, providing a sketch of the sort of society that might emerge, is best approached by describing briefly three of the proposals that have been put forward at the seminars covered by the papers presented here. They are:

(i)   the two-tier economy;
(ii) the less conventional third-tier economy;
(iii) 'small nests in the hierarchical tree'.

Economies of scale

To understand these iideas it is necessary to recognise in manufacturing industries and also in many other forms of organisation, economic and otherwise, the existence of what are known as 'the economies of scale'. For the moment these may be seen to be of two kinds: (a) *the physical economies* which give immense advantages to very costly and extensive plant and machinery, provided a market exists within economic distance to purchase its products, and (b) *the service and administrative economies* which enable one central management to provide, or to hire, the services of specialists and administrators and the economies of buying and selling in large quantities to a very large number of separate units – factories, shops, offices, hospitals, schools, etc., etc. The influence of these two economies favours large-scale organisation and tells against idealised small-scale solutions to the work-problems such as presented by, say, Weil, Oakeshott or Garaudy. On the other hand, there are the diseconomies of scale which show that, generally speaking, men and women do not work well in large groups and that the more extensive the tentacles of a central management become, the less effective it is: 450 men is about as large a number of individuals as can work together efficiently, two coachloads for the annual party is much better; a group of 22 is incalculably more flexible than one of fifty or a hundred, but a section of 7, as the army has proved, is even more effective in situations where initiative, quick decisions and improvisation are needed. Such advantages of small-scale organisation as these tell against large organisations; but also they constitute the basis of demands for different kinds of tools, and in this way are a large influence in favour of Weil's philosophy of work.

To return for the moment to the mass manufacturing sector of industries, it will be seen that some features of the economies of scale make very cost effective the mass production of certain basic consumer goods as well as some 'semi-durables' such as cheaper kinds of furniture and motor cars. The introduction of electronic and other automative devices will add enormously to this effectiveness, as well as to the boring and repetitive quality of the work itself. However, capital goods such as automated and semi-automated plant machinery, assembly lines and electronic equipment are very expensive to install and can only be afforded when there really is a huge and sustained mass demand for their products. Mass production methods on a large scale are only justified by very extensive mass markets, indeed on a continental, if not inter-continental, scale.

(i) *The two-tier economy*

This argument leads to the first proposal. Let there be a *two- or three-tier economy*,[1] the first of which would be made up of those capital-intensive and increasingly automated organisations in which it is recognised that the majority of those working in them, except managers, engineers and other technicians, will increasingly find continuous periods of work monotonous and boring. Those who favour this proposal suggest that most ordinary workers would wish to be employed in such plants for no longer than, say, a third or even a quarter of their working time in any one year, arranged in any way agreeable. In the rest of their time they would be free to do less monotonous, possibly more creative, work. In general terms it might be thought desirable for the wages in the first tier to be equivalent to a subsistence standard – this was Gunnar Adler Karlsson's suggestion;[2]

but others would pitch the remuneration deliberately at a figure well above that necessary for subsistence, so that the surplus might subsidise work in the second or third tier.

The second tier would consist of ordinary manufacturing and commercial work but organised according to the standards of size set out above – firms or collectives of between 150 and 450 workers, but divided out into operating units of between 22 and 50 men and then again into sections of initiative of no more than seven to nine. If the predictions in Gimpel's paper[3] are right, its firms or collectives would, over a period of time, almost certainly find themselves having to work with less capital than now. They would tend, for reasons given below, to use more labour-intensive machinery, probably of the type sketched by Weil; or small, sophisticated, all-purpose industrial robots obedient to their user's thought and intentions as described in Macrae's paper.[4] Another likely consequence of a world-wide shortage of capital is that a large proportion of it would be absorbed into the first-tier economy providing essential goods and services on the scale of the mass market, leaving the second tier to develop its own ingenious technology out of whatever small doses of capital were available to it.

Also included in the second tier would be producers' co-operatives, groups of contractors and sub-contractors, firms of craftsmen, small specialist shopkeepers and, of course, the many types of organisation making up the service industries.

(ii) *The third tier*
Examples of enjoyable work likely to be found in the third tier of the economy are given in Peter Harper's paper[5] and also in the various articles by Ray Pahl and Jay Gershuny[6] on the neighbourhood and household economies in the United Kingdom: these are described extensively in Krishan Kumar's paper.[7] These activities are at present financed either by cash surpluses derived from work in the first or second tier or by social security payments. Another sector of the third tier might accommodate the 'hidden economy' where services and favours are exchanged on a non-cash basis or 'the black economy' which exists frankly to avoid paying taxes or complying with other regulations.

More clear-cut and successful examples exist in Italy. Here the 'economia sommersa' moonlighters (ie people doing second jobs in evenings and afternoons); the proprietor worker; the small merchant; small teams of designers; work contracted out to groups of women (and some men, too) often to do at home and once larger firms now broken down into groups of less than twenty workers, constitute an exceptionally thriving third sector of the economy in sharp contrast to the almost bankrupt first tier, consisting mostly of large state-owned industries. These small enterprises are greatly helped by the fact that many union rules and local authority regulations are relaxed in their favour. Using the terminology of the two-tier and three-tier economies, it could be said that individual enterprises and small family firms operating in the third tier of the Italian economy, and the small market-conscious and design-conscious firms in the second, have been decisive in giving Italy a faster growth rate than the rest of Europe.[8]

(iii) *Small nests in large hierarchical trees*[9]

This proposal is more elaborate and ambitious than the other two. In effect it is for the reform, or sometimes even the break-up of the giant-sized organisations, financial empires and conglomerates of both capitalism and state enterprise, and then for their reconstitution in such a way as to allow their previous subsidiary firms and departmental units much greater independence than before: sometimes their total independence. An alternative approach to understanding the principle behind this idea would be to say that at present the co-ordinating hierarchical command structure of large corporations, 'hires the services' of a large number of operating subsidiary companies, specialist departments, as well as of specialist personnel – finance officers, designers and so on, but especially bosses or managers. The change involved would be two-fold: (i) to slim down the hierarchical structure from that resembling a pyramid to that resembling a tall tree; this would happen if subsidiary companies and branches ceased to be dependent on each other, although staying within the same family network of firms; (ii) the firms thus released from the control of the hierarchy would then make contracts with what was left of the old co-ordinating structure – now hierarchical tree, and instead of being hired as previously, they would 'rent the services' they needed from those provided by the hierarchy.

It will, perhaps, help in understanding these ideas to bring in a fuller examination of the economies of scale than that above, which confines itself to the economy of large, complicated, labour-saving plant and machinery. To this should be added the capital economy, that is the enormous financial resources, investments, and facilities for credit enjoyed by the larger firms; it is this which provides them with all the facilities in the market that enable their products to become familiar household names and gives them their immense bargaining power as well as the resources to survive when smaller firms would fail. However, the advantage of this economy may sometimes be exaggerated; for example, transport costs and impersonal dealings might well in future reduce its geographical range.

A fuller examination is also needed of what earlier in this chapter have been called the service economies. In every large firm, or under contract to them, are specialist groups and departments performing services for all the various units making it up. There are research departments, market survey units, drawing offices, employment and personnel offices and so on. One particular service economy is very important indeed, it is known as the *information economy*. This rather cuts across descriptions of the other economies and covers information of every kind which is of use to individual firms and subsidiary firms within the larger firm or hierarchy: for example, the possible range of applications of scientific discovery to their activities; general information about the industry, its markets and sources of raw materials; information about sources of finance and the credit worthiness of people wishing to borrow or obtain credit from the firm, and the work records of employees wanting to move across the firm or from one department to another. Almost invariably in a large corporation information of this kind is reliable and unbiased; what economists call 'clean'' in contrast to the information given by individuals outside the firm or territory of the hierarchy, say by people applying for jobs, by companies wanting contracts or asking for credit, or by salesmen trying to boost their products.

The argument for small nests in hierarchical trees acknowledges the force of these economies offered by very large corporations to their constituent firms. It recognises no less confidently the effectiveness and resourcefulness of well-organised, small, self-contained units of enterprise; and in contrast it points to all the bureaucratic frustrations and the very great difficulties of managing a very large firm as a single unit.

When the two separate sides of this larger argument are put together an excellent case can be made out for the expertise and services of the hierarchy (the service departments, for example) to be considered independently from the initiatives, skills and projects of those working in the typical intimate, small-sized firm or collective. The result of doing this is to be able to see clearly the advantages of either (a) the hierarchies constituting themselves as bare trees with boughs or branches and renting the services of smaller teams, firms or contractors – 'nests' in the branches (or the other way round); (b) the members of the various small nests renting such services of the tree as they need – for example, renting a boss or manager; or (c) the contractors and sub-contractors looking upon themselves as nests of a particular tree. The idea will be understood as long as it can be seen that it is the birds in the nests, the living creatures, who have independence and are free to say what services (a) they are willing to provide, or (b) which they wish to rent.

Finally, it is important, therefore, to spell out the boss or co-ordinating function.[10] It is the job of bosses to make purposeful economic activities successful. They co-ordinate the separate activities of units, departments and divisions. They review plans and ensure that there are no gaps between the initiation and the completion of a project. They have overall responsibility for financial arrangements and prosperity of a project. In the schemes that have been put forward here, either bosses and hierarchies rent the services of workers and specialists, or the workers and specialists, formed into viable small units, rent the services of bosses and hierarchies. In either event the commands of bosses have to be reasonable and bosses have to be obeyed so long as their contract of employment lasts.

The problems of free men in a non-alienating economy

Might the firms, co-operatives or other kinds of collectives in the second- and third-tier economies, and might not the members of the small nests in the hierarchical tree, too, work in ways such as Weil, Macrae, Kumar and Harper describe, using, moreover, specially designed tools and machinery appropriate to them? These would be tools, machines and techniques that would overcome the alienation and estrangement of mechanical mass production work and the oppression of large, complex places of work: tools sufficiently sensitive to the changing ends which men set themselves and that do not brutally distance the workers both from each other and from their own work as well as nature. Philip Abrams suggests that this would be unlikely. He has a separate section of his paper devoted to soft, alternative technology and he uses Illich's 'tools for conviviality'[11] as examples for his argument rather than Weilian tools as described above. The difference may be crucial, because Illich's paradigm tools resemble those of an extremely intelligent, simple-living South American culture as yet hardly affected by the excesses of industrialism or utilitarianism; whereas Weil, or for that matter Macrae, write in anticipation of greater sophistication – of scientists, philosophers, humanists and inventors, as well as sharp-witted, intelligent workers concentrating on making tools that are more precise and more suitable for use by individual workers or small collectives.

Abrams recognises that what he calls the 'tools of alternative technology' tend to reduce the scale of social tools and disperse power. But they do not represent practical aims within the reach of workers devoted to freedom. Their introduction within the structure of existing society would be virtually impossible:

> 'The achievement of widespread alternative technology seems to call for just those forceful tools that alternative technology is designed to reject.'[12]

So Abrams would seem to be suggesting, as does his earlier criticism of the introduction of experiments of communal enterprises, that existing society must be broken up first, possessive individualism destroyed and the means of production socialised. But this is just what happened in Russia and few would deny the justice of Garaudy's, Birou's and Braverman's criticisms quoted above. Changing ownership has not reduced alienation and oppression one jot; due, mainly to bureaucracy and the secret police, it has somewhat increased both.

Could it be that in introducing change we are overlooking the importance of time and timing – for example, the crucial time when the actual conditions of production are ready, or will be ready for the introduction of the new technology intended? Above all, time is needed to develop practically those systematic changes in working methods and tools that will truly reflect the view of work as a series of well co-ordinated actions directed towards the achievement of serious purposes. Timing, too, is needed to synchronise those changes in the art of working, with new forms of organisation.

The solutions will not be in terms of ownership. Possibly they will be appropriate to both socialist and private enterprise. In any event they will, as soon as applied, modify each.

To address oneself adequately to the question of time and timing one might at this stage abstract four principles from Weil's thought in order to summarise and apply what has already been discussed:

(i) The reality principle: men must understand, before attempting to solve their problems or even to work on them, the exact material conditions which determine their various possibilities of action.

(ii) The utopian principle: a utopian goal of activity for Weil is ' a sharply defined limiting case, grounded in a careful analysis of necessity'.[13]

(iii) The transformation of necessity as an applied principle: in what ways is mankind as a whole, or groups of men in different collectives, at present transforming the winds of necessity as they are blown on to the world's surface; or how might they be doing so in a few years' time? How might the character of these transformations be changed so as to be more favourable for the realisation of utopian ends?

(iv) The work principle: work itself should not be undertaken for the sake of satisfaction or providing the means of happiness. These will come about if the conditions of work are themselves real and dignifying. The crucial question is 'how to organise our system of production'.[14]

In view of these four principles, is it not realistic to see these schemes – the two- and three-tier economies and the small nests renting the services provided by hierarchical trees – as the practical beginnings of the changes needed towards achieving an unalienated society free of oppression? They represent real tendencies in the organisation and forward planning of many sectors of western industry. Already it is conceded that there is only a limited area in which even the wealthiest industrial organisation can afford the huge outlay needed for investment in automated and semi-automated mass production plant and assembly lines. Very extensive markets and massive advertising are required to make them paying propositions. Those at the margin are exceedingly vulnerable to depressions and to the frosts of variable economic climates. Moreover, as has already been demonstrated above, not all intelligent current economic thinking presupposes that the influence of all economies of scale invariably favours monolithic, large organisations. The influences of many of the economies of scale favour smaller units of initiative and production. When diseconomies of scale are also taken into account, the size of the most viable operating unit is reduced still further. In firms using primarily mental skills, or mental and manual skills in union, as in building work, the most successful units are very small indeed: two coachloads at the most for the annual outing!

The functions of the diseconomies of scale have in recent years been reinforced by the consequences of education and by the new feeling of self-confidence that the workers have acquired from unionisation. The difficulties of communicating through the networks of large hierarchies is an even weightier example in favour of smaller scale units. However, the more crucial question that besets us returns to the importance of timing. It is to ask when will the legal and institutional means be ready for small nests in industry to rent the services they require of a chosen hierarchy: or a group of men working as a producers' co-operative and the right form of contact to hire a manager?

Change of technique as part of change on a grander scale

It is tempting to suppose that some of the changes now happening, and others of the same kind that we would like to see happen, bear a resemblance to those that occurred in the century before the Renaissance flowered fully. But it is mistaken to suppose that dramatic changes in society can be reversed step by step or will even follow the same pattern twice. New circumstances and new beliefs create the conditions for new stances, for new normative standards, new assessments of values and new moral attitudes. The final lesson to be learned from Weil's writings, in the sense that these have been taken as a book of texts which might be seen as giving unity to the papers appearing in this volume, is that changes in moral attitudes and rules are part of the chain of conscious responses of hard-working men and women, naturally informed of human virtues and methods of thought, to changes in the way that the forces of necessity are transformed in the human world.

The winds of necessity blow on to the outer crust of the world all the time; but it is only through their transformation into the forces, the problems, the perils, the issues of our contemporary life that we experience and perceive change. Facing these transformations we decide, sometimes unanimously but most often only after suffering great differences and debate, to take new and appropriate moral stands.

This is our situation today. And it is to various aspects of it that these papers are addressed. The forces of necessity are presented to our generation and with little doubt to the next, in the form of a rapid growth rate in the world's population, in shortages of oil and other energy supplies; in the threat to civilisation through its application of new knowledge in forms that can be used as destructive weapons, or as means of centralised political power; in the indiscriminate spread of industrialisation from country to country, each making the same claims on the same essential raw materials; in the likely preponderance throughout all areas of the world of educated young people under the age of 25, of whom a majority, unless there are great changes soon in the accepted modes of industrial production and distribution, will be unemployed.

There is the further likelihood, also previously discussed, which could eventually have an even more decisive effect than all these others in speeding up the introduction of alternative technologies – the sophisticated, thoughtful varieties advocated by Weil and Macrae, or possibly the more simple varieties advocated by Gimpel and the alternative technology movement generally, and perhaps, too, some of Thring's imaginative proposals. This is the probability that the supply of capital throughout the world, but especially in the capital-generating industrial countries, is likely to become increasingly scarce. Money will become in short supply. It is probable, too, that the demands of labour for a larger and larger share of the profits or surplus value of enterprise will increase and the proportion of capital for reinvestment especially outside the mass production industries will diminish. In that event, enterprises in the second and third tiers of a three-tier economy will simply be forced to devise new labour intensive techniques; techniques to correspond with the demands of new generations of educated workers requiring to possess the appropriate hand and machine tools for non-alienating work.

The proposals in this chapter and a great many like them are, perhaps, doing little more than making virtues out of necessity; applying principles thoughtfully to trends and tendencies that are even now evident. Mass production plants are already being established in, or transferred to, South America and South-East Asia; strikes, boredom, conservative habits and high labour costs in the old industrial countries already begin to give advantages to new manufacturing industries in developing countries. It must be emphasised that in most industrialised countries, manufacturing work, work carried on in factories, accounts for less than half all economic acitivity. Nevertheless, as Braverman shows,[15] office work and retailing are increasingly becoming organised and mechanised in the same way as factory work.

It has also to be emphasised that the ideas of small nests in hierarchical trees and of a three-tier economy are by no means put forward as panaceas. They are best regarded as examples of new structures which might develop mostly out of older ones and help forward some of the more profound changes of condition needed to bring about a less alienated and more human society. But in any event, even if fully implemented, there would be a great many activities falling outside their scope. Probably firms in the second tier at present resourcefully conducted with a contented workforce sharing the aims of the owner or manager will be the last to want changes which might upset their settled working habits and relationships.

Krishan Kumar concludes the section devoted to thoughts about future work styles with a comprehensive survey of the British industrial scene and brings to attention those specialised and bespoke manufacturing processes that fit British skills and temperament.[16] Many of these already exist on a considerable scale; others, with a little institutional and legislative help, could be put on a much more thriving basis. Yet one must also ask what is wrong with conditions in Britain that prevents the carrying out of very many good ideas that British inventors and designers undoubtedly still do have. Apart from some very convincing arguments for third-tier activity, especially in the neighbourhood, or one might say in 'the informal community economy', much of Kumar's emphasis is upon the revival of the skills for which Britain once was famous, or doing 'the thing that Britain has always been good at':[17] in particular the service industries which, with a little imagination, could be widely extended: much more could be made of not only the famous 'invisibles' such as insurance and banking, but also our medical and educational services. Both hospitals and universities, broken down into suitable small units, could be imaginatively adapted, provided the investment could be made available, to cater for the needs of patients and students from abroad. If his proposals were adopted, no more would be heard of campaigns to close hospitals and universities, or of large numbers of doctors and scientists emigrating for more suitable or better-paid work abroad. On the contrary, the services of our well-trained doctors and academics would be required to help adapt these to world-wide needs in hospitals and teaching establishments in England.

But life is not all work

Sira Dermen's paper shows that Weil's conception of work is a fitting model for any human activity with a specific end in view. 'Even the apparently freest forms of activity' such as 'science, art, sport, only possess value in so far as they imitate the accuracy, rigour, scrupulousness which characterise the performance of work and even exaggerate them.'[18] Although this is the way, wherever appropriate, in which the word work has been used throughout this section, it will be prudent to conclude with its usage in the narrower, more conventional sense of a gainful or productive activity. In that sense Birou concludes that human beings are not simply, or even essentially, productive agents, as the logic of reasoning must lead us to believe is what Marx thought they were. Such a view would neglect other material and equally necessary aspects of human life; dependent personal relationships, the experience of love, friendship and parenthood; mental and physical states and 'the experience and knowledge of the world that men must have before they can work.'[19]

By looking at men and women from these and many other angles we can see why Marx thought that human society could only be changed through the agency of the productive system, using indeed 'the forceful tools' of revolution. However, in his early years, Marx himself saw the danger to humanity of mechanical invention employed by man estimating himself solely as a productive agent.

'All our inventions and our progress seem to have only one consequence: to endow material goods with life and intelligence, and to turn man into a material force.[20]

It is this fact which Weil opposed with the force of her whole being; and commenting on this passage, Birou concludes that 'Marx the humanist is sounding a warning note here. In the name of man faced with death today, let us hope that we may understand what is at issue'.[21]

But do we understand what is at issue? Men, it is true, have made mechanical monsters with life and intelligence: their organisations have become machines with a life of their own. However, machines break down; machines stop; organisations die. The crisis goes deeper. It can be approached from three quite different angles. The first includes the general subjects raised in the first chapter: energy, population expansion, technology, unemployment, social violence, intolerably sized cities and so on; alongside these there is the crisis of capitalism, the crisis of socialism, the crisis of communism and the crisis of the Third World.[22] The second view of it comes from the standpoint given by the character of the means, methods and organisation of industrial production and allied activities. From these two perspectives emerges a single issue of great importance. This is whether people are self-conscious, imaginative and adaptable enough to see themselves as the creatures affected by these techniques and organisations and if so, whether they can understand that the worldwide emergency is not a temporary crisis, but one made up of the very means that they have chosen to solve the problems presented to them by the forces of bare necessity.

'It is man who creates the systems of production, forms of technical civilisation, utopias of future progress, programs of social organisation of human life.'[23]

But this is only a beginning. The basic essentials of life, it is agreed, have to be produced and distributed fairly in order that people have the means to live their full natures as human beings, and this serves to draw attention to the third part of the crisis that Birou perceives. Preoccupation with the values and issues of production, its machinery, organisation and control, threatens to take up, if it has not already done so, all the energies of society and to take over all its beliefs. Man, as Marx foresaw, has become a material force; he is now an out-and-out materialist; a worshipper of material success and progress in the West and a philosophical materialist in communist countries. But, as Birou emphasises, material appetites with their accompanying productive systems, represent only one part of human nature. It should be seen that man also needs material things to enable him to pursue and enjoy his other values: he needs them for the sake of his affections, responsibilities and ideals, as well as to play his part in the world of his fellow men. It is here that the life of public activity stressed by Arendt is relevant.

The worldwide crisis has roots very deeply embedded in the tradition of Western thought. Immediately underlying it is the utilitarian tradition with its confusion between two meanings of good; the morally good, the worthwhile, the inherently good – good as an end; and good or goods in the sense of things made and sold for use. Goods in the second sense are one of the means for attaining good in the first sense.

But further down is a much older dualism implicit in the Christian system which itself contains two contrasting strands of thought concerning the nature of freedom. And, although contrasting, both are exceedingly precious. The first emphasises the absolute need of giving to the human person the education, the upbringing, the opportunity, the material means and formal conditions to enable him to discharge his responsibilities as a person. This, in the course of history, has ended in the more or less traditional view of freedom in which the conditions of freedom and progress are identical. It may then be developed by a writer such as Weil stressing the value of the freedom gained through realisation; or it may be developed, as it is by present-day political activists, to stress the conditions necessary to provide a favourable climate for economic development and progress more widely defined.

The second strand of thought gives this neo-classical freedom a moral and supernatural dimension, seeing it as a part of the essential link between the person and the community: that is to say family, extended family, village or any natural group within which one individual recognises another by name or look, or other personal quality. This link is essential and combines together the material and moral aspects of life. Even without the wealth or property claimed for him by formal liberty, the individual still has the support of the community and a place in it. He cannot be excluded by the community; even if the community be geographically widespread and only linked by common interest. This view may be developed so as to include some of the stimulating thought and research into antiquity with which Arendt surrounds the *vita activa* – public life. But in most industrialised countries, although not Latin ones, the idea of public life of the community, which is not the same as social life, lacks positive interpretation. In order to see the practicality of such interpretation one has only to think of some of the functions which could be performed more agreeably and sometimes more economically by decentralised bodies under the aegis of local communities than, as at present, by governments and the centralised agencies that they sponsor. Individuals should have more say in the planning of the environment in which they live, and there is a strong case to be made for their very often having a decisive voice in the choice of the form of energy supply appropriate to the area. When national services break down or deteriorate there is no sound reason why they should not be undertaken at a lesser cost and more efficiently through the local community; spontaneous efforts of the locally organised delivery of letters, for example, or local transport arrangements to meet local need. The community in these respects would be making itself a part of the third tier of the national economy. One can also think of ways in which individuals could show their concern for the sick and the elderly and help provide the young with the training and opportunities for suitable careers in life. For these and similar purposes the need for having a balanced variety of local enterprises is once more stressed.

People ought to be able to look to their community for the means of fulfilling their personal aspirations. Of those whose being is expressed in this way Pope Wojtyla writes: 'They seek their own place and a constructive role within the community; they seek for *that* participation and *that* attitude to the common good which would allow them a better, a fuller, a more effective share of the communal life.'[24] It is in this context that the idea of the community as a political entity can be developed, and the needed changes in moral values and assumptions sought by a new outlook can be discussed. The interests, affections and loyalties, traditions and belief of people in the community extend into one another and constitute something close to common identities. Similarly, the attitudes and interests of individuals are conditioned by their families and the network of relations which they throw out. They have a common background and history. Above all, and this has been true since the time of the city states of which Arendt writes, members of the same community share the same sense of justice and fairness applied both to general and to particular events. Hence it is the ideal forum for the discussion of ideas. Few ideas are accepted wholeheartedly at first. Like strangers, they come from the world outside and have to become known and evaluated before they are accepted or rejected.

Put into such a setting voluntary, yet organised, communal effort of a genuinely political kind could be brought into play and society itself be protected against such evils of centralism as, for example, bureaucracy and subservience to the power of one or two highly organised trade unions. This need be no recipe for anarchism. The idea of small nests in large hierarchical trees could well serve as a model for what ought still to be done centrally and what might be more happily done in the well-knit and politically active community by responsible, informed individuals anxious to share at least in the discussion of the issues of public life. Nor does it exclude important roles for centralised bodies. Surely all intelligent anticipations of the future must include the idea that decentralised bodies on the rim of the wheel will be connected to the centre by novel and highly efficient forms of communication forming the spokes. In the same way, hub will be connected to hub.

Human life needs restored to it the balance that it once had and has now lost. This is what we really mean by alienation. We now live mainly through systems and processes together with the plans and disciplines of work they produce. This creates artificiality in our lives and our relationships. Thus, our first need is to correct the imbalance between our brains, our minds, our bodies and our true emotions; no less between them and their physical and their immediate social environment in the community. What industrial man living in sophisticated modern society misses is that characteristic of more primitive communities, that sense of oneness with environment which was 'a living, inwardly realised participation'.[25]

It is in the community of family and neighbourhood or the community of those sharing our interests, our pleasures, our politics, our problems, our recreation, values and concerns that we can rediscover the image of the whole man that we have lost.

From these real feelings and authentic human values, surely it will be possible to solve some of those problems of industry and work posed in this and the earlier chapters. From this start, the right balance of industry, trades and crafts and agriculture must emerge; the right size of enterprises and the right balance between satisfying local needs and those of the market. Surely, too, will emerge the flexible forms and methods to overcome alienation, as FitzRoy has already been quoted as predicting: moreover, they will have ' . . . relevance compared to more dogmatic "radical" doctrines . . . touted as panaceas for all social ills'.[26]

Founded in genuine relationships, the most suitable forms of co-operation and participation will emerge in response both to the nature of work and the character of the worker. Participation in larger firms will be realistic and responsible at all levels in all tiers, where it can be genuinely effective. And these forms of enterprise will be balanced by others – the individual enterprise, the family firm, the firm of less than 20 workers, as have sprung up in Italian communities and proved such a boost to the country's growth rate.[27]

Here, in communities is the basis for many of the other changes mentioned in this book. It is through being voiced in the community that other ideas canvassed at present such as equality, solidarity and rights of personality which have proved illusive under utilitarianism, will find expression and definition. If civilisation is to develop a different moral outlook with new assumptions and attitudes to environment and work, surely this is the most practical forum in which to discuss the values on which the community places the most importance and what form individual aspirations should take to express them.

ENDNOTES

1. References to the 'bi-modal' and two-tier economy can be found in Robin Marris, 'A New Model of the Process of Business Concentration with Special Reference to Public Policy towards Small Firms', Acton Society Occasional Paper No. 7, Siena Series 1977/79 and in the following transcripts: No. 23 (discussion following Robin Marris's paper); No. 2 (discussion following Gunnar Adler Karlsson's paper). These transcripts may be referred to at the Acton Society, 9 Poland Street, London W1, provided an appointment is made.
2. Gunnar Adler Karlsson, 'Technology, Population and Power', *The Future of Industrial Society*, Vol. II.
3. Jean Gimpel, 'Small Units – A Danger to Civilisation,' p. 111 below.
4. Norman Macrae, 'The Next Stage in Lifestyles', p. 195 below.
5. Peter Harper, 'Stay Alive with Style', p. 207 below.
6. R. E. Pahl, 'The Industrial Societies and After', *Universities Quarterly*, Autumn 1976; J. I. Gershuny, 'Self-Service Economy', *New Universities Quarterly*, Vol. 32, no. 1, Winter 1977/78.
7. Krishan Kumar, 'Thoughts on the Present Discontents in Britain', p. 260 below.
8. Julia Bamford, 'Small Business in Italy: the submerged economy', p. 243 below. See also *Time* magazine, August 1981.
9. The idea of the hierarchical tree and its nests originates from Professor David Teece's paper presented at Siena in 1977, 'Some Relative Efficiency and Comparative Institutional Properties of Markets and Hierarchies', Acton Society Occasional Paper No. 4, Siena Series, 1977/79. This paper and the subsequent discussion owes much to the book of David Teece's mentor, Professor Oliver Williamson, *Markets and Hierarchies: Analysis and Antitrust Implication* (New York Free Press, 1975).
10. Stephen A. Marglin, 'What do Bosses do? The Origins of Hierarchy in Capitalist Production', *The Review of Radical Political Economics*, Summer 1974, Vol. 6, No. 2, pp. 60-112.
11. Philip Abrams, 'Tools versus Values', p. 120 below.
12. Philip Abrams, ibid.
13. Sira Dermen, 'Necessity, Oppression and Liberty: Simone Weil's Thoughts on Work', p. 172 below.
14. Sira Dermen, ibid.
15. Harry Braverman, *Labor and Monopoly Capital: the degradation of work in the twentieth century* (Monthly Review Press, 1974).
16. Krishan Kumar, p. 260 below.
17. Krishan Kumar, ibid.
18. Simone Weil, *Oppression and Liberty* (Routledge & Kegan Paul, 1958), pp. 84-85 quoted by Dermen, p. 172 below.
19. Père Alain Birou, 'The Productive System as the Agent of Social Change', p. 142 below.
20. Marx, 'People's Paper', April 1856, quoted by Père Alain Birou, ibid.
21. Père Alain Birou, ibid.
22. Père Alain Birou, 'Open Letter to Edward Goodman', p. 288 below.
23. Karol Wojtyla, *The Acting Person*, translated from the Polish by Andrzej Potocki (Dordrecht: Reidel, 1979), p. 297, quoted in Edward Norman, 'The Moral and Political Attitudes of Pope John Paul II', *The Cambridge Review*, 1 June 1981, p. 197.

24. Karol Wojtyla, *The Acting Person*, p. 286, quoted in Edward Norman, *op. cit.*, p. 196.
25. F. C. Happold, *Religious Faith and Twentieth Century Man* (Pelican Books, 1966), p. 168.
26. Felix FitzRoy, 'Alienation, Freedom and Economic Organisation', *The Future of Industrial Society*, Vol. II and p. 50, Chapter III above.
27. Julia Bamford, p. 243 below.

The moral economy of the rat race

Tom Burns

Fred Hirsch's brilliant book *Social Limits to Growth*,[1] supplies the occasion for these thoughts; the idea of there being a *moral* economy is taken, of course, from E. P. Thompson's essay.[2] I would like to try to extend Hirsch's diagnosis of our present situation by supplying some account of how we got there – i.e. to indulge in the kind of historical aetiological exercise which makes sociologists so unpopular with historians.

But since the only method available to sociology is that of critical comparison, resort to the historical past for comparisons is often unavoidable.

It is at least common ground that there are two categorical, and fundamental, differences between the present day world and the pre-industrial world. The first consists in the simple and familiar facts of population expansion, economic growth and changed values – religious, moral, political, social. The second category, equally familiar, but in fact rather more dubious, is the acceptance of change itself as part of our condition.

Perhaps the most consequential of all these differences lies in the sheer weight of numbers the world now contains. Braudel rightly begins his account of the pre-industrial era by heavily underlining the fact of accelerated growth in population. 'World population doubled during the four centuries (1400-1800) covered by this book; nowadays it doubles every thirty or forty years'.[3]

Beyond this, there is the further difference that this increased population has also been able to increase its capacity to produce material goods and services. The data base is more contrived and more crude, of course, than in the case of population, but in Britain alone the national produce *per capita* reckoned at constant prices, quadrupled during the eighteenth century, when the population of Britain multiplied itself three-and-a-half times. Population increase has slowed down in Europe since then, but economic growth has not.

Modern societies are founded on industrial capitalism, the first mode of production to guarantee, in Habermas's words, long-term economic growth.[4] But along with mastery of material and social technologies which have made this possible, human values and purposes have also, perforce, been transformed. Familiar as this third, immaterial, aspect of the Great Transformation has been made for us, the familiarity is still one of the lecture room and the text book; the change, though obvious enough, is amorphous, and, above all, immeasurable. Some mental, imaginative, effort is needed to grasp the relevance to our contemporary predicament of the change in moral values which either accomplished or were wrought by the onset of industrialism. It is these simple facts of population expansion, economic growth and change in moral values which have combined to land us in the Catch 22 predicament – the paradox of affluence, as Fred Hirsch calls it – which we have to escape from or reconcile ourselves with.

Readers of Hirsch's book will recognise the 'Catch 22' reference. His general thesis is clear enough: the drive for economic growth, for more of everything for everybody is as powerful as ever it was and probably even more so; but there are limits to economic growth, and they are pressing on us now, not waiting for the Year 2000. For the constraints imposed and the deprivations those limits inflict are social, not physical. So what we have to solve are the problems not so much – or not only – those of limiting population growth, or controlling pollution, or discovering alternative sources of energy and other finite resources, or inventing new social technologies for effective public control, wider participation and codes of distributive justice. The central task, according to Hirsch, requires us to change social norms and not moral values.

To understand this central task, we have, I believe, to go back to the Great Transformation[5] itself – the social, economic and political revolution which culminated in (rather than started with) the historical events of the decade of the French Revolution and the fifty or sixty years ordinarily allotted to the fulfilment of the Industrial Revolution. And if Hirsch is right, and I think he is, it is to the third aspect of the Great Transformation that we have to turn, and treat the slow transformation of values – of what people aspire to, seek satisfaction in, prefer, approve – as the matter which we must seek to understand and get straight.

What I want to do is assemble, revise and amalgamate the kind of historical explanation which might afford a starting point for the discussion of remedies. For I am convinced, with George Lichtheim, that the first problem for us is not so much to change the world, for that is being done fast enough without our help, but to understand it.

The shift in values associated with the emergence of the liberal-democratic nation state and with the industrialisation of Western society has been tagged with a variety of labels over the past hundred years: from status to contract, from *Gemeinschaft* to *Gesellschaft*, from prescribed status to achieved status, from the fixed order of 'the Great Chain of Being' to the idea of progress, from a monarchic, aristocratic or oligarchic political system to plutocracy, pluralism or socialism, from the duties and burdens of subjects to the rights of citizens. In more personal, and more fundamental terms, the shift might be rendered as one from self-respect to self-esteem. The respect owed to oneself and to others as equal of the children of God, or in Kant's secular version, as ends in themselves and never merely as means, which (at least notionally, ideally and normatively) may be said to have held good in medieval and post-reformation society, became regard for a person's possessions, abilities, competence, qualities – in short, for personal attributes, especially alienable and marketable attributes.

The change, more simply, was one from equality to inequality. This is somewhat difficult for us to grasp (though perhaps no more difficult than Whitehead's designation of the corresponding mental and cosmological historical shift as being a shift from the medieval and renaissance age of reason to the modern age of belief).[6] For the inequalities in all practical senses which differentiated people in pre-industrial society – inequalities even more gross and manifest than those which prevail nowadays – were inequalities which were institutionalised in the *société d'ordes* or *Ständegesellschaft*, legalised by sumptuary laws and property laws, enforced within the political system and even sanctified by Christian teaching. *Nevertheless*, three hundred years ago, before the Great Transformation, the essential equality – or the equality in essentials – of men, even in terms of their attributes, were no more than plain common sense:

> 'Nature hath made men so equall, in the faculties of body, and mind; and that though there bee found one man sometimes manifestly stronger in body, and of quicker mind, then another; yet when all is reckoned together, the difference between man, and man, is not so considerable, as that one man can thereupon claim to himself any benefit to which another may not pretend as well as he . . .'[7]

And Hobbes even goes on to brush aside objections as the product of vain conceit 'of one's owne wisdome, which almost all men think they have in a greater degree than the Vulgar; that is all men but themselves and a few others, whom by Fame, or from concurring with themselves, they approve.'

Social inequality prevails everywhere, and in all historical periods. This is not to say that it is, or has been, universally acceptable, but in all societies there are arguments, principles and values invoked to defend the inequalities which exist, to explain them, to defend them and to 'legitimate' them – i.e. to render them legally, politically, and, ultimately, morally defensible. This is so, naturally enough, because there are also arguments, principles and values which may be, and often are, invoked to challenge them.

The moral axioms from which both sides argue may change, as they have from Augustine and John Ball to Hobbes and to Tawney, as to the dimensions and the degree of inequality. But the paradox implicit in Hobbes' statement remains curiously constant: thus Harold Lydall, opening up his inquiry into what he calls the 'structure' of earnings, writes:

'Why is it that human beings, all of one species and starting at birth with fairly equal endowments should develop by middle age a dispersion of earnings with a proportionate range as wide as fifty or even a hundred to one?'[8]

In most Western societies these days, inequalities resulting from differences in achievement or prowess through specific aptitudes and skills are accounted worthy and defensible, and those deriving from inherited privilege, power or wealth, or from patronage are accounted unfair and unworthy and morally indefensible. This is not universally true, but during the past two hundred years the extension of achievement as the determining principle for social position, and the erosion of other means by which power and privilege may be obtained has come to be regarded as a dominant criterion of social improvement or 'modernisation'.

'It seems at least that in industrial societies "achievement" is in no way merely a regulatory and distributive norm for economic work, but rather it is becoming more and more the evalued principle that regulates all areas of life. One can say . . . that achievement is well on the way to becoming the only over-arching value category in industrial societies.'[9]

It seems very unlikely that there has ever been a time, in any society, in which the 'legitimacy' of the unequal distribution of rights, privileges, power, wealth and income won absolute and universal acceptance. This is one reason why it is difficult to swallow Habermas's contention that there is, in contemporary Western society, a crisis of legitimation.[10] This existence of crises of this kind seems to be established by hindsight after historical episodes seen later as 'revolutionary': in 1519, 1942, 1789 and 1917. What does happen is that there is a shift in the values and principles on which legitimate inequality is founded and it is common ground that, nowadays, entitlement to preferred positions derives from successful competition with others – or is at least regarded as more securely founded, less challengeable, more 'legitimate' than entitlement by inheritance, luck or force.

In consequence, therefore, it is arguable that the idea of equality inherent in the sense of common humanity, or of 'equality before God' which prevailed in pre-industrial society (which was, of course, anything but egalitarian in all practical senses) has been displaced, or, in fact, destroyed, by the idea of equality of opportunity. Further, the kind of self-respect and respect for others which went with it has been replaced, or destroyed, by self-appraisal and appraisal of others in terms of attributes which are in the broadest sense economically marketable. In Weber's view, the essential prerequisite of industrial capitalism was the creation of a free labour market, and this view is universally accepted; it is the implication, connotation and consequences of a free labour market under industrial capitalism which are matters of debate. Yet the model of the market which Weber had in mind was a rather special one, and he does not seem to have been aware that there were other kinds of market. For the point about the labour market so essential to industrialism is not merely, as Weber insisted, that it is free and open, but that it is competitive. This is crucial. In the frequent discussion of the development of the market society in England and Western countries generally, the distinction between a market and a competitive market has been lost. But the distinction is of the utmost importance. 'In the Middle Ages,' says Holdsworth, 'economic dealings were regarded rather as a series of personal relationships than as a mere exchange of commodities, with the result that the ideal aimed at was a moral ideal – honest manufacture, a just price, a fair wage, a reasonable profit'.[11] And economic dealings of this kind took place in the market. One can also, within limits, speak of a medieval labour market, too. But the conception of markets which prevailed in the Middle Ages, of marketing, and of the relationship of the market not only to the economy and to society at large, is quite different from the competitive market which makes its appearance as the dominant force in the nascent industrial society of the eighteenth century. Karl Polanyi is quite right to see the Great Transformation as centred in the way in which market economics became seen as of vital importance to society. 'Instead of economy being embedded in social relationships, social relations are embedded in the economic system.'[12]

The clearest indication of this is the long series of legislative and judicial acts which 'freed' the labour market in eighteenth-century England. This transformation is documented by Holdsworth from 1702, when the House of Commons, responding to a petition of weavers and woolcombers about untrained or half-trained workers coming into their trade, said that trade ought to be free, and declined to take any action. By 1759 Lord Chief Justice Mansfield voiced a wholesale disapproval of the old statutes which gave entitlement to practise crafts only to those who had served their full seven-year apprenticeship (and forbade employers engaging semi-unskilled or unskilled labour);

> 'If none must employ, or be employed, in any branch of trade, but who have served a limited number of years to that branch, the particular trade would be lodged in a few hands, to the danger of the public, and the liberty of setting up trade, and the foundations of the present flourishing position of Manchester will be destroyed. In the infancy of trade, the act of Queen Elizabeth might be well calculated for public weal, but now it is grown to that perfection we see it, it might perhaps be of utility to have those laws repealed, as tending to cramp and tie down that knowledge it was first necessary to obtain by rule.'[13]

When, at long last, the statutes of apprentices were repealed in 1814 they had long been very largely inoperative in practice.[14] By then, England had successfully been transformed into a competitive market society, one in which market relationships 'so shape or permeate social relations that it may properly be called a market society, not merely a market economy'.[15]

It was the persuasiveness of the image of society as essentially a market, of social relationships being governed by competitive market dealings, of the evaluation of qualities and people as well as things as commodities which provides the clue to the distinctive character of the new social institutions which gave birth to the Industrial Revolution. If one substitutes for Hobbes's sardonic rendering of man as driven to rivalry by power, fear and the desire to be conspicuous, Locke's 'uneasiness', or 'desire for some absent good', the transition to a philosophically and morally sanctioned competitive market society is complete.

The ability to sell, and to buy, labour as a commodity in a free market, an absolute prerequisite for capitalist industry, was fully institutionalised in early eighteenth-century England; even by 1700, more than half the occupied adults were wage earners. Land had even earlier become treated as an alienable commodity. On the basis of these two economic institutions, which developed slowly but deliberately during the sixteenth and seventeenth centuries, the institutional life of the country relevant to all kinds of economic enterprise became permeated with the value-system and the characteristic patterns of relationships and actions of a competitive market society. Competitive achievement is no more than an essential complement to the institution of a free market in land, capital goods and labour. And, aptly, it is the life of Richard Arkwright, whose name is so indissociably tied up with the Industrial Revolution, which testifies most clearly to the fact that this whole complex process of institutionalisation came to maturity towards the end of the eighteenth century. His whole life is evidence of the freedom with which inventions and improvements could be bartered and become the subject of contracts – were, in fact, marketable; it is also testimony to the success which attended one who, like Arkwright, 'was anxious to better himself', who 'had fertile brains for devising means of rising in the world and . . . knew how to drive a good bargain, the sort of diplomacy in which he had been trained to being akin to that of the pedlar or the horse dealer'.[16]

It is this same eighteenth-century world which accepted the traffic in electoral votes and parliamentary seats as part of the machinery of politics; politicians might be condemned as venal, but the market system was as defensible in that respect as in any other. Votes, ideas for inventions, a capacity for business enterprise were all saleable resources, as was land and labour, and as were the products of literary and artistic effort. The system of patronage which had supported the writer and artist and musician gave way to commercial publishing and the academy market.

One must not exaggerate the extent of the change; profitable dealing was nothing new, and selling goods or one's services to the highest bidder had always been regarded as reasonable, if not entirely proper in some respects. But there had been a tight limit to the kind of goods or services which could be disposed of in this profit-maximising way, and to the circumstances in which it could be done. Above all, whatever the realities of the situation or the historical trend which hindsight allows us to discern, there was a traditional moral consensus about selling and buying which affected the necessities of life. This consensus was articulated in law which dates from the fifteenth century and which itself converted customary practice into positive law. There was, as E. P. Thompson puts it, a 'model of the marketing and manufacturing process . . . appealed to in Statute, pamphlet or protest movement – against which the awkward realities of commerce and construction were in friction'.[17]

This model applied most clearly and strictly to cereals. Corn had to be marketed direct, so far as possible, from farmer to consumer, being brought in bulk to the *local* market. Farmers 'should not sell it while standing in the field, nor should they withhold it in the hope of rising prices. The markets should be controlled; no sales should be made before stated times, when a bell would ring; the poor should have the opportunity to buy grain, flour or meal first, in small parcels, with duly supervised weights and measures: At a certain hour, when their needs were satisfied, a second bell would ring and larger dealers (duly licensed) might make their purchases.'[18] All dealers were subject to restrictions designed to prevent speculation on price rises and on different prices in different markets.

It may well be that such regulations were framed by merchant guilds and enacted by burghs in order to protect local dealers and millers from 'foreigners', but it seems equally true – and makes equal sense – that the interests of local consumers, poor as well as rich, were protected by the same regulations, and were intended to be so.[19] For over and above all these provisions, there was an equally elaborate set of rules for consumer protection. 'Millers and – to a greater degree – bakers were considered as servants of the community, working not for profit but for a fair allowance,'[20] and, for London and the larger towns, where such rules were impracticable, there was the Assize of Bread which assigned a price to the loaf related to the ruling price of wheat.

What Thompson sets out to document in this essay is that the 'breakthrough of the new political economy of the free market' spelt the 'breakdown of the old moral economy of provision'.[21] Just what is the force of the distinction between a moral economy and a political economy is not clear; it seems to me self-evident that both are normative conceptions of the principle which has governed economic practices, and thus both are equally 'moral' just as both are equally 'political'. For, to revert to a point made earlier, the transition from a market economy embedded in the social order to a social order embedded in the market economy did not just happen. It was made to happen by the social action of groups and individuals moved by values and purposes more in accordance with the latter order than the former, covered by infringements of the law as well as of traditional moral principles, and eventually by political decisions which changed the law so as to promote conditions favourable to the operation of free competitive markets and to the new values of maximising profit and promoting competitive enterprise. Peter Mathias makes this a critically important factor in his assessment of the reasons why the Industrial Revolution took place in Britain in the eighteenth century, and only in Britain:

> 'When the statement is made, therefore, that the crucial distinguishing mark of the Industrial Revolution in Britain was that of the "market economy" or "responsiveness to market forces" or "institutionalising market forces" or "the smallness of the subsistence sector", we are making a positive statement about political decision-making in England; not implying simply the absence of political decision-making. A market is always politically determined in the sense of requiring a legal framework.'[22]

The dismantling of the laws which regulated markets and protected consumers, artisans and employees was already well under way before Adam Smith gave his blessing to the process. But this was only a beginning, and before its completion by the middle of the nineteenth century, industrial capitalism was well into its second phase.

I have to dwell on this for a moment. When I speak of 'phases' in the development of capitalism, I am not referring to stages of growth or development marked by such terms as 'early' or 'entrepreneurial' capitalism, mature capitalism, or 'late capitalism', 'monopoly capitalism', the 'corporate state', or 'corporatism'. Terms such as these, whether used by Liberals or Marxists, seem to me to overrate the sheer inertial force of industrial capitalism, and to underrate its dynamic capacity for change and regeneration – something which Schumpeter at least grasped at when he wrote of 'the creative destruction' which characterised the historical development of capitalism. One of the more distinctive features of industrial capitalism is its ability to take on new life when its obituary has been written[23] – as it has been so frequently since 1848, up to the Second World War (out of which the last thing we expected was the emergence of a resurgent, even triumphant capitalism, creating economic miracles in one country after another, and an affluent society even, so we were told, in Britain). The point, of course, is that it is a different capitalism which emerges out of these crises from that which suffered them; and what emerges is not a capitalism one step nearer the grave, or capitalism with a new mask, but a regenerated capitalism, one with a new, or at least reconstructed, *modus operandi* and structure.

If we look at the historical development of industrial capitalism in this light, we can see how it was that even before 1800 strict limits were placed on the free competitive market in labour by the Combination Acts and the Conspiracy Laws, which prohibited any union of workers which might counter the bargaining strength of the quite public combinations of employers to control wages and conditions of labour.

During the early nineteenth century, a whole series of private acts enable entrepreneurs to appropriate common land, to acquire monopoly rights, and to reduce investment risks.[24]

Legislation again provides an indicator for the initiation of a third phase of industrial capitalism in, for example, the Companies Act of 1862 – the Magna Carta of co-operative enterprise as it was called – and, thirteen years later, Disraeli's Trade Union Act, which finally freed trade unions of their worst constraints. Taken together, both acts not only legitimated but encouraged the agglomeration of capital and of manpower which the new, larger and more complex industrial enterprise needed. For it was at this time – the third quarter of the nineteenth century – that industrialism underwent its second major change – partly the result of the entry into full scale industrialisation of Germany and the United States, but more the consequence of a new wave of industrial innovation which comprehended and followed on the chemical revolution, the communications revolution, and, most important of all, the armaments revolution of the 'fifties and 'sixties. But these developments relate to the material technology side of industrial capitalism. The special mark of this third phase, though, comes from two quite new developments on the side of social technology: first, there is the discovery of bureaucratic organisation, in the strictly Weberian sense, as a universally applicable instrument of the administration of large scale undertakings:

' . . . the changes that were taking place within the more advanced societies . . . reflected a pronounced trend from *laissez-faire* towards combination in economic enterprise, towards collective self-help among wage-earners, towards state regulation in the economic and social fields. Like the movement towards greater material output and like the advance in technology and production methods, processes with which it is intimately connected, the drift towards greater organisation among men, as specialised groups and as total communities, has been virtually continuous and continually increased throughout modern times. But it was in the generation after 1870 when the drift was so much accelerated by the interaction of the greater problems and the greater opportunities with which societies were confronted that those forms and attitudes first took the clear shape which exists today.'[25]

But the rapid acceleration in the growth of bureaucratic organisation which the *New Cambridge Modern History* rightly notes as the distinguishing mark of the last quarter of the nineteenth century was prompted by motives beyond those for devising adequate machinery for coping with growing complexity:

'Of all the expanding governments at this time it may be said that it was not only in the interests of society that they were intervening in the social sphere, and not only in the social sphere that they were adding to their competence and their powers. All, the least, as well as the most authoritarian, were improving in executive and administrative efficiency; all relied on this development – on the growth and professionalisation of the bureaucracy, the army and the police; on the vast improvement in weapons and transport; on the increased possibilities of controlling public opinion and securing public loyalty to the press, the widespread adoption of conscription and the provision of state education; and all these causes and consequences of increased centralisation – for the maintenance of stability.'[26]

The impetus for the acceleration of the movement from social organisation proper[27] to bureaucratic organisation undoubtedly came from the new phase of industrialisation. The incorporation of the production of complicated articles, and the development of complex industrial processes, while it did not absolutely call for large scale organisation, provided opportunities for larger manufacturing plants in which a whole series of processes could be carried out and co-ordinated, and for corporations able to amalgamate, or attract, the necessary capital. For the specific function of the new corporation was to impose stricter and more expensive limitations on the competitive market system out of which industrial capitalism had grown, this time by including the manifold transactions required by the increasing technical division of labour to make large lots of individual products within a single span of control, exempting them from the costs and vicissitudes of the 'free competitive market'. The self-same process is seen more publicly and crudely at work in the development – in the same period of time – of cartels and trusts, with Germany and the United States again taking the lead. The development of the modern corporation between 1870 and the mid-twentieth century is the crucial phase in the shift from the values, the politics, and the legal consensus on which the competitive market economy has been founded. And it is as well to remember that the competitive market economy was but half alive as a practical reality before it was fairly quickly walled up and canonised; at this distance, it is tempting to say that it was called into being only to affirm the demise of the traditional, 'moral' economy.

While the more spectacular manifestations of the third phase of industrialism – bureaucratic, large-scale, corporate – lay in the rapid spread of big engineering and chemical production plants and in the cascade of innovations in communications and transport, its more socially and economically consequential character lay elsewhere, in enormous expansion of the sheer range of goods and services available for consumption,[28] in the emergence and rapid growth of mass education systems, and, thirdly, in the transformation of the capital market and the labour market. For it is on these developments that the present phase, to which I am attaching the label 'Institutional Capitalism', is founded.

All three developments are familiar enough. Perhaps the one way in which it is proper to regard the progress of industrial capitalism as a simple progression is in the accumulation of capital itself. The principle reason why Britain is still relatively affluent is 'not that it has a lot of land, nor yet that Britons are unusually skilled, nor yet that Britons work unusually hard. The explanation is to be found instead in the vast accumulation of national capital that Britain has inherited as a result of its high rate of savings in the past'.[29] Capital accumulation over a period of centuries, from well before the Industrial Revolutions, was transformed from sheer asset accumulation by the mechanisms, created largely in the nineteenth century, for putting savings to profitable use by industrial investment at home and abroad (before 1914, one pound in every ten of Britain's gross domestic product was invested abroad), lending to governments, or lending to individuals and to private or public institutions. During the present century, as the volume of capital has grown, so it has passed more and more into the hands of institutions and away from individual persons; saving itself has become institutionalised in life assurance, pension funds and building societies; by the surrender of private investment to investment trusts and, last of all, by the investment of tax revenues by government in building, services, procurement and direct investment in industry. Industrialism now supports a vast superstructure of money management, and industrial capitalism itself is now largely controlled by money empires controlled from the finance capitals of New York, London, Frankfurt, Zurich and Tokyo.

It is within this new world system of financial (not 'monetary') imperialism that the two other familiar developments have worked themselves out. The multiplication of consumer goods and services which marked the closing decades of the nineteenth century (and its connection with the deceleration in the growth of the birth rate) is now a sociological commonplace. But the bounty provided by corporate capitalism was even more strikingly manifest in the escape of working people and their families from the categorical imperative which dominated the whole of their lives during the first and second phases of industrial capitalism – 'pas mourir'. The opening of the twentieth century is marked by the advent of consumer choice, actually of *patterns* of consumption, something which Alain Touraine has remarked upon as inconceivable before the nineteenth century.

And this increasing flow of goods and services which large-scale production under corporate capitalism has made possible has both demanded and paid for[30] the two other fundamental changes – the mass education systems we now have, and the conversion of the competitive labour market into an occupational system. The provision of compulsory primary education for all by the State during the latter part of the nineteenth century had the twin purposes of equipping the new urban industrial work force with the essential rudiments of literacy and numeracy and of 'gentling the masses'.[31] The subsequent construction, separately from that base, of systems of secondary and tertiary education, the rapid expansion of the range of subject matter taught, and the cultivation of an increasing specialisation within that range is wholly the work of the corporate phase of capitalism. A new world of educational provision was called into being to meet the demands of corporate capitalism for clerks, secretaries, government officials, technicians, managers and scientists, not so much to redress the balance of the old educational world but to fill the enormous gap which had opened up between its extremities.

There is no question, of course, of the educational system that we have being brought into being as the product of some comprehensive, far-sighted plan to match the emergent needs of corporate industry and bureaucratic government. But there certainly has been a long-term strategy of plugging holes and meeting needs for categories of labour and types of specialists, a strategy culminating in the official manpower policies adopted by most Western countries in the 'fifties, 'sixties and 'seventies of this century. And in tune with this is belief in achievement as a moral good and as a social necessity which has become a central article of faith. Complex societies such as ours are seen as made up of individuals with important, if not measurable, differences in the amount of competence, ability, skill, creativity (enterprise, adventurousness) and information which societies such as ours need for their own survival. It is because of this that the complex systems of educational and occupational promotions open to merit are designed so as to maintain a flow of the best qualified people to fill places in society where the best talents are most needed and best rewarded. Setting up a system of promotions of this kind is not, however, enough. Beyond this, it is essential for every member of society to enter the race and compete as best he can. To this end, we are all indoctrinated to regard success – in society's own terms – as among the highest personal goals of our lives, if not the paramount goal. Confirmation of this is visible everywhere, in that the distribution of goods, facilities and privileges accords more and more with the differences in the social positions achieved in this way.

The educational and occupational systems we now have are complementary and mutually supportive. Recurrent reforms of the educational system have spread the assumption that the more intelligently capable children are now effectively separated out and funnelled into suitable secondary schools and high schools and that, out of these, the cream separates itself out and passes to the universities and technical colleges. So the labour market in which corporations seek for recruits is ready graded. And since, for corporations and government departments, investment in a recruit has to mature for many years before yielding a return, it is necessary both to select the most suitable candidates and to hold on to them. And recruits themselves, as well as corporations, see themselves not as 'taking up a job' but 'starting a career', and careers thus begun are presented as enclosed for life within the corporation; indeed, in their endeavours to attract the right kind of candidate, corporations tend to advertise careers rather than posts.

Inevitably, the career system which has to a large extent replaced the competitive labour market has assumed greater and greater importance. And since, for most of us, the career ladder we find ourselves on is fairly short – indeed, for the mass of people, may have only two or three rungs – we have turned, white collar workers, technicians, Angestellten, cadres, and the new cohorts of semi-professionals, to organised trade unionism as *the* instrument by which the length of the ladder may be extended, at least in money terms.

Corporate capitalism is, of course, powered by the managerial capitalism of Robin Marris.[32] Managerial capitalism is an engine for sustaining economic growth *and* the growth of career structures; both movements require more and more refinement in the division of labour and the multiplication of occupations, together with scales of rewards. And it tends to do this, as recent work has shown, in a curiously compulsive way, sustaining growth in scale through mergers, takeovers and foreign investment well beyond the point at which they can be justified in terms of economies of scale,[33] (which relate to plant size and not to size of firm, anyway) or relief from the threat of price wars.

But while the engine of institutional capitalism, which has now taken over from corporate capitalism, may be faltering on its economic growth curve, it remains wholly successful in involving the whole population, manual workers along with the rest, in the achievement system.

This has now become the political dilemma confronting most Western societies, and it is what makes Hirsch's book so extraordinarily well timed. For it is not yet one more attempt to solve the dilemma, but an attempt to demonstrate that it is a false, or at least unnecessary, one. It is, he says, about three issues: he calls them 'the paradox of affluence', 'the distribution of compulsion', and 'reluctant collectivism'. Most of us sense rather vaguely some interconnection between the three issues, but they are commonly regarded and treated as separate – they surface in different pages of our daily newspaper. Hirsch's principle thesis is that all three spring from a common source – the rising expectations with which centuries of economic growth have successfully indoctrinated us all. True, wars and depressions have interrupted the growth curve, but whenever they occur, they have been treated as crises, as deviant or irrational assaults on normality by pressures or events *external* to the system.

It is hardly news that satisfaction has not increased with affluence; Durkheim made the point 80 years ago. But it is only recently that we have caught on to the fact that there are ways in which striving for affluence can be self-defeating. At the beginning of the century, to take a familiar circumstance that Hirsch dwells on, suburban living offered clean air, gardens and the delights of rural living combined with a short rail journey to the well-paid jobs in the city centres which enabled people to afford them, and as well as to the theatres, shops, concert halls and galleries and other forms of social and cultural nourishment. Economic growth lowered the relative cost of suburban living while enlarging its facilities, on the one hand, and increased the proportion of incomes which made suburban life possible.

The result is the familiar leap-frogging process which, by mid-century, had reduced the delights of suburban living to a brief honeymoon period between living on a building site and being cut off by the tide of bricks, mortar and tarmac as it reached the crest of the next stretch of rising ground; the city centres themselves became progressively decayed, deserted and dangerous; and commuting became a nightmare. Increased affluence has brought the delights of foreign travel to more millions every year, and it has made the summer beaches of the Mediterranean – which the *Sunday Times* recently called the sunniest sewer in the world – as pleasurable a holiday resort as the terraces of football grounds, with entry costs about the same; most of the great paintings of the Louvre and the Uffizi are invisible to anyone less than six feet tall from June to October; Venice is sinking under the weight of countless tourists' feet; the more attractive landscapes are disappearing under, or marred by, the spreading rash of weekend cottages, holiday homes, *pavilions* and caravan sites.

Not all the goods and services which are the mark of affluent societies carry this kind of inbuilt self-destruction device. Goods like vacuum cleaners, washing machines and television sets are consumed, so to speak, privately, without adverse effects for other people. But whatever balance is struck between private goods and public bads is, in fact, irrelevant. It is, of course, production of material goods that we have chiefly in mind when we speak of economic growth; but the enjoyment which comes from possessing material goods becomes more and more dependent on possession unalloyed by the social bad which comes from other people possessing them, too. Goods other than purely private ones become progressively contaminated through their sheer multiplicity. And, what is more, as purely private goods – from square meals to hi-fi sets – add up and become available to more and more people, as more and more working class individuals and families compose their lives in terms of the pursuit of affluence through the acquisition of strictly private goods (and so live 'privatised' lives), so demand intensifies for merit goods and for those public goods and services which can be fully enjoyed only if they are available for consumption on much the same basis as purely private goods – i.e. are free from public bads like congestion and pollution or are available free from the rationing restrictions which apply to major public goods like health services and education. To free oneself from suburban congestion means either moving further out or acquiring both a town apartment and a country home and an extra car; in Britain, to avoid waiting a year for essential but non-emergency surgery may mean paying for private hospital service; again, the same entry ticket to pleasanter and better paid jobs which a university degree gave to a few people a generation ago means paying for intensive educational care nowadays, so that one's children may gain entry to the more prestigious establishment, or extend full-time education into postgraduate work for higher degrees or professional qualifications; even the time needed to enjoy merit goods has to be bought with more goods and services – more gadgets, a second car, taxi fares, restaurant meals.

But all these are the more superficial consequences for the paradox of affluence, as they are the more familiar. 'As demands for purely private goods are increasingly satisfied, demands for goods and facilities with public (social) character become increasingly active. These demands make themselves felt through individual demands on the political system or through the market mechanism in the same way as do the demands for purely private goods . . . these demands in themselves appear both legitimate and attainable. Why should the individual not spend his money on additional education as a means to a higher placed job, or a second home in the country, if he prefers these pleasures to spending on a mink coat or whisky, or to a life of greater leisure?'[34]

That question has been voiced more loudly and more frequently in the mid-'seventies as the middle class backlash has gained strength in the United States and in Britain. Coupled as it is with slogans defending individual liberty, still a central value of Western society, it becomes a very powerful voice – powerful enough to create the current almost equal balance between broad right and broad left in Western Europe which commentators seem to read as a prescription for political instability, and which, in America, stokes resentment among both middle classes and lower classes so as to multiply individual and collective acts of violence and of repression, calls for 'law and order', and, more generally, a 'revolt against the masses'.

These consequences are evidence of the increasingly costly, but inevitably vain endeavour by individuals to escape the costs of economic growth. For the endeavour by individuals to escape these social costs increases the demand for material goods and for services which can either cut the cost to the individual or improve their chances of those higher paid jobs which will yield a higher income and therefore greater purchasing power, and therefore the means of escape. Inexorably, individuals and organised groups are drawn into greater competition not merely to accumulate these material goods which economic growth produces but to gain that extra edge on others which will put them in an advantageous position so far as the social costs are concerned. The 'revolution of rising expectation', therefore, of which we have heard so much, has to be construed as a consequence, and not merely a cause, of increased consumption. Expectations 'rise' in defence of existing positions and standards of living relative to others.

Fuelled in this way, consumer demand, related as it is to the desire to be 'better off' in terms of position rather than in material possessions, is insatiable, and necessarily so.

Hirsch ends his book not with a solution but with a plea:

'the prime economic problem now facing the economically advanced societies is a structural need to pull back the bounds of economic self-advancement. . . Society is in turmoil because the only legitimacy it has is social justice; and the transition to a just society is an uncertain road strewn with injustice. . . For the overriding economic problem discussed in this book, the first necessity is not technical devices but the public acceptance necessary to make them work.'[35]

Hirsch presented the problem, and left it with us, as a moral problem. But this does not mean that it is insoluble in terms which are economically irrational. Economic activity becomes more rational the broader the range of theoretically known and practicable alternatives among which a choice can be made. The task we have is to show what a choice can be made. The task we have is to show what rational, practical alternatives exist at this time, and in our society, and what we can do to favour that increase in rationality which will make them feasible.

ENDNOTES

1. F. Hirsch, *Social Limits to Growth*, A Twentieth Century Fund Study, Routledge & Kegan Paul, 1977.
2. E. P. Thompson, 'The Moral Economy of the English Crowd in the Eighteenth Century', *Past and Present*, No. 50, pp. 76-136.
3. F. Braudel, *Capitalism and Material Life*, 1400-1800 (trans. M. Kochan), Fontana, 1974, p. 1.
4. J. Habermas, *Technik und Wissenschaft als Ideologie*, Suhrkamp, 1968.
5. K. Polanyi, *Origins of Our Time* (first published in the U.S. under the title *The Great Transformation*), Gollancz, 1945.
6. 'Science has never shaken off the impress of its origin in the historical revolt of

the later Renaissance. It has remained predominantly an anti-rationalistic movement, based upon a naive faith.' A. N. Whitehead, *Science and the Modern World*, C.U.P., 1933 edn, p. 20.

7. Thomas Hobbes, *Leviathan*, 1651, Pt I, chap. XIII.
8. H. Lydall, *The Structure of Earnings*, O.U.P., 1968, p. 68.
9. H. Kluth, quoted in C. Offe, *Industry and Inequality* (tr. J. Wickham), Arnold, 1976, p. 41
10. J. Habermas, *Legitimationsprobleme im Spätkapitalismus*, Suhrkamp, 1973.
11. W. S. Holdsworth, *History of English Law, Vol. XI*, Methuen, 1938, p. 389.
12. K. Polanyi, *op. cit.* (1945), p. 63.
13. quoted W. S. Holdsworth, *op. cit.* (1938), p. 420.
14. W. S. Holdsworth, *op. cit.* (1938), p. 421.
15. C. B. Macpherson, *The Political Theory of Possessive Individualism*, O.U.P., 1962, p. 48.
16. P. Mantoux, *The Industrial Revolution of the Eighteenth Century*, 13th edn, Methuen, 1961, p. 221.
17. E. P. Thompson, *op. cit.*, p. 83.
18. E. P. Thompson, *op. cit.*
19. A. B. Hibbert, 'The Economic Policies of Towns', M. M. Postan, G. G. Rich and E. Miller, *Cambridge Economic History of Europe, Vol. III*, Chap. IV, C.U.P., 1963, p. 172.
20. E. P. Thompson, *op. cit.*, p. 83.
21. E. P. Thompson, *op. cit.*, p. 136.
22. P. Mathias, 'British Industrialisation: Unique or Not?', Colloques Int. du CNRS No. 540: *L'Industrialisation en Europe au XIXe siècle*. Edns du CNRS, 1972.
23. An idea suggested by a remark of Professor Gianfranco Poggi's at a seminar at the University of Glasgow in April 1977.
24. 3,360 Enclosure Acts were passed during the reign of George III and 'Acts were passed to give enlarged powers to trading corporations, and to the companies which supervised special trade. Sometimes inventors got special Acts to give them a monopoly in the sale of their invention.' See W. S. Holdsworth, *op. cit.* (1938), pp. 625-9.
25. F. H. Hinsley, Introduction to *New Cambridge Modern History*, Vol. XI, *Material Progress and Worldwide Problems*, C.U.P., 1962, p. 17.
26. F. H. Hinsley, *op. cit.* (1962), p. 32.
27. By this I mean precisely what Adam Smith, in an unfortunate and quite unwarranted flourish of rhetoric, referred to as the 'hidden hand'. Smith had already written at length of just what kinds of rules governing public behaviour and social relationships were involved in the maintenance of social order in a civilised society without resort to an elaborate bureaucratic machinery of public control. v. Adam Smith, *The Theory of Moral Sentiments*, 1759. J. Ralph Lindgren's *The Social Philosophy of Adam Smith*, Nighoff, 1973, is a courageous attempt to rescue Smith from two centuries of misinterpretation.
28. v. C. H. Wilson, 'Economy and Society in Late Victorian Britain', *Economic History Review* (2nd series), Vol. 18.
29. N. Macrae, *The London Capital Market*, Staples, 2nd edn., 1957, p. 11.
30. There is quite a blatant symbolism about the fact that State-supported secondary education in Britain was paid for out of revenue raised by the imposition of new excise duties on whisky.
31. D. V. Glass, 'Education and Social Change in Modern England', in A. H. Halsey, J. Floud and C. A. Anderson, *Education, Economy and Society*, Free Press, 1961.
32. R. Marris, *The Economic Theory of Managerial Capitalism*, Macmillan, 1964.
33. See L. Hannah, *The Rise of the Corporate Economy*, Methuen, 1976. L. Hannah and J. A. Kay, *Concentration in Modern History*, 1977. G. Meeks,

Disappointing Marriage: A Study of the Gains from Merger, C.U.P., 1977.
34. F. Hirsch, *op. cit.* (1977), p. 4.
35. F. Hirsch, *op. cit.* (1977), p. 190.

Giving enterprise a human face
(Créer des Mutants)

Roger Garaudy

The basic problems facing economic entities (private or state enterprise, co-operative, collective, team or purposive group) are not organisational problems, they are problems particular to the community: nation, state, army, church and university. Facing these problems in so many different circumstances constitutes a crisis: a community crisis is, above all, a crisis which makes us examine the question of ultimate ends.

What is in question is the ultimate aims of communities, and, naturally, the organisational problems involved, for organisation is the setting-up and setting-in-motion of the means for reaching an already determined objective. Today's controversy about economic undertakings of whatever kind is found at four levels: (i) their purpose, their ultimate end; (ii) allocation of profit; (iii) organisational and structural problems, and (iv) how power is transmitted: is it to be centralised or is it to be decentralised and enjoyed by smaller units balancing each other? These four levels are interdependent. The last three derive from the first, that is, the true purpose of organised work in the economic sphere.

The ultimate end, or purpose, of organised economic activity

At the economic level, the problem of 'finalities' arises under the global forms of 'growth model' and 'planning'. If enterprise is defined very widely as 'an activity for selling a product or a service on the consumer goods or capital goods market', it is not at all evident that this activity is in the general interest, as postulated by optimistic economists such as Bastiat, who claimed in his *Economic Harmonies* that if everyone pursued their own interests, the public good would be assured. Adam Smith, of course, also puts forward this idea of enlightened self-interest. When growth models are imposed upon the planning and organisation of ordinary economic activity, it becomes evident that this providentialist conception of an 'invisible hand' harmonising personal interests with the public good is more and more open to doubt and dispute.

When the managers of an enterprise, be it public or private, decide on an investment, they do so in order to encourage their organisation's growth which each business justifies as being in the general public interest. The sum of such decisions adds up to a pattern of blind growth, of growth considered as an end in itself. This in no way leads to the truly humane end of enriching the lives and personalities of men and women.

In order to emphasise the fact that it is the system in its entirety that is responsible for this, let us take two examples, one in the private sector, the other in the public. Every year in France, 13,000 slot machines are sold. This represents 120 million francs worth of business. The financial importance of this enterprise, which deals basically in inhibiting youths' mental development, is on the same imposing scale as the budget of the Maison de la Culture (The Organisation for Promoting Culture). The situation is about the same in a State enterprise: for example, the receipts of the French Tobacco Organisation (Regie Française des Tabacs) total as high as seven or eight billion francs, increasing minimally five per cent per annum, a sum roughly corresponding to the budget of the Public Health Department.

The complex created by the automobile, the petrol industry and the road system is of prime importance and affords another example of this. In France, our road transport system costs us 110 billions per annum out of a total national budget of 260 billions (ref. year 1971). It is represented by an organised pressure group which aims to give road transport the means of repressing the national rail industry. It influences public opinion and industry to patronise the long-distance road transport of goods; and this costs more, both in terms of energy expended and manual work, than does rail transport.

With the 22 billions that it cost to develop the Concorde, public transport in the Paris area could have been radically transformed; that is to say, the conditions of life of three million salaried Frenchmen could have been changed. This project would have created a thousand times more jobs and required infinitely more innovative scientific research – and more centres of research workers, too – than did the development of the Concorde.

A United Nations report on health and the astounding study of Dr Predal have shown that not more than three per cent of pharmaceutical products on sale are really effective; whilst the real aims of the pharmaceutical industry can be discerned in the fact that it turns out the same products under a variety of labels, or in the fact that it manufactures products that are ineffectual and, indeed, sometimes harmful.

We could endlessly continue this enumeration showing the contradictions between growth-aim peculiar to certain industries and the general public interest. What can one say, for example, about armament industries whose huge profit margins encourage investment in order to multiply the most illusory military symbols in France, and all to make our country the third largest arms supplier in the world. As Goodman said, scientific research itself is corrupted when the State and captains of industry are the impresarios and financiers of scientists,[1] thus making science dependent upon the system.

I have tended to multiply these examples to show how disputable the aims of industrialists can be – their sometimes blind and ill-conceived designs for development – which contribute to an overall policy of global growth. It is this overall policy which drags the whole industrial world into spending some of its time doing useless work, encouraging the consumer to multiply, beyond his needs, his consumption of goods symbolically linked with prestige, as well as his consumption of 'magic' that he hopes may compensate him for the frustrations engendered by the system. Another very grave objection is that it increases, to no real purpose, the working hours of the worker, which he could employ much more enjoyably doing something else. The theories of radical economists in the US, notably Hardesty, Morris Clement and Clinton Jenks, and the studies made in France by a group of Saclay researchers, have established that the diminution, alone, of senseless activities within the system would reduce by half the working hours of the citizen in his role as worker, whilst improving the quality of his life as a citizen and individual. The thirty-hour week would release men from their struggles for employment and their anxieties centred on their place of work. Less encumbered by useless and unwholesome products, and consequently having more leisure time, they would be able to rediscover the spirit of a more real humanity to devote to their personal development and to their relations with others.

As to the ultimate purposes of working establishments, I want to make six remarks:

1. I don't pretend that all these changes can take place immediately. One can't wave a magic wand and change the values and needs of a people who have been manipulated and conditioned for four centuries; one can't bring them to reject their present artificially stimulated desires overnight. It is important, however, to illustrate that economic studies offer the possibilities of other ultimate ends to which purposive activity can be directed. But these alternatives are not conceivable unless the possibility of another economic order is concretely drawn first. There remains, for example, the political

problem of a cultural revolution, i.e. a new choice of civilisation for countries like ours, for which I will suggest the means later.

2.   I am not at all a champion of the 'zero growth-rate' because there can be no question of stopping expansion when there are billions of people in the Third World and millions in the rich countries without the means of living a truly human life. The direction of growth should be toward the humane enrichment of all, not toward augmenting the power and profits of the few. The aim is that expansion should serve needs; and not needs, expansion.

3.   The sole aim of a work-place or business should not be realising a profit. It has a social, human and moral function, namely to aid the 'opening out' of a man, rather than to contribute toward his alienation.

4.   Work, even when organised along the least alienating and most modern lines, is not the only end of man: he can't wholly fulfil himself by work alone. The reduction of working hours, which can only be brought about by critical changes in the growth model, is the royal way to liberty.

5.   From 1896 to 1976 in France, productivity increased 900 per cent (i.e. where a week of fifty-six hours was necessary eighty years ago, only seven hours are necessary today), while working hours diminished by only thirty per cent. In other words, the growth in productivity essentially served to increase the quantity of products and consumer services produced but only to give workers a very little more spare time.

The principal problem now facing us is this: in this anarchy of production in which planning is only an illusion (for the plan is no more than the result of compelling relations between different pressure groups), is there no other alternative but imperative, authoritarian planning where 'les finalités', e.g. the policy of the firm, its production programmes and its allocation of resources at its disposal – are exclusively determined by a political decision from the top?

6.   The energy problem plays a determining role with regard to all other economic problems. With the petrol crisis and the distress provoked by the nuclear age, energy has become our principal problem, and the answer to it implies a choice of society, a choice of civilisation. All great historic breakthroughs are born of the discovery and development of new forms of energy. The link between the industrial revolution, marked by the invention and application of the steam engine, and the French Revolution affords one of the best examples of this.

Doubtless, there is no mechanical connection between these two phenomena. Karl Marx, after having written in *The Poverty of Philosophy* that the water mill created feudal society with lord and serf, and that the steam mill created capitalist society with manager and worker, became his own critic. This he did when he wrote of 'the relative autonomy' of superstructures in relation to base. Nevertheless, the fact remains that different forms of energy serve as infrastructures on which different social and political relationships are based – some structurally and some more loosely.

It is a remarkable historical fact that an era in which coal was the principal energy source and railways the driving force of growth, was succeeded by one in which petrol was the principal energy source and first the car and lorry industry the driving forces, then air transport became an added force. On top of this came the age of electricity in which domestic equipment played its role. A particular form of capitalism, a particular form of crisis and a special conception of socialism has corresponded to each of these phases.

During the last decades energy consumption has doubled every ten years, and we are supposed to believe that this is a law indelibly written into the nature of things. These extrapolations lead us to absurdities: consuming an average of 5 Tep (tons of petrol equivalent) per capita per annum, the European and the Japanese consume an average ten times more than an inhabitant of the Third World, and two-and-a-half times less than a North American. If the whole world consumed the same average as North America it would not only lead to an upheaval in nature – climates, etc. – and in social organisation, but also to the exhaustion of energy resources (uranium as well as petrol) in the coming fifty years. Even if the expiry dates cited in the Club of Rome's apocalyptic report[2] are disputable, an undeniable truth has emerged: physical limits to growth do exist.

The *San Francisco Chronicle* justly wrote that energy consumption is probably the best index for measuring damage caused by an individual or a society to the environment. That is, beyond the mini-crisis born from the higher prices so justly demanded by oil producing countries after a colonisation period when scandalously low prices were paid for petrol, there exists a mega-crisis for which the excessive quantity of energy used by consumers in the so-called 'developed' countries is fundamentally responsible. For this reason, deceleration in energy consumption imposing a fundamental and critical change in the global growth model, also in the models of organised society and of civilisation, becomes essential. This is not a question of choice, but of necessity.

It is a dangerous illusion to believe that the 'tout au nucleare' will allow us to dodge the basic problem and escape expiry terms. However, before tackling the energy resources problem in detail, we ought to consider an even more serious problem raised by the nuclear programme. This is *political* pollution, which is as dangerous as *physical* pollution.

Although the political problems are immense and obvious, extreme centralisation and nuclear immeasurability also pose an ecological problem. In fact, the risks of sabotage or theft of fissionable materials such as plutonium (allowing the possibility of trifling with 'rustic' bombs), which giant nuclear centres run, are such that the necessity of avoiding them will inevitably lead to a policing framework such as no country has ever known before. This doubles the necessity for decelerating energy-consumption and decentralising sources of energy production. The question then is, need the urgency of tackling such problems take us back to the candle and stagecoach?

I think not. We must denounce the myth of growth for growth's sake, of growth at any price because it is supposed to raise the standard of living for all men. Twentieth-century historic experience proves to the contrary. (1) Growth aggravates inequalities, and (2) inequalities are the driving force of growth. Growth is a self-perpetuating myth invented for the benefit of economic and political power holders.

The allocation of profits

This brings us to the second problem, that of the allocation of profits in enterprises of various kinds, in society and the world as a whole.

By virtue of the simplistic axiom 'the bigger the cake, the bigger the slice for everyone', we have complacently developed the myth according to which growth – as it is conceived today – increases everyone's standard of living. This has now been revealed as being entirely false. It remains, however, behind the inhuman abstraction of the 'real national product per capita', which measures 'development' in individual countries and international institutions.

As far as the planetary problem is concerned, it is easy to state, as I have done in my *Dialogues des Civilisations*, that the very underdevelopment of colonised countries (and nowadays formerly colonised) is the primary condition for, and the unavoidable corollary of, the primitive accumulation and development of the colonising countries and multinational firms. Pope Paul VI made a point of this phenomenon in encyclical *Populorum Progressio*.

In countries of the Third World, integration of the Western growth model gives rise to privileged and parasitic minorities. In the so-called developed countries, the gap increases also between the thin layer of privileged and the vast number of unfavoured masses. For example, in 1975 in France, the average income of a couple with two children was 500,000 old francs a month, while 3 million Frenchmen had less than

2,000 old francs a month and the most favoured 5 per cent had an income of more than 3 million francs a month. And the real gap is even larger because we are talking here about figures taken from tax declarations and everyone knows that the likelihood of cheating and fraud grows with the size of income.

This inequality in life continues all the way to death. Out of every 100,000 members of the more-favoured classes (managers, executives, liberal careerists, etc.) 500 die before they are 50; out of every 100,000 labourers, 1,300 (two-and-a-half times more) die before the age of 50.

Not only has the growth model failed to reduce inequalities up till now, but it will never resolve them, for the fundamental structural reason that in this model *inequality is necessary because it is the driving force behind growth*. It creates, among the less-favoured, the desire to imitate the more-favoured, and this desire increases continuously because the frustration cannot decrease.

The social consequences of this growth concept are murderous to the nation. They divide it irremediably because they imply opposition – not contingent but structural – between the capital-providers and work-providers.

In this hopeless situation the trade unions are led into continual and quantitative struggle in their demands for the lowest incomes to be adjusted to match the purchasing power of higher-income groups. A system based on the demand for permanent growth of economic activity implies that the worker's interests and those of the work-providers are divergent. A market negotiation for allocation of profits no longer exists. The market-logic applied to the offer and the demand for work leads, therefore, to a clash, almost to the point of war, between the two coalitions of interests: it is a class struggle which is not an invention of the workers' movement nor of organisations of capitalists, but an undeniable fact born out of the structure of the system.

Giving workers an interest based on profits does not resolve the problem because they require calculation and division applied to the profits alone, and not to the efficient results. Besides, more than a third of all undertakings in France declare no profit whatsoever.

This contradiction is aggravated by a contradictory increase in money lending. Until the beginning of the twentieth century loan rates were established at under 2.5 per cent, which assured a doubling of capital in 30 years. Russian borrowing after two wars brought this rate up to 4 per cent and then to 7 per cent, which allowed a fortune to double in ten years. Between 1968 and 1975 loan rates went up to 14 per cent and more, so that, leaving aside provisions for tax, a fortune could double in 5 years.

The consequences are catastrophic, not only because the basic and defective characteristic of capitalism – the possibility of enrichment without work – is encouraged, but also because this increase, which could be justified (though not in this proportion) in a period of expansion, continues irreversibly during a depression; then, as a result of inflation, also becomes a cause of magnifying it. The firm becomes committed to paying interest rates which it can only afford by increasing prices – thus fuelling the inflation and debasing the value of money all the more. Moreover, this encourages a lazy use of capital whilst failing to reward hard work and risk taking commensurately. The figures given by the 'Comptes de la Nation' for 1966-1973, show that the amounts paid to money-lenders multiplied by four, while those paid as salaries, and to risk-taking companies owned by equity shareholders, multiplied by only two and two-and-a-half.

Let me make one remark to avoid a misunderstanding. There is no question of my condemning the notion of profit. Even in a socialist regime it must remain as a criterion for measuring the efficiency of a production unit, such as an energy surplus created by human work and co-ordination. What is being disputed is the method of re-employing this profit and of allocating it in our society, which has become one of blind growth.

The level of work organisation

This leads us to the third argument. This is at the level of the organisation of work. On this level most of the criticism is taken up with the slowness of most managers of businesses in shedding their old mechanistic conceptions of work organisation born of Frederick Taylor's theories of the scientific management of labour.[3] These conceptions have the following characteristics:
1.   The centralisation of the decision-making process.
2.   Refusal to discuss the application of the idea of the scientific organisation of the work process to the job in hand with the workers.
3.   The radical separation of information from its dissemination. The information remains, just as the resulting decisions do, the exclusive property of the manager; whilst actions at all levels are reduced to no more than the process of transmitting to each worker so many bits and pieces of information as concern the detailed specification of the work he is set to do, and the actions he is actually carrying out. In the same way that worker participation fails to solve the problem of allocation of profits, different authoritarian and paternalistic methods – job enlargement, job enrichment and so on – fail to solve the problem of work organisation.

Necessary decentralisation would hardly be effective if it were conceived in a mechanical way, if it consisted only of diminishing the size of production units by dividing up the enterprise. The golden rule for all decentralisation is that each problem should be resolved at the level where it is set, where it first arises. This is perhaps the best definition of self-management, for self-management consists in continuing to the limit the present irreversible tendency of civilisation, which demands that each problem should not necessarily be resolved from the top, but from the level where it arises.

4. At the base of the pyramid of the typical complex enterprise of modern industry work is becoming increasingly fragmented, detailed, repetitive and alienating. There results a mechanistic model of the firm; one which moreover is linked to the typical positivist's conception of planning for the future. This itself is nothing more than quantitative extrapolation – selecting certain known facts of the present in order to conceive of a plan for the future and to present it with the undeniability of a scientific statement. Experience has increasingly shown that this type of firm, this system which is closed in on itself, is unable to adapt itself to demands for changes from within, where it faces growing opposition from the workers and even from some levels of management. It has also shown itself incapable of adapting itself to meet the needs of a changing outside world.

The law required diversity; Ross Ashby in his *Introduction to Cybernetics*,[4] states that an extremely diverse environment can only be dealt with successfully by a system of equivalent diversity.[5] This law makes it possible to appreciate the defects of any crude, simplistic, mechanistic conception of the organisation of the firm. It is not flexible enough to respond to an ever-changing environment. Here again, although work-interest does not solve the problem of how the benefits of work are to be shared out, a number of anti-Taylorist methods were being put forward as early as 1959 in a book by Frederick Herzberg on work motivation. In its approach, this book is opposed to Taylor and his theory of scientific management; instead it calls for the enlargement and enrichment of tasks, from which emerge certain ideas concerned with participatory forms of organisation based on particular objectives. Yet neither set of proposals solves the problem of work organisation itself.

To their credit, these proposals do recognise that, even from the point of view of productivity and no other, at the present stage of technology the motivation of the worker is more important than contriving even the most perfect mechanical system of typecraft. The decentralisation which is needed would have little effect if it were conceived in a mechanistic manner, that is to say if it consisted merely in subdividing the firm into smaller units of production. Genuine decentralisation implies that small units have access to their own means of information provided, for example, by small computers, instead of the mirage of so-called organisation held together by giant computers. It also implies that these units should be allowed the maximum of decision-making powers over their own affairs, thus reducing control from above, and more important, making possible feedback from the base. This feedback should cover both the workers' views on internal work organisation, and a permanent re-evaluation of the needs of the social environment within which the enterprise is operating.

The golden rule of this sort of decentralisation is that *problems should be solved at the level at which they arise.*

I would like to stress two important ideas related to this subject.
1.   That this golden rule does not apply only to the firm but is valid for all organisations in a given society, be it for example, the running of a hospital or a university, a housing complex, or a transport system.
2.   That the systematic application of this rule without any obstacle is perhaps the best definition of workers' control (autogestion). It has nothing to do with that utopian picture, very easy to characterise, wished on it by its adversaries from all sides, of everybody taking decisions about everything all of the time. This is absurd. No organisation of whatever type would last a fortnight with that sort of anarchy. Workers' control is simply the pushing to the limit of that weighty and irreversible tendency which characterises the current phase of civilisation, namely that it is not inevitable that every problem should be solved from the top; but, on the contrary, it should and can be solved at the level at which it arises. This is what Kant would call the regulating principle, the specific yet ultimate aim of all the attempts made to meet a demand which characterises the present epoch. In the same way that on the eve of 1789 the demand for political rights had reached maturity, so now each citizen should be recognised as having his or her own economic rights. But there is a difference. Citizenship can no longer be exercised by power becoming estranged from the mass of the people and then delegated. This is what has characterised and continues to characterise the so-called democratic system with its parliament and political parties. There is absolutely no intention of applying the parliamentary system to the firm which is one of the unfortunate tendencies to be found in the Sudreau report on factory reform in France. Today it is bureaucracy, technocracy and traditional concepts of hierarchy which are being questioned. It is they that are under fire and their functions should be delegated to no one.

Bureaucracy is a sort of Parkinson's disease with the following syndrome: to the extent that the centralised firm develops, the administrative apparatus grows faster than the number of people being administered. This first leads to all decisions being taken at the highest level in the firm, and then to the absurdity of the decision-making process rising through the top of the firm to the State itself.

Technocracy has these two aspects:

(a) It uses a 'scientific' pretext based on the absolute superiority of inviolable rationality and science as a sacred reality transcending everybody, over and above those to whom it is applied. This means that any dialogue with the base such as the base of the pyramid structure is out of the question, as is any feedback which the base might generate.

(b) In the name of this same scientific positivism, the question *how* is always posed, but never the question *why?* This blind technocratic approach results in a real fetishism of means, a religion, as if the running of the firm and its quantitative growth was the end of life. The question of what are the ultimate aims and purposes of the firm and those in it is never considered. Thus technocracy comes to imply a type of organisation formed for its own worship and a kind of clericalism devoted to its growth and to the cult of growth in general.

Hierarchy in the traditionally accepted sense, implies both bureaucracy and technocracy. It is very significant if we consider the etymology of the word hierarchy: it evokes both the idea of giving orders and the idea of something sacred. In its very principle it is a theological notion. The purpose of organisation of work is imposed in a sort of transcendental manner from outside, from on high. But this model of the transcendent, based on spatial exteriority and dualism, is out of date even in theology. Father Chen in his 'theology of work', attacks the dualist conception of hierarchy whereby God has His plan and man's labour is nothing but its faithful realisation. 'Work,' he writes, 'is a free and active participation in creation and sharing in the divine ordering of the world.' It would be paradoxical if certain captains of industry were to claim to be preserving, in their conception of hierarchy, forms of dualism and of transcendence that theologians no longer claim for their God!

At the level of the devolution of power

In point of fact what is being challenged is the unwritten law whereby the owner of the capital asset gives orders, or at the very least is the only one who can appoint the person who will give orders, namely the manager. It is he only who is responsible to the suppliers of capital. The very least that can be criticised is that it is by no means obvious that the ability to lead (or to choose leaders) and the ownership of assets necessarily go together. (It is another question to know whether, in any actual situation, it is all the shareholders or just the big shareholders who have this privilege. However, this is outside the scope of this particular essay).

I would just like to emphasize the link between the way power is distributed within the firm at the present time, and the growth model. If power resides solely with the owners of capital, or with the managers whom they have appointed, the final aims of the firm will, of necessity, be subordinated to its returns in terms of profit and power, and the head of the firm will be chosen according to this criterion alone.

This is why, when thinking about the growth model, the application of the principle that the firm is a society of people and not a society of stocks and shares, is so important. Basic power can only emanate from meetings bringing together everybody who works for the firm.

Thus what we have called economic citizenship becomes possible.

We can make the definition more precise at a fourth level by stating that it means that every worker, intellectual or manual, has the possibility of reaching the highest level of decision-making on condition that *the only criterion in the choice of leading members of the firm is their contribution to the ultimate ends of the whole society* (and not just in relation to financial returns).

This is another aspect of the definition of workers' control. What then are the obstacles to designating responsibility according to the sole criterion of *contribution to the ultimate ends of society as a whole*? One of the obstacles may be that the devolution of economic power, the nomination of top people in a firm, is undertaken by a *political party*, according to the criterion of party membership. I take this as a starting point because, historically speaking, the starting point in recent times for thinking about workers' control has been Yugoslavia, where in 1948 they found an alternative, not to capitalism, but to Stalinism.

But it is also true that capitalism raises enormous obstacles to the appointment of leaders of a firm solely on the basis of their contribution to the ultimate purposes of society as a whole. I will not go over again what I have already said about the inadequacy of the aims of the firm to meet the aims of society as a whole; I would, however, like to emphasize one aspect of this which represents a strong tendency within our present system. For a growing number of bosses, it is not their initial personal qualities which legitimise their position but their performance as managers.

The key problem of the devolution and exercise of power within the firm therefore has two aspects:
1.   Are the leading members of the firm responsible solely to the

suppliers of capital and nominated by them? Or are they responsible to all the workers, manual and intellectual, and nominated by them?

2. How is it possible to make people aware of the absolute necessity of the ultimate ends of the firm being subordinated to the ultimate ends of society as a whole?

It is thus possible at this level to develop further the idea of *workers' control*. We can see that it is less and less of a utopian idea, and is in fact the expression of this weighty tendency which characterises the times in which we live: we are moving towards a society which demands for its survival that the sole criterion in the choice of economic leaders (and political leaders for that matter) is their contribution to a plan which encompasses all of society.

The central problem at the present time is perhaps whether we will slow down or facilitate this irreversible development. This is a central problem because, depending on what choice we make, the result will be either a convulsive or a constructive development.

Solutions

If we now take the same four problems sketched at the beginning, we can summarise the answers that we have found at each of the levels of organisation. Regarding what I have called 'les finalités' – the ultimate aims or purposes of organisations and of organisation itself – the problem consists in allowing new ends to emerge.

A classic response has until now been to demand that political decisions should be taken from above instead of in the economic anarchy of the market. This is roughly the Soviet model. I have analysed it in my *Project Hope*[6] where I showed the reasons for its failures, namely (a) it has adopted the growth model of traditional capitalism; (b) it has reproduced, at a political level, the power and management structures born from the capitalist system; and (c) it has been proven that while socialisation of the means of production may be a necessary condition for ending alienation, it is not the sufficient condition for doing so; still less when the socialisation is of the kind that has been reduced to nationalisation. State capitalism does not diminish the alienation of the worker.

The lesson to be drawn from this experience, so far as capitalist countries are concerned, is that a programme of systematic nationalisation cannot really be a solution to its problems. Nationalisation is not a socialist measure, but rather a democratic one where the undertaking is a monopoly, and a national one where a vital national activity is dominated by foreign capital.

Except in cases where nationalisation is the last recourse, the public sector cannot serve as an efficient pilot for orientating the system toward the satisfaction of everyone's needs rather than toward the profit and power of a few. For instance, in France, the Renault factory, in spite of brilliant management, has not contributed at all to reversing the tendency for the private car to prosper to the detriment of the profitable development of public transport.

The French government has at its disposal the necessary means for redirecting the economy without nationalisation: (1) because 30 per cent of French investments are already State investments (the figure is even higher in Italy, Britain and Austria) therefore it can exert an influence through a price policy and an income and wages policy, through direct loans from its nationalised banks and by direct aid and capital-sharing; and (2) because taxation is an instrument of the State for directing growth and changing the form of society.

Regarding the energy example, differential taxation imposing heavy prices on exhaustible energies can have a very dissuasive effect on large energy masters, whether they be business firms (such as long-distance road transport, whose lobby groups in France play a determining and treacherous role in undermining the railway network for their own profit) or private individuals (by discouraging use of private cars and moving people toward the use of public transport).

On the other hand, tax stimulation can be efficient by lightening the tax load on businesses, collectives and private individuals who invest in their own energy production via the soft technology field, i.e. small solar units, windmills, geothermic, water power, etc.

Up till now we have spoken only of governmental intervention. However, the necessary changes in our society and its objectives cannot flow only from above, because it is not the state which dominates the economy and culture. On the contrary, well-organised pressure groups at every level (only initially at the top) impose blind growth models conceived strictly according to their own interests. Therefore it is impossible, in the present system, to hope that the state can direct production toward the needs of the many rather than the profit and power of the few. On the other hand, powerful trade unions, or professional and workers' organisations, together with executives and intellectuals could form what I have called elsewhere – borrowing an expression from Gramsci but giving it a different sense – 'the new historical block'. If sufficiently conscious of its historic goal, this block could constitute a powerful lobby and play a very important political role. It could propose, impose or experiment with new forms of self-determination of ends, and self-management of means, in every field of social life. Self-management, it must be understood, is not only a new form of business management, but also a way of altering the management of every form of social activity. Self-determination of goals and self-management of means can and must become the basic principles of any organisation, whether it be economic, political or cultural. Understood, then, as the will to resolve each problem at the level at which it is set (and not only from the top), self-management is fundamentally distinct from the Proudhonian anarchy of co-operatives: it is a political structure forming part of the whole of society and at the same time in a more narrow sense it is an economic structure characteristic of business as such. This is the main topic of my *Project Hope*.[7]

One step that can immediately be taken in this direction is to oblige the state to become less legislative and more contractual in its economic policy. Until now, in the economic interventions of the state, the legislative has outweighed the contractual approach. What has characterised the law has been that it has been a directive not based on a discussion between two parties, eventually impartially sealed by a third. Instead the legislative method has been characterised by the imposition of the will of one of the two parties.

The contract thus constitutes a new form of human relations. It substitutes an organic link, a permanent link, almost a biological one, for the hierarchical subordination of the parties concerned. It is a really human contractual link limited in time to the performance of one specific project.

Thus the contract can constitute a bridge between liberty and coherence, between programme and the market, between self-management and indicative planning. It can likewise be a method of economic regulation, whether it concerns the organisation of work, or a prices and incomes policy, or the objectives desired by the government for private enterprise to follow. It is by no means impossible that by such methods the state can lay down a general framework for business which would enable firms and collectives of this new type to be created.

Something of this sort has already happened. In France in 1973, a legal proposal was put forward by an MP of the Right majority, supported by an important section of young employers and managers. This aimed at providing a new way for capital to be raised by businesses. In essence it provided for 'men to rent capital' instead of the present state of affairs whereby 'capital rents men'. The mechanism for this innovation was a simple one; it extended mortgage techniques so that working groups or teams could enter into contracts by which they rented the means of production, research and development, and the capital needed to finance inventories of stock. This project gave the renting interest no right to intervene in management. And this is an important element in any strategy of change from a system in which capital buys work, to one in which work buys capital.

Do not mistake this solution for socialism; but it is an important transitional step.

Thus the problem of devolution of power can be resolved. Any power is based on a consensus. This consensus can be obtained by several means, often initially by force and fear. Nevertheless, these methods have narrow limits. In St. Helena, Napoleon, summing up his political experience, said 'the great lesson of my life is that you can do anything with bayonets except sit on them'. Consensus can be obtained through demagogy, paternalism and material stimulation, as they do in the Soviet Union. It can also be obtained through competence and performance and willing agreement.

The central problem of self-management is to create a real economic and political democracy, that is to say, to give everyone at every economic, political and cultural level the possibility of being a creative and responsible person, or as Karl Marx said 'to create such conditions that every child or adult who bears within himself the genius of Raphael or Mozart, can become Raphael or Mozart'.

There is no need to create creativity; it exists in everyone. It is sufficient to withdraw the obstacles to its flow, and this cannot be decreed from above – a method that would be contrary to its very principle. Self-management is not just a new form of management, the precise image of which we must have in our pocket in the form of some model stature for all businesses. The problem is to create conditions under which a new embodiment of civilisation and society can emerge from below: conditions in which individuals will want freely to give their best.

How shall we begin?

In order to bring about the necessary changes, it is essential not to exclude arbitrarily any initiative, whether it comes from the state, from business, from collectives or from individuals. The only criterion with which to judge any particular activity in a political regime, the functioning of business or a collective, or for judging the value of a leader in any sector, is the following: *what opening does it allow for social experimentation and innovation?* This is because piecemeal social experimentation and innovation is the only way of allowing the emergence of new aims and a new sense of purpose from below. From this will follow the invention of new forms of organisation of work, and new ways both of devolving power and distributing profits. It would be contradictory to the principle of self-management to try to make decisions governing it from above. The state or private initiative must help stimulate the creation of a great many centres of social experimentation and social innovation. This could be done in a state which set about creating a ministry or foundation for social experimentation and innovation. What would the primary objectives of such a ministry or foundation be? I think they would be mainly two, one at the economic level and one at the cultural.

At the economic level, the prime target would be to encourage the creation of small or medium-sized enterprises producing decentralised and inexhaustible energy, that is to say energy other than nuclear, oil or coal based. The advantages would not be only ecological, but also political, such as the decentralisation of energy sources and the consequent avoidance of political pollution which necessarily follows in the wake of their increasing centralisation.

Such an approach allows a multiplying economical effect. Even small loan investments could exert such an effect because they would very often act as a supplementary spur to the expansion of small, already-existing enterprises whose proliferation would be rapid. One can think of firms specialising in providing solar or wind heating in homes, schools, isolated farmhouses or villages; or of businesses whose managers want to assure their autonomy in energy; or of research centres studying, let us say, the development of a means for producing liquid hydrogen economically as a fuel of the future for the interal combustion engine. A second and very important advantage to be derived from this economic objective would be its contribution to the establishment of new relations with the Third World. For example, the multiplication of small solar-production units of energy for water supply pumps in isolated villages could profoundly change the economy, indeed the very life of many countries, especially in the desert and arid areas of Africa and Asia. A third advantage would be that these small units, thanks to researches adapted to specific local needs (for instance, the prototype of the solar pump at the University of Dakar), would open a huge market which would be at the same time operated on a human scale and allow the apprenticeship of new forms of co-operation and self-management.

At the cultural level, the effect of a ministry or foundation for social experimentation and innovation would be a huge and multiplying one because of the link established (for instance, through a bulletin or audio-visual media) at low cost between isolated researchers and great research centres. Thus thousands of initiatives and discoveries would no longer be left fallow but would grow by cross-fertilisation and co-ordinated study.

This brings us again to our central objective: how to bring into being and train pioneers of creative change (*Pioneers of Mutation*). I propose that we should begin to think of establishing new small universities dedicated to this purpose. Until now the universities – and teaching generally – have had as their essential objective *the integra-*

tion of the young into the existing order. In these germinal centres of new culture, the end-purpose would be radically different. It would be *to prepare men and women to invent the future* – to create the conditions for systematic change. The animators of such an innovation would rarely be professional teachers, specialists from other spheres of life or professors. They would be, instead, those who had proved their concrete imagination or efficiency in any enterprise of a new type; or in their research (as exemplified either in works on the creation of new forms of energies, or on the application of these discoveries in radically new conditions); or pioneers of new forms of management stimulating the aptitude to create in every worker, and so on. Primarily they would create interest first and transmit knowledge second. This University would employ artists who would have considered the creative act in terms of its relation to social life, who would consider a work of art not as a reflection of existing chaos, but rather as a project for a new order in the process of being born; an instrument for awakening a creative participation in every individual.

We should solicit the Third World to help us to make a critical appraisal of our Western model of civilisation, to help us enter into a new relationship with Nature, with our fellow man and with God. Likewise, we should issue such an invitation to men of differing religious experiences and different experiences of reality, men with whom we would have shared the common characteristic of having meditated on the ultimate goals of life.

Then we should be able to share with them a vision of the necessary changes in our society and of the pioneers needed to achieve them.

ENDNOTES

1. See also Gunnar Adler-Karlsson, 'Technology, Population and Power'. *The Future of Industrial Society,* Vol. II.
2. *Limits of Growth,* The Club of Rome, 1973.
3. Frederick Taylor, *Shop Management* (1911), Principles of Scientific Management (1911). See also Hugo Münsterberg, *Psychology and Industrial Efficiency* (1913).
4. Ross Ashby, *Introduction to Cybernetics,* Chapman & Hall, London, 1958.
5. A term which he borrows from the vocabulary of cybernetics to refer to the degree of complexity of a given system, which in turn means the number of different forms it can take.
6. Roger Garaudy, *Project Hope,* Paris, 1976.
7. Roger Garaudy, *op. cit.* (1976).

Small units – a danger to civilisation!

Jean Gimpel

I have always been rather opposed to the idea that Small is Beautiful. In the 1960s I was delighted to come and live in England where the sports arenas were larger than those in France. Colombes, the largest French stadium of the time, only seated 60,000 spectators. As soon as I arrived in Britain I rushed to watch a match at Twickenham which seats 70,000. I then went to Wembley which has a capacity crowd of 93,000. My unfulfilled ambition is to watch a match in Glasgow at Hampden Park which seats 134,000. And my ultimate ambition is to visit Rio de Janeiro where the stadium has a record capacity of 230,000.

I love mass media, in particular the mass medium of television. I think it wonderful that millions of people can be watching the same programme as I am. I love great cities and their traffic jams. They are a proof of the prosperity of the West. When there are no traffic jams, that will be the day when the West will be witnessing a terrifying economic depression. And I love high rise buildings. I have always been fascinated by the world record-breaking spirit which pushed the American people to build ever higher skyscrapers. Although the highest skyscrapers were put up in recent years, the competition really ended in the 1930s with the Empire State Building, 1,472 feet high, and with 102 floors.

Now I mention my liking for large structures not simply because of the pleasure I derive from them, but because they often seem to be symptomatic of the vitality of a society. In the inexorable rise and fall of civilisations, one thing which stands out is that the highest point of a civilisation's cycle usually coincides with its maximum technological power. Indeed, the spiritual greatness of a civilisation is only possible because of its technological achievements. One might almost say that technology *is* civilisation.

When technology ceases to progress – as it does when a society's psychological drive weakens – that is when a civilisation begins to die. It does not, of course, happen suddenly. A gradual evolution takes place as a society moves from its youth to a period of maturity and then finally to old age and decline.

I believe the Western world today is in the later stages of this process. But before examining the present, let us look at a few historical precedents. In the past, societies have usually been at their most creative in the earlier stages of their development. It is then that they seem to be animated by the same world record-breaking spirit that we see in the American skyscrapers of the 1930s. It was the first Egyptian dynasties which built the Great Pyramids. Medieval France was equally prepared to attempt the most ambitious technological feats. Wishing to impress visitors to their cities, the French bourgeoisie erected soaring arches and spires, culminating with the project to vault the choir of Beauvais Cathedral 157 feet and three inches above floor level in 1247. (In fact, part of the vaults collapsed not long after.)

In tackling such projects, contemporary engineers were continually driven to the discovery of new technical methods.

But in their declining years these societies started to build smaller units. By the end of the thirteenth century the French economy had ceased expanding. There were no more pioneers and fewer self-made men. The yield of the land was no longer increasing and the climate was changing for the worse. The population growth was levelling off. In place of magnificent vaults and spires, the bourgeoisie built themselves private chapels. Small had become beautiful. Unfortunately, these small units required no new technical know-how – and thus the impetus to push back the frontiers of knowledge diminished.

What happened to France in the Middle Ages seems to be happening to the Western world, and specifically to the United States today. In medieval France all the great innovations – and by innovations I mean inventions which have been financed, developed and marketed – had been made by the end of the thirteenth century. By then some sort of technological plateau had been reached, and for the next hundred years or so there were no major innovations except in the important field of military technology where the cannon and other firearms were developed (continuing emphasis on military technology is a feature of declining societies).

The same pattern can be seen at work in our age. The modern industrial revolution began in England in the eighteenth century and has been carried forward in the twentieth century by the United States. Various parallel characteristics exist between early medieval France and twentieth-century America. Medieval faith, for instance, compared to the modern ideal of democracy; the cathedral compared to the Automobile; Beauvais to the Empire State Building; the Cistercians compared to Henry Ford; the Gold Louis to the Dollar.

But by the 1940s the United States had entered its period of maturity – a period which did not last long and which already possessed such features of imminent decline as a levelling off of the Gross National Product, a tendency towards self-interest, a resistance to change, a loss of interest in record-breaking and so on.

It was in 1971, in my view, that the United States finally entered its period of old age and decline. That was the year when Congress refused to allocate funds for the Supersonic Transport, the American Concorde. This anti-technological vote represented a complete reversal of traditional attitudes to innovation. And, echoing the declining period of the Middle Ages once again, the United States has continued to invest heavily in armaments while neglecting civilian technology. In recent years the United States' level of investment in non-military technology has been one of the lowest of the eighteen most advanced industrial countries in the world.

Now the eclipse of the United States is bound to have profound consequences for the whole of Western civilisation. In the past there was always some new nation ready to take over: Spain inherited the mantle of Italy in the sixteenth century, to be followed by France in the seventeenth and Britain in the eighteenth and nineteenth centuries. But today there is no new power in the West to succeed the United States, so it looks as though Western civilisation itself is in jeopardy.

It is not yet clear what the immediate cause of the collapse will be. It might come from an increasing deterioration of the present world recession. That will inevitably lead to protectionism. Countries will rush to put up trade barriers, and once they go up, they never come down – except after a war. It is, in fact, already happening: apparently even the mushroom industry in America has asked for protection – an event which prompted one journalist to headline his report of the news 'protectionism is Mushrooming'.

Alternatively, Wall Street might crash, leading to a long depression. A crash on Wall Street could be triggered off by a major financial failure such as almost occurred with New York City in 1975. Today, there is a very real possibility that one of the Third World countries might go bankrupt and default on its debts. Zaire almost went bankrupt in 1976 and today the financial world worries about Peru. If it does not happen to Peru, it will happen to another Third World country – there are many who want a moratorium on their debts, not quite realising the terrifying financial consequences it could provoke both for them and for the world at large.

A Wall Street crash might lead to a thirty per cent fall in industrial production in the West. The number of unemployed could quadruple. Deflation would take over from inflation; and when deflation arrived, governments would regret the good old days of inflation.

One by-product of these events would be a steep fall in the cost of energy which would automatically deprive the oil-rich Arab world of much of its current political power. And there would, of course, be other equally dramatic political consequences. A complete breakdown of law and order would not be improbable. It would be a real heyday for terrorists all over the world. Minority groups would threaten the integrity of European nations, and the Soviet Empire would probably break up: countries like Poland, which are already in economic and political difficulties, would revolt. The least affected people would be those who lived in the Third World. Their standard of living would fall only marginally, and thus the gulf between the Third World and the advanced industrial nations would close appreciably.

How should today's governments prepare for such an economic holocaust? I think that the Western nations would do well to start studying the effects of deflation. The Third World should try to make its economy less and less dependent on the West. It should cease importing Western technology, which invariably builds up astronomic debts, and concentrate instead on developing the traditional industries which many Third World countries are fortunate enough to possess. These will inevitably be small-scale enterprises, and not, alas, the record-breaking technological achievements which are the symbols of a great civilisation. But in the dark ages which lie ahead, they are probably the most realistic means of survival.

To recommend them is not to suggest that the future is completely bleak. In time, of course, a new civilisation will emerge. Quite probably it will be Chinese since they almost alone seem to have succeeded in breaking from their past. Meanwhile, the rest of us must prepare as best we may for the approaching cataclysm.

Technical resources of the history of invention

René Alleau

It was Arthur Buckley, a contemporary of Newton, who once wrote that modesty obliges us to speak of the ancients with respect since we know so little about them. Newton knew their writings virtually by heart: he had the greatest respect for them, regarding them as men of profound and superior minds whose inventiveness was much greater than is suggested by what remains of their writings.

Far more ancient texts have been destroyed than have survived. Today's new discoveries may be inferior to those which have been lost – a speculation which has a certain amount of historical basis. What, after all, remains of the hundreds of thousands of manuscripts from the library at Alexandria? What became of the two hundred thousand words in the library of Pergamum? Or the collections of Pisistrates in Athens. Or the library of the temple at Jerusalem? Or Memphis? What treasures were contained in the thousands of volumes on ancient Chinese science which Emperor Ts'in Che Houang-Ti ordered to be burnt for political reasons in 213 BC? People have tried to minimise the gravity of the Emperor's gesture, and so it would seem worth quoting the actual text of his decree:

> 'Anyone preserving a copy of a forbidden book will be tatooed and sentenced to forced labour for life. Anyone discussing or analysing one of the destroyed texts will be executed and his corpse exposed in a public place. Anyone alluding to texts of the past in order to complain about the present state of the Empire will be executed along with all his relatives.'

Evidence for the amount of ancient knowledge lost to us is overwhelming. It is as if we are faced with the ruins of a huge temple of knowledge of which only a few stones remain. But if we look closely at these few remaining stones, we glimpse truths too profound to be attributed simply to the intuition of the Ancients.

First, and contrary to popular belief, it was not Descartes who invented the rationalist method. 'Those who seek the truth,' said Descartes, 'must, as far as possible, doubt everything.' This seems very new. But if we look at Aristotle's second book of metaphysics we find the following sentence: 'Whosoever looks for instruction must first of all doubt, since doubt enables the mind to discern the truth.' Not only did Descartes borrow this crucial sentence from Aristotle; he also borrowed the four famous laws governing the mental process which are the basis of the experimental method. Clearly Descartes had read Aristotle, a fact which is often ignored by modern Cartesians.

'If I am wrong, I therefore know that I exist, for someone who does not exist cannot be wrong. By the very fact that I know myself to be wrong, I know that I exist.' This is not Descartes either: it is St Augustine.[1] The principle of the need for scepticism and doubt in the observer was taken to its extreme by Democritus, who would consider valid only those experiments which he had personally attended, and whose results he had authenticated by sealing them with his ring. This is very far from the naivety and credulousness we normally attribute to the Ancients. One of Democritus' most interesting theories was the idea that a universe could be constructed from one atom. Although many more recent works on atomic theory owe much to Democritus, Leucippus and Epicurus, this particular idea is even older. Sextus Empiricus tells us that it was traditional wisdom by Democritus' time, and that he himself learnt the theory from Mosous, the Phoenician, who in a very strange marginal note, claimed that the atom was divisible. This, of course, is more accurate than the notion of indivisibility which Greek physicists were later to adopt. Here, as in so many other cases, ancient wisdom passed into obscurity; when fragments were later brought to light they were claimed as genuine new discoveries. Examples are legion.

It is a curious fact that in the field of cosmology, the older the theory, the more likely it is to be accurate. For instance, Thales and Anaximenes believed the Milky Way to be composed of stars, each of which represented a world with a sun and planets situated in an immense space. Lucretius knew about the uniform rate of fall of a body in a vacuum, and he, too, believed that space was filled with an infinite number of worlds.

Later, when attempts were made to explain the law of gravity, the cause was sought in the reciprocal attraction of all matter – the explanation arrived at was that the earth attracts all terrestrial bodies to itself, and the sun and moon attract all their own particles to themselves, and thus stabilize them in their particular sphere. Galileo and Newton expressly acknowledged the debt they owed to the Ancients; similarly, Copernicus states in his preface addressed to Paul III that the idea of the rotation of the earth was suggested to him by ancient texts. Of course, the reference to these earlier sources in no way diminishes the genius of Copernicus or Newton or Galileo. It is tempting, however, for a dwarf sitting on the shoulders of a giant to believe that he himself is great; and it is tempting for us to forget that we are being carried by just such a giant, by the whole of scientific tradition from antiquity to the present.

The history of invention is well illustrated by the famous anecdote about Mlle Bertin, Marie-Antoinette's milliner. One day, in the Queen's presence, Mlle Bertin took an old hat, altered it, and turned it into a beautiful and fashionable one. Then, turning to the Queen, she said: 'The only new things are those which have been forgotten.' The history of invention frequently bears this out. In 1618, for example, there appeared a short pamphlet entitled 'The Natural History of the Burning Fountain near Grenoble'; the author was a doctor of medicine from Tournon, one Jean Tardin. Not only did Tardin study this fountain's natural gasometer but even went so far as to reproduce the observed phenomena in his laboratory. He put some of the water into a closed receptacle, raised it to a high temperature and produced flames whose origin he could then study. He explained quite clearly that the basic material for these flames was a kind of bitumen which had to be gasified into an 'inflammable exhalation'. Nothing was done with this information. So for two whole centuries an important discovery lay lost and forgotten simply because ancient texts had not been studied. Had this discovery not been forgotten, it would have had an early and highly important effect on industrial development.

Let's take another example. Claude Chartes published his report on optical signals in 1793. But a hundred years earlier, in a letter dated 26th November 1695, Fenelon had written to Jean Sobieski, secretary to the King of Poland, describing experiments in optic signalling and telephony. Earlier still, in 1636, Schwenter, in his 'Physico-mathematics', examined the principle of the electric telegraph and described how two people could communicate by means of magnetised needles. Yet it was not until 1819 that Oerstaed's experiments on the deviation of a magnetised needle were published. In this case, too, the discovery was lost for almost two centuries.

In 1729, Tiphaigne de la Roche described image photography and even colour photography with extraordinary precision. This scientist, who is now virtually unknown even to historians of science, wrote: 'The impression of the image occurs in the very first instant the canvas receives it. It is removed immediately and placed in a dark room; an hour later when the paste has dried, the finished result is a true reproduction of the original.' And here is how he described the physical details of the experiment:

'1. The nature of the gelatinous substance which intercepts and preserves light rays must be studied.
   2. Description of difficulties in the preparation and use of this gelatinous substance.

3. The interaction of light with this dried substance.'

The properties of chemical substances capable of fixing light impressions were recognised long before Tiphaigne de la Roche: as early as 1566 Fabritius gave a precise account of these chemicals in his classic work 'De Rebus Mecanicis'. And yet it was not until January 7th 1839 that Aragon announced Daguerre's invention to the French Academy of Science.

It is difficult to establish connections between Antiquity and the Middle Ages on the basis of available documents, particularly since we have so little information about Arab manuscripts. But one more example should help to illustrate the lack of knowledge about earlier scientific activities. On 16th October 1826 Moreau presented the results of his experiments on vaccination to the French Academy of Science in the following terms:

'Retain the liquid from the pustules on the point of a lancet and introduce it into the arm, mixing the liquid with blood. Smallpox fever will ensue. The induced illness, however, will take a mild course and will not be dangerous.'

He described all the symptoms that occurred and although he was not sure of the exact nature of the injected liquid, he thought that it might be an anaesthetic. There are similarities here with Denis Papin's work (published in 1681) on surgery without pain; with the experiments on anaesthesia carried out in May 1772 in the presence of Queen Maria Theresa and her physician, Rowersby; and with ancient Chinese experiments using plant extracts and mandrake. The effects of mandrake were known during the Middle Ages, totally forgotten in the eighteenth century, and then rediscovered and used with great success by D'Auriol, a doctor from Toulouse. No one has ever taken up these experiments again.

On 17th December 1897 Ernest Duchêne, a student at the École de Pharmacie at Lyon, submitted a thesis entitled 'Contribution à l'étude de la concurrence vitale des micro-organismes antagonistes, contre les microbes'. In this study, he gives a detailed description of the action of penicillum glaucum. If such discoveries in the field of antibiotics had been developed at the time, it would have made an enormous difference to First World War casualties.

Many, many more examples could be given of experiments and discoveries which anticipate developments not made until years or even centuries later. But there are also instances of specific discoveries, such as gold mines, which were subsequently forgotten. In June 1848, Marshall discovered some nuggets on the banks of a river where he was carrying out surveying work for the construction of a mill: the nuggets turned out to be gold. Many years before, Fernando Cortez had passed that way in search of the Mexican's Eldorado and its fabulous treasures. Cortez had turned the country upside down, ransacked every hut he came to, but had never for a moment thought to collect samples of river sand. Spanish financiers and Jesuit missionaries trampled the gold-bearing sands of this Eldorado underfoot for three centuries. In 1737, however, more than a hundred years before Marshall's discovery, a Dutch newspaper carried a report about the gold and silver mines of Sonora, giving their precise location. In 1767 'L'Histoire Naturelle et Civile de la Californie' was published in Paris and recorded testimonies from a number of explorers about these gold nuggets. No one took any notice of it. There are also the tales which the old Arab explorers brought back from their travels: these would have been a good source of information about prospecting, but they, too, were ignored.

It seems to me that a practical lesson must be drawn from all this. To say simply that some discoveries are overlooked and forgotten about is no excuse. Every industrial technique ought to be worked out according to three essential rules: Experiment, Science and History. It would be both presumptious and naive to ignore history, and to concentrate on attempting to discover something totally new rather than trying rationally to adapt and improve a technique that already exists in an imperfect form. Before committing itself to costly investment an industry ought to be aware of every aspect of a problem: a simple patents search to establish sole priority is not enough to give a full picture of the state of development of any process or technique. It is very much in the industry's own interest to research the history of a particular process as thoroughly as possible.

There are certainly gaps and distortions in the information available: lacunae in the preservation and transference of knowledge were inevitable in ancient civilisations. But nowadays such gaps can be avoided, thanks to developments in information storage and retrieval techniques. With computers, and well-organised new libraries offering the possibility of vastly extended research and selection of information, it is unforgivable that we should fail to make up the ground previously left uncovered by historical research. This systematic research should not be left in the hands of a few scholars – a co-ordinated European Service should be set up with adequate funds and the interdisciplinary co-operation of historians of science and technology from different countries. Such a research service would be of untold practical benefit to industry. Let us hope that it may one day become a reality.

Translated by Anne Green.

ENDNOTE

1. S. Augustine, ed. Pascal, *La Cité de Dieu*, XL, 26 p. 193 (ed. Citée).

Tools versus values: notes on the possibility of communal work

Philip Abrams

> 'Man ceases to be recognisable as one of his kind when he can
> no longer shape his own needs by the more or less competent
> use of those tools that his culture provides.'
>
> Ivan Illich, *The Right to Useful Unemployment*

By 1975 it was being argued throughout Europe that the
counter-culture had died. The experiments of the previous decade
were judged to have failed; the new consciousness had manifestly not
been realised in effective new social practice; the alternative society
remained a hypothesis. Nevertheless, there were some continuities.
One of the most challenging was the widespread attempt to renew the
counter-culture on the basis of a more positive involvement in work.
The revolution of the individual was replaced by a less flamboyant,
often very carefully planned, effort to reconstitute social relationships
by way of new styles of collective production. A simple materialist
lesson appeared to have been learned. From the disasters of the highly
individualistic, expressive and usually retreatist projects of the 1960s
there seemed to have grown an understanding of the sense in which
work is a generic human activity, the foundation on which society,
including the new society, must be built if it is to be built at all. The
counter-culture remained alive but its new programmes sought to
realise radical values not in new forms of private life, politics or play
but in new forms of work. Specifically, the distinctive projects of the
new phase were to be attempts to provide goods and services to the
markets of the surrounding 'real' world on the basis of co-operation,
co-ownership, profit-sharing and worker control. Such experiments in
alternative relations of production were often coupled with an interest
in and search for alternative technologies as well, means of
scaling-down and restoring human practice to the immediate
experience of work. Exemplary demonstrations of the serious
possibility of re-appropriating work as a human activity were
proposed.

It is becoming possible now to begin to assess the achievements
and the difficulties of these projects. A wide-ranging appraisal,
Working Communally, has indeed been published already by David
and Elena French. The assessment I shall attempt in these notes will

be more modest, centred on the extent to which the experience of 'working communally' has brought to light unavoidable tensions, perhaps even contradictions, between the technical requirements of effective work (tools) and the more general, underlying purposes for the sake of which communal work is attempted in the first place (values). In particular I shall look at two arguments. First, there is the argument that the type of demand for meaning in work which has commonly inspired experiments in collective production is in fact incompatible with sustained use of the sorts of tools, techniques and procedures of work that must be used if the seeds of communal work are to be planted fruitfully in the soil of advanced industrial, mass-consumption societies – the argument that for compelling technical reasons work in such societies *must* be organised in ways which make that sort of meaning unattainable. And secondly, there is the more fundamental argument that insofar as the most basic values of those who take part in experiments in collective production or communal work are essentially values of private consumption (my income, my way of life, the quality of my experience) the projects are necessarily doomed; the argument that collective production cannot coexist with private consumption. Both arguments have been advanced by critics of communal work. Both have a certain prima facie plausibility. And both if made good would tend to suggest that work cannot be re-appropriated as part of the meaningful experience of the worker until a powerful undercurrent of individualism in the culture and ideology of our society has been stilled.

Of course, it is widely believed that the recovery of meaning in work is now a lost cause, unalterably blocked by the division of labour and the technologies which advanced industrial economies must embody. Writing twenty years ago about 'Work and Its Discontents', Daniel Bell came regretfully to the conclusion that there were no intrinsic rewards, meanings or satisfactions to be expected in most of the work that had to be done in industrial societies. The efficient organisation of production entailed fragmentations and estrangements which no amount of job-enrichment could counteract. In the face of the unavoidable banality of the experience of work the only rational relationship to work was now ruthlessly instrumental; work had become the necessary idiocy one endured in order to be a human being away from work. Minimising the hours spent at work and the attention seriously given to it, and maximising the income and benefits wrested from it became the logical strategy for industrial man. The enactment of that logic is the 'flight from work' discovered by Goran Palm in Sweden, by Goldthorpe and Lockwood in Luton and by an army of industrial sociologists throughout the industrial world. It has become an orthodoxy of that literature that work in industrial societies is indeed normally meaningless and that life is the time between clocking-out and clocking-in. Many texts now urge us simply to bracket work aside as nasty, brutish, but with luck also short and well-paid.

Through the large picture windows of the office block on the opposite side of the street I can see as I write fifteen audio-typists bound hand, foot and ear to the machines that enable them, in a continuous electrical flow, to process the disembodied words of employers they never meet. It does not matter that the content of the messages that pass through them are to them normally meaningless. All that matters once they are wired up is that they are given unambiguous instructions. That is all the transmitter-transcriber machine of which they are part requires. Insofar as jobs are constituted so that workers are tools, and for the job to be done properly must not be more than tools, the flight from work becomes a human imperative. What is remarkable given the extensiveness of such a uniquely alienated state of affairs in industrial societies is that some people should still think it worthwhile to try to recapture communal forms of work which express and realise whole lives. But are such projects constructively radical or merely utopian dreams?

The counter-cultural critique of work and the related search for new forms of work have proceeded on two grounds. One emphasises the relations of production; capitalism, state socialism, bureaucratic management, the mass market – the fact that audio-typists are not just shackled to machine processes but are doing a job created for them by scholars and publishers who can impose the terms on which they want the work done. The other concentrates on the forces of production, the domination of the worker by the tools of work quite independently of the relationships within which jobs are created and defined. The former view is perhaps the more familiar, having been argued in a powerful body of marxist and marxisant critiques. The latter, the claim that workers have become victims of their tools, that it is technique that engenders alienation, is in fact more widespread although usually less overtly articulated, a taken-for-granted assumption legitimating the taken-for-granted flight from work in which most of us are engaged. The intellectual basis for such a view has, nevertheless, been very well expressed by a number of writers, notably by Peter Berger. People produce an endless variety of tools and use them to modify their physical environment and bend nature to their will. But once a tool has been forged it also bends its user to the limits of its technical possibilities. 'Once produced,' Berger maintains, 'the tool has a being of its own that cannot readily be changed by those who employ it. Indeed, the tool may even enforce the logic of its being upon its users.' Thus, we invent language and our very thought is at once entrapped and structured by its rules – that, after all, was Hegel's original instance of alienation. Or again: 'Man produces values and discovers that he feels guilt when he contravenes them. Man concocts institutions which come to control him as powerfully menacing constellations of the external world'. Advanced technology simply carries such relationships to an extreme. The social demand for maximum efficiency of production is met by technical forms of production – process work, the assembly line, bureaucratic routine, ever larger units of production, the relentless intensification of the division of labour – which must progressively eliminate the individuality of the worker as a significant or even a possible factor of production. Tools become social facts.

These two views of what is wrong with work are not mutually exclusive. David Dickson, for example, in his *Alternative Technology* has sought to combine them in the argument that technological necessities are not ineluctable facts of nature but rather cultural facts of a man-made history, necessities of particular systems of social power. To him the tools of work are first and foremost the instruments by which relations of domination are forged and enforced. The forces of production are forceful in the life of the worker precisely because they embody the relations of production. Audio-typing is vile work because the worker is governed by a relationship between machines. But people become audio-typists as a result of their position in a market in which they cannot command better jobs. Yet in the movement towards communal work in recent years Dickson's type of analysis has been eccentric. Most of those involved have tended to emphasise the malignant effects of *either* the tools of work *or* the relations of work, not both. This in turn has provoked two fairly distinct types of proposal as to how the human recovery of meaningful work might proceed. Those who are most impressed by the constraints of the forms and forces of production look towards a renewal of craftwork and/or some form of alternative technology. Those who emphasise the relations of production look instead to co-operation, commune-ownership or worker-control. Each of these possible escapes from the idiocy of work into a collective work-based alternative thus demands consideration.

But a last preliminary word is necessary. It is, in fact, quite difficult to find examples of any of these types of envisaged counter-cultural re-entry of society which are stable enough, productive enough, coherent enough to constitute fair tests of the viability of communal work. The attempt to construct an alternative world through enterprises that are primarily orientated to work, primarily new ways of organising the forces and relations of production is, in the capitalist societies at least, much talked about but little practiced. In 1974, some colleagues and I completed a study of communes in Britain. Several of the groups we had visited seemed to me to have had a driving central concern with work, to have understood their main purpose as being the achievement of a collectively ordered mode of production around and through which the values they cherished could develop. My first thought on being asked to write this paper was to go back to half-a-dozen of these groups and look at them more closely. All but one of them had ceased to exist. The one that survived had turned into a flourishing business – organised on the basis of private ownership and a strict and hierarchical division of labour. Most of the far more promising 'communities of work' established in France, above all, the watch-making collective at Boimondau, seem to have gone the same way. David and Elena French have described their own very similar frustration in looking for appropriate objects of study in the United States: 'communal workplace after communal workplace shimmered briefly on the horizon, only to vanish at our approach.' Thus:

> 'A Colorado design commune had disbanded in anger by the time we discovered its address. A Massachusetts woodworking commune proved to be an assortment of largely unrelated people sharing a loft full of machinery. A Canadian game-making commune on closer look became husband and wife and some interesting ideas. An Illinois law commune disintegrated just before our letter of inquiry reached it. An elusive Vermont candle-making commune had not produced a candle in five months when we finally tracked it down . . . Ultimately, we were forced to conclude that we were chasing something that by and large did not exist.'

The situation is not quite that hopeless in Britain; there are just enough projects of each of my form types to permit at least a provisional empirical discussion. But on balance the general message is clear: extensive and stable development of communal work is not probable within long-established capitalist economies. For the real thing one has to look to Tanzania or Israel, Yugoslavia or China. Meanwhile, *Alternative England and Wales*, Nicholas Saunders' guide to the counter-culture devotes a mere 2 of its 336 pages to work for a quite simple reason: 'This section was going to be a comprehensive guide to work outside the economic system – not only employment but the whole business of setting up alternative work organisations. But apart from individuals and small, closed groups of people there isn't much happening.'

The dream of craftwork

What *is* happening, and it is minutely recorded in *Alternative England*

and Wales, is a massive search for craftwork. The movement includes both the renewal of ancient crafts and the development of new ones: leather-working, moulding plastics, weaving, potting, working with polystyrene, batik, inflatable buildings and domes, mosaics, gilding, glass-blowing, candle-making, working with silver, copper, pewter, precious and semi-precious stones, printing, book-binding, engraving, micro-electronics. And the resources for learning crafts, pursuing them and marketing their products seem amply to match the demand for opportunities to live like that.

From Schiller and Marx to Ivan Illich and Goran Palm, assertions of the alienated meaninglessness of work have rested implicitly or explicitly on an ideal of the possible meaningfulness of work culled from the folklore of craftsmanship: every man his own Benevenuto Cellini. Much of the energy that has been turned towards communal projects in Britain in recent years has plainly been fired by the same ideal. Indeed, the attempt to reconstruct work as craft is probably the common form basis of all the attempts at reconstruction I am going to consider. The object has been to win self-realisation through work which expresses highly personal skill, through the creation of products the value of which lies precisely in the extent to which they embody the individuality of the producer. A number of communes and collectives founded on that principle now exist in Britain; some, such as Taena in Gloucestershire, have existed for many years. Yet what such groups most strikingly reveal is the degree to which craftwork is a private not a collective matter; the potter, the silversmith, the poet each do their own work, with their own tools, in their own space, for their own customers. Solidarity is achieved by meticulously dividing labour on the basis of idiosyncratic skills, not by concerting it. Integration springs from shared religious beliefs, or a highly instrumental understanding of the practical advantages of collective residence, or simple friendship. The whole point of such communes is that they do *not* involve communal work; rather, they permit an intense privatisation of work.

Despite their communal form such enterprises are saturated with individualism. Insofar as they succeed they do so by providing retreats from society in which highly talented individuals can specialise in the production of luxury commodities for the markets of the very society which has ostensibly been so firmly repudiated. When they fail, and most commonly craft collectives of this sort do fail, they fail because such individuals find the constraints of genuinely communal work, including a measure of banal routine and a deliberate suppression of individualism, a violation of their personal integrity; or because realisation of their continued entanglement with the philistine mass market drives them to some yet more esoteric, more strictly private retreat. The real momentum in these projects is 'freedom for me'; work is valued not because its essentially social nature is grasped and appreciated, but on the contrary because it is understood as a private activity.

It is often argued that craftwork is committed, by its inherent technical characteristics, to individualistic ideologies of this sort. Certainly it can be a vehicle for individualism. No less certainly much of its contemporary appeal lies in the fact that it is seen as such a vehicle, a means to recapture the self. But the technical necessity of the relationship is less obvious. Is there really some intrinsic property of craftwork which requires the craftworker to treat task, tools and product as inviolable extensions of self? Can craftwork really only be done on that basis? To have watched at least four craft communes fall apart in the face of the disillusioned discovery that 'all we're really doing is selling bric-a-brac to tourists,' or 'anyone can make candles,' coupled with intransigent assertions of the right to self-expression in work is to be more than half-convinced that the answer to such questions must be yes. The collective arrangements, co-ownership, co-residence, profit-sharing and subsidy simply prove too fragile to contain the tension that results. The commune at the Bridge in Airedale is a pertinent example. This was a group of eight people who had pooled their resources to buy and restore a large, deserted farmhouse and to establish a collective making pottery (mainly mugs and jugs) and kitchen furniture (tables, cupboards, wall-units and chairs). The pottery, a simple but distinctive design, sold rather well from the start and after two hectic years the furniture was also beginning to command regular sales in local markets. At that point the members of the group gradually became aware of a serious problem of strategy and values. Both sets of products could prospectively be produced and marketed quite successfully on the basis of what were in essence standardised, mass-production techniques. In particular there appeared to be a steady demand for a steady supply of identical mugs, identical jugs and identical wall-units. The economic logic of the venture urged development in that direction. But the sense of craft skill that had brought the group together and motivated them thus far rebelled against the conditions of their own economic success. What was to be done?

After several anguished months the potters decided to insist on breaking with the market and branching out into more refined, skilled, esoteric 'art' work – which indeed was, at least initially, almost impossible to sell. Appalled by this irresponsibility the furniture makers for their part then insisted on withdrawing their capital from the project and went on to establish themselves as directors of a quite conventional small manufacturing company trading very nicely in an increasingly national market. None of the possible compromises implicit in the division of labour within the group had proved acceptable to its members. The farmhouse is now once again deserted. Surely this sort of history, which would be repeated many times, does point towards a principled incompatibility between craft work and collective production?

The dilemma of the craftworker has been especially well described by Christopher Caudwell in a famous analysis of English poetry. For Caudwell, and in this sense his is an orthodox view, craft is doomed by capital and the craftworker's typical response, escape into an ever more private world of skilled craft, is only spuriously radical. Thus: 'The development of capitalist production remorselessly turns the craftsman into a labourer. The machine competes with and ousts the product of his skilled hands. The effect is . . . to make him revolt against the demands of a commercialised market by setting up his skill as a good in itself detached from social uses.' The whole of that pattern can be found again and again in the experience of the craft communes. Time after time the careers of the members of such groups seem merely to follow the pattern Caudwell traces among the English poets:

> 'The poet is the most craft of writers. His art requires the highest degree of technical skill of any artist; and it is precisely this technical skill which is not wanted by the vast majority of people in a developed capitalism. He is as out of date as a medieval stone-carver in an age of plaster casts. Because of the conditions of his life the poet's reaction is similar to that of the craftsman. He begins to set craft skill in *opposition* to social function, 'art' in opposition to 'life'. The craftsman's particular version of commodity fetishism is *skill fetishism*. Skill now seems an objective thing, opposed to social value'.

Technique, one might say, becomes the value of a valueless world, the worth of a worthless culture, the opium of the craftworker. But the fetishism of technique is as Caudwell also points out (and as did F. R. Leavis), really a fetishism of the craftworker. Once the product is valued for its technical content regardless of social content the real object of value is not the product at all but the producer. The essence of what Leavis called the 'illusion of technique' is the demand that the craftworker should be esteemed for the skilled use of his tools, not for what he or she makes. 'In revolting against capitalism the poet . . . simply moves on to an extreme individualism, utter "loss of control of his social relationships", and absolute commodity production – to the essence in fact of the capitalism he condemns. He is the complete mirror-revolutionary.' Self-fulfilment is found in the sale for enormously high prices of objects which express nothing but the personal skill of the individual craftworker.

It is impossible to deny that historically this is what has happened to craft work – and to poetry. But we may still ask whether it has to happen? What we find in the craft communes is typically that craft is being used as a means of escape from routine, the mass market, the rat race and the stereotyped world by people who for all the communal form of their escape are profoundly caught up in an ideology and a complex of values that equate freedom with unfettered self-expression and identity with the separation of self from others (independence from, not identity with); their values are the values of possessive individualism. Such people are indeed trapped in the illusory projects described by Caudwell and Leavis. Or, rather, given a modicum of talent they can indeed realise craft work as an alternative to process work, for themselves – but only on the basis of a mode of working that is thoroughly private. The impossibility of collective craft production is not something that is imposed on them by the nature of craftwork; it is something they themselves bring to and impose on such work. The work itself is no more than a tool of their values. Could it then be a tool for other, more genuinely social, collective values as well?

What matters of course is how the producer relates to the product. If the product is to have value only as 'mine' the producer will tend to appropriate work and its tools in a closed circle of personal skill. If the product is merely 'their work and tools alike embody an alienation which can best be lived with on the basis of a cold instrumentalism in which the abstract worker as object becomes a tool for the sensuous worker as subject. But what if the product is 'ours'? Would not working together in an organic division of labour then be the appropriate mode of production? Such reasoning is familiar within the contemporary craft movement and so far as it goes it is surely correct. The essentially collaborative workshops, studios and schools of Renaissance fine art perhaps exemplify such a collective mode – it was after all Leonardo who felt impelled to 'insist that drawing in company is much better than alone'. More certainly, if more humbly, the community of workers, and of producers and users, described in George Sturt's *The Wheelwright's Shop* affirms the practical possibility of collective craft production. The trouble is that petty bourgeois refugees from advanced industrialism cannot change their values at will or on the strength of a purely theoretical understanding of their predicament. So they use the tools of craft production to intensify their isolation, not to conquer it. Sometimes, though, they learn from experience. The history of the Earthcraft commune near Cambridge is a case in point.

Earthcraft was perhaps the most work-oriented of all the communes we visited in the course of our earlier study. Run as a limited company with equal shareholdings distributed among the co-residents it always contained a diversity of practical craft projects together with an overriding, strongly asserted sense that 'working for the place' provided the basic rationale for the collective as a whole. Considerable commitment to this principle was always demanded by the core members of the group. As a result, there was a high and rapid turnover of new, fringe members unwilling or unable to subordinate their private needs and purposes to the economic and emotional patterns the core group judged necessary. Yet within the core group itself there were profound disagreements as to just what working for the place should mean. Should there be a single concerted communal enterprise; and if so, what should it be and how should it be organised? Or should there perhaps be some main project – horticulture, sheep and catering were all tried at different stages – with other more individual work loosely related to it? Or should everyone do whatever work they personally chose to do with a system of rules for sharing chores and income in the background as a loose framework for holding the ensemble together? The members of Earthcraft never managed to find an enduring answer to these questions. Or rather, their membership changed and changed again endlessly as different answers were attempted. The ideological attraction of the third possibility, each member working separately to realise her or his own potentialities, proved subversively strong. But the counteracting sense that the essentially socialist values that had underpinned the venture from the start could only be realised on the basis of at least some measure of working together could not be dispelled either. Gradually, in the face of much profound unhappiness, many departures, and innumerable explosive rows, two main proposals for a central work project emerged. One involved the growing and marketing of organic foodstuffs; the other, a workers' co-operative engaged in the design and manufacture of precision instruments for medical research. As these purposes came to be more clearly formulated and recognised within the core group Earthcraft became steadily less willing to function as an all-purpose refuge for what they now termed 'dropouts, hippies and people with personal troubles', and steadily more concerned to recruit members with relevant, practical experience and proven skills. In the end the collective fell apart in three directions. One group, repudiating the idea of any sort of economic or cultural engagement with the external realities of capitalism, moved to a commune in Devon in which self-sufficiency is ensured on the basis of a genuinely collective but also highly authoritarian organisation of farm work which also enables members to pursue a variety of highly idiosyncratic craft projects of their own – from Tibetan dance to abstract expressionist engraving. A second group have devoted themselves to supplying and staffing a wholefood shop. And a third have formed a small scientific instrument company on the basis of co-ownership and the pooling of some extremely advanced technical skills.

The experience of Earthcraft thus seems to me aptly to summarise the possible destinies of craft-radicalism in contemporary industrial societies. Craft-radicalism can lead one out of the world into a collective retreat which is in essence no different from the private retreat of the highly talented craftworker, except that the pooling of resources makes it available to the less talented or more wilfully eccentric. Or it may lead back into the world in one of two ways: through collective production based on distinctively modern, rather than traditional, craft skills and a positive search for social function; or through a demonstration of the feasibility of alternative technology, the substitution of what Illich has called 'tools for conviviality' for tools of manipulation. It remains to consider how viable either of these seemingly more constructive outcomes of craft-radicalism actually is.

Alternative technology?

The advocates of alternative technology are the most wholehearted devotees of the belief that the sickness of industrial society is essentially a matter of the relationship of the worker to her or his tools. The tools of large-scale industrial technology are seen as despoiling nature, dehumanising the worker and brutally distancing workers both from each other and from their own works as well as from nature. The call is for new technologies which reverse these patterns. Thus Dickson suggests that alternative technology could be characterised as, 'a technology which is satisfying to work with, can be controlled both by the producers and the community by whom the products are used, conserves natural resources and does negligible damage to the environment'. In the same manner Illich tells us: 'Convivial tools are those which give each person who uses them the greatest opportunity to enrich the environment with the fruits of his or her vision. Industrial tools deny this possibility to those who use them. . . Most tools today cannot be used in a convivial fashion.' And in *Towards a Liberatory Technology*, Murray Bookchin appeals for a technology in which, 'the tool amplifies the powers of the craftsman as a *human*'. A world reorganised on the basis of alternative technology would be a world, accordingly, of smaller units of production, less specialisation, craftwork rather than mass production, labour intensive work rather than capital intensive work, the relative self-sufficiency of relatively small communities, widespread mastery of the science and technology appropriate to these social forms, lower energy consumption and, probably, lower standards of living'. It is a curious combination of medievalism and a condition in which very advanced, but scaled-down technology is to 'provide the means by which the individual could fulfil and experience his full human potential'; a landscape, in Robin Clarke's phrase, 'dotted with windmills and solar houses'.

Attempts to enact this vision, as distinct from programmes for it, are as yet few and far between. Most, like the wholefood project that grew out of Earthcraft, the Eco-house commune in Wales or the Street Farmers group in east London, have concerned themselves with ways and means of changing the relationship of individuals to their natural environment so as to secure self-sufficiency rather than, in any direct way, with the possibility of transforming relationships and processes of production between individuals in society as a whole. The social unit with which the majority of experiments have been concerned is the private home not the workshop or market. On the whole, alternative technology projects are demonstration projects in the possibility of life without electricity bills or ecological rape, not attempts to identify the structures of a new type of economy. Noting this marked one-sidedness, this emphasis on private self-sufficiency rather than collective social innovation, Dickson, in a manner quite representative of the alternative technology movement as a whole, blandly dismisses it as an almost improper consideration: 'Such decisions would be left essentially to the workers and the community involved.' It remains to be seen whether this sort of neglect of what must be called the politics of alternative technology makes sense in the light of what a-political alternative technology projects seem able to achieve.

It has been shown that you can run a car on methane gas. The gas gives slightly less power than petrol and were it taxed in the same way as petrol would be slightly more expensive. It has been shown that you can heat a house, to a bearable temperature in sunny climates at least, by solar energy. You can make bread using nothing more than wind, water and muscle power. The Street Farmers, before they were evicted by the local planning authority, claimed to have shown that a whole large household of vegetarians could subsist in an urban terrace house with the aid of nothing more than sun, rain, wind and organic waste. The Technical Research Division of the Department of Architecture at Cambridge University is spending a good deal of public money on a more elaborate version of the same project – an 'eco-house' of 60 square metres with one acre of land (for goats, chickens and vegetables) within which it is proposed to show that nature can provide three-quarters of the needs of an average family. A turkey farmer in Norfolk heats his house with methane gas, although as Nicholas Saunders notes: 'John has to wheelbarrow the turkey shit through the house to the back garden which makes the whole place stink for days.' In sum, actual alternative technology remains at a very primitive level, largely frustrated by the second law of thermodynamics. The most promising projects are massively capital-intensive – such as the billion dollar attempt to mobilise solar energy for industrial purposes being funded by the United States Government. For the rest, alternative technology is for the moment and in practical terms almost entirely a matter of finding bases for private self-sufficiency within a framework of ideals of craftwork and harmony with nature. The social meaning of such projects is well illustrated by the experience of Ceres, the organic food enterprise that was spawned by the disintegration of Earthcraft.

Ceres has its public face in a wholefood shop located in what a geographer might call the zone of transition in Cambridge. More relevant to its success is probably the fact that it is situated halfway between the swimming pool and the technical college and on a strategic route between the university and a massive concentration of bed-sitter accommodation. Originally, in 1970, it was both shop and restaurant and functioned as an outlet for the produce of the Earthcraft commune. The restaurant collapsed because the members of the commune found the drudgery of preparing food, waiting on table and washing up incompatible with the notions of self-realisation that had brought them into the commune and because the project as a whole was not profitable enough to employ non-members of the commune at wage levels that could compete even with those offered to college servants. The shop, which is of course much less labour-intensive, has survived and seems at present to be a modestly successful business. Its self-consciousness is firmly that of the alternative technology movement – at its point of contact with straight society. Behind Ceres stand a whole array of producers who have embraced craftwork with nature as an alternative to process work on nature. The shop asserts the moral integrity and economic viability of such work. Thus:

'Our aim is to present an alternative to the supermarket. . . We feel that large-scale technology has become insensitive to the environment in which it operates. We wish to encourage a more gentle technology, aware of its effects on nature. . . We will strive to provide food of the highest quality at the lowest possible price.

By high quality we mean: unrefined, produced without exploitation of man or nature, organically grown where possible, and if
processed, processed in the most natural way and free from
additives, i.e. wholefoods.'

The link with the commune is severely attenuated now although a
small supply of vegetables still comes from that source. On the other
hand the shop has become an important retail agency for a wide range
of macrobiotic and other organic, ecologically natural products –
soft-textured, pink, recycled lavatory paper was being promoted on
my own last visit – primarily from market gardens and workshops all
over East Anglia but increasingly from national and international
sources, too. There are a number of related projects which cluster
around the grocery: herbal medicines are promoted as part of a
campaign against 'the industrialisation of health': 'we aim to create a
healthy people freed from their dependence on drugs, drug companies, hospitals and doctors . . . we want our store to become a focal
point for . . . ideas concerning natural medicine'. Courses, classes and
discussions on alternative farming methods (not using artificial ferti-
lisers and insecticides), recycling and energy-saving are arranged and
advertised. The shop functions as an important information centre
and meeting place for a variety of counter-cultural projects including
Gay Liberation, Womens' Liberation, Abortion Reform and numerous self-help community organisations. It is run as a producers'
co-operative with members' (shareholders') earning proportions of
the profits related either to the amount of work they do or to their
contributions to capital.

On the other hand muesli can be bought more cheaply half-a-mile
away at any of three supermarkets. Their much-valued wholemeal
flour is frequently out of stock because the miller, who works from a
windmill in a village fifteen miles away, got bored or tired or
interested in something else or simply couldn't control the wind that
day. The cheap and delicious raspberries are likely to be full of
healthy organic maggots. And you can often wait half-an-hour to be
served because the staff don't see themselves as shop assistants and
are engaged in something more worthwhile. It is ideological commitment, values, not economic success, an effective alternative technology, that keeps Ceres in business. Cambridge, of course, contains a
quite disproportionate number of mildly prosperous consumers
ideologically sensitive to the appeals of wholefood; one of the very
few other successful projects of this type in Britain happens to be in
Oxford. The profit-margin is about comparable to that of any other
small, local, independent grocery, that is to say, quite low; the project
survives because it gratifies the values of those who run it, not because

it gives them comfortable incomes or because, as a shop, it constitutes a technological alternative to either the corner store or the supermarket. Actually, because the core members of the group find running the shop tedious or distracting, wage-workers are constantly being taken on to handle an increasing proportion of the routine drudgery the project entails. Ceres is more and more just another business. And increasingly the shareholders, as in so many other producer-co-operatives, expect it to be just that.

The problem of income is unimportant, of course. The point of places like Ceres is not to make money but to indicate the possibility of a different way of life. But is that being achieved either? In relation to their own ambitious programme the members of Ceres admit that their experience is a mixture of success and failure. Variety has been injected into the market. The possibility of producing and consuming organic foods rather than convenience foods within an equivalent range of costs has been demonstrated. Radical ideas and questions have been disseminated to a young and socially sensitive population. And a handful of people have found that the division of labour involved in alternative agriculture can provide them with a satisfying way of life. Yet the whole project is contained and flourishes inside the terms of the capitalist economy to which it is supposed to be an alternative; is increasingly assimilated to that economy. Capitalism has always permitted small entrepreneurs with interesting new lines to make good – modestly. Such developments complement and renew the system rather than threaten it. The fact that in this instance the pursuit of profit is subordinated to other values merely means that Ceres and projects like it will never become very powerful as institutions in a capitalist world. How does one move from functioning as an accepted oddity on the margins of a detested social system to being a manifest alternative to that system? Especially as insofar as 'radical' values are substituted for profit and economic efficiency, those values are themselves also values of the system: self-sufficiency, self-expression and self-fulfilment – all conceived as thoroughly individualistic purposes. This seems to be the heart of the problem. The people who turn to alternative technology are for the most part profoundly committed to the idea of private consumption – for themselves and for others. Their effective unit of consumption is 'I' not 'we'; production and technology alike are subordinate to that principle.

Yet the relationship between tools and values in alternative technology projects is more complex than in the craft communes. The intention is to design tools by which a new social world could be built. But in one important sense at the level of values the social world that is envisaged is not new at all but merely a purified version of what already exists, a world of private individuals. As a result the technical possibility of the tools is demonstrated but the realisation of their social possibilities remains unaccomplished. Socially, the development of alternative technology remains at the level where the individual is given control of some aspect of her or his destiny. The further move to any sort of extensive collective or communal control, a convivial society as it were, is not made. But this failure is not just a matter of values. Or rather, it seems that the diffusion and establishment of alternative technology implies a *political* process which the sorts of tools and institutions those who believe in alternative technology are able to forge cannot begin to encompass. The whole tendency of alternative technology is to reduce the scale of social tools and institutions and to disperse power. Its natural origins are in modest enterprises. But how, then, does alternative technology engage with, pit itself against and overthrow a society organised precisely in terms of massive institutions, long-range manipulative tools and enormous concentrations of power? In the face of that paradox perhaps David Dickson is right to substitute the term 'utopian technology' for alternative technology: utopian not in the sense 'that the tools and machines described are impracticable, but to indicate that their introduction on a significant scale would be virtually impossible within the existing structure of society'. The achievement of widespread alternative technology seems to call for just those forceful tools that alternative technology is designed to reject.

Common ownership

The scientific instrument company which was the third venture to survive the dissolution of Earthcraft was in many ways both more radical and more conventional than either of the other two. It was more radical in its attempt to renew the idea of craftwork through distinctively modern skills presupposing technologically advanced precision tools in research, design and development. And it was more radical in opting for relations of production involving common ownership and thoroughgoing internal democracy – even though those relationships were no more than the obvious counterpart of the divisions of skills and labour between experts which made the project technically possible in the first place. But it was much more conventional in the values which led its members to define the purpose of the company quite simply in terms of the efficient pursuit of an established social function within the existing society around them. Here, possibly, is a recipe for communal work which could be at once meaningful for the individual worker and engaged in a larger social world.

It is, perhaps, not surprising that, given the values and purposes of the people who have typically been recruited to counter-cultural enterprises, sustained attempts at socially valued work based on genuinely collective relations of production are of all communal work projects the hardest to find in contemporary Britain. Nevertheless, there have been some and there has been a certain pattern to their experience. The building company Sunderlandia is one of the best known and in many ways its history seems to be representative. It came into being in June 1973 and at the time of writing in November 1978 seems to be on the point of liquidation. In those five years a great deal of building was done and some serious lessons about the viability of communal work in societies such as contemporary Britain were painfully learnt.

Sunderlandia began as a privately financed experiment launched by a journalist, a shop steward and an architect to combine common ownership with the development of a medium-sized building firm playing a special role in the training of apprentices in the building trades. Sunderland seemed an especially appropriate site for such a project, having both a serious housing shortage and high levels of unemployment among school leavers. The organisation of the firm was modelled quite closely on that of another well-known common ownership enterprise, Scott Bader Limited (who also provided some of the funds to help Sunderlandia get started), and conforms in general terms to the model rules laid down by the Industrial Common Ownership Movement (ICOM). Thus, the company has no shareholders and those who invest in it have no voting rights or share of profit, receiving interest on their investment at a fixed rate. The membership of the company is restricted to those who work in it and contribute to capital through weekly subscriptions. A board of directors is elected by a general meeting of the members which can also dismiss the board. Wage differentials are restricted to 1:2. However, within this framework, and again in line with other projects associated with ICOM, a fairly clear hierarchy of management, tradesmen and apprentices was envisaged with a considerable expectation of definite leadership on the part of management and discipline on the part of the workforce. This effort to combine common ownership and hierarchical management is perhaps the distinguishing feature of ICOM – as distinct, say, from the projects inspired by the Institute for Workers' Control or the Co-operative Union.

The element of leadership is seen as important given the larger purposes the firms seek to realise. Thus, in the case of Sunderlandia, over and above the strictly business purposes of wanting the company 'to become a model for other medium-sized building companies providing a design service when required, providing good quality workmanship and commanding a respected position in the market' – ambitious enough in themselves – the founders hoped to realise four more general objectives. They wanted to revolutionise the division of labour in the building industry by making the design function an integral part of the work of the builder instead of a separate professional expertise. They wanted to generate new attitudes to work based on the revival of craft skills and the formation of 'multi-trade' work teams controlling their own work. They wanted to demonstrate that unemployed and unskilled school-leavers could be trained as craftworkers on the job in such terms, developing in time both job-commitment and a flair for leadership within the framework of common ownership. And most generally they aimed 'to practice social justice, democratic procedure from the bottom upwards; to establish leadership and an appropriate management structure; to encourage participation in decision-making despite class cultural barriers.'

From the outset Sunderlandia ran into opposition both from the Local Authority and from the Federation of Building Employers – not least because in order to obtain work at all the company had to 'hustle' for contracts in ways which disturbed the conventions of normal practice between local builders and local government. Nevertheless, work was found: initially, modernising working-class cottages, then a contract to build four vicarages, then modernisation and improvement work for the North-East Housing Association and Newcastle City Council, eventually the building of new housing developments. By 1977 one of the founders could say that at least as a building firm, 'the project has been a success and has established Sunderlandia as respectable housebuilders and members of NHBC' – which gives the purchaser a ten-year guarantee of the quality of their work. The training experiment has also been reasonably successful; that is, Sunderlandia has shown that training can be efficiently carried out with a far higher ratio of apprentices to tradesmen than any conventional firm would tolerate.

In almost all other respects, however, the project had by the end of 1977 gone badly wrong. There is no agreed account as to why this should have been, but among the disagreement certain crucial themes stand out. Centrally, the problem seems to have been the impossibility of reconciling the internal tension between the principles of leadership and equality and the consequent impossibility of forging a tool, the company, which could function effectively in an unfavourable external market. The unfavourable external market – a fact of life for all small- and medium-sized building firms in contemporary Britain – was decisive. Finding enough work merely to stay in business was no basis for securing the commitment of members when membership was based on the expectation of profit – let alone for realising the larger ambitions of the project. Yet by mid-1977 'the company had not yet had a share of profit because there had been no profit' – actually a trading loss of £9,350 in the previous year. Members were subscribing £1 a week to capital and were understandably reluctant to share losses by cutting wages. Management appeals to the members to save fell on deaf ears. In such circumstances a conventional company would have pursued market efficiency by giving management more room for initiative and introducing productivity incentives for its workers in the form of bonusesl wage differentials and threats of redundancy. In Sunderlandia all moves in such directions were contentious, divisive and normally in the end blocked by the majority vote of the general meeting of members. Democratic control proved to be the effective enemy of collective production in a capitalist market. In a social context which demands hierarchy and inequality it produced a suicidal insistence on equality. Few of the members offered themselves as leaders and those who did found it almost impossible to secure support for measures they wanted to take. Two of the founders had given up active participation in the company by the spring of 1977 and the third had come to the conclusion that:

'Possibly a group who have equal power suddenly thrust upon them and who have no ideology to follow and who are not used to investing their trust in leaders from their own class, will always tend to discourage the one who sticks his neck above the rest. Practically all those who have shown entrepreneurial inclination have left, discouraged by the lack of respect among members for Sunderlandia's aims, and discouraged by the lack of reward for the extra responsibility undertaken, particularly when they have known that better material rewards are available to them elsewhere.'

Specifically, the members insisted on equalising pay, the best trades-men left and management could find no way of managing that did not lay them open to virulent attacks based on the egalitarian values they themselves espoused.

Although the three founder members of Sunderlandia now claim to have three very different versions of what went wrong there is in fact impressive agreement among them as to the crippling dilemma at the root of their experience. The irrefutable and ideologically irresis-tible proposition 'we don't have gaffers here' was applied mercilessly by the meeting of members to all proposals to create the sorts of inequalities market success seemed to the managers to demand. In effect, a cultural gulf between the social classes involved in the company was opened-up by the perceived (and I would say real) requirements of the market in which the firm had to operate.

Management simply could not understand why the tradesmen objected to bonus schemes ('they set people against each other'); the members were baffled and enraged by management appeals to save and to show 'responsibility' to the firm. On both sides a sense of being back in a familiar struggle with an alien class built up in the wake of a seemingly endless series of crises, rows and confrontations. Robert Oakeshott, one of the founders and manager of the company in its early years, attributes the decline of the firm to 'a sharp increase in antagonism between the company's blue- and white-collar workers', and the resulting paralysis of management in a position of 'responsibility without authority'. Other accounts stress the sense in which to succeed the company had to embrace 'capitalist values' which the workers refused either to share or to respect. Eventually the tradesmen (those who had not left for better paid or more responsible jobs elsewhere) seem to have come to see common ownership as just another 'bosses' con', one more management device to get them to work in poor conditions for inadequate pay. Thus, as one close witness has remarked, their constitutional position as owners of the company did not prevent 'laziness, bad workmanship, cheating on site, pinching materials, abusing company transport for private ends, not turning up to general meetings . . . the easing-out of apprentices, dismissal of unpopular members of the workforce'. In sum, 'the structure did not alter their work attitudes' – any more than it had really altered those of the middle-class, idealistic founders and managers of the project. Values dominated tools.

Sunderlandia was not, of course, in any sense typical of the common-ownership projects that existed in Britain in the 1970s. Indeed, the most striking thing about the dozen or so projects of which I am aware is their diversity; it is not at all clear what would be 'typical' of them. The distinctive features of Sunderlandia were its relatively small size (never more than 50 members), the fact that it grew out of a principled egalitarianism rather than out of the failure of a capitalist enterprise or a conflict between workers and managers and the fact that it did not enjoy any privileged position in the market in which it had to operate (that is, there was no acute demand for its products, no established trading position on which to build and no safety net of public or private subsidy). In other words it was a singularly pure and in that sense realistic experiment in constructing a small-scale unit of communal production. Its failure must be judged in those terms.

Conclusion

Many interesting and important projects and experiments have been

ignored in this discussion. To have included them would not, however, have altered the conclusion at which I feel any consideration of
the possibility of communal work in contemporary Britain must
arrive: namely, that it is hard to see how communal work could be
successfully institutionalised in a society organised psychologically and
structurally on the basis of private consumption. In such a society the
tools of collective production, in whatever form they are developed,
seem to be ruthlessly blunted and distorted by the values of possessive
individualism. Sixty years ago, Beatrice and Sidney Webb had already
accurately observed the fate of such projects:

> 'Democracies of producers, as all experience shows . . . have
> hitherto failed with almost complete uniformity whenever they
> have themselves sought to win and organise the instruments of
> production. In the relatively few instances in which such enter-
> prises have not succumbed as business concerns they have ceased
> to be democracies of producers managing their own work and have
> become in effect associations of capitalists . . . making profits for
> themselves by the employment at wages of workers outside the
> association.'

But there is more to it than that. It is not simply that the requirements
of democratic work (or of meaningful, unalienated, human work) are
at odds with the requirements of competent business. The experience
of recent craft communes, alternative technology co-operatives and
common-ownership industrial companies suggests rather more than
that. It suggests that that incompatibility of personal value and social
function in work is a necessity of a society organised in terms of
individualistic values and profound structural inequality. Craftworkers fly from such a world into the fetishism of their private skill;
producer co-operatives turn into owner-dominated businesses; common-ownership companies become battlefields of class conflict; the
tools of revolution are subjected to the values of the old order. Other
particular destinies are available to such projects, but none of them
give the lie to the general impression that small-scale attempts to
reconstruct work as a social activity are doomed in a world where the
powerful structures of society, the decisive tools in Ivan Illich's sense,
are all functioning to enforce the idea that the point of work is private
consumption. However, Illich's conception of tools must be seen
finally as masking an all-important distinction. The fate of the
counter-cultural work projects I have discussed surely indicates that it
is not the strictly technical characteristic of work, whether pottery or
organic farming or building, that make collective production unattainable in our sort of society. Rather it is the structure of social
relationships within which the meaning and value of the products of

work are defined and by which the use of tools is accordingly determined. Tools in the sense of institutions not of techniques are our problem.

The productive system as the agent of social change: work, structures and techniques

I. Work as the Driving Force in Society
II. Techniques (aux racines de la raison technique)

Alain Birou

I. Work as the driving force in society

Here we shall deal with a problem which is absolutely fundamental, but in general very badly perceived – i.e. the recognition that work is not simply the driving force but also the 'raison d'être' of life in society. Broadly speaking, one can say that this belief is typical both of classical capitalism and of Marxism. This is a philosophical vision characteristic of the Age of Enlightenment and an anthropological option where men as subjects of activity, in other words humanity, make themselves and are creators of their own needs: they create, too, their own usefulness, significance and happiness. This belief was made possible as the result of the introduction of the new process of industrialism. Modern industrialism, Marx thought, could multiply wealth indefinitely. We can find one of the first expressions of this in *The Fable of the Bees* (1705) by Bernard de Mandeville, which characterises the new psychology of work, opposing simple diligence to the spirit of industry.

Where Marxists differ from liberals is that the liberal sees the infinite increase in wealth as being able, within this new system, to satisfy the needs of all, whereas Marxists point to the alienating division of labour as being the essential feature of this new form of society, a feature which will increase until the consequences of it smash the existing order of capitalism and create a reconciled society – with no division of labour.

Marx considers the productive act to contain and determine the whole of human existence; so that every aspect of our existence emerges from our own creativity:

'Men believe that there are things which are given to them or are imposed on them. In reality they ought to realise that it is they themselves that have produced these things.'[1]

From 1845 Marx realised that it was the organisation of production that essentially characterised society. For him, men were more than mere subjects conforming to this process, they were themselves part of it; both moulders and moulded. In 1849 he wrote:

'The social conditions in which individuals produce, and the social conditions of production change and transform themselves as the means of production and productive forces themselves change and evolve. The general effect of the conditions of production form what one calls social conditions – society – and, notably, a society in a stage of determined development.'[2]

J. Habermas has defined very well how the category of work is, for Marx, truly the foundation for the human being. It becomes the central concept of his way of thinking about humanity. 'By way of the process of work in society and through mediation with man's subjective nature, the nature of the environment becomes objective. Thus work is not only a basic anthropological category but no less an epistemological category. . . . By understanding Man as belonging to the particular category of an animal that makes tools, we have in mind not only a scheme for action but also a conception of the natural order. Work as a natural process is more than a simple process; it regulates material exchange and elaborates a world.'[3]

For Marx in his early manuscripts, a resumé of which is given below,

'Nature is neither objectively nor subjectively, immediately or adequately, at the disposal of the human being.'

Work is not, however, a transcendent reality for Marx, nor an absolute praxis constituting the world. Work in society is fundamental as a means of mediating between objective and subjective nature. Therefore,

'Man, or Humanity, is an historical subject which generates and reproduces itself through an act which is undertaken in consciousness and which because of this must develop and transcend itself. History is the true natural history of Man.'[4]

This concept of work is the symmetrical respondant for Marx of Hegel's concept of the Idea. The unity of Man does not realise itself through thought, but through action. The basis, the substratum of real life and of a concrete humanity is not logic, but economy. It is material production and the appropriation of products which define the scope and content of consciousness.

'The synthesis no longer appears as an activity of thought, but as a material production. The production of nature rather than of the mind becomes the model of the process of natural reproduction of society. That is why the critique of political economy in Marx takes the place of the formal logic in idealism.'[5]

Praxis is the supreme notion for Marx, the foundation of all categories and all theory, because it is precisely this practical activity which makes the creative capacity of man emerge. Praxis is thus tied to the priority of making and producing. It is through work, by producing his means of existence, that man forms himself and in consequence knows himself. Thus, for Marx, work is in some way at the origin of the human being and even explains him genetically.

'Individuals are what they manifest in their life. Therefore, what they are coincides with their production, with the objects they produce as well as with the way in which they produce them. What individuals are depends on the material conditions of their production.'[6]

In a text of 1844 Marx said that,

'Man is not distinguished from his essential activity, but makes of it an object of his will and consciousness. He is conscious of it as vital activity and alienated labour destroys this relationship.'[7]

Later Marx was to abandon this concept of the essence of Man, but this expression betrays his fundamental anthropological conception; work identified with vital activity defines the human being. To the extent to which he becomes a means, it is Man himself who is abased to the level of an instrument. If, therefore, the activity of mastery over and transformation of, the external milieu is one which constitutes the human being, then any subdivision of this 'universal' labour is bound to be a fragmentation of Man. It is a separation from his total being.

Let us now look at the primordial importance of the division of labour for Marx.

The division of labour as the fragmentation of man

Mandeville, in 1729, from studies of the techniques of clockmaking and naval shipyards, reflected on the sense and the importance of the division of labour. Diderot takes up the argument in his Encyclopaedia (under the word ART) and we know that the first chapter of the first book of *The Wealth of Nations* is devoted to this theme. The problem of the division of labour is without doubt the most central problem for Marx – the one which obsesses him radically; from it arise the other problems such as private property, growth of Capitalism, class struggle, etc.

As labour constitutes the human being, the reality of the historical division of labour is, in the eyes of Marx, a scandal; a process doubtless necessary, a driving force of history, but something which must be 'resolved'. It is for him the centre of the fundamental contradiction. With still Hegelian overtones, Marx tells us that 'the series of the economic evolutions of eternal reason begins with the division of labour.'

Private property is not for him a consequence of the division of labour; in reality it is the same thing under a different name.

'The division of labour and private property are after all identical expressions. . . The different stages of the development of the division of labour represent just as many different forms of property; in other words each of the divisions of labour determines also the relationship of individuals with the materials, tools and products of work.'[8]

To recognise the reality of the division of labour is to affirm the necessity of commercial exchange. The value of exchange is thus the consequence of the social division of labour. 'Exchange and the division of labour condition each other mutually.' Individual production only becomes social when it is exchanged in the impersonal forces of the market.

'The study of the division of labour and exchange is of the highest interest because they are the concrete and alienated expression of creative activity and power.'[9]

All the text which follows is noteworthy for the fundamental preoccupation which Marx seems to affirm here – that 'the division of labour and exchange are the creations of private property'.

But there is throughout Marx's thinking a wish to overcome the situation created by the division of labour. As it produces the fragmentation of Man, it is essential to overcome it so that Man can rediscover his lost unity. Thus Marx maintains an ethical goal in which 'production would be immediately social; the fruit of an association which would allocate work co-operatively amongst its members'. Therefore, instead of 'being subjected to social production which exists outside them like fate' individuals would render production subject to themselves and would 'manage it as an act of their communal power'.[10]

Work in material production can have an attractive character and can contribute to self-realisation 'if its social relevance is assured, if it is recognised to be of a scientific nature and if it becomes at the same time general work'. Work in this way can become 'an activity regulating the forces of nature in a rational process of production'.[11]

To see his conception of history and the passage to communism we will refer to the German Ideology.[12]

The division of labour is thus the driving force in the historical process, but only to a point, since once it is abolished it will cease to have relevance. However, it will not start from the presupposition of divided labour imposed on producers by owners, whatever division there is will come about through purely human choices: human assent. The present division of labour imposes on each individual an exclusive and already determined sphere of activity 'whereas in communist society, where no one has an exclusive sphere of activity, but may perfect himself in any area he pleases, society regulates general production and creates for me the possibility of doing today something, tomorrow something else . . . as is my pleasure'.[13]

The self-administration of labour in which the general will coincides with individual aspirations, parallels the presuppositions of the perfect market of liberal economics; that of the perfect mobility of factors of production. Liberal economics sees perfection at the point of market equilibrium. Marxism sees it in the revolutionary process as an ideal of reconciliation bringing together all the forces of evolution together with the transformation of capitalism wrought by the consciences of the workers.

Marx's final aim is communal labour, or immediate association, the free choice and distribution of necessary labour tasks rather than its distribution through the market:

> 'Let us imagine a union of free men working with communal means of production and expending, according an agreed plan, their numerous individual forces as a single force of social labour. All that we have said about Robinson's work is reproduced here, but socially and not individually (the products are an object of immediate usefulness).'

After having defined how the method of distribution will operate, and what is the double role of the time of work in this communist context, Marx adds:

> 'The social relationship of men in their work, including the useful objects which result, remains simple and transparent in production as well as in distribution.'[14]

Marx recognises there will be a residual 'empire of necessity' even once communism has been established, but it will be reconciled with the rule of liberty:

> 'The associated producers – the socialised man – regulate rationally their organic exchanges with nature submitting them to the common control of all, instead of being dominated by the blind power of these exchanges; that is the empire of necessity. . . '

But the rule of liberty only begins when work ceases to be dictated by necessity and by aims imposed from outside; it is situated therefore by its very nature beyond the sphere of material production, properly speaking.

> 'It is beyond necessity that the blossoming of human power, which is its true aim, begins.'[15]

Literally, this suggests that even in community society some work is undertaken *from necessity* and therefore not freely. But we should compare it with the famous text on a similar subject in the 'Critique of the Gotha Programme', written ten years later.

> 'In a superior phase of community society, when the subordination of individuals to the division of labour has disappeared and in consequence the opposition between intellectual and physical work; when work has become not only the means to live but the first necessity of living; when, with the universal blossoming of individuals, the productive forces have grown and all the sources of wealth burst with abundance, only then will we be able to escape once and for all from the narrow horizon of bourgeois law and society will be able to write on its banners, "From each according to his capacity, to each according to his needs".'[16]

It seems that it is only the social division of labour and private property that flows from it, which produces the really undesirable effects that Marx describes. The other consequences of industrial production can be coped with.

The essential thing, for him, is the concrete material content of men's lives. But this cannot be effected simply by teaching them, making them conscious of, the universal values of goodness, justice, equality, etc. Marx goes further than previous philosophies when he stresses that the problems of men's material lives are not solved by the mere recognition of ethical and legal norms. These norms are themselves dependent on laws that govern the material life of a people, and for the origins of these laws we must look to their deep roots bedded in the division of labour.

The division of social labour creates an objective web of interdependence in society, and produces particular types of human beings whose natures are determined by these interdependencies. Consequently, all sorts and forms of associations in society are to be traced back to the fundamental relationships and mentality produced by the division of labour. It is thus the fundamental explanatory facet of society.

In such a perspective it can be seen how economic power legitimises itself and makes itself master of the productive system; also how it serves as a principle for changing the social system arising, as it does, from the ways in which the division of labour is co-ordinated and forced on the workers by external forces: private capital. Techniques and methods of production evolve incessantly within a consistent structure of control and co-ordination, which men call capitalism, and which is embodied also in State Socialism, albeit in a different way.

Elements for a critique

This requires an examination of the fundamental presuppositions of Marx's thought;

1.   Marx first rejects any idea of overcoming any limitation of man's independence, either from other men, or from nature. True, it is important to point out that men can control their own destinies. Marx elevates the human creative act above all else; it is given ontological priority and absolute universality. All other things are subordinated to it and it is, in this sense, totalitarian.

Marx thus neglects, or takes no account of other dimensions of human nature and human life, which are no less important and no less material to them: parenthood, their physical and mental state, love and dependency, as well as experience and knowledge of the world that men must have before they can work; these are just as primordial aspects of man as his labour, yet Marx makes them dependent on it, or else ignores them.

2.   In an existentialist view Marx is right to reject abstract philosophical concepts but wrong to oppose Hegel's idealism *solely* with the concept of productive labour.

Through this mono-conceptual approach Marx himself is guilty of a kind of abstraction typical of Hegel and the Enlightenment. He transposes into the principle of production what Hegel had said of the state:

> 'The State is the external necessity and superior power of civil society, but furthermore it is at the same time its immanent end.'

In the *German Ideology*, Marx says:

> 'If it is clear that production offers externally the object of

consumption, then it is clear also that consumption offers ideally the objective of production as an interior image, as a need, as an instinct or as an end.'

Consumption, the end of production, is how society defines itself for Marx, just as for Hegel it is defined in terms of the State, the end inherent in civil society.

3. Marx's only understanding partially man's nature results in a very partial conception of man's liberation, which is, in fact, utopian.

The view of socialised man, or humanity, in which the division of labour is harmonised, is itself a result of a mixture of two conceptions of social organisation. One is the idea of total man, or of reconciled society, in which there is a very limited division of labour reduced in quantity according to social necessity. The other is an 'a posteriori' scheme for planning this 'post-revolutionary' division of this residual labour.

This 'single-cause' notion of man's social reality and the ignoring of other factors leads, therefore, either to a utopian vision or else to State Socialism.

4. The limit of Marx's aim is the total man and the liberated society. The voluntary division of labour envisaged by Marx in *The German Ideology*, *Capital* and the *Critique of the Gotha Programme* characterises 'achieved communism', yet it is an aspiration that is already present in free society. In fact it corresponds to what liberal economists or capitalists would call 'the perfect mobility of factors of production'.

In a liberal system, the theory of perfect competition is anti-institutional in character. So is its aim. In the same way, in Marxism, the harmonisation of the division of labour operates within the free spontaneity of the associated workers. It is also anti-institutional. Both perfect competition and Marx's utopian view of labour are unrealistic visions born of emergent industrialism.

5. If one accepts the production-consumption relationship as the only true or possible basis of society, one cannot mount an effective critique of capitalism since it is built on the same foundation. Marxism shows how under capitalism the system of private property and division of labour limits and contradicts the productive process, how a dominant and controlling class emerges. But given all this there is the fundamental problem: how can we *direct* change in any way which is not simply an already determined product of the productive forces? The will for liberty must be located outside the system of social determinism: how else can the system be deflected? Only so can judgements be made about 'seizing the laws of social change'.

6. The question raised by Marx's central idea of ending the division

of labour by the concept of united labour, is the extent to which it can be finally achieved under socialism. How can production be regulated without classes? Is it by everyone spontaneously taking on whatever he pleases to do each day; or by direction of central authorities? If the latter, we are allowing the existence of a privileged group who wield power equivalent to that of capitalists.

Handing over productive power to the workers does not insure against either of these eventualities. The freedom of manoeuvre enjoyed will still be constrained by the 'regulating power of the economy as a whole'.

Conclusion

If man is defined essentially through his work it is impossible to escape from the Marxist dialectic of socio-cultural determination, unless:

(a) We reject the hidden philosophy and false anthropological premise that work determines everything else in man's life.

(b) We return to the roots of the concept of technical reason which Marx uncritically accepted.

(c) We assert that Marx did not get to grips with the heart of capitalism, that is the capitalisation by privileged groups of their scientific knowledge and technical power.

(d) We accept the importance of the division of labour but see its roots in a cause which lies further back; the way men see themselves, the way in which they want to exist in society, and the way in which they look for the means of living in society.

'All our inventions and our progress,' Marx once said, 'seem to have only one consequence: to endow material forces with life and intelligence, and to turn man into a material force.'[17]

Marx the humanist is sounding a warning note here. In the name of man faced with death today, let us hope that we may understand what is at issue. It is a warning that applies to what lies beyond capitalism as well as Marxist 'pseudo-science'.

II. Techniques (aux racines de la raison technique)

By 'technique', I do not mean the various skills which together can achieve a specific result, but all methodical processes, based on scientific knowledge, which are used in production, in information and in communication. Why not keep the word 'art' or the word 'metier', which are the French translations of the Greek 'techne'? It is precisely because by going back to the Greek root one wants to express the new reality, which emerged in the 18th and 19th centuries from scientific learning being applied to new instruments and machines, and processes which were independent of men. Diderot's Encyclopaedia only refers to technique in terms of belles-lettres.

Marx did not consider technique

The concept of technique is not a central category for Marx. He sees it neutrally, simply as an instrument. It is the human form of praxis that he understands as Man's work. What determines human, social existence is the organisational side of work. That is why (in a manner never very well defined) he attributes historical causality to work, to the productive process, the technical means of production as well as to human development. All these forces, when reclaimed by the workers, will inevitably inspire the self-generation of a new society, reconciled both with itself and with nature.

Marx considers that the conditions of production (which are for him social conditions) are determined by the productive forces which themselves determine methods of production. He justly criticises capitalist society because the means of production (the capital hoarded by the bosses) becomes separated from the workers and thus dominates them. As he sees it, this private appropriation changes what ought to be a technical process creating use-values, into an economic one of creating exchange values. On this view, workers in association could organise themselves collectively so that, as masters of their means, they could dedicate production to use-values. Marx never wondered about how this mastering of the means of production would come about – either because the techniques used in his time seemed fairly simple and accessible, or because he considered that scientific and technical know-how was in itself positive and did not conceal any latent power. All harm was already inherent in capitalism.

Finally, this appropriation of technical instruments by the workers themselves coincides with the only political aim which Marx would admit; that is the free community of workers self-managing their entire social existence.

Outstanding questions

Marx is obsessed with the 'formal and real subordination of labour to capital'.[1] As he sees it, capital is more the appropriation of the means of production than the scale and nature of these means. Marx understood the development of mechanism, but he did not inquire into its meaning; he considered it positive, and only attributed negative qualities to capitalist appropriation. The continuous perfecting of machines is analysed as a factor which allows the growth in the rate of profit and this hides any better understanding of the relationship between 'techniques' and the nature of work.

Having said that, everything needs to be explained; technique is itself the accumulation of intellectual capital. How can workers, as such, appropriate the power to create technological knowledge? The fact that one is materially master of machines does not liberate one from the oppression caused by having to ensure their continuous functioning and by still being employed in their service. From another angle – where does the impulse come from which, starting with working conditions, would compel Man to fulfil himself and to evolve into a fraternal social being? Is it certain that men only evolve through their work? Are production and work alone responsible for human and social change? Are they the sole determinants?

Thus Marx, obsessed with the injustices of a savage capitalism has essentially criticised the inequalities of the productive system, technique being a neutral means which depends on the kind of society in which it exists.

New lines of research

Other thinkers have considered the technological phenomenon, and for Hans Freyer, Jacques Ellul, Schelsky, technique has become an independent force having a dynamism of its own which it has itself imposed on the entire social order. According to Freyer, we have at our disposal a certain abstract ability (Können) which comes to us incessantly in successive waves thanks to progress which has now become automatic. For Schelsky, technical progress itself produces unforseeable methods independent of any conscious planning, and independent of any use to which they may be put.

Technical progress is directed by its own will. One is astonished to see how many supposedly enlightened minds show themselves incapable of understanding what the 'determinism of technique' means. Indeed, unable to understand what 'original technical will' signifies, they still exclaim that technique is, in itself, good – or at worst completely neutral. Technique does not exist in isolation. Nor is it true that it had an heroic era when scientific and technical activities developed and became organised essentially 'as a function of their true ethical criteria'. In the minds of some, technique has become a tool, which, neutral in itself, is contrasted with the culture and the economic and political forces which use this tool for their own ends. Only industrial bourgeois society is 'historically responsible for the perversion of sciences, techniques and their products'.[2] Science and technique are therefore supposed to have become victims of a politically motivated misappropriation. The 'political economy' (and the 'economic politics') of Liberalism, which seeks growth and maximum profit, is claimed to be responsible. With such objectives, science and technique have progressively become 'zealous servants of the system'.[3] 'The organisation of scientific technology in recent times has moved away from the traditional autonomy of scientific research and from the principle of the efficiency of technique, to place itself under the control of political, economic and military forces. This tendency is in no way inherent in scientific and technological development – it is a deviation and abuse of it.'[4] Such a position avoids the fundamental issue; what is the basic intention inherent in the network of machines? What is the power of the technostructure?

Towards the roots of technical reason

Technique in the modern sense refers to a new relationship between Man and nature through applied science. At the outset we have a new 'episteme', a totally new manner of knowing the universe. This manner is the 'methode', inaugurated by Descartes: 'We can say that it is from the dawning of existence as method that the modern world enters into the era of technique.'[5]

But technique remains in the minds of most people, even the most learned, as a neutral of more or less good means, whose effects depend on the good or bad use made of it. To think of technique as an instrument, as a means to an end, was still possible in Marx's and Hegel's time. They revealed many hidden forces in existence but did not ask themselves, except Hegel and he only momentarily, about the real nature of technique.

One must look back to discover the rational source of technique. For what is the essence of technique is in no way technical; it is the combination of a will with a method of knowledge which arouses a new type of ability. Those who discuss this theme by starting with the techne of the Greeks, of Plato or of Aristotle, and then pass on without solving the problem of continuity to modern technique, have not understood the epistemological and ethical ruptures which took place in the 17th century.

At the outset, technique is methodologically a system of rationality, all the elements of which are linked, and which is capable of linking all elements of reality. It is presented as the ability to multiply indefinitely the possibilities of the growth of production without using up time and extra muscular energy. It is thus presented as a concrete universal which can be attained through the power of human reason. Through it, man has the capacity to do everything (*potens omnia facere*), and simultaneously the capacity to become everything, after a certain fashion (*potens omnia fieri*). Thus, technical ability is not only a power to 'do' nor a power to 'have' but a power to 'be'. Technique is the essential value which has priority over being and becomes the basis and criterion of all other values. Its implementation through work is that privileged place where the value of all human existence is formed: economic value is only the social expression (through production) of this first value.

Technique certainly does not exist in isolation. What is very real is the sum total of technical projects which contain an overall technical aim. But, little by little, these projects assume a social power – they become an objective reality of social existence which has its own dynamism and its own logic. It is not going to be enough to destroy a working order of this established socio-cultural technostructure (i.e. the capitalist system or indeed of the communist system) so that there should appear automatically an appropriation by each and everyone of the technical skills which command social structures.

Translated by Simon Carter

ENDNOTES

I. *Work as the driving force in Society*

1. Marx, *Grundrisse*.
2. Marx, *Labour, Wages and Capital*, 1819.
3. Jürgen Habermas, *Erkenntnis und Interesse*, Italian Translation, p. 30.
4. Marx, early manuscripts.
5. Habermas, *op. cit.*, p. 33.
6. Marx, *German Ideology*, 1846.
7. Rubel, M.C.I.-III.
8. Marx, *German Ideology* (Milhau, 1846).
9. Marx, Outline of a critique, *Pleiade II*, p. 104.
10. Marx, *Grundrisse*, Rubel, M.C.II, pp. 219-220.
11. Rubel, M.C.II, pp. 212-213.
12. Marx, *German Ideology*, Milhau, p. 123.
13. Marx, *German Ideology*, Milhau, p. 107.
14. Marx, *Capital*, Vol. I, Garnier, pp. 73-74.
15. Marx, *Pleiade II*, pp. 1487-8.
16. Marx, *Pleiade II*, p. 1852.
17. Marx, *People's Paper*, April 1856.

II. *Techniques* (aux racines de la raison technique)

1. Marx, *Materiaux pour l'economie*, Rubel, II, p. 365.
2. Bernard Vincent, *Paul Goodman et la Reconquête du Present* (Seuil, 1976).
3. Paul Goodman, cited by Bernard Vincent, *op. cit.* (1976).
4. Paul Goodman, cited by Bernard Vincent, *op. cit.* (1976).
5. Jean Beaufret, *Dialogue with Heidegger*, II, p. 165.

Military organisation and leadership as paradigms for industry

Major-General A. E. Younger, D.S.O., O.B.E., in an interview with Edward Goodman

E.G. *As you will recall, I am anxious for you to throw light upon the suggestion often made that the structures of economic organisations follow the pattern set by the military some years before. I think also the size of effective business unit may some years later follow the size of army units; but these are only tentative correlations. By talking I hope we can establish whether there is any substance in these ideas and what conditions there are: training, information-flow, etc. At our last meeting when we discussed modern armies' systems of command hierarchy you started by saying that the problem in the early 19th century was to find a substitute for military genius. Marlborough in England, Napoleon in France, and before him Frederick the Great in Prussia, had shown how the fortunes of a state could be transformed most dramatically by a leader of true genius. Then the German intelligentsia got down to thinking, 'We can't guarantee to produce any more military geniuses; genius is a random thing. How can we, therefore, produce a dependable substitute?' The answer was organisation; the general staff and high command structure. Could we go over that again?*

A.E.Y. Yes, the answer was the formation of the Prussian General Staff. Before then, you see, you didn't have the idea of a general staff. Staff work was less complicated and it all took place in the great man's brain (at least you hoped he was a great man). Marlborough had a great friend in Prince Eugene who was the only man Marlborough ever discussed his battle plans with. The two of them, for instance before the Battle of Blenheim, went up into a church steeple together to view the French dispositions. They discussed them and made their plans; just the two of them. Luckily Marlborough was not only very experienced, but a highly original thinker on military matters and Prince Eugene was exceptionally experienced in warfare and between them those two were able to run a major battle which affected world history. So you see the problem was to recreate what went on inside that church steeple, but with ordinary people and not geniuses. After being defeated by Napoleon, the Prussians said, 'Well now, we can't depend on having a Marlborough, a Frederick the Great or a Napoleon every time, so we must get people who we know have got high grade brains and make them sit together to do the detailed planning. Then the man at the top really hasn't got to waste his efforts on the detailed work because it has been done for him'.

There are four names to remember: von Scharnhorst, who became the director of the newly-founded elitist War Academy in 1801 and carried through many army reforms; his friend and associate, von Gneisenau and their contemporary, the military theoretician, Carl Clausewitz. In 1808, at Clausewitz's suggestion, the War Academy was reformed into the General Staff College and he himself was put in charge. Clausewitz emerged as an outstanding teacher and his original thought undoubtedly played a large part in the success of the staff system that subsequently developed. The idea behind it was to screen the actions of all the officers in the Prussian army so as to collect together the most able men to make efficient and effective plans for any eventualities that might happen in war. They were housed in a large building in the centre of Berlin, far away from possible battle-fields.

The fourth name of importance emerged later; it was the elder von Moltke, who made the General Staff into an instrument of great efficiency and was himself able, by telegraph from Berlin, to command the Prussian army in the Austro-Prussian war of 1866. The same staff system again proved its mettle first against the French in the Franco-Prussian war of 1870 and later in the swift defeat of Russia in the early months of the First World War. Even after the ultimate defeat suffered by Germany in the two World Wars, the General Staff could argue that these resulted more from political than strictly military factors.

E.G. *Thank you; that gives a pretty good background picture as a start. Actually, what you have described interestingly goes beyond the topics we have set ourselves. I think you have uncovered the origins of the cult of planning – military, economic and political planning; the substitution of teams of brainy people for genius!! Sorry for that aside. Let's get back to the subjects of leadership and training for staff officers. These may well have lessons for industry.*

A.E.Y. Before we do that, let me just say that the position of Chief of Staff has no exact parallel in industry. He should be fully in the mind of his Commander and responsible to him for the efficient performance of the staff. The Commander is thus free from the mass of day-to-day decision-taking and can concentrate on whatever he considers to be of most vital importance. Confident that his Chief of Staff will keep him informed of any important development, he can visit subordinate or neighbouring commanders, or make future plans without interruptions. Even more important, he can project his personality to the men under him, so that when they have to do something really unpleasant, they will feel the confidence that comes from the belief that a leader really knows what he is doing.

E.G. *Yes, I see that; nevertheless, every chairman or managing director in industry needs apt information. Perhaps there is a need for something similar to a general staff. Are there any other general lessons?*

A.E.Y. Yes, there is one. Perhaps there are good reasons for it, but hearing that some firm has decided to close a factory without consultation always strikes those with military staff training as amazing. It would be unthinkable even to halve the size of, say, a battalion without detailed preliminary discussions with the men concerned and their commanding officer. The battalion's overall Commander would undoubtedly visit the unit to discuss the effects of the decision. It would be automatic to obtains the views of the men affected, if only because long experience has shown that quite often they have the best ideas.

E.G. *That makes it seem if I may say so, that in many respects the modern British army is more liberal than industry. But perhaps we can discuss that later. Can I now go back to the staff officers and start with their training?*

Staff training and general knowledge

A.E.Y. When I was serving we had three levels of training for the staff officer. At about seven-year intervals we thought that it was good for him to be pulled back to 'school' to discuss affairs with his peers, under an instructor – that's what brings out the star people. The first level was the Staff College at Camberley for officers at the senior captain or junior major level, at about 28, 29, 30; that sort of age. We did it again at the National Defence College at Latimer at age 36 to 39; and then we had a final level, designed really for the stars; only ten officers from the army went there each year. That was at the Royal College of Defence Studies, in London, and the age was in the middle to late forties. The system has been changed slightly now by the introduction of an earlier stage, where officers after they reach 26 attend a basic course of a mainly organisational nature. They must pass this before they can be promoted to major. This in turn raised the age of the Staff College student to 32-34.

E.G. *I think I have seen the RCDS people coming out into Europe sometimes, would that be right? I think they visited Florence recently. . .*

A.E.Y. Yes, they do world tours. The idea is to expose them to a generalist view of world problems, some of which are economic, political and social, so that defence matters can be put into a better perspective. We started off at Camberley on a purely army basis where we taught the officers the rudiments of their profession. How many people and what equipment is held in the basic unit of the different arms of the service, infantry, armour, artillery, etc? How do you write an administrative order? Who do orders go to? What are the branches of the staff, and so on? We made sure they had a grounding in their profession before they went on to apply that knowledge as junior staff officers, which would be their next postings.

E.G. *Their knowledge at that time is, therefore, mainly organisational; do they learn other units' capabilities and weaponry as well?*

A.E.Y. Yes, but even more importantly, all the time they're also being taught how to think; how to make appreciations of difficult situations and to decide what are the various courses of action open to them, and which is therefore the best course. They also get their first formal introduction to the Royal Navy and Royal Air Force students at Camberley. In this way a genuine understanding of the three Services is begun to be achieved.

E.G. *What about the next stage of training at the National Defence College? What does that achieve?*

A.E.Y. The object of the NDC is to educate the 'middle piece' staff officer, i.e. those that have already successfully completed one staff job, in the requirements and workings of the Central Staff in Whitehall. The students include nobody from foreign countries, unlike the other levels where some foreign students are considered helpful in giving a wider view of military and political thinking. The course is cleared for discussion of all problems up to and including the Top Secret category. After it a student should be capable of entering one of the responsible positions on the Central Staff in Whitehall and knowing how to operate without further training.
ould that kind of training be relevant for industry?

A.E.Y. To answer your question comprehensively I would first have to analyse the problems to which the top management occupants of industrial tower blocks in London address themselves, and compare these with the problems being looked at by the Central Defence Staff in their big buildings. I am sure these would be quite different. However, if we looked at the difference between the problems of the manager of an outlying industrial plant and those of the head office in London planning their activities and then compared that difference with the difficulties of 'middle piece' commanders in the Defence field and those of the Central Defence staffs, I suspect there would be considerable similarities. Therefore, there would be a similar need for teaching potential top managers, who had already received experience in the field, something about central planning.

E.G. *Of course, managers do not start in the field as young officers do. And that is an important difference. Then rightly you say training after early experience is another. What is there then for industry to learn?*

A.E.Y. I think the thing for industry to ask itself is that, at least where there are organisations which are as big as the army, and some of them are bigger, should they institute some similar form of a staff system, backed by staff courses? I have talked to leaders of industry about this and they usually say, 'We can't afford it.' Superficially staff training may appear expensive in time and salaries, but perhaps one should ask, 'Can you afford *not* to have it?' We feel we can't do without it and therefore *have* to afford it, possibly at the expense of something else. In fact the smaller an army gets, the more it must strive for excellence – there's no place for a poor performance in a small army. A huge army can accept a few poor units, because there will be others to replace them if they make a mess of things, but a tiny army cannot; all the units have got to be high grade.

E.G. *You also said that re-education is something that some firms do and some don't. Very few in fact do it.*

A.E.Y. Some do, and, of course, there are other organisations, such as the Henley Staff College and the Civil Service Staff College at Sunningdale which run courses, so it doesn't only have to be the firm itself. I believe there are some firms, for instance British Oxygen, which run a type of staff college.

Size of unit

E.G. *Can we jump now to the question of size? You were more or less taking the view that because of the fire power of the enemy it would no longer pay you to have big anything; big warships, big tanks and certainly not big sub-units or big platoons.*

A.E.Y. Every factor of modernisation goes against the old idea of masses of men, and the tactics used on the battlefield are very much related to the weapons being used. For instance, if a big block of men got together, as they did at Waterloo, on a modern battlefield, a few shells would kill the lot of them, so they must be dispersed. Now once you start dispersing them you cannot use the old words of command, such as 'Form square', because the soldiers would be out of earshot and wouldn't hear you say it! The more powerful weapons get, the fewer you need and the more you must disperse people. In order to dominate an area you therefore require fewer and fewer men. For that reason as well the trend is towards smaller units and more dispersion, but these units must still be able to concentrate closer together at short notice should the situation need this. Communications are vital here.

E.G. *You did explain that a unit was a battalion in your terminology.*

A.E.Y. Yes, in the British Army we call the battalion the unit, and this has always been something of the order of a thousand men. You can trace it straight back to the Roman legions, although the size of the unit has for some years been getting smaller and smaller. Below battalions we talk about sub-units.

E.G. *Yes, you explained that in the 1914-18 war the unit would have been 800 strong, excluding cooks and others, whereas in the last war it was down to about 600 or 650, and is it less now?*

A.E.Y. In actual fighting men in an infantry battalion it is now down to more like 350; the rest are staff including those with specifically administrative duties. This has happened for a number of reasons. The complexity of weaponry has increased and hence its repair and replacement are more complicated; the number of radios to maintain communication at all levels has had to go up; the vehicles for moving around the battlefield have become more sophisticated, be they tanks, helicopters, infantry carriers or engineer tractors. All these have led to a large increase in the number of men specifically needed to look after them and keep them serviceable. However, although the main function of these men is administrative, they are all trained to fight and will do so if the need arises.

E.G. *Is that what happened at Goose Green?*

A.E.Y. Exactly.

E.G. *Could you explain a bit about the organisation of armies into battalions, companies and so forth?*

A.E.Y. The basic organisation – shall we go from the top down – of the army is best started, I think, at the division level. A division is an independent organisation of about 10,000 men, which contains in it all the fighting troops, which are the tanks, artillery, infantry and engineers, and all the support troops that those require, such as medical, transportation and so on. It has a sizeable headquarters. So that's the division. Now a division breaks down normally into three brigades, each of three battalion-sized units supported by artillery and engineers.

E.G. *Yes, now how many divisions make armies and so forth, going up from the division and then the high command?*

A.E.Y. Normally, when in doubt, it's the rule of three. However, we in the British Army have always made our corps headquarters very flexible. On the whole, you give the corps a mission which, harking back to the 1939-45 war could be, say, to attack and capture the town of Caen out of the Normandy beachhead. Now for that mission the corps may well be given five divisions, because it looks like being difficult and dangerous, with a requirement for two extra armoured divisions. So that this corps may have its five divisions, the next-door corps, which is perhaps just holding a front and not fighting, may well be down to only one or two divisions. So a corps is a flexible headquarters and can take as many divisions as are required for a particular mission. But, when in doubt, remember the rule of three. A corps, say, in peacetime in Germany will have three or perhaps four divisions. Now corps are made up into armies, again on a mission basis. An army may have two corps or may have five. Armies are made up into army groups, and if there is a big front, there may have to be groups of army groups. The Russians certainly had them, the Germans did and we did after Normandy. There was a British army group and two American army groups.

E.G. *Now can we get back to the battalion? How does that break down into sub-units?*

A.E.Y. The battalion – let's call it about 650 men – breaks down into four companies which are commanded by majors and these will be about 140 strong.

E.G. *The same size as a school house?*

A.E.Y. Yes, perhaps. Companies break down to platoons and a platoon will be about thirty strong; this is the lowest level commanded by an officer. The first command for a young officer when he comes out of Sandhurst is a platoon. Platoons split into three sections, each commanded by a corporal and will have about eight to ten men. That basically is the organisation.

E.G. *I imagine a higher quality of leadership is needed.*

A.E.Y. Yes, the young officer must live, eat and if necessary die with his men. He will be neither better nor worse off than any of them. Under operational conditions this breeds a sense of comradeship which can last for a lifetime.

E.G. *What about leadership at NCO level?*

A.E.Y. The sub-unit leader must be capable of making his own decisions and taking his own action, knowing the overall commander's plan, and what part that commander expects him to play in it. Things will go wrong and he will have either to adjust his dispositions or his actions or else he'll have to go back to his commander over the radio to ask for help because something's gone wrong.

E.G. *What happens if a battle goes wrong?*

A.E.Y. Battles never go according to plan, but a commander is unwise to make a plan that is inflexible, because he will be in trouble when the unexpected happens. For instance, he keeps a reserve up his sleeve so that when something goes wrong in one place he can put in that reserve to make it go right.

E.G. *Then is he more or less back on line?*

A.E.Y. That's the idea. But he must always leave some flexibility in his plans in order to deal with the unexpected. Commanders and staffs must not be too rigid in their outlook or else they will be quickly thrown off balance and will find it difficult to recover. The essential point is that the commander should be free to concentrate on where things are most difficult or most critical and if necessary go there himself. Then he is absolutely in the right place to take the vital decision with his mind uncluttered by matters of detail. It doesn't mean that things can't go wrong elsewhere, but then his staff takes in that information and relays it to him, knowing where he is and knowing, themselves, what their commander is striving to achieve.

E.G. *The commander you are talking about now; is he at unit level or at formation level?*

A.E.Y. Either, but the commander at formation level is the key man.

E.G. *To what extent are the smaller staffs you were talking about, at the unit level, aware of the overall plan?*

A.E.Y. Oh, they will be aware of it all right. That's very important, because the plans call for much co-operation between the various types of units. Timings in particular are critical. For instance, taking one example, I'm sure you can see that the gunners would be totally unable to give proper artillery support unless they knew precisely where everyone is at every moment. So if someone gets ahead of the timetable, as often happens, it's no good the gunners going on with the old plan or they'll be landing shells amongst their own troops. They must be aware of the aim of the plan and must be able to switch to a revised timetable.

E.G. *So communications are important right the way through?*

A.E.Y. Yes, they are vital, and become even more so the further spread out units are and the faster the pace of the battle.

E.G. *Is there still such a thing as military etiquette, if I may use that expression? I mean that a General would not mind being consulted by a corporal if it was necessary, or would he have someone else to refer to?*

A.E.Y. There is a military chain of command and the corporal would go to the sergeant. . .

E.G. *Oh, he would do that, even in battle?*

A.E.Y. Oh yes, unless there was a breakdown, in which case there would be nothing wrong in the corporal going to the colonel. But normally, if the thing is organised properly the chain of command still works. If a platoon is in trouble the battalion does something to help that, and so on. Each man refers back to his immediate boss, more to get help to achieve whatever it is he's been told to achieve, rather than to get an order varied; the point being that it is better to keep to this chain of command if you can, so that a problem isn't raised to an unnecessarily high level for solving.

E.G. *I remember when I first saw you you were telling me about street fighting in Northern Ireland where you operate with sections of about a dozen men.*

A.E.Y. Yes. A patrol usually consists of three 'bricks' to use the current jargon. Each 'brick' has an N.C.O. and three men, and the actions of the three 'bricks' are co-ordinated by the platoon officer. This represents half his platoon; the other half, similarly organised, will be co-ordinated by the platoon sergeant. I think there are two points about that. One is that in such a situation it emphasises the importance of the junior N.C.O. In the First World War the junior N.C.O.'s responsibilities in battle did not extend much beyond ensuring that the men under him were dressed correctly and had their bayonets fixed at the right time. Now he can be placed in a position of potential disaster. Whilst out on patrol he might, for instance, see a Protestant child being accidentally run over by a Catholic-driven car, whereupon a small fight starts. What he does then can be absolutely critical. He can either damp the whole thing down or he could panic and shoot somebody and thus be instrumental in initiating a major outbreak of violence. So that's the first thing – he's got much more responsibility. Now the second point is to get away from the idea of the only order being, 'Right, follow me' – it isn't at all like that. If there's an armed IRA suspect in a house and the patrol has been told to get him out, quite a complex little plan has to be made which has to be done by the corporal. 'You two men go round the back, you two round the side, and we'll go to the front. I want you to go on top of that house and cover us as we go in there.' It's a detailed little plan which he must make, and all his men must know what all the other men are doing or they'll make a nonsense of it. The whole thing is much more difficult than it used to be and is only possible by having better-educated soldiers and better-trained junior commanders.

E.G. *As you were saying earlier, communications are vital. But information is something important in itself as a category, isn't it? How is it conveyed? You were just saying that this little group in a street, going into a house where there's a suspect, has got to know what the other people are doing.*

Information and communications

A.E.Y. Information always goes both ways. It comes down from on top and it comes up from the bottom. Whatever form of operation you're fighting, a tiny little one in a street in Belfast, or a major river crossing with a lot of troops involved, things will go wrong at the bottom. Information must be passed upwards as to what has been found. 'There's an extra machine gun here – we weren't planning on that, we didn't think it was going to be there. Something's got to be done about it because it's holding us up.' That kind of information comes up from the bottom. Other information comes down from the top. The Colonel gets in touch with a company commander and says, 'Now look here, there's a crisis further to the left. I know you're doing well, but I have to take half your men away in order to hold that position'. So always there will be conflict of priorities, and this will arise from information coming up from the bottom from the people who are being shot at by the new machine gun, or down from the top from the commander who is seeing the wider picture. Information must also go sideways so that equivalent-sized flanking units know what is going on and are not taken by surprise. Care must be taken that not too much information is passed, otherwise units or formations will be swamped by it and will not be able to evaluate it properly.

E.G. *Yes. I wonder whether you remember one of the papers Joe Stiglitz gave at Siena on information economics. He said, 'I think that some economists regard industry as founded on military models', and talks · of 'command hierarchies'.[1] A command is defined as encapsulated information in Joe Stiglitz's language, and he says that it is more economic for the information from below to go back to the top and be incorporated by the commander into one piece of information, i.e. literally one command. I, myself, am a little critical of it. What do you feel? It is rather like 'By the right', isn't it?*

A.E.Y. Yes, of course, I haven't got the advantage of knowing what goes on in industry but . . .

E.G. *No, but he was saying that this was good military sense, too.*

A.E.Y. All I would say is that in every military operation I've had anything to do with the plan is being modified all the time. This is because where the enemy is actively involved, changes of plan may be forced on you. His reaction to your moves could be different from what you predicted and force you into modifying the plan in a major way. As I have said before, the secret is to keep your own plans flexible with various options open so that you can alter things without too much fuss should the need arise.

E.G. *What is the consequence, do you think, of what we have said on my original set of questions? Is it, for instance, true that the organisation of industry follows that of army command hierarchy and general staff organisation? Hastily, I would think one first ought to define the period between the army perfecting a form of organisation and industry imitating some parts of it. For example, which army organisation were industrialists and economic empire builders copying in the 1950s: those of the mass armies of the 1914-18 war and up to Stalingrad – or of the armies that fought in North Africa and Western Europe in 1945?*

A.E.Y. I don't wish to be rude to industry, which I know is striving to make a success of its endeavours. However, as I mentioned earlier (see bottom of page) the orders given by top management sometimes appear more like those given by World War I commanders in the army than their modern counterparts. Then the order would have been to 'go over the top' at a certain time – no questions and no more orders. This order would then descend through each level of command until, ultimately, the company commander led his men over the top. As I have explained, it is quite different today.

E.G. *So when some economic text books refer to the theory of command hierarchy they are not referring to the present day at all?*

A.E.Y. Industrial corporations with hierarchical command structures through which orders and, as it were, pre-packaged or detailed managerial directions come do not belong to the present day era of military practice. Instant obedience to a command such as 'Form Square' (which would have been given 150 years ago when the cavalry were seen to be charging at the unit) would be totally impractical today. Instead of orders instantly to be obeyed, the trend now is for directions to be given through the military hierarchy outlining certain objectives; so that each commander on the spot has an objective to attain, using the best means available to him. He will translate the objective he has been given into either actions or further objectives to be passed down the line until finally the corporal says, 'Follow me.'.

The Battle of Malaya

E.G. *Can we switch to Malaya very quickly. When we first talked, more than a year ago, nearly two years ago, you were telling me that it was the small unit that really helped win Malaya, plus the rule, which again you talked about at Siena, of the army behaving humanely and not throwing bombs at women and children.*

A.E.Y. Yes, since it was basically a political war in which one group, who were Communist and Chinese, was trying to gain control of the country or at least to have a say in the control of the country, it was realised fairly early on that this was quite different from a normal war where the enemy is any male of the opposing country. In order to get at him it was considered justifiable, for instance, to bomb the war factories in Hamburg and the people who worked in them. Whether this was really justifiable is another matter, but in the war it was *thought* to be justifiable. Now, in the process of bombing Hamburg, many women and children would get killed. In Malaya the expression 'hearts and minds' was introduced, I think, for the first time. It was seen that to stop the attempt by the Chinese Communists to take over the country the Army had to have the hearts and minds of the population on its side. Taking that as a guiding principle, it obviously becomes pretty futile to use as a tactic the bombing of a village in which there are thought to be some Communist terrorists. If even one little girl is killed or maimed what will those villagers think about the Army? They're going to hate it and justifiably so, and it will have lost their hearts and minds. The object was to gain their approval, not to lose it, so we had to fight the war in Malaya under severe ground rules in which no village was allowed to be shelled, let alone bombed, unless we were certain that no women and children were going to get hurt. Even if we knew there was a Communist cell in a village, we could not attack it by bombing and shelling unless in some way the women and children were moved out first. So that was the first rule. The second new development was that it was seen that the ordinary Malayan peasant, a rubber tapper perhaps, really didn't care too much who ran the country as long as he was able to do his job, get his pay, and from that provide food for his family. If a Communist group came into a village or even came up to a villager in the jungle with rifles and so on and said, 'Comrade, tomorrow you will provide me with a sack of rice' he would automatically do it. The threat would be, 'You will be shot', or 'Your family will also be shot, unless you do this'. So what the authorities in Malaya felt they must do was to place a barrier between the terrorist and the ordinary working population who, as I say, really couldn't care less who was in charge of the country as long as it worked sufficiently well. What they did was to build totally new villages in the open, where they could be watched, surround these villages with barbed wire and move the people from their own villages in the jungle into these controlled villages. They were all given a pass and all had to go in through a guard. There were also posts with machine guns in them guarding the barbed wire. The terrorists, of course, did not get passes and in a village the guards themselves got to know people well and when a strange face appeared and said he wanted to stay with his auntie in house number so and so, immediately the guard was suspicious.

E.G. *How many men did you have guarding the village? A platoon?*

A.E.Y. Yes, but they were police really, not the army.

E.G. *Platoon size?*

A.E.Y. About a platoon, yes. There would be a sergeant in charge of it.

E.G. *Only a sergeant? And he would be under an officer?*

A.E.Y. Yes, a group of these would be commanded by an officer.

E.G. *Some distance away, and he would be in communication on walkie-talkie?*

A.E.Y. Yes, indeed. Of course, these were Malays, they weren't British. The British battalions were used more in the jungle to seek out terrorist hideouts, then surround them and watch them. The main tactic was to put an ambush on every track out of the village and then put in an infantry attack on the village. On the whole the communists would run for it and the Army would pick them up in the ambushes.

E.G. *Again, small numbers. A platoon?*

A.E.Y. To attack a village you would use a company, but it would be spread out right round with one platoon probably going in to do the attack and two other platoons round the village setting up the ambushes. Quite small numbers were involved, just three or four men on each track out of the village through the jungle. It was very much a corporals' and sergeants' war and it was where the war would be won or lost, by the corporal in the ambush. If he was awake and alert and on his toes when the people came running towards him he would just get a few seconds to take them prisoner, or if they shot back, to shoot them. If he relaxed for a few seconds, they'd be gone, because people move fast and it's very thick country.

E.G. *That was where we first started talking about the man on the spot having to make the decision because he couldn't get in touch with his commander quickly enough.*

A.E.Y. Yes, they've got to think, these sergeants or corporals. They've got to be trusted and they've got to trust their superiors. They've got to be trained and when given responsibility they react to it and they do it marvellously. The army is justifiably proud of the way they operate because they don't panic, they don't pull triggers and shoot people unnecessarily.

E.G. *When did these developments start?*

A.E.Y. Historically, it was Sir John Moore before the battle of Corunna who had the original idea, but the full implementation of it has been a fairly new development, and indeed we're learning all the time. It didn't happen like that in Amritsar in India between the wars. There General Dyer gave the order to shoot, and a lot of people died as a result. And I think we've learnt from that. We've been learning all the time.

The responsibility of the small unit

E.G. *The beginning of all this was the idea that the effective unit of initiative, which is different in economics language from military language, is getting smaller and more effective in the army, and trusted – that was another important point – and if the man wants help, he radios for it. Of course, if he's doing wrong, he's told so, but generally speaking, he's trusted, and this is something which I think industry just has to learn.*

A.E.Y. I think perhaps the thing that illustrates it most directly is the tank unit. There you have a weapon, one tank, with a huge gun of tremendous destructive power, and in it you have four men, sometimes three, probably commanded by a corporal or a sergeant. Now here is a group capable of enormous things. Their next superior commander may well not be able to see them at all because they are separated by a wood or houses, but they've got communications and can be in touch for instructions very quickly. I think that describes the change best, because there's a very small unit of four men controlling this tremendous fire power, out of the physical control of their commander, other than by radio; i.e. small is beautiful in that case.

The same thing happens in the air; one plane can carry an atomic bomb. A small group of men up in that plane – probably four men – controlling a vast destructive power, and only on a radio link with their base.

E.G. *Now, how do you fit that in with what you've said about the responsibility of the man with his finger on the trigger? The man with his finger on the trigger is the sergeant in the tank perhaps, or the commander of that plane.*

A.E.Y. Yes, in the tank or the plane it will be a sergeant or a junior officer who will be in charge.

E.G. *And the pilot's the man you would make culpable for dropping the bomb?*

A.E.Y. Oh yes.

E.G. *Not his superior, and* his *superior?*

A.E.Y. Well, it's both. The pilot's got his orders, just as the tank man has got his orders, and if he does something different, you either pin a medal on him or you court-martial him depending on whether it's been successful or . . .

E.G. *Yes, but if he were to drop the first bomb, and it were to start an atom war, he's the man you would hold responsible, the sergeant or the pilot?*

A.E.Y. Ah yes, but this is rather different. You see, as I put in my Leadership paper,[2] we have now different rules about obedience, in that, not only can you disobey a command if that command is to commit a crime; not only that, but you are committing a crime yourself if you don't disobey it. So, what is a war crime? Well, usually it has been defined as killing women and children. That's one of the definitions. So, if you toss an atomic bomb on to a city like Hiroshima, are you or are you not committing a war crime? It's difficult to see how you can possibly say that it's not a crime. Now, it comes back to who's responsible for this. There again, I think we have to say the responsibility would be split. The man who actually pulls the lever in the plane and lets this thing go must accept more responsibility. But equally if he lets it go on the target he was told to knock out, then who told him this? Whoever his commander was must share responsibility.

E.G. *But if he didn't push the button to release the bomb he'd be up for court-martial and probably shot? However, that's a serviceman's risk.*

A.E.Y. This is a difficult problem. The chances are that, because our military system is based on discipline, the man would pull the trigger because he would have confidence in the integrity of the man giving the order. I just don't know whether he would be shot nowadays if he claimed, 'This is a war crime. I cannot therefore obey it'. I'm not sure what the outcome would be. It's never been tested in law.

E.G. *So your approach to disarmament might be quite an interesting one. A really moral, Actonian one. That letter of Acton's to Creighton does raise these points, doesn't it?*[3]

A.E.Y. It does indeed. It does not quite cover my approach to disarmament, which is rather different. It's more a question of developing a climate where people get to know each other and therefore trust each other. I think that's where the answer to disarmament must lie; somewhere in there. Somehow the use of nuclear weapons must be banned, because of the potential threat to life on this planet.

E.G. *But this approach is still moral?*

A.E.Y. It is moral in that we need to change our attitude to warfare. Science is developing weapons that are just too dangerous. I think the hope lies in the sort of arrangement that, for instance, England developed with Scotland. They fought each other for countless centuries until, by chance, a Scotsman became king of England and the border gradually disintegrated so that now it would be ridiculous to have a war between these two. Similarly, the European Community has made the border largely disintegrate between France and Germany. This is how a proper climate for disarmament starts and, hopefully, the leaders of the French forces will never again start planning a war against Germany, and vice versa, because they're all part of the same family.

E.G. *Yes, and if there's no plan, then there's no war. You can't have one.*

A.E.Y. No, but you can have all sorts of other things, crises, but not wars. Whether the Iron Curtain could be bridged in a similar way I don't know, but if we can make a start with the EEC and never have another war in Western Europe, that is something.

E.G. *I suppose learning each other's languages helps and is along those lines.*

Conclusion

E.G. *Have you anything in mind to say in conclusion which is* *applicable to both army and industry; something about leadership probably?*

A.E.Y. Yes, man-management. I don't want it thought that we Army people are arrogant in our belief that we are the best man-managers. Let me simply say that unless men at all levels have confidence in those above and below them, especially in times of emergency, then things are bound to go wrong. If you have to waste time and mental effort wondering if the orders you have been given are right, and morally right as well, you will never get things done efficiently and in time. There is a definite distinction between, on the one hand, carrying out orders unthinkingly in blind obedience, and on the other hand of not having to ponder an order too deeply because you have faith in the man who gave it. In the Army there is a command structure and everyone knows his place in it and by and large accepts his place. Commanders know their men well, and the men know their commander and a spirit of trust and comradeship is built up, fostered by traditions in regiments and units. Of course, the Army has one priceless advantage denied to most of industry; that is lack of competition in its work between the various parts of the Army. Naturally, there is competition between units at sport and in training and there is intense and usually healthy rivalry, but there is no profit motivation as in industry where one firm will be positively trying to do another down to capture his market. It could be said, I suppose, that the Army would therefore lack ambition and hence real dedication. My answer is that there is plenty of rivalry and a striving for excellence in the Army, but it is not at the expense of others in any vindictive way.

ENDNOTES

1. See Joe Stiglitz, 'Some Reflections on Information Economics and Information and Economic Organisation', Acton Society Occasional Papers 2 and 3, Siena Series, 1977/79.
2. Tony Younger, 'Military Organisation and Leadership', Transcript 9, Siena Seminar, 1977.
3. 'I cannot accept your canon that we are to judge Pope and King unlike other men, with a favourable presumption that they did no wrong. If there is any presumption it is the other way, against the holders of power, increasing as the power increases. Historic responsibility has to make up for the want of legal responsibility. Power tends to corrupt, and absolute power corrupts absolutely.' Extract from Lord Acton's letter to Bishop Mandell Creighton covering his review in the *English Historical Review* (1887) of Vols III and IV of the Bishop's own *History of the Papacy during the Period of the Reformation*. Lord Acton, *Historical Essays and Studies* (Macmillan & Co. Ltd., 1907), p. 504 (appendix).

Necessity, oppression and liberty: Simone Weil's thoughts on work

Sira Dermen

Simone Weil was born in Paris in 1909 and died in England in 1943. In 1931 she graduated from the École Normale and worked as a teacher of philosophy. But her concern for the condition of the workers and her desire for direct knowledge led her to take a year's leave of absence in 1934 to share the lot of the unskilled workers in the Renault works. She spent several months of 1936 in Spain to judge the civil war at first hand. In 1940 she left Paris, went to Marseilles, then New York and finally to London, where she worked with the Free French Group. Most of her writings were published only after her death, and many have not been translated into English until recently. Her early writings are on politics; her last ones are more concerned with religion.

Until recently Simone Weil's thought was neglected, at least in the English-speaking world. On any count she is not one of the influential modern thinkers, even though she has analysed with brilliance many aspects of contemporary life. Anyone familiar with her thought will find her relative obscurity unsurprising: there is nothing comforting in her thought, no concession to 20th-century shibboleths. For every sentence which could win her party allegiance, we find another which would repel the potential adherent. Here is a thinker who identified with the plight of the working class, yet disbelieved in the possibility of the working class revolution; a woman who felt deeply for the sufferings of her fellow men but was the most hard-headed of realists. She admired both Marx and Machiavelli. While growing increasingly religious she chose to remain outside the church. She was an advocate of the overriding importance of meaningful work, but had little in common with what we have come to call liberationist movements. She deplored the disjunction between science and religion. Her concern was for meaning, justice, dignity, and unlike most social critics she was precise in her use of the idea of utopia. For Weil, a utopia was a sharply defined limiting case, grounded in a careful analysis of necessity, which could be used as a touchstone for evaluating present and possible societies. Passionate as she was for human fulfilment her intellectual development represents a struggle against all simple-minded and *ersatz* solutions to human suffering. What she hated above all was that intellectual habit whose psychological description is wishful thinking. And this brings us to the subject of this paper: her thoughts on work.

Simone Weil saw work as essential to a meaningful and dignified life – not just necessary to supply us with the objects of our needs and desires, but positively indispensable to our acquiring a true conception of the realities of the world, and the supreme corrective to fantasy and wishful thinking. Work is the great educator.

This is not a fashionable claim. Psychologists tell us about the Pleasure Principle and the Reality Principle – but modern consumer societies are built in part upon fantasies of pleasure. We believe that we can imagine an ideal world in which reality conforms to our wishes. And then the machine is the answer to the Reality Principle.

Weil's outlook is a repudiation of all of this.

'To desire is nothing; we have got to know the material conditions which determine our possibilities of action; and in the social sphere these conditions are defined by the way in which man obeys material necessities in supplying his own needs, in other words, by the method of production.'[1]

Her insistence on the Reality Principle does not stem from a killjoy temperament. (Her letters disprove such a supposition.) Rather she was exceptionally aware of the tragic consequences of social actions informed by aspirations based on wishful thinking: the consequences are human suffering and death for the sake of the mere replacement of one form of social oppression by another. From the start, she had a sharp eye for oppression of any sort: see for instance an early article written for *Revolution Proletarienne*:

' . . . we are obliged, if we wish to look reality in the face, to ask ourselves whether that which is to take the place of capitalism is not to be a new system of oppression, instead of a free association of producers. . . We can say, to put it briefly, that up to the present mankind has known two principal forms of oppression, the one (slavery or serfdom) exercised in the name of armed force, the other in the name of wealth thus transformed into capital; what we have to determine is whether these are not now being succeeded by a new species of oppression, oppression exercised in the name of management.'[2]

She was twenty-two when she wrote that.

To return to Simone Weil's vision of work. If we see work not only under its instrumental aspect but intrinsically as supremely valuable – in that it protects us from illusion and educates us in truth and reality, then our thinking about work will be markedly different from most current discussions, whether conservative or humanist-radical. Given Weil's approach, worker-satisfaction will not be our *direct* concern. For an obsession with how we can make workers satisfied with their jobs – whether to increase efficiency or happiness or both – betrays the tacit assumption that most work is somehow undesirable and in itself unrewarding. But if we see work as Weil did, our main concern will be: under what conditions is work real and therefore dignifying, instead of degrading? Solve that problem and workers *will* be satisfied. It is an objectivist philosophy. We need not bother so directly about satisfaction – the world will take care of that. What we do need to bother with – and Simone Weil was the last to underestimate the difficulties here – is how to organise our system of production to embody real work. Our approach to art could furnish a useful analogy. No one writes books on how art might be made satisfying to the artist – there simply isn't a problem. But we are familiar with the picture of the frustrated commercial artist. He is a man who has to practise a degraded version of his work. And we criticise some societies because their very organisation does not allow for the possibility of real art.

What, then, justifies Weil's vision of work? What justifies the belief that given certain realistic arrangements work can be not only satisfying, but the supremely valuable experience? To answer this question we need to turn to her view of the human condition.

For Simone Weil the starting point is that man is a part of the natural world and as such is subject to necessity.

' . . . as long as man goes on existing, that is to say as long as he continues to constitute an infinitesimal fraction of this pitiless universe, the pressure exerted by necessity will never be relaxed for one single moment.'[3]

To survive man has to satisfy his needs. These constitute a prime example of the necessities he is subject to. And so he has to manipulate his environment, which is itself governed by other necessities. The most abstract formulations of these latter necessities are to be found in the sciences of matter; from a more anthropocentric point of view they are all those man-independent forces we encounter in ploughing, harvesting, fishing, wrenching minerals from the earth, transforming coal into gas, manufacturing objects. Now, in primitive conditions of existence, necessity is transparent: first, man is more conscious of his basic needs, because he experiences hunger, cold, etc., in the second place he constantly bumps up against the unyieldingness of the world. Thus he is in no danger of underestimating the forces that control him – control him, that is, by dictating the conditions of his existence.

As societies become more complex it becomes increasingly easy for us to forget our subjection to necessity. Our conditions of existence become opaque to us. But the basic facts remain unchanged – necessity reigns, as it must – but our perception of necessity becomes murky, and illusions about our place in the world set in. In modern industrial societies people seldom encounter 'naked necessity' as Weil puts it. The way we satisfy our needs is through a highly complex chain of activities that no one person understands. So the progression from a simple to a complex economy can, for our purposes, be characterised as follows: man moves from a state where he is directly in touch with nature and necessity to a state where social life interposes itself between man and necessity. Our dependence on nature is replaced by our dependence on other people and on social institutions. And since for Simone Weil there has never existed a form of complex social organisation that is not oppressive, this amounts to saying that the yoke of nature is replaced by the yoke of society. Man only escapes subjugation to nature to find himself subjugated to the collectivity. Her view of man's gradual dominion over nature is, as already indicated, two-fold: first the price paid for our apparent escape from natural necessity is social oppression; second, escape from nature is an illusion, we are still subject to natural necessity, but now indirectly. And this is where her claims about work fit in. Work is, under certain conditions, the very encounter with necessity that we have lost sight of. It is the supremely educative experience in that it teaches us the truths about our conditions of existence. It is the only way we can train ourselves in truth generally and in realistic social thought in particular. For responsible social speculation doesn't take the form of believing that with enough goodwill everything is possible; it consists of finding out what our limited degree of freedom is in a world of inescapable necessity.

We may find this transition too swift. One might grant the truth of Weil's view of the human condition, and grant her analysis of our societies as opaque, without accepting her doctrine of work. Why should a correct view of our condition necessarily be earned through work? Why can't we come at it through contemplation, intellection, reading and so on? Then again, why shouldn't other activities – art and science, for instance – fulfil the function that she assigns uniquely to work? I think these are legitimate questions. Her answer may be gleaned from the following passage:

'We have only to bear in mind the weakness of human nature to understand that an existence from which the very notion of work had pretty well disappeared would be delivered over to the play of the passions and perhaps to madness: there is no self-mastery without discipline, and there is no other source of discipline for man than the effort demanded in overcoming external obstacles. A nation of idlers might well amuse itself by giving itself obstacles to overcome, exercise itself in the sciences, in the arts, in games; but the efforts that are the result of pure whim do not form for a man a means of controlling his own whims. It is the obstacles we encounter and that have to be overcome which give us the opportunity for self-conquest. Even the apparently freest forms of activity, science, art, sport, only possess value in so far as they imitate the accuracy, rigour, scrupulousness which characterise the performance of work, and even exaggerate them. Were it not for the model offered them, unconsciously, by the ploughman, the blacksmith, the sailor who work *comme il faut* . . . they would sink into the purely arbitrary. The only liberty that can be attributed to the Golden Age is that which little children would enjoy if parents did not impose rules on them; it is in reality only an unconditional surrender to caprice. The human body can in no case cease to depend on the mighty universe in which it is encased; even if man were to cease being subjected to material things and to his fellows by needs and dangers, he would only be more completely delivered into their hands by the emotions which would stir him continually to the depths of his soul, and against which no regular occupation would any longer protect him.'[4]

I turn now to her characterisation of real, educative work. To try to understand this is to try to understand her conception of liberty, since real work is essentially free work. We can consider her thoughts on freedom under the headings negative and positive liberty.

Negative Liberty is freedom from constraints. As is clear by now, Weil's is a philosophy that sees man as greatly constrained by necessity. The question is what sort of necessity and the degree of freedom allowed. First, there is natural necessity. This is essentially inescapable; but we have some freedom, witness the different ways of satisfying our needs embodied in different systems of production. Human organisation gives us a measure of freedom, not strictly from natural necessity, but from feeling constantly its pressure upon us. Next, there is social necessity. To the extent to which this is grounded in natural necessity, it makes for inescapable constraints. But institutions can be changed. And although Simone Weil had no faith in revolutionary change, she did think that, with lucid thought, we could aim at a system of production and a set of values embodied in a living culture, that would minimise social oppression. The problem is to

' . . . know whether it is possible to conceive of an organisation of production which, though powerless to remove the necessities imposed by nature and the social constraint arising therefrom, would enable these at any rate to be exercised without grinding down souls and bodies under oppression'.[5]

The third major constraint, which we can to a degree overcome, is internal to man – what she calls 'blind passions' – insatiable desires, terrible fears and so on.

Now, one striking feature of her descriptions of these three major constraints is the recurrent use of the epithet 'blind'. She talks of man being freed from 'blind nature', 'blind collectivities' and 'blind passions'. The opposite of 'blind' in this context is action guided by thought. And here we have in essence her conception of *positive liberty*. The free man is one whose relation to the world is informed by continuing thought.

In Weil's conception of positive liberty we find what is at the same time an intellectualist and an activist view of freedom. The rest of my paper will consist of a summary with comments of the section in *Oppression and Liberty* entitled 'Theoretical Picture of a Free Society'. It gives us her characterisation of free, and hence real, work and a sketch of a society embodying such work.

> 'True liberty is not defined by a relationship between desire and its satisfaction, but by a relationship between thought and action; the absolutely free man would be he whose every action proceeded from a preliminary judgement concerning the end which he set himself and the sequence of means suitable for attaining this end.'[6]

Man can choose between blindly submitting to the spur of necessity (servitude), or he can adapt himself to the inner representation of it that he forms (liberty).

These are ideal limits. Here are some examples which approach these limits.

First, servitude: (a) primitive man, governed by the spasms of hunger tearing at his belly, with a minimum of planning and forethought; (b) the slave who jumps to the orders of the overseer armed with a whip; (c) the modern manual worker on a production line.

Weil's central example of liberty is a person engaged in solving a problem in mathematics. All the means necessary are available to him – he can look for assistance only to his own judgement. A completely free life would be one where all work consisted in a conscious and methodical combination of efforts as in the solving of a mathematical problem. A life of this kind would liberate one from the blind grip of the passions, would give a clear view of what is possible and what impossible, what is easy and what difficult. It would eliminate insatiable desires and vain fears. In this way he learns moderation and courage, indispensable virtues. This ideal gives the standard by which we can judge present societies and proposals for their improvement.

Weil gives a careful discussion of obstacles to positive freedom – that is to freedom conceived as the continuous linkage of thought and action:

Chance Chance is seen by Weil as an aspect because of the size and complexity of the world. Consequently, through the workings of chance, action does not always achieve the expected end. But, by understanding, chance can be limited and liberty is therefore possible, insofar as we exempt our *actions* from chance by placing them under the control of the mind. Even if our understanding is insufficient, and our actions have elements in them of the provisional and the instinctive, and even if we use trial and error, these elements can be progressively reduced with time, as insight deepens with scientific and technical progress. Her belief is that the provisional and instinctive can be subordinated to method.

The second obstacle to freedom is internal. It comes from the *mystery of our own body*, and especially the obscurity of the relation linking our thoughts to our movements, and the unruliness of our thoughts. But there is a way out of this dilemma: the more tools are shaped to the task, the less they are extensions of our bodies, the less will the vagaries of our mind interfere.[7] Good tools are linked to the task and are therefore incorruptible. Once we use them they will transmit those thoughts, and those only, which are relevant to the task. Good tools help eliminate the non-functional aspects of thought and feeling. Primitive man, however skilful, sees the link between man the world under the aspect of magic, not of work. This changes as, in the struggle against nature, the living body becomes less important than passive instruments. And these instruments gradually become fashioned according to the task rather than by the shape of the human organism. Their operation is external and freed from the passions.

The difference between theoretical speculation and actions In theoretical speculation the mind first solves the problem by its own particular methods which may involve reading discursively – or even daydreaming – then the solution can be applied to the action. The analogy between the problem of actions and of mathematical problem-solving often fails because (i) theoretical problem-solving proceeds from what is simple to what is complex, whereas the movements of the manual worker are merely sequential[8] and (ii) often different persons carry out speculation and action, or the same person does both, but at different times. We can see this latter case as an internal division of labour. Now unchecked division of labour, whether internal or external, is inherently ominous in that it can sever the link between thought and action. Hence we can have work that is not methodical but is merely in accordance with method. We can have method in the motions of the work, but none in the mind of the worker.

Increasing complexity of work, things, organisation This is linked with 'The difference between theoretical speculation and action' above. Blind operations, sophisticated instruments used according to instructions, wrong division of labour – all lead to opacity, to the subordination of the mind of the worker and hence to loss of freedom.

'The only mode of production absolutely free would be that in which methodical thought was in operation throughout the course of the work.'[9]

Other men Strictly this is the only factor which leads to servitude. Other obstacles (such as inanimate nature, chance) can inhibit the development of freedom, but cannot actually impose servitude. Characteristically, it is the particular interaction between obstacles to positive liberty and the activities of men that create the conditions of servitude. The complexity of the world can be exploited by men so that they corner privileges for themselves. (For Weil it makes very little difference whether these are privileges of priestly status, ownership of means of production, or monopoly of knowledge.) Only man can enslave man. Even primitive men would not be the slaves of nature if they did not people her with imaginary beings comparable to men. Being dependent on other men leads to pleading (for the slave) or threatening (for the master), instead of contriving and acting.[10]

'The soul is plunged into bottomless abysses of desire and fear, for there are no bounds to the satisfactions and sufferings that a man can receive at the hands of other men.'[11]

Worse than being dependent on other men as individuals is what happens besides in all oppressive societies: one is dependent on the blind play of the collectivity. The collectivity is completely abstract, wholly mysterious, inaccessible to the senses and to the mind; its acts seem arbitrary to the second power. The collectivity is enormously strong and arbitrary. We have two main ways of limiting the power of the collectivity over the individual and managing with it as we manage with the necessities of nature: (i) fixity of social organisation, tradition, e.g. the family with all its rules; (ii) written law. But no law or tradition can adequately foresee and control the potntial damage done to a child by cruel parents. These aspects are exacerbated when human beings combine into a collectivity.

(Consider the difference between the relationship between a servant and his master and a man and the collectivity. However shockingly arbitrary an action of the master's may appear, the servant can give some explanation – if only that his master is in a bad mood that day. There is no analogy with this in the operation of decrees of the state – whether ruthless dictatorial ones or the plans emanating from legally constituted committees.)

The list of obstacles to freedom are formidable. But there is a way out of the impasse. Collectivities are infinitely stronger than individuals in all spheres except that of the mind. Here the relation is reversed: collectivities do not think, and cannot compel thought. A collective life where men would not be subject to the collectivity could come about if material existence were such that 'only efforts exclusively directed by a clear intelligence would take place'.

In more detail this would mean:

1. Each worker himself controls, to a significant extent, both his own efforts at a task, and their co-ordination with the efforts of others.
2. Technique must be such as to demand from the worker continual use of methodical thought.
3. Techniques must be sufficiently similar, and education widespread, so that one could have a clear idea of all specialised procedures.
4. Co-ordination of specialised efforts must be at a similar level of simplicity and transparency.
5. Collectivities must be small to be encompassed by the mind.

(The ideal size of the working unit should never be sufficiently vast to pass outside the range of the human mind.)

6. Community of interests must be sufficiently patent to abolish competitive attitudes.

Here at last men would be bound as always by collective ties, but only in their capacity as men. They would not be treated as things. We should have, then, not only liberty, but love (friendship) – an even more precious good.

The ideal picture can serve as a standard for the analysis and evaluation of actual social patterns.

Here are examples of evaluation of different kinds of work using Weil's criterion of liberty in work. In the sphere of individual action: A fisherman in his little boat – high. Manual worker on a production line – low. Craftsman of the middle ages – high. Fully skilled worker, trained in modern technical methods – high. In the sphere of collective action: A team of workers on a production line under a foreman – low. A handful of workers in the building trade, pondering some difficulty, then unanimously using the method conceived by one of them – high.

If Weil's conception of work and the analysis of obstacles to freedom are correct, then 'the most fully human civilisation would be that which had manual labour as its pivot, that in which manual labour had the supreme value'. What we have here is not a religion of production.

> 'It is not in relation to what it produces that manual labour must become the highest value, but in relation to the man who performs it; it must not be made the object of honours and rewards, but must constitute for each human being what he is most essentially in need of if his life is to take on of itself a meaning and a value in his own eyes.'[12]

Culture should be a preparation for real life and not an escape, so that one may maintain both with the universe and with one's fellows relations worthy of the greatness of humanity. Labour must be at the centre of culture.

Science is regarded by some as a set of recipes (this degrades the intellect), and by others as a body of pure speculation (this degrades the world). When it becomes impossible to understand scientific notions without at the same time perceiving their connection and applications, and impossible to apply them without understanding, then science will have become concrete and labour-conscious, and each will possess its full value.

Art in the above ideal society would inform and be informed by the balance between mind and body, between man and the universe, which can exist in action only in the noblest forms of physical labour. Sport would aim to give the body that fluidity which would render it pervious to thought and hence make it possible for thought to enter directly into contact with material objects. Social relations would be modelled directly on the organisations of labour.

Weil's analysis is similar to Marx's analysis in that it starts from the relationships of production. It is different in that, where Marx seems to have wanted to classify modes of production in terms of output, this analysis would classify them according to the relationship between thought and action.

Simone Weil saw herself as containing a tradition of thought which appears in the works of men such as: Descartes, Bacon, Goethe, Rousseau, Shelley, Tolstoy, Proudhon and Marx.

> 'The idea of labour . . . as a human value is . . . the only spiritual conquest achieved by the human mind since the miracle of Greece.'[13]

Instead of the 'heartbreaking curse in Genesis' we have Bacon's words:

> 'We cannot command nature except by obeying her. This simple pronouncement . . . suffices to define true labour, the kind which forms free men, and that to the very extent to which it is an act of conscious submission to necessity.'[14]

ENDNOTES

1. Simone Weil, *Oppression and Liberty* (Routledge & Kegan Page, 1958), p. 45.
2. Simone Weil, *Revolution Proletarienne* (Paris, 1933).
3. Simone Weil, *op. cit.* (1958), p. 84.
4. Simone Weil, *op. cit.* (1958), p. 84-5.
5. Simone Weil, *op. cit.* (1958), p. 56.
6. Simone Weil, *op. cit.* (1958), p. 85.
7. Weil's idea that it will not suffice for a tool to be a mere extension of our body exemplifies the severe intellectuality of some of her conceptions of freedom. The cyclist, driver, pilot who feel their vehicle as an extension of their body surely experience a sense of freedom. It is an unthinking, sensual sort of freedom, through union with the world. (Knowing how, knowing that).
8. Note Weil's Cartesianism here. Not all theoretical knowledge proceeds like this. Mathematics, science, technology, certainly do, and this is essentially an indispensable method for understanding matter. But not for understanding human beings, or for the humanities. Theoretical speculation about the human condition has to proceed organically, by reference to the whole.
9. Simone Weil, *op. cit.* (1958), p. 95.
10. This is a somewhat exaggerated statement. It suggests an extreme individualism – a view I don't think Weil ever held. Certainly in her later thought (Need for Roots) it is balanced with explicit descriptions of how men need to belong to a social group, be rooted, in order to satisfy all their needs. (The need for obedience is listed as a vital need of the soul.)
11. Simone Weil, *op. cit.* (1958), p. 96.
12. Simone Weil, *op. cit.* (1958), p. 104.
13. Simone Weil, *op. cit.* (1958), p. 106.
14. Simone Weil, *op. cit.* (1958), p. 106.

Labour, work and the public world: Hannah Arendt's 'Human Condition'

Margaret Canovan

Few recent critiques of work in modern industrial societies have been as striking as that offered by Hannah Arendt in her book on *The Human Condition*.[1] Arendt, a German Jewess, fled from Hitler's regime and eventually settled in America. There she turned her formidable powers of reflection upon the public world of action and politics which had traditionally been despised by German intellectuals. She concerned herself particularly with two opposed kinds of political experience; on the one hand totalitarianism, to which her best-known book was devoted,[2] and on the other hand, free politics carried on amongst equal citizens, each of them capable of spontaneous action. In *The Human Condition*, however, she sought to clarify what she meant by free 'Action' of this kind by distinguishing it from other human activities. She contrasted the realm of politics in which men can act freely among their fellows with the less free realm of social and economic activities; and within this latter category she made a sharp distinction which is our primary concern here – the distinction between 'Labour' and 'Work'.

Arendt had learnt from Heidegger to take words seriously as repositories of forgotten experience. If 'Labour' and 'Work' are indistinguishable from one another, as most social theorists appear to think, why are there two words in so many European languages,[3] one of them having close verbal associations with pain, trouble and effort and the other not?[4] Arendt suggests that the ordinary use of 'Work' and 'Labour' as synonyms obscures a vital distinction which modern developments have hidden from our attention. Let us look at her accounts of the two.

Labour

Arendt's 'Labour' is the toil involved in staying alive, reproducing the species and serving the process of nature.[5] There is nothing specifically human about this, for all living creatures share it. Just as cows spend their lives eating grass and chewing the cud, so many of the activities of men are dictated by sheer natural necessity. In modern societies it is easy to forget this. Not so in pre-industrial societies, where the endless business of tilling the soil, gathering the crops, grinding the corn and making the bread was inescapably exhausting and time-consuming. In such a society, one man could free himself from the bondage of natural necessity only by forcing another to serve him. To quote Arendt,

> 'Because men were dominated by the necessities of life, they could win their freedom only through the domination of those whom they subjected to necessity by force.'[6]

The freedom of Athenian citizens, for example, was bought at the expense of their slaves.

The particularly bitter and inhuman characteristic of Labour is its endlessness. Like the process of nature to which it belongs, it is never finished. The corn is grown to be harvested and eaten, whereupon the field must be tilled and the seed sown again. The product is consumed as soon as it is produced, leaving nothing to show for the toil that has gone into it. The primary meaning of Labour, then, is ministering to the necessities of life, an activity that is both futile and inescapable. Arendt's description of this must ring true to every woman who has spent hours preparing a meal, seen it eaten, and realised in baffled frustration that it is all to be done over again. However, she extends her category to include a number of other activities, and we shall have occasion later to consider to what extent her categorisation is justified.

One of the human activities that Arendt assimilates to Labour is childbirth, the perpetuation of the species. This is warranted by the many languages in which the same word is used for the painful toil of birth and the exhausting business of tilling the fields. To parents of two-child families in modern societies the association may seem odd, but for most of human history women have been in thrall to nature, subject to a long succession of pregnancies, many of which would not even produce a surviving child. For women, as for serfs, a free life was not an option.

Another form of Labour consists not exactly of producing for consumption or serving nature, but of endlessly keeping nature at bay. Arendt has in mind all the tasks necessary to maintain the human world: the cleaning, painting, road-mending and general maintenance which is, like production for consumption, necessary but futile. Such labour does not achieve anything tangible, since it has constantly to be done all over again. Arendt refers to the Greek legend of Hercules cleaning the Augean stables, and remarks that this feat was heroic only because it was a once-for-all event:

> 'unfortunately it is only the mythological Augean stable that will

remain clean once the effort is made and the task achieved'.[7]

The types of labour we have so far considered have two things in common. Firstly, they are obviously hindrances to a free life, at any rate if extended over the sort of hours usual in pre-modern societies; and secondly, although modern society has by no means abolished them, it has vastly reduced both the physical toil involved and the proportion of any individual's life that need be spent on them. We might suppose, therefore, that Arendt's category of Labour gives us cause to congratulate ourselves on the progress modern industrial society has made towards freeing mankind from inhuman drudgery. This is not, however, the conclusion that Arendt draws. While she would agree that Labour in the senses we have discussed is much less inexorable than ever before, she lays her emphasis on two other kinds of activity which she also assimilates to the category of Labour, and which are, she claims, on the increase.

First of all, she claims that *any* human activity can be reduced to the level of Labour if it is done simply 'as a job', for the sake of making of living.[8] In the modern world, she suggests, all values except the labourers' values of keeping alive and raising one's standard of living have been devalued to the point where politicians, philosophers and artists accept that the only reason for their activity is 'to make a living', just as if they were serfs toiling to keep the species going.

Secondly, she includes within the category of Labour any production that is carried on for the sake of consumption, and she stresses that in modern industrial societies it is not just food and bodily necessities that are consumed, but all the 'consumer goods' of modern industry – cars, washing machines, three-piece suites and the rest. This means that modern industrial workers are Labourers just as surely as their peasant ancestors. Before we can properly understand the emphasis Arendt places upon production for consumption as a criterion of Labour, however, we need to look at her contrasting category of Work.

Work

Arendt insists that although the two have been confused in all previous theories,[9] human experience bears out the hint contained in the linguistic distinction between Labour and Work. In contrast to Labour's futile, repetitive bondage to nature, Work is *un*natural, and free and human precisely because it is unnatural. A man engaged in Work is not forced by his need to consume to go on doing the same thing in endless futility. Instead, he thinks of something he wants to make – a durable, non-consumable object – and he masters nature in order to do it.

Contrast, for example, a peasant labouring in the field, serving the process of nature in a never-ending cycle, with a craftsman working to make a piece of furniture. The Worker does not adjust himself to nature: in fact, as Arendt stresses, his attitude to nature is masterful and violent.[10] When he carves wood into a shape he has decided upon, he breaks into nature's processes, and is left with something solid to show for his effort. For the defining characteristic of Work is above all that it produces something solid and durable. The products of Labour exist only to be consumed, giving rise to more Labour in an endless cycle: but the results of Work are *things* with a durability of their own, objects which can survive their maker.

It is impossible to understand Arendt's ideas unless one appreciates the stress she lays upon durability as a characteristic of the products of Work. She agrees, of course, that the things Work produces are usually meant to be used, and that in being used they will eventually wear out. However, it is not in their nature to be consumed as it is in the nature of food and 'consumer goods' to be consumed and constantly replaced. Work creates something out there in the world as a visible testimony to the human effort and thought that has gone into it, and, taken together, the products of Work create a specifically human world with a permanence of its own to shield man from the meaningless flux of nature:

> 'Work and its product, the human artifact, bestow a measure of permanence and durability upon the futility of mortal life and the fleeting character of human time.'[11]

This notion of the man-made world which provides human life with a background against which individual uniqueness can become visible is a key concept in Arendt's thought.

The salient characteristics of Work, then, are that it gives rise to a durable product; it contributes to the human world which stands between us and nature; and it is an expression of human mastery over nature, not (like Labour) of human bondage. Within Arendt's theory, Work holds a place above Labour but subordinate to Action. She opposed the common modern belief that human fulfilment is to be found in suitably transformed work. According to her view of things, the crown of human activity (understood by the Greeks but lost and forgotten since their time) is public life, that Action among one's equals in which each man can show his own uniqueness and strive to leave the memory of his deeds behind him.

Arendt does *not*, then, regard Work as the highest human activity. Its proper function, to her mind, is to provide a durable human world to form the setting for Action among free men. Nevertheless, she leaves no doubt at all of her views on the relative merits of Work and

Labour. She suggests, indeed, that certain psychological qualities correspond to each form of activity, and the qualities of the *animal laborans* are greatly inferior to those of *homo faber*. Man so far as he is a Worker does develop many qualities that are characteristically human and not animal. He is dominant, individualistic and ingenious; he creates things that had no previous existence; he is rational, adjusting means to ends, and he establishes a system of utilitarian values which, while excessively instrumental and not enough in themselves to bestow meaning on life,[12] are at least an advance on the merely animal satisfactions of the Labourer.

The *animal laborans*, by contrast, is hardly human at all. He is immersed in the endless cycle of nature; he has no experience of freedom or of individuality and his ideals are dreams of endless consumption. While recognising that this represents an aspect of every human existence, Arendt has nothing but contempt for a life devoted only to the values of the Labourer.[13] The proclaimed intention of modern societies to maximise 'the greatest happiness of the greatest number' by 'raising the standard of living' seems to her to demonstrate the triumph of the Labourer's outlook over the higher human capacities.

Labour, work and the modern world

In *The Human Condition* Arendt deliberately chose to set her categories of Labour, Work and Action in the context of pre-industrial society, and in particular the society of the Greek *polis*. This allowed her to make sharp distinctions between the separate worlds of Labourers, Workers and Actors. The Labourers were slaves without rights, sunk in the misery of subjection both to nature and to their masters, providing for the bodily life of the higher classes; the Workmen, free artisans, contributed their products to the durable world which provided a setting for Action; while the crown of the edifice was the privileged class of full citizens devoting their time to Action among their equals.

The obvious query which this historical model provokes is, what has this to do with modern industrial society? Arendt's answer is to claim that her model pinpoints what is wrong with our society by demonstrating that Work and especially Action have been devalued in the modern world, whereas Labour and the values of Labourers have replaced them. On the face of it, this is a very odd claim to make. After all, as we have seen, the core of Arendt's concept of Labour is the idea of bondage to nature. How, therefore, can Labour be dominant in a society like ours, in which most activity is so thoroughly *un*natural? How can modern man have lost his human world, as Arendt claims,[14] when so much of our environment is man-made? Let us consider Arendt's answer.

First of all, as we have stressed, Labour is production for consumption rather than use: and if fewer men are now employed in producing food, the most elementary item of consumption, modern industry has enormously increased the number of things that are consumed. In place of the comparatively sparse but durable and permanent products of Work with which civilised men were formerly surrounded, modern men are engulfed in an endless stream of consumer goods: vehicles, furniture, machines that are deliberately not made to last. Man-made objects have been turned into the same kind of comestible as food, destroying the human world and imitating the flux of nature. We still produce and consume in endless futility, even though our items of consumption now include cars as well as food.

Furthermore, according to Arendt the process of production in modern factories represents a very passable imitation of the inexorable process of nature. Just as the peasant was forced to adjust his life to the rhythm of the seasons, so the modern Labourer has to adjust his life to the rhythm of the assembly-line. Most of those employed in modern industry have no opportunity for Work, the realisation of an idea in the creation of a durable object; only the engineers who design the machines have that satisfaction. From the point of view of the Labourer, machines are not a triumph of mind over matter but only an artificial, mechanised pseudo-nature to which he is in thrall.[15]

We may, of course, object that comparatively few people in modern societies are actually employed on assembly-lines. Arendt claims, however, that so dominant has the outlook of the Labourer become that virtually everyone now does his job for the same reasons that the serf slaved in the fields: to keep himself alive and to be able to consume more and more. Maintaining and increasing one's standard of living is now regarded as the highest end in life. Arendt admits, of course, that Labour in modern societies is not so back-breaking as in pre-industrial times, for the machines created by Work aid the Labourer's toil. What they cannot alter, however, is the fact that most men spend their lives in Labouring in order to consume, without freedom or significance.

Finally, Arendt maintains that modern masses prove their kinship with ancient serfs by showing no interest in anything except increased consumption:

'the spare time of the *animal laborans* is never spent in anything but consumption, and the more time left to him, the greedier and more craving his appetites'.[16]

The strengths and weaknesses of Arendt's position

It must be emphasised that by focusing on Work and Labour rather than on Action, the present paper necessarily gives a rather distorted impression of Arendt's principal concerns. *The Human Condition* is in no sense a programme for the replacement of routine Labour by creative Work, for Arendt is quite clear that the proper function of Work is the subordinate one of providing a durable setting for the public life which can alone do justice to the unique qualities of men. All the same, it is obvious that her theory does include a critique of modern industrial employment.

The first notable point is the originality of Arendt's position. The grounds on which she objects to modern industrial work are quite different from those commonly cited. We are accustomed to attacks on modern industry which contrast the meaninglessness and alienation of factory work with the satisfying, non-alienated life of the peasant. It is often claimed, and much more often assumed, that what is wrong with factory work is that it is *unnatural*, in contrast to the life of the pre-industrial worker who lived in harmony with nature.[17]

By contrast, Arendt in effect denies that men *can* be in harmony with nature. Either they are slaves to nature, like animals, peasants and pre-modern woman, or else they are nature's master as a craftsman is. As a result, and in sharp contrast to many critics of modernity, Arendt does not suggest that there is anything new or specifically modern about futile, meaningless Labour. She does not subscribe to the view that Labourers have become worse off since the advent of modern industry. On the contrary, she sees quite clearly that they are better off now than ever before.

It is important, therefore, to be clear what her complaint against modern industry is. Part of it is, of course, that with the advent of mass production, craftsmen have been replaced by machines and Work replaced by Labour. Arendt never pretends, however, that most men were craftsmen before this. The point of her image of ancient Greece is that although the vast majority of the population of the *polis* Laboured in misery, and although even the Workmen were liable to be despised,[18] nevertheless those few who did enjoy freedom in Action understood what human life was about and what its true values are. They knew that Work and the durable world it produces are superior to Labour and the meaningless flux of nature, and above all they knew that free political Action within this human world is the highest activity of all.

Arendt's ideas are always interesting. Like Socrates, whom she revered, she acts as a 'gadfly', goading others into thought, if only by forcing them to consider why they do not agree with her. Let us therefore conclude this paper by considering why her ideas are unacceptable as they stand, and what amendments might be made to them.

There are, I think, two main areas in which Arendt's theory of Work and Labour is open to attack. In the first place, we can criticise her concept of Labour on the grounds that it lumps together too many different kinds of experiences, thereby obscuring the differences between them. Secondly, we can try to show that her notion of Work is not internally consistent, so that if she were to pursue the intimations of her own concept she would arrive at a rather different conclusion. Let us look first at Labour.

It must surely be counted among Arendt's virtues that she brings such unsentimental realism to her account of the back-breaking toil which most of humanity have always suffered, avoiding the familiar trap of romanticising the 'natural' life of the peasant. Nevertheless, her category of Labour blurs important distinctions. To begin with, her emphasis on the Greek city, where labour was carried out by slaves, gives the impression that slavery to nature and slavery to man are virtually the same thing. We can see the fallacy of this if we consider one of the rare cases of free peasants without lords, medieval Switzerland. In a sense the Swiss peasants were certainly in thrall to nature, obliged to labour long and hard in a country where snow-storms and avalanches constantly reminded them of the limits of their control over their environment. Nevertheless, they could see a great deal of difference between Labouring for themselves in freedom and Labouring for a lord.[19]

Again, if slavery to nature and to man are not equivalent, slavery to the 'artificial nature' of the assembly line is different again. The analogy is a vivid one, but it cannot be carried very far. If we compare a modern car worker with a peasant, then it is true that in a sense each is subject to the rhythm of something outside himself. Nevertheless there are great differences, and advantages and disadvantages on both sides.

The peasant has the advantage of seeing an immediate personal relevance in what he is doing,[20] since the food he grows will mostly be used to feed his own family. Also, within the limits set by the seasons he organises his own work. The car worker, on the other hand, is not normally building a car for himself, and cannot organise his own work because the machines dictate their own tempo. Nevertheless, there are important respects in which he is much freer than the peasant.

Most obviously, the peasant cannot stop the process of nature. If the harvest is ready, he must get it in or lose it. But the car worker can (and frequently does) stop the assembly line. He can go on strike, bringing his capacity for Action into his Labour, and break his subjection to the machine in a way that cannot be emulated by the peasant. Furthermore, the modern industrial worker does not depend upon the machine for his livelihood in the unqualified sense in which the peasant depends upon nature and the slave upon his master. In a modern society equipped with unemployment pay and social security, he can leave his job without running the risk of starving. The financial consequences of unemployment are unattractive, but they do not impose labour upon him with anything approaching the stringency of necessity in pre-modern societies.

Something else which Arendt's analogy between Labour and slavery leads her to neglect is the world to which the Labourer goes home at the end of his shift. The Greek slave was a slave all day and all night and on Sundays; but the modern labourer can clock off and go home, with the opportunity to exercise other human faculties in his spare time. To some degree, employment in modern societies acts simply as a base, a way of earning a living so that a man can then get back to the really important business of life: to building his own private world in the home, making his own garden, constructing his own Hi-Fi set, or engaging in the other multitudinous activities that make modern private life so busy and absorbing.

Arendt's dismissal of leisure as sheer consumption is connected with her conviction that a free and truly human life must involve action *in public*. She stresses over and over again the subjectivism of modern men, who are immured in their own experiences, thoughts and perspectives, and lack the judgement and sense of reality that can come only from moving among one's equals. There is, however, a curious incoherence in her thought on this point. On the one hand she emphasises that it is Work that gives rise to a common human world to house mankind, but on the other hand, her account of Work seems too individualistic to be suited to this public purpose.

Work, as Arendt stresses, is an essentially individual affair. In contrast to Labour, which lends itself to being carried on in unison by gangs, the paradigmatic Work-situation is that of a craftsman alone with the idea that he wishes to realise, able to exert sovereignty over his material.[21] Furthermore, creation implies destruction. The new product of Work is realised at the expense of the material that was there before.[22] As an account of the experiences of making something, this rings true; and when it is applied to the builder of a *private* world it creates no problems. The man who realises his ideas in his own back garden can be sovereign over his material without impinging upon the creations of others. But it is not this kind of private world that Arendt is interested in. Alongside her stress upon the durability of Work's products, she also insists that their significance lies in the contribution they make to a durable common world. The difficulty here is that in so far as each individual Worker enjoys his prerogative of creation, then he is bound not only to add objects to the common human edifice, but also to destroy what was there before. The architect who knocks down a Georgian terrace in order to realise his own idea of a tower-block in all-too-durable concrete is certainly engaged in Work in Arendt's sense, but it is by no means clear that he is contributing to the stability of the common world.

What seems lacking in Arendt's account is an idea of conservation, or a trace of the ecological attitude that has become commonplace in the years since *The Human Condition* was written. She tends to see nature as raw material to be shaped and mastered, although a more conservationist attitude towards the human world seems to be demanded by her own theory itself. If each Worker regards everything that is given as so much raw material, then a stable human world cannot last long. It could, therefore, be argued that the modern loss of stability in, for example, the buildings by which we are surrounded, can be attributed quite as much to Promethean notions of creativity among architects as to the Labourers' passion for consuming everything that seems to Arendt to dominate the modern world.

Arendt's distinction between Labour and Work does not in fact seem to fit her separation between nature and the human world. A durable setting for human life requires some degree of creative Work, but not too much: to a far greater extent, what it requires is care and respectful maintenance – activities which Arendt includes under the heading of Labour.

Can Arendt help us in thinking about work in contemporary society? With qualifications, much that she says can be illuminating. Her distinction between Work and Labour has much to commend it, provided we stick to the central cores of the two concepts and avoid confusing analogies. There certainly is a difference between repetitive, fruitless toil on the one hand and the creation of a durable object on the other. The two do not by any means comprehend all kinds of jobs, but they certainly describe recognisable activities. It is interesting that the distinction corresponds to what tend to be regarded as 'men's' and 'women's' jobs in private life: the husband commonly does the jobs that leave a durable trace – the carpentry, amateur building, patio laying – while the wife cooks, cleans and washes up. It is in private life, too, that the notion of Work as a 'world-building' activity carries most conviction: for (analyses of 'Mass Society' notwithstanding) the inhabitants of identical houses on identical housing estates are not content to behave like interchangeable atoms. Within their own boundaries they do indeed create their own unique worlds, stamping their own imaginations on houses and gardens.

Where private life is concerned, then, Arendt's categories have a good deal of descriptive power. But her categories are not, of course, designed to apply to private life, since her main interest is in the common world and in public Action. Much of what she has to say about the need for a durable common world is persuasive: as we have seen, however, it is not entirely in accord with her accounts of Work and Labour. If we take seriously the need for a durable world then we should regard individualistic creativity with some suspicion, except in private life: while on the other hand we should treat with great respect the Labour involved in *maintaining* the common world. The drift of Arendt's own thought calls for a further distinction here between different kinds of Labour. There is a difference between spending one's life washing dishes and spending it cleaning St. Paul's Cathedral. Both jobs are repetitive, but maintaining one of the monuments of the common world does not have the soul-destroying futility of simply serving the needs of the body.

Finally, how do Arendt's categories apply to modern work in general? Do they have any relevance to most jobs in a post-industrial society? Clearly, the occupations that most people now engage in for a living are not Work: but are they Labour in Arendt's sense? What about the very wide range of employees, from car mechanics to computer programmers, who are frequently called upon to solve a problem and exercise a skill? Their activities are neither creative Work nor mere repetitive Labour: they are perhaps more akin to *performances* than to anything else.

But what of all the jobs that are apparently just ways of 'earning a living', and therefore fall under Arendt's category of Labour because they are subservient to mere Life? I think that in dismissing employment in this way Arendt is missing much of its significance, and, furthermore, failing to recognise something her own categories can help us to describe. For it is surely true that the significance of going to work for many modern employees, from typists to bureaucrats, from factory workers to managers, is not simply that it allows them to make a living, but above all that it takes them out of their private lives into a *public world* of Action, a place of dramatic events and confrontations to which the actual job to be done is often secondary.

This is a point that is often forgotten by critics of modern work. Using the model of the mythical peasant who was in harmony with nature, or of the almost equally mythical craftsman finding daily satisfaction in his creation, they look at employment from a subjectivist point of view and fail to notice the significance of the work-place as a public world. For an office, shop or factory is not just a prison into which one must enter to earn money to consume at home: it is also a place where things happen: a place where the absorbing drama of individual interaction can be enjoyed. The unemployed person or the housebound mother, is, like Arendt's ancient slave, pushed out of the bright public space into the darkness of private life.

As we have seen, Arendt herself did not see modern work in these terms. It may be, however, that her categories have applications beyond those which she suggested. Her concepts of Work and Labour, if suitably qualified, provide illuminating descriptions of activities that take place chiefly in private life, in the home while, paradoxically, it is neither of these, but instead her concept of Action between individuals that can perhaps do most to alert us to the public and communal aspects of modern employment, and therefore to one of the neglected costs of losing one's job.

ENDNOTES

1. Hannah Arendt, *The Human Condition* (University of Chicago Press, 1958). References below are to the paperback edition (New York: Doubleday Anchor Books, 1959), and refer to the book as H.C.
2. *The Origins of Totalitarianism*, first published under the title of *The Burden of Our Time* (London: Secker and Warburg, 1951), and republished with amendments in 1958 and 1967 (London: Allen and Unwin in both cases).
3. H.C., p. 72.
4. H.C., p. 44.
5. Arendt quotes Marx's definition of Labour as 'man's metabolism with nature'. (H.C., p. 86).
6. H.C., p. 74.
7. H.C., p. 87.
8. H.C., p. 43, p. 110.
9. She devotes a good deal of time to discussing the views of Locke, Adam Smith and Marx.
10. H.C., p. 122.
11. H.C., p. 10.
12. H.C., p. 134.
13. H.C., p. 115.
14. H.C. passim, but e.g. p. 231.
15. H.C., p. 114.
16. H.C., p. 115.
17. On this point, see A. Clayre, *Work and Play* (Weidenfeld and Nicholson, London, 1974).
18. H.C., p. 137.
19. Expressed for example in a village inscription beginning, 'We have by God's grace a lovely freedom', quoted by Benjamin Barber in *The Death of Communal Liberty – The History of Freedom in a Swiss Mountain Canton* (Princeton: Princeton University Press, 1974), p. 142.
20. And, of course, the disadvantage of chronic anxiety about the failure of his crops.
21. H.C., p. 141.
22. H.C., p. 122.

The next stage in lifestyles

This is based on the talk given by **Norman Macrae** *at the Siena Seminar, 1977, and on subsequent answers to questions. The wording is not Norman Macrae's, but he broadly agrees with the script.*

I am an optimist in the sense that I believe that an era dominated by big business corporations and big government is coming to an end of its own accord. I agree with those modern and much-criticised socio-biologists who say that Man is an animal who has a genetic urge to hunt in packs, but also to make those packs less than 100 strong. Big corporations are now too large to inspire people to hunt together in packs. Therefore, behind many of their façades the employees from just below the managing director to those around the shop steward are forming packs to hunt each other within the organisation itself. In the West it is not possible to persuade people to enjoy working in super-size herds – by beating the drums of economically orientated ideologies or of any other of the industrial religions, whether they be socialism, free enterprise or something else. Not even Welsh miners can be set to singing Japanese-style company hymns in love of the National Coal Board, 'Land of my coal mine, you belong to me'.

The top forty or so executives in a really big corporation do hunt together as a pack for the good of the dear old firm, even when stock options do not tie their personal fortunes to its prosperity. The reason is that forty or so can (with good management) be a natural sized pack to make co-operative work into fun, even if it does sometimes have to hunt with other unsympathetic people. However, this loyalty runs into contradictions. Healthy rivalry with other great corporations is the driving force behind most efficient international companies. The proof of victory is to win more territory and to grow bigger than your rivals. But the winning pack then finds that the faster its firm grows, the more obvious is the tendency for a decline in its efficiency.

Examples of inefficiency increasing with size are numerous and everyday. In Britain it is almost incontrovertible that the larger the workplace, the more frequent and acute are the industrial disputes, the higher the absenteeism and the greater bogus (as well as genuine) sickness. This shows itself in the idealistically motivated social services as well as the unidealistic British Leyland Company. Hospitals with under 100 beds show between half and two-thirds the sickness rates among nurses as those with more than 100 beds. Nurses are rarely malingerers. Therefore, there may be useful material for industrial psychologists and medical researchers to study here. The same deterioration is apparent in industry.

Big business becomes bigger and usually badder through processes of growth and takeovers. It is customary to blame the badness on to middle management. But this criticism can hardly be sustained; middle bureaucracy is so intent on rising to top bureaucracy that it is careful to be no more than an imitator of its present betters, knowing that by so doing, it stands the best chance of getting into their shoes. Nowadays most middle managers can disguise their obsequious natures by using computers and computer models to fit their changing patterns of advice to the known prejudices of the changing mix of the top people in their organisation. This is what is called planning.

Alternatively, a large middle management may be used, not to justify the initiatives that correspond to the prejudices of those who fix their salaries, but rather to block any initiative at all. The result is an increasing lag between the conception and completion of investment projects. This is absurd because one of the few things that computerised planning should be able to do is to cut sharply the time between the design of a new product and its coming off the production line. Thus bureaucracy within the organisation will ultimately bring down the big corporations.

The remedy for big business inefficiency and bureaucratic failure cannot be nationalisation, or some other form of public ownership. When the chips are down even bureaucratic big business is more efficient than either Whitehall or Town Hall enterprise. Compare, for example, the washing of clothes as a private industry and crime prevention as a public monopoly.

In the last three decades launderettes, washing machines and 'biological detergents' have cut by something like three-quarters the toil and time taken by the British working-class woman to do her wash. At the same time the productivity per policeman in every rich country has declined by around 75 per cent. Crime rates have typically trebled while police establishments have risen by over a third. Throughout the developed world, prisons have achieved the almost unbelievable of being able to show negative gross production; most penitentiaries now succeed in creating recidivists more than they cure criminals.

The failure of this kind of public service hits hardest at the poor, because it is in poor areas that the danger of being mugged or raped has risen many times during the past thirty years. In the Inner City schools the sickening apprehension has mounted that one's son may be being taught to become a delinquent, or one's daughter made into a slut.

In some rich countries, such as Britain, the proportion of GNP taken by public expenditure has gone fantastically over 50 per cent. Progressive governments look on public squalor amidst private affluence, and want to curb the squalor. Therefore, they move net labour resources out of the more productive private sector into the public sector, where marginal productivity is now often negative. They are then puzzled that things are worse than before. Then conservative governments come in and contemplate the mess caused by the high public expenditure. They cut this whilst trying to maintain public sector employment, i.e. by putting production for a public servant lower still.

A second reason why any form of bureaucratic production of services and goods doesn't work is that, in an age of advancing technology, the decision-maker must ask every day: what is the best tradition-busting technology that I can introduce? If the technology is labour-saving, he has to decide daily how many of his colleagues ought eventually to lose their established jobs. In a non-market orientated bureaucratic organisation anybody who keeps asking those questions is regarded as a bad colleague who is constantly rocking the boat. In many big business corporations with one layer of management laid upon another, the decision-making function has been transformed into the power of decision-blocking, and this power has fallen into the hands of the same sort of bureaucracy as enables a minister to stonewall. In the end these big businesses will go bust.

We are probably at the end of the Henry Ford revolution, when top people could sit at the top of big business organisations and decide exactly how the chap down there on the shop floor should work with his hands. Now two fundamental things have happened. First, as soon as a country grows rich, people down there on the floor say they do not like to be ordered about from the top. And surely they are right. This is what I call the '*people problem*'. Some of my friends do not like this label, but I still think it is the most striking one to say what I mean. Secondly, there is what I call the '*enterprise problem*' in an age when automation is due to turn the ordinary worker from a manual worker to a brain worker. But people at the top of big business are still behaving in their old bossy ways as though they were top brass in the First World War. They are trying to plan how the workers in the office below should use their imaginations. This cannot succeed.

The tradition of the last thirty years has been to take three bashes at the 'peoples' problem: (1) import workers from the poor South, who temporarily do not mind being put on the shop floor, and told what to do by a remove boss; or (2) sending the whole organisation to the poor South in a multinational company; or (3) waving the flag of worker democracy and self-management on the home ground. None of these three will work.

Immigrants arriving at Willesden for work on London Transport are told that they must integrate into the customs of the other menials with whom they are set to work and live. So, also, with the immigrants arriving to work in the factories at Birmingham, Bradford and Eindhoven. In English, integration means 'Become bloody-minded like your fellow workers, as quickly as possible, please'. The first generation Jamaicans, accustomed to the English sense of humour and brought up to expect that Willesden and Birmingham were centres of the civic virtues, will swallow all this in a bewildered way, hoping that it will all be explained at the Citizens' Advice Bureau, the Police Station, or at the next local election. Further indignities will be piled upon them, exacerbated by the absurdities of Britain's class-consciousness and ridiculous system of rent control. These and more will be borne meekly by the adults in the hope of getting in more of their families by legal or illegal means. However, these will not be the reactions of their children, who will gang up into small packs. Some will go mugging, believing it to be revenge for four hundred years of slavery, while bashing some old lady in the park whose sense of historical guilt is understandably small.

Whether enfranchised or disenfranchised, whether a legal or illegal immigrant, many of these people are not loved. The result is that anti-immigrant feelings tend to surface at awkward moments. On continental Europe there has been less of an effort to integrate immigrants as welcome settlers, doing the manual work for which they came; instead, many have been employed on a short-term basis. This adds to the instability of an already jittery society.

The second remedy for the alienation of ordinary workers in rich Northern countries was supposed to be to export manufacturing industries to the poor South. This will continue, though in an erratic way. The most successfully-exported industries will be for disguised re-import, like the American consumer electronics industry. This departed entirely to Asia in the 1960s, but is now coming back to America for automated and computer-controlled production, because the American trade union restrictions, which would have prevented its return, have in the meantime disappeared.

One factor which will encourage the setting up of new industries in the poor South in the 1980s will be the changing age structure in those countries where a majority of the population today is below the age of 21. Children largely produce nothing and teenagers largely produce riots. The age bulge will pass on ten years over the next decade. By 1988 these countries will have lots of under-employed cohabiting couples in their twenties. I think that some factories are likely to emigrate towards them in some countries, although their governments are unlikely to be at all obsequious.

It will, however, be surprising if these factories are established by another southward safari by multinational corporations. There will be a search for local entrepreneurs and profit-sharing arrangements, based on hiring out the know-how through some licensing agreement. Multinational corporations have learned from earlier lessons when they failed to notice that, just as their emigrant boom took off, material ownership was becoming no longer a source of economic or political power, and was probably indeed becoming a source of loss of both. So their interest in south-bound safaris should wane.

The third remedy for worker alienation was thought to be worker participation or 'producer democracy' in the rich countries themselves. We will not solve the 'people' problem by workers electing a committee to run the firm. It is untrue that people love their politicians whom they have elected; still less do they love the representatives elected by the majority whilst they voted for the minority.

Once you have created a committee to run a business by elections of this sort, the committee falls back on precisely the same sort of bureaucracy as does not work in any other organisation. Basically, I think that voting anyone to run anything in the twentieth century is like Monarchy in the nineteenth century. It is where the world is coming from; it is not where it is going towards. In this twentieth century the way in which the world is going is towards consumers' freedom. At the moment we have a marvellous choice of goods at the supermarkets but we have no choice at all of the lifestyles we each wish to follow. It is to this choice among lifestyles that any sensible system must move.

*   *   *

The data-processing revolution will allow us to record the sort of lifestyles we want and to set up a real market in these. Let me give some examples.

Robertson may want £50 a week, provided he can work only a few hours a week at a place of his choice at times chosen by him. Mrs Biggs may want to gossip on the production line; Miss Jones may enjoy working under a father figure. Browne may be a lazy productive genius; and von Braun a frenetically ambitious one. Smith may loathe having a foreman standing over him, and Jones may be equally intolerant of a shop steward trying to bully him to join a protection racket. What all these people have in common is that, when applying for a job, none of them is enabled actually to state these basic requirements.

On the other side there is the employer, who knows what jobs he has available and may have slots which each of these people could fill. But the tyrannies of conventional politeness and job classification prevent him from establishing contact in interview or conversation with these prospective employees so that they are happy and he is well-served. Instead, he usually advertises for somebody with experience. He will then get an inadequate person whose experience has been gained from being shifted from one relieved ex-employer to another. Had the means existed for prospective employer and employee to communicate their true requirements, at least one school-leaver would have found a career.

Databanks will improve all this. Before long the applicant for work should be able to sit answering questions from a computer console. 'Is flexitime important to you, and do you want some individual say in choosing your own working hours, immediate companions, targets for work?' My personal answer: 'Usually, yes'. 'But in emergencies do you mind sudden periods of frantic working for a day-and-night on end?' 'No, actually I rather enjoy that.' 'Do you object to calling your superiors Sir or Herr Doktor?' 'If they pay me more I'll call them Your Excellencies if they wish.' 'If this firm is at least as successful as the rest of the economy and it is possible to double everybody's real income every 15 years, do you want your next doubling in twice your present accumulation of material goods or six months' extra holiday a year?' My answer: 'I'd like to decide as this advance progresses, so don't tie me into any generalised trade union wages and hours agreement please.'

If there were a glut on the market of obsequious anarchists like me I then would be offered a less profitable contract than the scarcer supply of ruder, but more easily regimented, women or men. But wise employers would then adapt their work schedules so as to be able to use more of us obsequious anarchist bargains. The marrying of job specifications, individually-varied and constantly-changing patterns of lifestyles will be a very major industry in the future. The result will be what I call the individualisation of work contracts.

I had hoped that some of this would happen in the last twenty years with the emergence of so many women from married life into the working force. I thought that as they came to be employed, so they would wish to negotiate individual contracts to suit the circumstances of their home lives as well as their particular talents and inclinations. Instead, they have just been re-employed in the old hit-or-miss, authoritarian way.

But another development is now on the horizon, and this gives another set of opportunities which I think will be taken. In the 1960s I used the phrase 'tele-commuting' for this. It is now probably about to come into operation. Several American insurance companies have been negotiating with the telephone companies to try to get bulk contracts. In a decade or so a large number of their white-collar workers may be working from their own homes, communicating by telephone or facsimile transfer or telex with the colleagues and computers with whom they work.

Eventually this should usher in a genuine social revolution, because basically the cost of telecommunications, once installed, need not depend greatly on distance. It should eventually be as cheap to ring up from China to New York as from the office next door in New York. This will mean that people can live in Tahiti if they want to and telecommute each day to their office in Milan.

Once that happens, all sorts of happy social revolutions can occur. For example, politics should become much less important because, instead of voting for people to rule us in a particular way, we can move to the societies where the ways of running things are the ways we like. If we are keen golfers or surf-bathers, we'll move to near a golf course or surf-bathing. If we are most earnest-minded people, we will choose to live in communes with the sorts of people with whom we feel most *en rapport*.

This should come for white-collar workers quite quickly. Thereafter, firms in rich countries will be bound by market forces to liberalise on the contracts they offer to blue-collar workers as well. Sometimes, a blue-collar worker may have six months' holiday a year, so that he can spend those six months where he wants to, although quite often he'll choose to moonlight into another job.

Often a firm will set a module of output which it will subcontract to a particular group of blue-collar workers to perform for a given fee; the firm will then leave the timing and the arrangements under which the group produces the module for the workers to settle for themselves within the broad framework of the contract. The workers will be able to organise themselves as they wish, for example, they could be an *ad hoc* team; they could be contracted to a single boss or partnership; or they could form themselves into one of the many types of co-operative ventures now discussed. Whatever the details, the contract arrangements will allow much more flexitime for the workers. That, I think, is the way in which we will move to solve the 'people problem'.

I, myself, believe that workers will choose different contracts, living in different places, even moving between blue-collar work with long holidays and white-collar tele-commuting from particular places, at different times of their lives. And oddly I think that this system will also move towards settling the enterprise problem as well. But first a tangential line of thought worth noting.

*   *   *

There has been another quite separate geographical development in the world's pattern of industry: namely, the shift in the centre of gravity in terms of business from the Atlantic to the Pacific. The century lasting from 1775 to 1875 was dominated by the British, whose pre-eminence was based upon the first transport revolution of the railways; next, between 1875 and 1975, it was the turn of the Americans with the motor car. The century which lies ahead will belong to whoever can master the third and biggest transport revolution of telecommunications. In this area the Japanese look like being the front-runners. Another reason for the shift from the Atlantic to the Pacific is the rapid transformation of Asia as a whole. Over the next 20 years there will be one billion people moving into the age group 20 to 45 in Asia. That is one billion people coming on to the labour market; the biggest sudden increase ever. For the first time in Asia, most of them will be literate. It is therefore highly probable that many manufacturing industries will move from west to east.

Another subject worth pursuing at a tangent in a paper devoted to future trends concerns energy. I do not believe the pessimists for a moment. Since the 1770s energy has been in elastic supply simply because technology, under the incentives of high rewards, has always been on the verge of finding new ways of releasing energy from matter. What is more, these new ways have been constantly less labour intensive and more easily transportable. Today there are many thousand ways already established, in theory at least, of releasing energy from storage in matter. The rise in energy prices since 1973 gives an incentive to find practical ways of using this theoretical knowledge.

*   *   *

Back to the enterprise problem. In my view we can already see the beginnings of it being solved now. When I visit business corporations in America, I notice a constant see-saw between perhaps a seven-year stint of decentralisation followed by a briefer period of recentralisation. The recentralisation becomes necessary when the people at Head Office discover that the various bodies out in the field are all going in wildly different directions. So decision-making comes into the centre, and the different divisions, or separate companies, have imposed upon them whatever has been discovered to be the most efficient modes of operation during the experiments of decentralisation. However, the recentralisation does not last long because people at Head Office, after three or four years, discover that they are writing memos which have no relevance to what actually goes on the field. So then they decentralise and these bouts last longer. The general, if erratic, tendencies towards decentralisation and towards smaller and smaller profit-centres, which grow more and more entrepreneurial and settle their own contract policies.

We might now have a look at the contract as a means of enlisting the initiatives of those who have initiative and want to develop characteristic lifestyles of their own.

In the period of exciting experimental opportunities which lies ahead, rich countries and rich companies can no longer rely exclusively on the entrepreneurship of those with rich families in the background to give them security. The aim must be to make sure that so-called ordinary people have the scope to become tycoons, as such people had when the Industrial Revolution was young.

Each progressive firm should define the modules of work that it wants to be done, and then invite bids from members of the staff who would be happy to achieve the module working as subcontractors, not employees. The bids will sometimes come from individuals and sometimes from groups of friends within the firm. When accepted, the parties will get down to working out the details of the contract forming the basis of the relationship between them.

In 'far-out' ventures the bidder will say how much of the corporation's existing services (production, marketing, etc.) he would wish to use; and how rights of decision eventually to sell of the venture, if successful, to an outsider should be shared. Some of these 'far-out' bids would be from employees willing to take a risk with their own security – in effect working for bare maintenance if the project failed, or even involving a loan which would have to be paid back to the firm over the years.

Computers will play a vital role in devising freelance contracts and enlarging the scope for them, so that eventually subcontracting will be used even in assembly-line industries. The key to this revolution is what the Americans call 'Customized production at mass-production prices'. What this means is that the computer-controlled production line can be used by the customer to introduce his own specification, adapting what would otherwise have been a mass-production model. A computer, unlike a human being on the assembly line, can decide that this or that modification will be made on items 293 to 417 passing down the assembly line. Once one gets that chance for product-variation, the experiments for deciding what variations to try out will not be found by a committee. On the contrary, they will much more sensibly be based on various entrepreneurial experiments tried out as subcontractors by individuals within the organisation. Big companies will rent out some time on their assembly lines in this way.

In future, experimental products will not only be easier to manufacture, but eventually easier to launch. Public reaction will be simple to assess by means of two-way telecommunication sets of various types which should become commonplace in rich countries' households by the 1990s. The new product, be it hardware, software, a service, a good, an ingenious package holiday, will be advertised on television offering substantial discounts for orders placed there and then. Customers will give these orders from their homes by pushing the right buttons on their consoles to make their commitment; simultaneously another button will be pressed, which will deplete their bank account in favour of the advertiser at the discount price. There will be further discounts for customers willing to make instant payments for deferred delivery, so that in effect they will be helping to finance the manufacture of their own purchase.

The same method can be used in reforming the internal organisation of a firm – say, the typing-pool. Using the principle of competition, most big businesses would already be wise to encourage their staffs to set up several separate secretarial or typing teams who can then compete to find the best way forward to tomorrow's paperless office.

Another interesting source of innovation favouring small businesses and the creation of a multiplicity of property rights will be industrial robots. It is more logical to call them all-purpose. They are machine-tools that can be programmed to work in a great many different ways. This means that a firm need have fewer machine-tools, and therefore smaller factories, especially when there will be a lot of second-hand jigs lying around.

The changes that I have been trying to explain are already in the pipeline. If society is enlightened enough to take them, they can become realities within a comparatively short time. But they will not affect all the world, rich and poor, intelligent and unintelligent, industrious and lazy, at the same time. There are some industries where there will be little scope for increasing choices available to those who have to work in them. In richer countries workers doing dull jobs will deserve and get even longer holidays than those doing fun-jobs. Anyway, workers will change occupations as soon as they are bored. More important, a lot of these jobs will move to the poor two-thirds of the world. The poor countries will move into the rich one-third's present lifestyle and the rich one-third will move faster into the telecommuting age.

The advantage will lie with those countries which have the right sort of cultural attitudes and business mechanisms to welcome change. My bet is that pacemakers in the rich world will be the Japanese, and in the poor world the Asian countries who most nearly adopt Japanese methods.

The failing industries will be those that try to protect themselves by cartels. I have been asked; what effects on my own industry of newspapers? The cartel here is run mainly by trade unions which oppose high technology, keeping in employment many more journalists and printing workers than any newspaper really requires. My guess is that confederations of entrepreneurs will nevertheless break through, using even more labour-saving technology than would have been used if the workers' cartel had not existed. (I could add, 'I see Rex Winsbury in his evidence for the Acton Society to the Royal Commission thinks this, too'.)

By the end of the century most of the new comment that a customer buys in written form, as distinct from on videotape, may come to him individually, probably by facsimile print-out from the back of his television set. The packages that readers order will then not be those put together by the editor of *The Times* or *Daily Mail*, but those ordered individually by himself. After seeing on a screen what is on offer, he will order, by pressing a button, one of several competitive summaries of the news, plus comment advertised that day by tomorrow's Bernard Levin or Scotty Reston, everything written about that day's racing at Ascot, book reviews by his favourite critics and possibly a pin-up of a nude redhead in leather boots (or whatever is his special hang-up). Advertisements will be attached, probably chosen by a computer which will have worked out from Mr Jones's other preferences what products will especially appeal to him, and to what way of their being presented he will be most susceptible. If he does not want the advertisements, his paper will cost him a lot more.

Most industries should be even more susceptible to groups of entrepreneurs working as confederations. Critics say that will not apply to capital-intensive industries, where those who put up the money for the expensive plants will want to appoint the people who decree how the workers in those plants shall behave.

The critics misunderstand what is happening. In the 1970s it has gradually become clear that the ownership of the means of production is no longer a source of economic or political power; indeed, it may be a source of powerlessness. Throughout industry, ownership increasingly means loss of control. So does direct employment. It is much easier for an organisation to achieve its end through taking action against subcontractors by cutting off contracts.

One sort of property-right that must be liberalised, however, is ownership of information. We have got to have a new Restrictive Trade Practices Act specifically to free the supply of information to small firms as well as large. I think that basically information has got to be made public, put on to computerised databanks and obtainable for a fee. This will mean that government departments, universities and research bodies of all kinds have to to be made to disgorge it as well. We do not want information systems to be under bureaucracies.

I want information to be a public good, from which we can all draw, as we do in a public library. No bureaucrat tells me what book I can read. He is not going to tell me what I cannot draw from a databank either.

An era of government monopoly of all kinds is, thank heavens, coming to an end. It is clear to me that much government in the past fifty years has been an unproductive job invented by intellectuals, who in the future will have many more interesting things to do.

Stay alive with style

Peter Harper

Work is about staying alive. But there's staying alive, and staying alive with style, which is what interests me. If you want to stay alive with style, there seem to be two basic possibilities for life and work. One, which is quite unusual, is to make work itself stylish. This generally entails doing it most of the time. The other possibility is to use work to make non-work stylish, and there are two basic varieties of this. One is to make non-work stylish by the sheer abundance of freedom; the other is to make it stylish by virtue of the goods and services work provides.

The kind of society I want to live in offers each of these possibilities in any mix I care to make. Is this possible? I'm not really saying anything extraordinary. Some people love their work, whatever it is, and everybody else agrees that what they do is useful and they get paid enough so there's no problem. For the rest of us it's not so easy, because actually we don't like working very much.[1] Faced with this, most of us accept it as a fact of life and work 'normal' hours in return for, by historical standards, good wages which we use to secure a high standard of living. If you're into high standards of living – a high level of material consumption – this is a very rational thing to do. Call it Option I. But if you're not unduly excited by high standards of living, other options are logically open. If what you most value is leisure, or freedom from work-disciplines, you could work a lot less and live on a much lower income. Call this Option II. If you're into doing nice work, you could spend most of your day at pleasant, craft-like activities, working hard with a small income, but enjoying yourself. Call this Option III.

Although Option I is overwhelmingly dominant in this culture, the others, which have always existed for special minorities, seem to be gaining ground. People are increasingly exercising their economic freedom to choose not only what to buy, but how to earn the money to buy it. And buying itself is becoming less important. Apart from empirical data which I come across from time to time,[2] I find myself encountering more and more people from all sorts of backgrounds who are 'sick to death of 9 to 5' and want a rational change, one which will allow them to fulfil their responsibilities, but live a much less constrained life. Very often they're not quite sure what this might mean in practice, but there is a general pattern. They don't want to do the same thing all the time, five or six days a week. They would like to spend, perhaps, two days doing a manual, clerical, retail, even professional job for cash; another two or three engaged in a craft which provides a focus for intense interest and skill, and also makes a bit of money; and the rest, non-money work with family and friends in the home and community.

In other words they want a bit of everything. And why not? In my life I've lived for substantial periods with each basic option and I can appreciate the benefits and disbenefits of each for different people in different life-situations. Why can't we choose freely and change freely? It ought to be possible, in a clever and efficient culture like this is supposed to be, to arrange any mixture anyone wants, within the general constraints of productivity and economic justice. The obvious response to this is that we are already perfectly free to choose these lifestyles if we want to, and furthermore in the longer term, advances in technology will make alternative choices progressively easier. Therefore, no drastic changes are needed: the market plus technology will suffice.

I'm not quite sure what to say to this. It's a strong point. The alternatives *are* growing anyway. But this kind of radical choice is much easier for certain groups of people than others. For many, although they might really like a change, unorthodox work styles are psychologically invisible or socially unacceptable. And there are severe economic and organisational disadvantages in a society set up to cater for a dominant Option I. As attitudes change among ordinary people, and in planners, officials, business people and government, we are likely to find ourselves constrained by a lag in the formal structures: planning regulations, tax laws, insurances, regional grants and incentives, unemployment benefits, retraining facilities, educational curricula, timekeeping, union rules, etc. These *will* have to be changed. As far as regular technological progress is concerned, it cannot be denied that in increasing productivity it can in principle reduce the amount of work we have to do for a given level of consumption, and thus increase leisure time; and it can automate routine and dangerous jobs, thus reducing many of the alienating aspects of work. Fine. But it doesn't seem to operate quite so neatly as this. Technology doesn't develop or function in a vacuum.[3] New consumer 'needs' arise to mop up extra production, and people end up working as hard as ever – that is, if they don't lose their jobs altogether, a fate which seems to befall people who, for the time being at least, don't want to be unemployed. And it's often skilled jobs (like in design and printing) that get displaced by automation, leaving the workers with less skilled work to do. This raises that chilling prospect which social satirists like to conjure with, of a ruling caste of technocrats who manage the automated production systems, set over a lumpen, passive, consuming population.[4] This is not to be laughed off.

My feeling is that this business-as-usual approach is not going to get where I and a lot of other malcontents want to go. To offer *everybody* the possibility of *drastically* reduced essential work and/or *greatly* increased scope for really enjoyable work, we need more passionate and wholehearted changes. What might these be?

I can group the changes I would like to see in three categories, roughly corresponding to the three options. First, the humanisation of the formal sector. I don't have anything unusual to say about this. Basically I'm sceptical about large-scale formal work ever being made really enjoyable except for a minority in particularly interesting roles or with just the tastes it takes (I once knew a power station worker who treated his workplace as a fairy palace, full of variety and unexpected wonders). But maybe I'm wrong. A lot can be done, ranging from the traditional shorter-hours-and-better-working-conditions, through the now trendy profit-sharing, flexitime, job enrichment, co-management, etc., to the meatier measures of job-sharing,[5] change of products,[6] 'the right to do socially useful work'[7] and honest-to-goodness workers' control. If this lot were combined with a considerable reduction in formal work so it became an interesting change rather than an overwhelming presence, then we'd be getting somewhere.

This is more or less the best I can envisage for people who are solidly into Option I (making non-work stylish by virtue of the material rewards work provides). What about the others? Theoretically, it's possible to identify, or at least imagine, whole sectors of the economy specially suited to their needs. For Option II (making non-work stylish by sheer abundance of freedom) for example, supposing we had special centres where absolutely basic goods were produced as quickly and cheaply as possible. Here people could work minimum hours for the minimum necessary income and consume the products of their own work. For Option III (making work stylish), suppose we took the most naturally human or 'convivial'[8] parts of the economy – the domestic, community and small business sectors – and increased their range and productivity. Here people could continue to work contentedly for long hours without drudgery and make a positive contribution to the rest of the economy.

In many ways these proposals follow ideas originally put forward by Paul and Percival Goodman in their book *Communitas: Means of Livelihood and Ways of Life*. This classic of utopian planning described three archetypal societies which correspond more or less to my three options. The first is called 'The City of Efficient Consumption'. Based on existing modern cities, it is more rationally organised to fulfil the dreams of a society of dedicated consumers

(Option I). The second scheme is called 'Planned Security with Minimum Regulation' and envisages a situation where work is reduced to an absolute minimum by universal induction into a state-sponsored 'labour service' whose task is to provide everyone with the basic goods and services. Thus the production of necessities (a small fraction of the total economy) is taken out of the market and constitutes the only regulated part of society. The rest can do what it likes, as can the people outside the small proportion of their lives spent in the labour service (Option II).

This scheme is an expression of one of the classic utopian dreams: to abolish work, or at least to minimise it, through technology, automation and rational social organisation. But, of course, the contrary dream also exists: to exalt work and make it central to the whole purpose of life (Option III). This is the basis of the Goodmans' third paradigm, 'The Elimination of the Difference between Production and Consumption'. The heart of the scheme lies in four basic principles which can be roughly summarised as:

(a) A closer relation of the personal and productive environments.
(b) A role for all workers in all stages of the production of the product.
(c) A schedule of work designed on psychological and moral, as well as technical grounds.
(d) Relatively small units with relative self-sufficiency.

Each of these visions will appeal to different people at different times in different moods – the same person may prefer one option now and another later on. He must be free to choose without feeling that he is prejudicing his welfare, his values or his aspirations.

In this respect the Goodmans' second scheme seems particularly interesting, because the basic necessities are taken care of in a relatively small part of anyone's life. The rest of the time can be spent loafing about or in any other 'unproductive' way, but equally could be devoted to Option I or Option III work-styles.[9] But there are obviously a lot of problems in trying to adapt this idea to our present circumstances. I'm imagining a special sector of the economy dedicated to basic needs and encouraged and protected by any legal or fiscal device that comes to hand. It produces things on a massive scale without styling, packaging, advertising: they are good and cheap but not pretty or charismatic. I don't know whether any private industry would be willing to do this kind of thing on a contractual basis (I'm thinking of utility clothing or military gear). The alternative, state-run factories might suffer the ills most nationalised industries seem to be heir to, but we ought to be able to work something out. Work in such centres would, of course, be voluntary but wages would be good; or maybe pay should be partly in tokens exchangeable for just these necessary goods. Workers could allocate their time any way they liked, with reasonable notice.

One thing is certain: in voluntary schemes like this, Option I freaks would be unlikely to participate, because they could get more money for *real* consumer goods in the regular economy. So a natural alliance of Option II and Option III people might emerge, and it might be politically sensible to orient some of the basic needs production towards the special requirements of the Option III population – particularly the special materials and technologies for their own preferred style of production. The part of the economy naturally connected with Option III is the small, and especially the 'informal', part. There is by now quite a literature on the growth of the 'informal', 'gift', 'domestic' or 'self-service' economy,[10] although personally I would put the focus on the collective-informal-plus-small-to-medium-formal which might be called the 'intermediate economy'. It is intermediate in two respects. In terms of scale, and in terms of organisational precision and work discipline, it lies between the two quarantined spaces in which most people spend the greater part of their lives: the home and the large, formal workplace. On this scale of work discipline I can distinguish six levels. (See Diagram 1.)

The domestic level includes not only nuclear households, but also larger 'families'. The collective informal level includes everyday neighbourly exchanges between households, 'bees', joint purchasing, tool pools, community work-ins, and might incorporate quite large numbers of people in co-operative projects. These two levels are essentially cashless. The 'black' level involves, in Robertson's delicate phrase, 'unrecorded cash transactions' which avoid tax, VAT or reduced welfare payments, and range from the simple purchases between friends which have more the flavour of barter, through moonlight odd-jobbing to (presumably) quite large-scale fiddles.

The small formal level includes unregistered sole-trader businesses and professional practices through partnerships with no employees up to medium-sized businesses with up to 100 workers. There would be co-operative equivalents of these as well, although at the larger end they would presumably be federations in order to retain their cosy, co-operative character. The large formal level doesn't really need explaining. I've put the Basic Needs sector at the most extreme level because I suppose it to be intrinsically large and rather rigidly organised, certainly not an idyllic place to work in – although I can't think of any real reason why it should be more highly disciplined than the large, regular formal.

The argument here is this: the intermediate sector is naturally the most convivial part of the economy, especially the informal and co-operative formal bits. But they need to be made more efficient and

Diagram 1

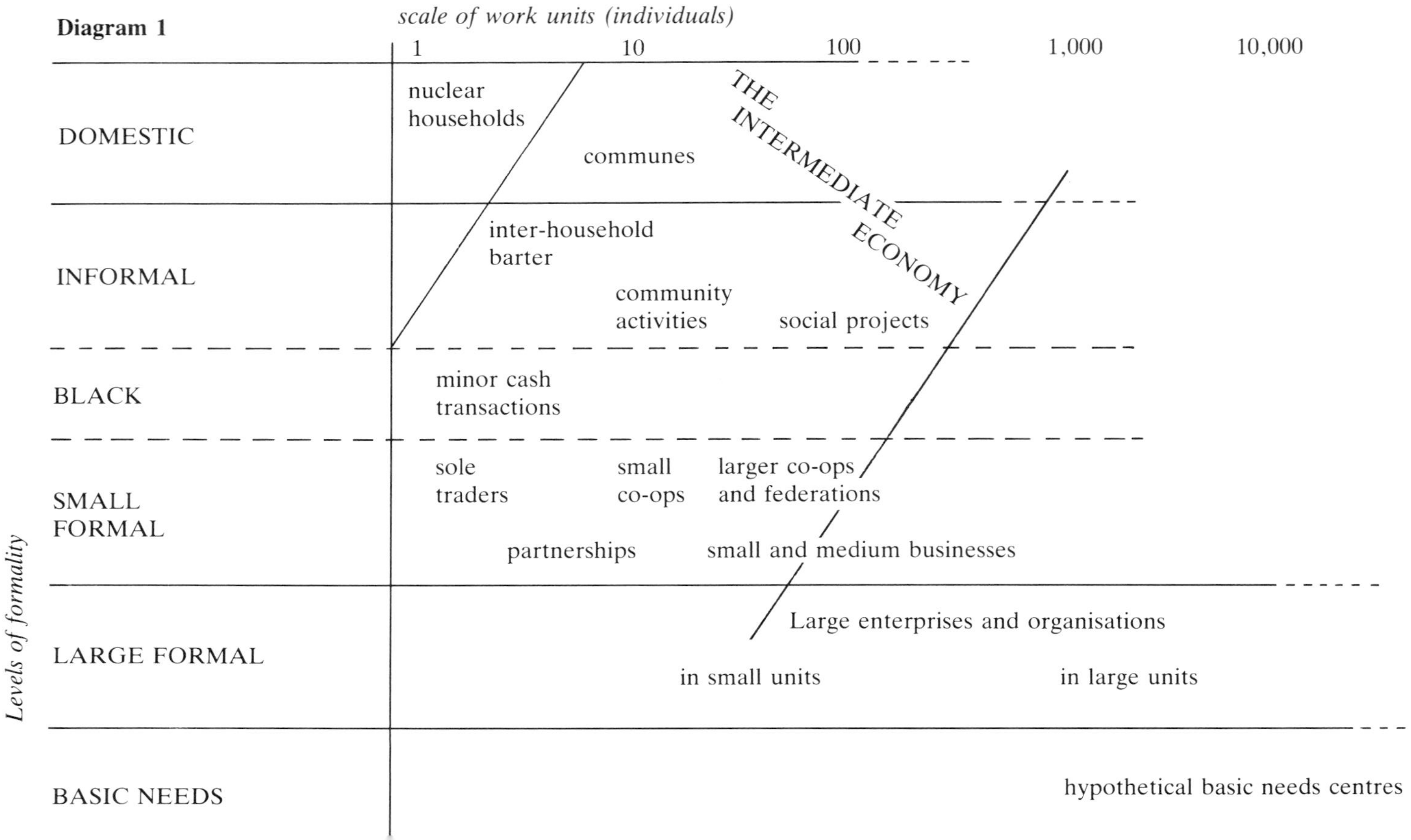

scale of work units (individuals)

| | 1 | 10 | 100 | 1,000 | 10,000 |

Levels of formality

DOMESTIC — nuclear households

communes

INFORMAL — inter-household barter

THE INTERMEDIATE ECONOMY

community activities

social projects

BLACK — minor cash transactions

small co-ops

larger co-ops and federations

SMALL FORMAL — sole traders

partnerships

small and medium businesses

LARGE FORMAL — Large enterprises and organisations

in small units

in large units

BASIC NEEDS — hypothetical basic needs centres

productive. This is partly a question of organisation and attitudes, and partly a question of technology. At the domestic level the effects of labour-saving devices have been quite profound over the last fifty years, and 'the Black and Decker Revolution' points further in the same direction. This process needs to be extended for larger groups of people. With careful thought and a lot more confidence, the intermediate sector ought to be able to supply a lot of its own appropriate technology. But it would still depend for many things on the large, formal sector, and this is where the basic needs element would serve: supplying cheap, appropriate equipment and materials and providing the basic security that will encourage free, even wild, experiment.

But what kind of experiments? Some ideas have been expressed in the form of drawings. Six drawings were worked out several years ago by a group of people involved in writing a book called *Radical Technology*[11] and interpreted by my friend and namesake Cliff Harper.

The general notion is, again, to move into the middle ground, sharing many things that are usually done on an individual or household basis, decentralising to a community level many things which are usually done by the large-scale formal sector. In general this means that consumption levels are lower, and fewer goods and services need be paid for in money. On average, less time is spent 'going out to work' and more time doing productive things in the community context, with or without cash transactions. The drawings have a utopian flavour about them, but they are all technically possible.

The Communalised Terrace This is too complicated to describe completely here. Imagine a row of, say, a dozen terraced houses of the kind you find in any industrial city. The Council has moved their inhabitants to some tower block in another part of the borough. It wants to knock them down and redevelop the site, but is short of funds for rebuilding, so leaves them. This is fairly common. A Housing Association approaches them with a proposal for rehabilitation, work to be carried out by the eventual occupants (which might include many of the former occupants) in return for partial grants, materials and skilled advice. The Council accepts.

The plan is to economise as much as possible on utility services (water, electricity, gas, sewerage) by rational redesign and the sharing of a number of facilities. First, various dividing walls are knocked down and the terrace converted into three or four larger dwelling spaces, to make better use of bathrooms, kitchens, hallways, etc. Two of the houses so combined are not lived in permanently, but are used for joint purposes which involve heavy expenditure of energy (bakery, laundry, sauna, workshop – metered separately). Other houses are designed for low energy consumption. They are heavily insulated on the outside to gain the benefit of the walls as heat stores, and heated by small gas fires. In the summer months, solar panels on the roof supply most of the hot water, feeding preheated water to gas-fired water-heaters which, of course, would do most of the work in the winter. Light cooking is done on a household basis, but baking centrally. Electricity is used only for lighting, small appliances and the workshop. 'Grey' (washing) water is saved and used, when necessary, on the garden. Toilets are of the composting type. Very little waste is passed into the sewers.

Living density is obviously up to the people who live there. If there are spare rooms, they might be used as creche, nursery school, library, workroom. Attics could be used as studio, mushroom-farm, hothouse, hydroponicum. Lean-to glasshouses at ground level would create extra space, conserve energy and grow food and flowers the year round. The garden would certainly not suffice to feed everyone, but could save a lot of money in fruit, vegetables and eggs, and would benefit from the waste water, and the output of the composting toilets.

Communalised Garden This might be the garden of the terrace described, or any collection of back gardens put together. There's nothing particularly extraordinary about it, just that it's often nice to work together in a big garden instead of alone in a small one. In this drawing the bits nearest the houses are left private. Tools can be shared; people can specialise in what especially turns them on; lots of seedlings can be grown in relatively few greenhouses or cold frames; composting is more efficient on a large scale; seeds are not wasted so much; garden materials can be bought cheaply in bulk; there's enough space and variety for experiments – and so on. It's worth remembering that, contrary to the plaints of some conservationists, when argicultural land is 'swallowed up' by housing developments, yields per acre go *up*, because horticultural productivity is so much higher than extensive farming.[12] Food production in cities could be greatly increased, to everybody's benefit.

Household Workshop If the informal economy is to grow and become more efficient, it must at least be able to maintain and repair its own capital. Each house should have the basic equipment for routine repairs, and knowing how should be everybody's birthright. A large house or a small group of houses might share a workshop such as this one, and it might even be possible to make things as well as repair them, for use or for sale. In this drawing you can see routine woodwork, metalwork and mechanics' tools, painting and decorating materials, equipment for making and repairing clothes – which you might have in any house, but also equipment for shoemaking and repair, weaving, pottery, silk-screen printing and wood-turning – all carried out at a very inefficient 'craft' level, but in these circumstances not needing to compete with formal economy equivalents. Notice that the equipment is, on the whole, very simple and uses little energy. The electric kiln is an exception and ruins the rhetoric: a larger, communal scale pottery with a large oil- or gas-fired kiln would make more sense.

Community Workshop This playground for the craft-conscious I find particularly inspiring, and where I live I have been trying for a long time to persuade my friends to help set one up – without much success. It's the same sort of principle as the household workshop, but on a much larger scale, accommodating the heavy machinery that a household space could not. In this drawing there is a metalworking lathe, a grinder, drill press, bender, forge, gas welder. The workshop would undertake vehicle repairs and general blacksmithing jobs; one-off or small-run manufacture of household items – repairs mostly – and perhaps things like solar panels or woodburning stoves; recycling car parts and electrical components, scrap metal, building materials, wood, perhaps glass. It would also lend itself to operations like engine rebuilding and reboring; fibreglass products; furniture making. Its running costs would have to be met either on a subscription basis by those who used it, and/or by payments for the goods and services it provided.

Community Media Centre Here is imagined the conversion of a disused church – easy enough to come by these days – into a place to gather for entertainments, festivals, meetings. The main nave is obviously a good space for concerts, recitations, parties, rallies. It could be divided if necessary by partitions. The crypt might be a quiet place for a recording studio. Elsewhere you might have, as in the drawing, a printshop or a community video centre, or whatever else took your fancy. You could even have weddings and funerals. There's some pretty fancy gear here, and such a centre would have to do quite a bit of commercial work in order to maintain it. But such electronic gadgetry is rapidly declining in cost, and it reminds me that the decentralised use of microprocessor technology might come to have a crucial role in the development of the intermediate sector.[13]

Semi-Autonomous Housing Estate This is different from the others because it's in the country, or at least in the outer suburbs. If it looks a bit too clean and neat, imagine that it's just been built and the planners tried to make it look as much like a conventional housing estate as they could, while accepting the general principles. The idea is that, without a great deal of extra investment, it is possible to create collections of family-scale smallholdings, perhaps twenty, independent of mains services and largely self-sufficient in food. Each site has a house, large garden and sheds for animals, equipment and storage; and land surrounding the estate is devoted to more mechanised, extensive production (e.g. grains, potatoes, hay) on a joint basis.

The houses are based on a design by Brenda Vale.[14] Being free from the constraints of other buildings or service runs, they can be designed optimally for their function. Some service needs are met at the household level, others at the communal level, depending on the scale appropriate to each. With solar heating for example, it makes no sense to collect, concentrate and distribute a form of energy which distributes itself and is only needed at a low density. Household kitchen and toilet wastes would be dealt with on a household basis and composted along with the extensive garden waste – plus muck from the animals. Actually, with this many animals (several cows, goats and lots of chickens and ducks), it would be worth collecting the muck and digesting it anaerobically for fertiliser and biogas – a process which only works on a largish scale. It would provide enough gas for cooking, used sparingly. Water would be provided centrally from well or spring, and pumped to a holding tank by windpump. If it were not pure enough to drink, this could be put right by filter-candles fitted to the household taps. Electricity would be generated by a pair of high-speed aerogenerators, feeding a central store of batteries with all the regulating and inversion gear to provide mains-like supplies.

The people living on such an estate could earn income from food surpluses and food processing – eggs, cheese, butter, vegetables, fruit, cream, preserves, herbs, etc. But they would need other sources of income, at least to pay their rent or mortgages! Workshops on the lines of the community workshop described above would be necessary to maintain the necessary equipment, and this might also be suitable for the manufacture of intermediate-scale farming equipment[15] for which there would be a growing demand. Otherwise I imagine that two or three days' work per week in the local town, or as a farm worker, vet or agricultural engineer, for example, would provide enough cash. The rest would be in the inhabitants' own hands, where it ought to be.

Some concluding remarks. The notions in this paper are rather utopian, but this doesn't mean that they are not practical. They are associated with a tradition of decentralist theory and practice which is undergoing something of a renaissance. Obviously, in its *extreme* form the neo-Luddite-back-to-nature-self-sufficiency move is not practical for large numbers of people, or even small numbers. I've been through enough of that trip myself to realise all too clearly its limitations.[16] A more vivid mix of the regular economic structures and the 'alternative' is needed. Maybe the middle ground is a good place to start.

ENDNOTES

1. Of course, there's an enormous literature on work alienation, notably in the Marxist tradition. Two excellent recent works are Harry Braverman's 'Labour and Monopoly Capital: The Degradation of Work in the Twentieth Century', *Monthly Review Press*, 1974; and Studs Terkel's *Working* (Wildwood House, 1975). Peter Brown's brilliant novel *Smallcreep's Day* (Paladin, 1976) deserves to be better known as an entertaining evocation of industrial alienation.

2. E.g. Jay Gershuny, 'The Self-Service Economy', *New Universities Quarterly*, 32 (1), 1977-78; Duane Elgin and Arnold Mitchell, 'Voluntary Simplicity', *Coevolution Quarterly*, No. 14, Summer 1977. Elgin and Mitchell estimate that as many as five million people in the U.S. are more or less committed to Options II and especially III.

3. E.g. David Dickson, *Alternative Technology and the Politics of Technical Change* (Fontana, 1974); Bob Young, 'Science *is* Social Relations', *Radical Science Journal*, No. 5, 1977, PDC, 27 Clerkenwell Close, London EC1 – or any number of Radical Science Journals.

4. E.g. *The Rise of the Meritocracy 1870-2033*, by Michael Young (Penguin, 1958); *Player Piano* by Kurt Vonnegut, Jr (Panther, 1974).

5. Robert Gilman, 'Job Sharing is Good', *Coevolution Quarterly*, No. 17, Spring 1978.

6. Mike Cooley, 'Lucas' Socially Useful Prototypes', *Undercurrents*, No. 26, February-March 1978.

7. *Lucas: An Alternative Plan*, Institute for Workers' Control, Pamphlet No. 54, Gamble Street, Nottingham NG7 4ET.

8. Ivan Illich, *Tools for Conviviality* (Calder and Boyars, 1973).

9. Elgin and Mitchell, see note 2.

10. James Robertson, *The Sane Alternative*, 7 St Anne's Villas, London W11, 1978; Peter Cadogan, *Direct Democracy*, 1 Hampstead Hill Gardens, London NW3, 1975; Scott Burns, *The Household Economy* (The Boston Herald American, Inc., 1976); Jay Gershuny, see note 2.

11. Edited by Godfrey Boyle and Peter Harper, Wildwood House, 1976. The rationale for the drawings is more fully explained here, especially in the section on 'Autonomy'.

12. Peter Kropotkin, *Fields Factories and Workshops Tomorrow*, edited with annotations by Colin Ward (Allen and Unwin, 1974).

13. John Garrett and Geoff Wright, 'Micro is Beautiful', *Undercurrents*, No. 27, April-May 1978.

14. Robert and Brenda Vale, *The Autonomous House* (Thames and Hudson, 1975).

15. Herbie Girardet, 'Small Tools for Small Firms', *Undercurrents*, No. 27, April-May 1978.

16. See 'Autonomy' in *Radical Technology* (note 11).

The group of Mondragon Co-operatives in the Basque Provinces of Spain as an intriguing and working model for small and medium-sized enterprises

Robert Oakeshott

Industrial co-operatives, democratically controlled enterprises, worker-owned businesses, what Mill and Marshall used to call 'Associations of Labourers', have not, on the whole, inspired either confidence or enthusiasm during the 150-odd years since the first experiments of this kind were launched in modern industrial society. More than that, any attempt, as here, to present a group of such enterprises as suggesting even partial solutions to the contemporary problems of how production should be organised is bound to run into considerable prejudice. It is as if solutions in this direction could have appeal only to people as remote from reality as Professor Galbraith's 'concerned nuns'. I shall, in fact, try to argue that one highly original and sophisticated group of co-ops, those centred on Mondragon in the Basque provinces of Spain, do apparently offer a working model particularly for small and medium-sized enterprises and a model which appears to solve a number of specific and pressing problems that enterprises in today's O.E.C.D. economies are increasingly running into. But before I do that I must deal briefly with the background to enterprises of this kind, with their record and with its interpretation. In the second main section I will present a sketch description of those Basque enterprises and how they work. In a third section I will suggest that there are several sets of problems to which they appear to offer better solutions than those vouchsafed by conventional enterprises, private or public.

As will be seen I am much indebted to the work of Professor Jaroslav Vaneck in this field as well as to one of his leading followers, Professor Derek Jones. In a different way I am indebted to the Joseph Rowntree Social Service Trust and to the Anglo-German Foundation for the Study of Industrial Society. The first has made it generally possible for me to work in this area over most of the last year. The second made possible a fairly detailed study of the Mondragon Co-operatives and of their celebrated banking and management institution, the Caja Laboral Popular – a study with which I was lucky enough to be associated.

Taking a broad view, support for enterprises structured in co-operative and/or democratic ways has been minimal in western countries since the Industrial Revolution. The capitalist and 'patronal' establishments, where they have bothered to notice such enterprises at all, have been hostile, tending to see them as a threat. The attitude of the full-blooded 'class struggle left' has tended to be hostile, too – seeing such enterprises as at best diversionary and at worst a betrayal of class unity and singleness of purpose. Marx himself was perhaps slightly more sympathetic. But he saw them as making, even when successful, at most a 'dwarfish' contribution in the struggle for the overthrow of capitalist arrangements. Essentially, he was dismissive. And if he valued such enterprises at all he did so *not* mainly as ends in themselves but as minor pawns in his class war.

The Fabian and bureaucratic socialist tradition has been perhaps the most hostile, anyway in Britain. The Webbs solemnly preached that such enterprises could never work: either their democratic structures broke down or they broke down as economic enterprises or both. The key argument in their writings is that to make management constitutionally subordinate to the workforce as a whole is to create an impossible set of relationships. But it can be plausibly argued that it was their own elitism and attachment to administrative solutions – as much as any practical argument – which determined their attitude.

The position of the trade union movement, at any rate in Britain and France, has tended to coincide with the Webbs'. There have, it is true, been cases of support by individual unions for individual enterprises of this kind. But because of their historic and continuing commitment to public ownership, the main stream of the union movements in both countries has been hostile, at least since the late 1880s.

Enthusiasm for such enterprises has, in fact, been confined on both left and right to small minority groups. There has been some support from Christian and libertarian socialists and from the 'respectable' anarchist tradition – from what Lenin would have dismissed as the 'infantile' left. And, of course, there is some implicit support in the writings of William Morris. Moving from left to right, and if we can strip off an outer layer of eccentric pre-raphaelite drapery, we can find some support for them in the catholic 'distributist' tradition – associated with Chesterton and Belloc. On a solider footing (and one perhaps closer to the Acton Society's origins) there has been some support from the progressive and reformist tradition within the catholic church, associated traditionally with Leo XIII and more recently, by extension, with Simone Weil.

As for the central and mainstream tradition of liberal economics, Derek Jones has admirably characterised the prevailing attitude as one of 'sympathetic pessimism'. There has been sympathy for the rationale of these structures and for the values which implicitly underlie them. But there has been pessimism about their ability to succeed as business operations. Their record has been read in such a way that pessimistic conclusions have been drawn.

The only long-standing and significant challenge to the conventional reading of the record has come from Alfred Marshall. He did not attempt to deny that the record of these enterprises, as it stood, was unconvincing. Instead, he argued that it was largely irrelevant. His key point was that not the genuine article but broken-backed alternatives to it were what, in fact, had been tried. If the genuine article was tried, he asserted, then it 'could not but succeed'.

Up to quite recent times Marshall has been almost alone in arguing that given the right conditions and right structures such enterprises would prosper. But in the late 1960s and 1970s the situation has rather changed. In the first place Professor Jaroslav Vaneck has, in a series of writings, tried to show what the pre-conditions for the success of such enterprises are; and has gone on to argue that, when those are satisfied, they may be expected to outperform their conventional rivals. Secondly, the empirical record has been re-examined, most notably by Derek Jones. For his part, Jones has argued that the record isn't nearly as bad as the Webbs and the conventional wisdom more generally have made out. For what it's worth I have, myself, attempted to compliment Jones' work by seeking to 'explain' – or indeed 'explain away' – the relative weakness of the record, particularly in Britain and France. I have tried to so do by showing that these enterprises have suffered from various handicaps (poor management, poor access to capital, poor shop-floor motivation), some almost deliberately self-inflicted, some resulting from mistakes of structure, some imposed by the environment, but all of which can in principle be eliminated.

This re-examination of the record of co-operative and democratic enterprises has more or less coincided with the great increase in the questioning of conventional enterprise structures, private and public, which has been going on since 1968. And its less pessimistic conclusions have been greatly buttressed by the 'discovery' of the Mondragon group of co-ops in the Basque Provinces of Spain. For they appear to have provided what has previously been lacking: a sustained and convincing success story. The upshot appears to be that Marshall's position is in the process of being vindicated in each of its two main thrusts. First, the non-Mondragon record can be fairly convincingly explained by special handicaps: i.e. the genuine article was not being tried. Second, where the genuine article has been tried, viz at Mondragon, it has succeeded.

The Mondragon co-ops

Both the cutting edge and the great weight of the extended family of co-operatives centred on the town of Mondragon in the Basque Province of Guipuzcoa in Northern Spain, is provided today – as it has been since the first co-ops started production in the middle and late '50s – by a highly successful group of industrial enterprises. In 1976 there were a total of 62 in this industrial group, employing together over 14,000 people and with overall sales of nearly Pesetas 24,000m. The largest concern in the group, ULGOR, was also the oldest. It employed nearly 3,500 people and was in its twenty-second year. Six of its associated industrial enterprises had workforces of over 500 in '76. But nearly 90 per cent of those in the industrial group were small- or medium-sized manufacturing businesses employing anything from 25 to 500 people.

Yet it would be wrong to conclude from any 'average' figures that what we are dealing with here is the type of artisanal, very simple and very low technology enterprise which has been characteristic of workers' co-ops elsewhere and in the past. We might think of them rather as 'good second division' manufacturing enterprises. They include Spain's leading producers of machine tools. In the shape of ULGOR they count within their ranks the country's foremost producer of machine tools – washing machines, refrigerators and so on; they include producers of bulldozers, bicycles and building materials. They include foundries and forging operations. And their single largest sub-group consists of 'intermediate goods' manufacturers, which supply components of one kind or another to buyers both within the group and outside.

The quality performance of these enterprises has not yet been fully studied by outsiders in detail. Nevertheless, the group's global figures, for sales and value added per head, certainly look competitive. And this is more or less confirmed for the group in general by the export sales – 12.5 per cent of total sales in '76 – and for the machine tool producers in particular: 20 per cent of total sales from exports in the same year. Moreover, since the early '70s there have been dramatic individual successes in foreign markets when contracts have been won to supply complete plants to produce consumer durables, in Mexico, in the Soviet Union and in Tunisia. It seems perverse not to take this evidence at its face value or to suppose that the quality of performance we are dealing with is not something of which more conventional enterprises anywhere would be proud.

But though the core of the extended Mondragon family of co-ops consists of these manufacturing enterprises, a whole range of supporting, complementary and other activities are organised on a co-operative basis as well. There were five co-ops engaged in agricultural production in '76. There were a dozen schools structured as co-ops and as many housing co-ops. There was a chain of co-operative consumer stores. There was a sophisticated and most unusual educational hybrid – an institution offering courses from apprentice to university engineering degree level. There was a social welfare service organised on co-op lines. Above all, there was the first ever really dynamic and successful co-op bank – the Caja Laboral Popular – which combined with its role of banker and savings mobiliser the functions of group leadership and co-ordination and the provision of back-up professional and management advice.

Mondragon is a small town with the kind of site in a mountain valley from which most conventional planners would want to exclude modern industry in the name of preserving a 'natural visual amenity'. It is roughly 50km inland from both Bilbao and San Sebastian on the Biscay Coast but seems further because the roads are steep and winding and there is no railway connection. It has an ancient steel-making tradition and its swords are said to have been famous even before those of Toledo. But in the early 1940s, back to which the origins of the co-ops can be traced, it was economically, socially and in almost every other way deeply demoralised. With their fellow Basques the men and women of Mondragon had sided with the republic in the civil war; and having been overrun by Franco's armies they had to accept virtual occupation as well as the suppression of all normal political and trade union liberties.

The origins of the Mondragon co-ops can be traced back to the work of a Basque priest, Fr. Jose Maria Arizmendi, who arrived in the town in the early '40s with a special mission from his bishop to attend to the needs of youth. As a result of his efforts and through an extraordinarily successful mobilisation of grass-root community support a new technical school was established; and the abler students were later encouraged to extend their knowledge and skills by studying for engineering degrees, 'after hours', at a neighbouring university. In the early '50s a first batch of these students were duly awarded their degrees. So there can be little doubt about the technical quality of the training they had received at Fr. Arizmendi's new school. But in his teaching at the school Fr. Arizmendi had always given as much emphasis to progressive catholic social and economic doctrines as he had to the importance of technical excellence. So it was not altogether surprising that, after a short abortive spell trying to reform conventional industry from within, five of the first graduating batch established ULGOR as an independent new venture in 1955.

It is worth referring back to these origins even in a brief description of this kind for two main reasons. First, it is important to be clear what a large part individual and community self-reliance – as opposed to Government and other bureaucratic intervention – has played in the development of the co-ops from the start. Secondly, it is worth emphasising that it was the reformist social and economic doctrines of the church, rather than the teachings of Marx, or of the Fabian Socialists or indeed of the Rochdale Pioneers, which provided the ideology on which the productive enterprises came to be founded. Our starting point, one of ULGOR's founders told me in the early '70s, was a belief in the primacy of productive work and the importance of technical excellence on the one hand and a belief in progressive catholic values on the other. It may be true that much of the driving force which explains the rapid subsequent expansion of the co-ops has come from sublimated Basque nationalism. But that has only been channelled in the direction it has been channelled, because of the co-operative structures that had been established and thus, indirectly, because of the values which underlie them.

What is certain is the dynamism of Mondragon co-op development since ULGOR was first set up. So far as I know it is without parallel in the history of co-operative industrial enterprise. When ULGOR started production, manufacturing simple heating stoves, it had a labour force of 23. By 1960, with encouragement and help from ULGOR, the total number of industrial co-ops had grown to 8 and the combined labour force was approaching 400. Thereafter, partly as a result of the extra impetus supplied by the Caja Laboral Popular – which had first opened its doors in 1959 – the graph of expansion looks almost exponential. In fact between 1961 and 1976 industrial employment in the Mondragon group increased at an annual average of 800 new jobs and new industrial enterprises were created at a rate of between three and four each year. Moreover, with the single exception of an abortive foray into co-operative fishing boats, there has not been a single case of enterprise failure. Again, with that one exception, there has been no single example of bankruptcy, bad debt or even of involuntary redundancy. So the gross expansion rates and the net expansion rates effectively coincide. And the policy of growth continues: new enterprise creation is still going on at a rate of three or four each year. A record of successful job creation may not be directly relevant to this seminar. But in today's world of much higher unemployment, it is an increasingly important criterion of economic and social worthwhileness.

More immediately relevant to the subject matter of this seminar are the structural arrangements of these successful enterprises – and the nature of their relationships with C.L.P., with their local community, and with each other. I will deal first mainly with the internal structures of the industrial enterprises and then with their various external relationships.

Starting from a basic commitment to democratic enterprise self-government, both the internal structures of the Mondragon enterprises and their external relationships can best be understood, or so it seems to me, as a set of highly sophisticated balances. In the first place there is a balance between the democratic principle and a principle of management and general discipline. Secondly, there is a balance between the need for individual self-reliance, responsibility and work incentive on the one hand and the need for enterprise – and group – solidarity on the other. Thirdly, there is a balance between the need for individual enterprise and group strength on the one side and the need for good relationships with the local community on the other. Fourthly, there is a balance between the need to reward capital and the need to reward labour. Fifthly, there is a balance between the needs of the present and those of the future. Finally and perhaps most generally there is a balance between the need for the enterprises to follow the imperatives of the market and the need of the individual workers for job security.

The control arrangements governing these co-operative enterprises can be easily understood. In accordance with the principle of democratic self-government sovereign power rests with a general assembly of which the enterprise workforce, its entire workforce, and only its workforce are members. The Assembly's chief operational powers are to elect a governing or control board, the Junta Rectora. In turn it is the Junta Rectora which appoints the general manager or chief executive. He or she, once appointed, selects the subordinate staff in the management team. The separate functions of management are specifically defined and protected by the co-op's constitution. In these ways and by provisions that the chief executive must be appointed for a period of years and cannot normally be interfered with in the normal exercise of his functions – but can only be removed if he proves incompetent – the principle of discipline is introduced. It is further buttressed, as we shall see later, by the enterprise's 'contract of association' with the C.L.P. In these ways, or so it seems, the Mondragon co-ops have got round the difficulty, identified by the

Webbs, of making management constitutionally to the workforce. Essentially, the arrangement is similar to the one which is said to prevail in Yugoslavia. The sovereign workforce takes the policy decisions; in all other main ways, except in matters of style, management behaves as it does in a conventional business.

The ownership and the profit (and loss) sharing arrangements are rather more complex. But here again we start from something like a modified version of the democratic self-government principle: the workforce, the entire workforce and only the workforce must be the owners of the enterprise. But ownership is not divided into absolutely equal portions as is power in the general assembly on the basis of 'one man one vote'. There are two modifications. The first is that an important ownership element must be collective and belong indivisibly to all the enterprise members as a whole. The second is that after an initial 'capital contribution' which is equal for everyone, individual capital accounts will subsequently be adjusted upwards or downwards – as the enterprise makes profits or losses – NOT on an equal basis but on the basis of individual earnings.

In 1977 the actual capital contribution figure was around Pesetas 120,000 for those entering existing co-ops and roughly twice that for those joining new ventures being started from scratch. In an immediate and irreversible transfer, 20 per cent of these capital contributions is shifted into a collective and indivisible enterprise account when a newcomer joins the enterprise and the balance credited to the capital account of the individual. Thereafter, at the end of each annual accounting period, both the individual accounts and the collective one are written up or down to absorb the net profits or losses of the co-op. In the case of losses the rule is that not more than 30 per cent may be debited against the collective account. In the case of profits the rules are more complex. Not less than 20 per cent must be credited to the collective account; and not less than 10 per cent must be spent on educational or social projects for the benefit of the local community. Thus a maximum of 70 per cent may be credited to individual capital accounts. But that percentage figure is reduced if profits are abnormally high, in which case either the collective fund, or spending on community projects, will benefit.

Two other key provisions associated with these ownership arrangements need to be mentioned. The first, which serves to protect individual interests, is that the individual capital accounts are periodically written up, in line with revaluations of the enterprise assets, to take account of inflation. The second, which serves greatly to enhance the financial strength of the enterprise, is that individuals may not normally make withdrawals from their capital accounts, except on retirement or if they leave the enterprise. Moreover, if a person simply chooses to leave – and is not forced to do so by circumstances which are beyond control – then he or she risks losing, at the discretion of the Junta Rectora, up to 20 per cent of the accumulated savings in his or her capital account.

More famous, and some would argue more debatable, are the rules which determine how wage rates are fixed. The first and most important lays down the general principle that the differential limit between the highest and lowest rates paid may not exceed 3:1, though this is qualified by the provision which permits payments of up to 50 per cent above their normal salaries in the case of senior management and professionals to take account of extra hours worked or of unusual responsibilities. The second lays down that the bottom rate 1 on the differential scale must be fixed in line with, or at a maximum of a few percentage points above, the going rate for similar work in the neighbourhood. The effect of the two together is, of course, that while the shopfloor is paid at rates comparable to or very slightly above those in neighbouring conventional enterprises, the top executives and professionals receive decidedly less than their counterparts in the private or public sectors. However, it is correct to point out that the co-ops see nothing particularly sacrosanct in either a 3:1 or a 4.5:1 set of differential limits. What they emphasise, on the other hand, is the importance of striking a balance between the constraints of the market on one side and the need for internal enterprise solidarity on the other.

In the Mondragon set-up, the heart of the ancient conflict between capital and labour is, of course, eviscerated by restricting relevant capital ownership to the workforce and by insisting that the entire workforce is made up of capital owners. Further, and in line with traditional co-op principles, the individual capital stakes are basically rewarded by a fixed rate of interest – which may not exceed 6 per cent. On the other hand the remuneration of capital is significantly enhanced in the Mondragon group by the rule which lays down that the allocation of profits (or losses) to individual capital accounts should be calculated on the basis not just of wage payments but on the basis of the sum of wage and interest payments together. There are ideological reasons for this – a desire to rehabilitate capital as a valued and acknowledged partner of labour in the production process. There are also practical arguments. For one effect of this provision is to strike a fairer balance between the claims of long-term workforce members and those of more recent arrivals.

But of all the rules which govern the arrangements of these co-ops perhaps the most important, from the viewpoint of the ordinary shopfloor worker, are those relating to job security. There is first the fairly familiar rule which lays down that the workforce must agree to work flexibly and 'out of trade' when circumstances require it. And this is frequently extended through either formal, informal or *ad hoc* inter-enterprise arrangements which allow workers to be transferred to work in a different co-op should the need arise. But, thirdly, under a key provision, a co-oper worker is guaranteed the indefinite payment of wages, at 80 per cent of normal rates in the event of work stoppage and when no alternative employment is available; and there are detailed provisions about how the required funds should be debited against collective and/or individually owned accounts should the need arise. It is this 'earnings guarantee'[1] which perhaps more than anything else reconciles the ordinary shopfloor worker to the operations of the market. It is said to explain why the co-op's profit figures appear to be lower than what their sales results would otherwise suggest.

One other set of provisions of special interest to the shopfloor needs to be mentioned. Notwithstanding the removal of the old conflict of interest between capital and labour, it is not assumed that the work process will be entirely conflict-free. The co-ops were, of course, first established and have very largely developed in a political environment in which independent trade union activity was illegal. To deal with conflict at work – and as a substitute for trade unions – elected social councils are a feature of at least all the larger co-op enterprises.

The relationship between the co-ops and the local community is given formal expression, as we have seen, both by the provisions which determine wage rates and, equally important, by the allocation of at least a 10 per cent profit share to community social and educational projects. But the overlap of interest is, in fact, seen in much wider terms. It is frequently emphasised that it is the local community which, by placing its savings with the C.L.P., has supplied he co-ops with the great bulk of all their capital requirements over and above what has been contributed by individual worker members. And it is partly no doubt as an acknowledgement of this indebtedness that the co-ops continue to commit themselves to what they call their 'open door' policy. By that they mean a policy of continuous expansion and job creation.

There is one formal sub-grouping, Ularco, which brings together ULGOR and five of the other enterprises in the industrial group. Essentially, it is a voluntary federation of autonomous enterprises. Its rationale is to combine the benefits of both larger and smaller scale. It allows for joint planning, joint purchasing and joint selling. It also allows for the redeployment of labour as between its component enterprises as we noticed more generally a moment ago. Progressively, too, the component enterprises have decided to pool and then average – for the purpose of individual capital account adjustments – their profits and losses. This last is claimed as an example of genuine grassroots solidarity arising spontaneously upwards from the bottom. Now the policy is to encourage similar voluntary federations among other members of the overall group, either on an industrial or local basis.

The Caja Laboral Popular

Yet the real key to the success and the dynamism of this extended family of co-ops in the Basque provinces of Spain is almost certainly provided by the Caja Laboral Popular. Its most conventional role is that of mobilising local savings to meet the capital needs of the group – needs which are obviously swollen by the group's commitment to the open door policy of continuous expansion. Right from its establishment in 1959 it has performed that task with remarkable success. And its success has, if anything, increased over time. Between '66 and '74 there was a 35-fold increase in its assets and a 22-fold increase in the numbers of its savings accounts. At the end of '76 its total balance sheet assets exceeded Pesetas 31,000m. and its own capital and reserves were in excess of Pesetas 1,500m. Even more important, since the early '70s, the expansion of the group has not been subject to any directly financial constraints. Perhaps for the first time in the history of co-operative industrial enterprises, the Mondragon group has come to enjoy access to capital which may well be superior to that of its competitors in the private and public sectors.

But much more unusual than the C.L.P.'s role as a mobiliser of local savings is its function as a management advice agency and a provider of back-up professional support. These specialised tasks are undertaken by its Empresarial Division, the staff of which numbers close on 100. There are accountants, engineers, economists, architects, people with experience of marketing and of the management of production, town planners and even psychologists. Alongside the management teams of the productive enterprises themselves, the professional staff of the Empresarial Division supply the essential management discipline which has so often been lacking in co-operative endeavours. The key instrument in maintaining this discipline is the 'contract of association' which all the other co-ops in the extended family must sign with the Caja. Spelled out in the contract are all the various rules – about capital contributions, profit (and loss) distributions, wage rates, the democratic control structure and so on – which determine how the co-ops are regulated. Spelled out, too, are requirements to discuss annual budgets and forward plans and to pass on monthly result figures for comparison with original projections. Of course, any co-op, as an independent enterprise, is free to negotiate its withdrawal from the contract of association with the Caja. But to do so would be to deny itself preferential access both to capital and to professional support. None of the co-operatives have so far attempted to move down that road.

The other very specific task which the Empresarial Division undertakes is the midwifing of new co-op ventures. Two considerations seem to dominate its activities in this area. There is first an almost absolute rule that the opening initiative in relation to any possible new venture must come upwards from the bottom, i.e. from the prospective workforce. The second is that any possible new ventures initiated in this way must be subjected to the most detailed feasibility studies and other procedures before any final decisions are taken about whether to go forward or not. In practice these procedures may take up to two years to complete. And in practice a positive decision is reached about not more than 40 per cent of the initiatives which come forward in the first place.

Finally, the C.L.P. is the main leadership body for the entire extended family of these Mondragon co-operatives. Up to quite recently its leadership role has covered, as well as general policy questions, technical and market oriented matters like product investigation and selection. However, these functions are being progressively taken over by a new institution which will have the main responsibility for technical research and development. Nevertheless, it seems probable that the Caja in general and the Empresarial division in particular will continue to be the main source of new ideas for the group as a whole.

In technical language the C.L.P. is a second degree co-op. Unlike the directly productive enterprises it is not controlled exclusively by those who work in it. Its sovereign general assembly contains two categories of members, bank staff on the one hand and elected representatives from the associated co-ops on the other and it contains them in equal numbers. These control arrangements provide an excellent safeguard against the risk that the bank will use its central position and its control over finance to accumulate an unacceptable amount of power. For it can always be held in check, in its own sovereign assembly, by the representatives of the associated enterprises. In practice the relationship between the bank and the associated co-ops seems to be a symbiotic one characterised by feelings of solidarity and of interdependent mutualism. Evidence of this is provided by the decision, taken some years ago, that the C.L.P. staff should not simply enjoy individual shares in its profits as happens in the directly productive co-ops. Because the bank's profits were consistently above the average for the associated enterprises, it as decided that individual capital accounts of bank staff members should be credited each year with the average individual profit share for the entire extended family of co-ops.

Some conclusions

It is easy to see that the Mondragon group of Co-ops offers *prima facie* solutions to a number of quite specific problems. One of the biggest handicaps under which small- and medium-sized enterprises are universally believed to suffer is inadequate access to finance. In its successful mobilisation of local savings the C.L.P. seems unquestionably to have solved that problem for its associated co-ops.

Small and medium-sized enterprises, whatever their structures, may also suffer from inadequate access to top level professional manpower. Industrial co-ops have been traditionally plagued by a further problem: management has been unable to exercise satisfactory discipline over the workforce. Here again the Mondragon group offers apparently successful solutions. A pool of high level manpower is available in the shape of the Empresarial Division of the Caja. Discipline is maintained partly through the mechanism of the 'contract of association' and partly by a careful definition of management functions at enterprise level. A reconciliation appears to have been achieved between the need for management to be constitutionally subordinate to the workforce and the requirement that it should carry out all normal management functions apart from basic policy making.

In the shape of Ularco the Mondragon group offers further an apparent solution to the problem of combining the advantages of both large scale and small scale operations. This is a voluntary federation of autonomous enterprises. At least in theory its component units enjoy some of the advantages of scale – joint sales, joint purchasing and so on – while retaining some of the advantages of their own separate identity. A most striking feature of Ularco is that the sovereign workforces of its component units have freely chosen to extend their co-operation into the most highly sensitive areas of profit and loss sharing. It seems perverse not to interpret these decisions as stemming from genuine feelings of solidarity.

But the really intriguing implications of the Mondragon co-ops seem to me to be a good deal wider and to extend outwards beyond the problems of small and medium-sized organisations with which this seminar is most directly concerned. In effect the Mondragon experience seems to me to point in a number of rather optimistic directions.

The first is towards the elimination of the ancient conflict between capital and labour and thus eventually towards the end of the class war. Apart from its historical and cultural content, that conflict stems structurally from the traditional assignment to capital both of enterprise control and of the ownership of variable enterprise income: viz profits. Break those links and, as at Mondragon, assign ultimate control to the workforce, restrict ownership to the workforce and insist on all the workforce being owners, and the whole basis of the conflict falls away. Of course, unless discipline is safeguarded, such arrangements can produce their own problems. However, we have already seen how the Mondragon group has overcome the traditional co-op difficulties of poor management and discipline.

The second is that the ordinary shopfloor worker can be reconciled to a modified market system. His chief objections have, of course, always been that the market system favours the stronger: that in its allocation of profits, in its determination of wage differentials, in its lack of concern for job security it unfairly exploits – discriminates against – working people and the weaker members of society more generally. Mondragon offers ways of dealing with all these objections. In the case of profits the solution is clear-cut. In the case of differentials it is sought as a balance between market constraints and the need for enterprise solidarity. In the case of job security it is achieved by the provision of an indefinite earnings guarantee.

Thirdly and more generally the Mondragon experience suggests that it is possible to strike a reasonable balance between the need to encourage individual self-reliance and responsibility on the one hand and the need to encourage fraternal arrangements and group solidarity on the other. We need not settle for a world in which virtue is exclusively concentrated at one or other of the two ends of this spectrum. We must not discourage self-reliance, as the bureaucratic socialists have done since the Webbs or even before. But nor must we discourage solidarity – as Mrs Thatcher and those who think like her seem compelled to do.

Fourthly, the Mondragon experience seems to suggest that arrangements can be devised which lead to a progressive spreading out of wealth and decision-making over time, rather than their progressive concentration: and that enterprises can forge real and close links with their local communities.

Finally, the Mondragon structure obviously allows the possibility that the workforce over time will have much more influence on the choice of technologies used. It happens that the initiatives already taken at Mondragon in this direction have been only partly a success. But there are exciting possibilities down this road in the long run.

Postscript 1982

The story of the Mondragon co-ops over the last years of the 1970s and into the early 1980s has essentially two aspects. First the statistics show an impressive record of continued expansion: the number of enterprises, the total of those employed, and overall group sales (and particularly export sales) have all increased substantially. Second, and especially over the last three years, the co-ops have had to cope with an increasingly ferocious recession. Unemployment in the Basque province had risen to 13.9 per cent of the registered labour force by the end of 1980 and was still going up. Bankruptcies proliferated throughout the region. Yet up to early 1982 no single member of the co-operative had permanently lost a job and the number of temporary lay-offs within the group remained negligible. Moreover, and in contrast to the experience of the private sector, there had been no co-operative bankruptcy.

By the end of 1980 the number of industrial enterprises in the group had risen to 83, and it has continued to increase since then. The most recent published statistics are from the annual report of the Caja Laboral Popular for the year 1980:

MONDRAGON INDUSTRIAL CO-OPS

	1977	*1978*	*1979*	*1980*
Employment (Nos.)	15716	16230	17129	18058
Sales (Pesetas Millions)	34119	43753	57099	68705
Exports (Pesetas Millions)	4115	5884	9040	13504

The figures for 1981, when they become available later this year, will certainly show that real growth has continued – that employment numbers are up and that both total sales and exports have increased at constant prices (allowing for inflation). It is also true that the current five-year plan projects further real expansion at least up to the middle of the decade.

The obvious immediate question is this. How have the co-operatives managed both to avoid bankruptcies and permanent redundancies and, in fact, to go on expanding when, all around them, the recession has been taking its toll? And the follow-up question is obvious enough, too. Is it realistic to suppose that the group will manage to weather the rest of the recession and to continue to expand in spite of it?

A combination of the group's key priorities and various special measures go far to explain what has been achieved over the last few years. Essentially, the group has given top priority to its employment objectives and has been prepared to do so at the cost of allowing its profits to be squeezed to almost nothing and even perhaps beyond. From a figure of 6 per cent of sales (or roughly Pesetas 2000m.) in 1977, profits have declined in each successive year and were only barely positive over the 12 months to the end of 1980. It is widely anticipated that profits in 1981 will turn out to have been 'negative'.

In giving a higher priority to employment and by a parallel policy of aiming to increase its market share during a recession, the group has obviously reflected the preferences of the great majority of its members. However, it is worth recalling that the larger Japanese companies tend to pursue precisely the same employment and share of market objectives during a recession and to do so, equally, at the expense of profits. It is also worth pointing out that, so long as these policies are pursued within safe limits, they are entirely rational, especially for businesses which, like those of the Mondragon Group, have no outside shareholders to worry about.

These general policies have been buttressed over the last 18 months by two important special measures. To begin with a majority of the co-operatives voted in their general assemblies last year to require all members to increase their capital contributions. Depending on salary levels the extra capital contributions, which may be sub-scribed in a number of different ways but must be fully paid within 24 months, range from Pesetas 55,000 to Pesetas 165,000 (or from roughly £250 to £750). In total something like Pesetas 700m. (or about £4m.) has been committed in this way and the money will significantly offset declining, zero, or 'negative' profits in the balance sheets of the individual co-operative enterprises.

Secondly, and during 1980, most of the co-operatives agreed to a small increase in the social security contributions paid by members to the group's own social security organisation Lagon Aro. Those contributions were raised by 0.25 per cent of gross income. The money so raised was set aside so that Largon Aro would be in a position to reimburse co-operatives for most of this expenditure in the case of temporary lay-offs – during which members are entitled to 80 per cent of their normal earnings. Up to early 1982 there had, in fact, been only negligible calls on these new funds.

Concurrently, with the introduction of these higher social security contributions, most of the group's co-operatives also agreed to participate in a new scheme for the switching of members to co-ops where business was strong – either on a temporary or a permanent basis. It is true that switching within Mondragon's various sub-grouping – ULARCO for example – has been going on for many years. The new scheme should be understood as a major extension of an old practice. Though the number of switchings or 'exchanges' over the scheme's first year – around 2000 'man months' – was quite small, the total of those affected was far greater than the number of those temporarily laid off. In other words the new scheme has made a real contribution to the stability of the group's employment.

Looked at together these special measures are evidence of a realism and maturity on the part of the ordinary membership of the co-operative. For they show that the members are prepared to impose short-term sacrifices upon themselves in order to strengthen the safeguards of their own long-term employment.

But though, therefore, what lies behind the achievements of the last few years can be quite easily explained it is harder to be sure about the medium-term future. That, of course, is because no one can tell how long the present recession will persist. There are certainly those at Mondragon who believe that more indirect measures may be necessary before it is over. The possibility that it will make sense to close down a few of the smaller and weaker enterprises – and redeploy their members elsewhere – cannot at all be ruled out. And there may also have to be some quite major redeployment of labour out of the largest co-operative, ULGOR.

But despite these uncertain and painful prospects the group's confidence in its long-term future seems well grounded enough. For it is based on two crucial comparative assets in relation to which the Mondragon co-operatives are clearly better placed than their private sector counterparts in Spain's population of small and medium-sized businesses. With their own bank, the C.L.P., behind them they are financially stronger than their average private competitor. And with the bank's 'empresarial or management services' division they can call on professional resources of an unusually high order.

One final point is worth adding to this postscript. Whatever else is true, the last few years have seen an astonishing upsurge of interest in co-operative or co-operative type businesses in general and in Mondragon in particular. The general species was powerfully commended during 1981 by such distinguished advocates as Pope John Paul II (in his encyclical, *Laborem Exercens*) and by the Nobel prize-winning economist, Professor James Meade (in his new book about 'stagflation'). Mondragon in the meantime has attracted quite exceptional attention and a growing army of visitors. Among the most notable of these last was a delegation from the Welsh TUC. As a result of their visit plans are now well advanced to launch a major Mondragon building initiative in South Wales. It seems likely that we shall see other similar attempts elsewhere.

ENDNOTE

1. Rather similar earnings guarantees are, of course, offered in many large Japanese companies.

'Autogestion'

Albert Meister

Although the word 'autogestion' is fashionable nowadays, the ideas which it embraces are, however noble, still extremely vague. For those who seek new revolutionary myths, autogestion means the end of exploitation of man by man, the abolition of the wage earning classes and the advent of democracy. For others, less idealistic and more interested in immediate results, it means simply participation in certain decisions. For yet others, who are interested in the mechanics of decision-making, it boils down to the democratic process, to consensus. In the extreme case, people refer to autogestion when the participants in a given area of human relations decide for themselves what to do during the few days that they escape from the constraints and inequalities of their daily lives and conditions of work.

To get a clearer view, it seems first of all necessary to distinguish between the way in which organisations function and the way in which they are structured – one can always find democratic structures the procedures of which are hardly democratic and vice-versa. Furthermore, since the word 'autogestion' is taken from real life, we must try to see what it means where it is used, i.e. we should start from an analysis of experiments which claim to be self-managing – to start from reality and not from hopes of what 'autogestion' might one day be.

I. Structure of 'Autogestion'

There are three basic types of self-managing structure.
a) *Co-operative 'autogestion'* which is what one finds in Western co-operatives. These enterprises are units of collective ownership and management of the means of production. The workers themselves are the bosses; power is attached to the individual, not to the number of shares held. Under this heading we can include the Israeli Kibbutzim which, like these other enterprises, are part of a liberal economy and make decisions which reflect the state of the market. However, in practice all types of co-operative (agricultural, industrial, financial, etc) today experience a progressive weakening of the independence of the worker-owner as worker-manager. This is so especially with regard to credit which is extended to them by centralised organisations headed by public servants. As we shall see with regard to Yugoslavian autogestion, the banks intervene in management decisions so that

important decisions come to be regarded as beyond the scope of the democratic process within the enterprise. It is no exaggeration to say that in France state intervention in the affairs of co-operatives is more noticeable than in Yugoslavia, where it is, however, more oppressive.

b) *Socialist 'autogestion' in a planned economy*. This was invented by Yugoslavia at the beginning of the 1950s and is, in reality, a combination of the typical features of a planned economy with the idea of having democratic structures within firms. The national plan is decentralised to republic level and thence to commune level. More significant in size than our Western communes, Yugoslavian communes exercise a planning authority over their territory and a trusteeship over their firms. The all-important linking mechanism between the democratic process in the firm and this planning authority is afforded by the procedure for the election of directors to the firm which is supervised by a mixed commission comprising both members of the workers' council and representatives of communal bodies. In fact this 'autogestion' is really a 'co-gestion' of state and workers' bodies: the state fixes the rules, including those of how the profits are to be shared at the end of the year. Naturally, the workers would like to participate in the allocation of these shares, so that it will be seen how severe a limit this sets to the powers of democracy at work. Likewise, the state controls fiscal policy, prices and credit. Thus, democracy within the firm is seriously limited, even though the elaboration of the plan and economic policies should result from the process of propositions and counter-propositions from the different levels of workers concerned in them. During the 1950s this system succeeded in making easy the growth of investment and in limiting consumption. Feelings of brotherhood and post-war egalitarianism facilitated this, but there were also times when it was necessary to give out some 'pocket money' (Tito's own words) so that the workers could have a share out to decide on in their assemblies at the end of the year.

c) *'Autogestion' of a socialist market economy*. Since the beginning of the 1960s, and notably after the reforms of 1965, state controls have been diminishing and the regulating function of a National Plan has been replaced by the banking system. We are not concerned here with the causes of these changes, of which the most important is, as I see it, the integration of Yugoslavia into the Western economy and the weakening of the faith in the construction of a Socialist society. Structures of democracy in firms appear reinforced because directors are at present named by workers' councils. Although half of all products (especially foodstuffs) have fixed prices, there is competition between firms. Public investment has not ceased, but credit is more and more the business of banks motivated by the prospect of profit. Communes still exist, but have increasingly less say in economic planning.

To all appearances, 'autogestion' emerges strengthened from the weakening of centralised planning. In practice, however, the banker wants to limit the risk to the money he has contributed by controlling its use and by intervening more or less directly in the choices made by the firms' directors. At the present time, although property remains nationalised in Yugoslavia, one is struck by the similarity between this type of 'autogestion' and cooperative 'autogestion' in a country like France. Yugoslavian firms have become competitive co-operatives: faced with the banks, the Treasury and different sorts of rules, they have hardly any say in their own management. Nevertheless, compared with Western economies, in which the co-operative sectors are very weak, the Yugoslavian market economy still distinguishes itself by the size of its self-managed sector. Side by side, the private sector is constantly growing and everywhere there arise more and more acute desires for individual accomplishment and promotion.

These three different structures of autogestion can therefore ultimately be reduced to two: that of the planned economy and that of the market economy. However, the choice of one or the other is not entirely free. If a subsidiary aim of the first kind of 'autogestion' was to break up the centralisation and bureaucratism caused by planning machinery, it was still true that the state intended to remain master of the economy. Decentralised and in harmony with businesses, the plan came closer to the people, but it continued to be regarded, in the best Soviet tradition, as proof of the state's crucial role in directing the economy. In fact it was an institutional symbol, in the same way that people still think of nationalisation as a signpost on the road to socialism.

Autogestion in a market economy, on the other hand, is no longer directed by a plan. It is a concept made up of a multitude of organisations, partners and centres of decision-making which channel the behaviour of self-managed firms in the direction of more or less clearly defined economic policies. These policies arrive precisely at the moment when the plan of yesterday's fashion appears too unsophisticated to direct the growth of an ever more complex economy. It is therefore the development of the economy, not the plan, which dictates the choice of struture of 'autogestion'.

Such a statement is less banal than it may at first appear if we think of the diversity of the centres of decision-making in a modern economy that extends beyond national frontiers. Previous distinctions between economics, society and politics are now much less clear-cut and unless society were to undergo a fundamental change by a re-think of its objectives or through war or revolution, changes only seem likely to arise from adjustments, repairs and corrections of detail. An overall view of everything is no longer possible and that is why national plans which claim to embrace all national change are essentially ineffective.

If one takes this context into account, then despite the enthusiasm and high ambitions of its protagonists, one must concede that the attempt to find new structures of 'autogestion' is reduced to reformism. It is just a question of finding the means to democratise the elaboration and control of economic and social policies or to reinforce and rearrange the structures of participation in businesses. There still remains the long-term problem of making these structures come alive. That seems the fundamental problem.

II. The Working of 'Autogestion'

If the structure of 'autogestion' plays a determining role as the framework of economic democracy, it is not a sufficient condition of it and we see self-managed firms which are no more than sorts of disguised employers' businesses; we see also entire sectors of 'autogestion' which are only organs of transmission of the national plan. Here again we will have to distinguish the problems on firm level from those which arise from the inclusion of the firm in a planned system or group stimulated by economic policies. On the level of the firm, the conditions of the operation of 'autogestion' are well known and we can limit ourselves here to a few reminders:

Whatever type of 'autogestion' there is – co-operative or of the Yugoslavian type – the founders have always believed that the suppression of class conflict, thanks to the socialisation of the means of production, would be enough to improve and transform the conditions of work. However, other conflicts have emerged which were previously obscured by the boss-worker conflict. Once formal equality is realised, natural inequalities only appear more flagrant and give rise to new stratifications, sometimes more odious than those which were based on money. For example, the triumph of the most intelligent who, when in power, are rarely the most human or the supremacy of those who conform most rigidly to official ideologies. Hence also the victory of comrades elected to posts of responsibility thanks to their popularity on the shop floor; and the increasing power of those who are most enterprising and whose initiative and business sense will be more useful to the growth of investments than to the workings of democratic procedures.

However benevolent the authority in the firm it tends, as time passes, to crystallise and, sometimes unwittingly, it opposes change. The very constraints of efficiency are invoked as obstacles to rotation and to the arrival of new men in the management teams. It is always unpopular to denounce this tendency as the protagonists of 'autogestion' seem usually to be men of the party apparatuses whose positions are threatened by this principle of rotation, as the Yugoslavian experience will bear witness.

It must also be said that the average man is conditioned by his upbringing, religion and education to trust and be led by his superiors, in this case his bosses who are reluctant to return to the ranks. One of the difficulties of democracy of self-management stems from attitudes of submission instilled by these 'institutions'.

Another point to raise is that of efficiency: I am not going to say that autogestion is inefficient, however 'autogestion' does signify the taking into consideration of other values in the firm apart from those that pertain to maximum profitability. To self-manage implies informing one's personnel and most often forming it in such a way that information can be received and made the basis of decision. To self-manage means to discuss, to debate and to control the way in which decisions are carried out. Even if the workers do not have to 'decide everything', it nevertheless follows that democracy uses up time and energy. It is expensive, and the price to pay includes that of time itself; the time taken for formulation, dialogue and propagation.

The first error of 'autogestion' was to believe that all these items cost nothing, as if they were an extra 'windfall' from the adoption of the socialist principle. It was because of this belief that people neglected to work out the cost of meetings, of information and of much else.

There was a second error of 'autogestion'. This was to claim that self-managed enterprises were to be at least as profitable as capitalist enterprises, even though they had to support (although not cost) the burden of democracy. It is not surprising that self-managed firms in a competitive environment have jettisoned every item which for the sake of pure profit has not been indispensable. This has meant in the longer term the abandoning of any attempt to make democratic structures come to life and of belief in any values other than profitability.

Then there is a third source of error – 'autogestion' in a planned economy means that many of the tasks of liaison and coordination between firms are executed by the administration – and we all know how socialist countries suffer from their bureaucracies! In the case of Yugoslavia, it has even been said that recourse to the principle of competition between firms was the only way to shake up the control mechanism of the administration itself. Autogestionary thought must therefore pose itself the problems of the transformation (rather than extinction) of the state.

If, on the other hand, autogestion exists in a market economy, the need for liaisons, coordinations and understandings between firms creates intermediaries of all kinds – agents, advisers, representatives, brokers, etc. Even if it does have the reputation of being parasitic, greedy for fees and commissions this class of middle men wields a good deal of power in firms. And the more complex the economy, the more this class grows in number and influence. These agents do not exploit a large staff (at the most a few secretaries) and do not have a high fixed capital (a telephone, a telex) and even in Yugoslavia they are considered harmless artisans. Yet it is perhaps they who are masters of the modern art of exploitation of man by man. It is they who understand how to use knowledge, information and the power of organisation to make profit out of their comrades toil.

People have always perceived the problem as that of making 'autogestionary' structures work. Could there be another way? Why not first encourage all the comrades, before they acquire prestige, status or position simply to show that they can live 'autogestionary' attitudes. Let them live autogestion before giving it structures!

III. Collective Management and 'Autogestion'

During the 1950s, some Yugoslavian firms invited the intervention of Western firms which specialised in staff education and human relations. Even in democratically structured firms it seemed necessary to set up new kinds of relationships between staff and management because the transformation of structures and the abolition of individual ownership of the means of production did not yet seem to have changed the attitudes of the bosses nor the authoritarian conditions of work.

If the socialisation of the means of production can still be thought of as a necessary preliminary to the creation of autogestionary structures, the facts clearly indicate that these transformations do not change daily life and do not alter the quality of social conditions. It may be true to say that changes in the infrastructure would determine changes in the way people feel and live together, but that is only true in the very long term, whereas people want a better quality of life right away.

In contrast to the structural 'autogestion' discussed until now, experimental attempts at collective management which intend to change the quality of life are being made at grass root level: more or less permanent communes, pressure groups on local or consumer issues, wild-cat strike collectives, more or less delinquent gangs, reciprocal teaching classes, religious celebrations without priests, extended families, etc. The motivation behind this attempt at a new quality of life is, crudely, this: We don't care about big structural changes because 50 years of socialism have changed nothing. We want to live differently right away and we don't care if our little experiments are considered insignificant, marginal and reactionary.

These experiments simply show another approach to 'autogestion' which gives precedence to the process of collective management over procedural change. There are those who suggest a rapprochement of the two tendencies, but this is to forget that the Church does not tolerate such heresies. The big organisations which are committed to autogestion will become bogged down in arguments about structural changes whilst ignoring the real reforms being carried out outside their scope. The example will not be heeded by those who are blinded by Marxist rhetoric and its belief in the all-importance of structural changes. They forget that it is with the limited and deficient men of today that the world of tomorrow will have to be constructed.

In contrast we find the pragmatism of those who try to make their structures of autogestion work – to educate, to inform, to create participation and to adapt what is done elsewhere. A good example of this order of priorities was given us in December 1972 at the conference of sociologists of autogestion in Dubrovnik. The Yugoslavs were finally able to have an easier dialogue with American industrial sociologists who came in large numbers, rich with their research into the working of organisations. Dialogues of reformists, it will be said with scorn, since it is the done thing to forget that autogestion is merely a reform of the centralised Soviet system which was justified, in the Yugoslavian case, after the break with the Soviet model. But then, do not the fruits of revolution always appear as insipid reforms in comparison with the desire to change mankind which inspired them?

So that, in contrast to other revolutionary myths, the dream of autogestionary socialism does not end up as a series of minor reforms or a system of 'co-gestions', should we not now examine what I have called above 'collective management'? We should try and learn from the experiences of those who want to live differently. At the same time we should penetrate big companies to analyse concretely what modern techniques of management mean – to see, for example, if participative management through objectives can come down to all levels of staff – and examine new modes of organisation of work – redefinition of tasks, personalised time tables, the dismantling of production lines, etc. We should encourage spontaneous 'autogestions' and instigate empirical studies of existing 'autogestions' in order to construct an 'autogestionary' practice for daily life. The great movements of humanity were great precisely because of their initiators' ignorance and because they refused to accept a certain world order.

Translated by Simon Carter.

Small business in Italy – the submerged economy

Julia Bamford

The contrasts and paradoxes of the Italian economy are a constant source of amazement for observers in other industrialised countries. The Italian economy is permanently in a state of crisis, so much so that for the Italians the very word has been stripped of all real meaning. New expressions have to be invented to cope with problems such as an inflation rate of over 20 per cent, a devalued currency, an unemployment rate of 1.5 million, wildcat strikes and mastodontic state corporations staggering under mountains of debt.

Nonetheless, amid this apparently hopeless situation, Italy has managed in recent years to consolidate its position as the West's sixth economic power and both in 1979 and 1980 achieved the fastest growth rate of any of the EEC countries. This is all the more remarkable in a country short of agricultural land and almost bereft of raw materials.

Italy defies most attempts at generalisation. It is a country of contrasts: both an advanced, developed country and an under-developed one, both Western European, integrated into the Common Market, and Mediterranean. Few visitors can fail to be struck by its visible prosperity, at least in the northern and central regions. Whereas sales of new cars in other European countries have declined sharply during 1981, in Italy they have increased by 3.7 per cent. Italy also leads the rest of Europe in the number of people owning second (holiday) homes. At the same time they save 24.5 per cent of their available income as opposed to 19.7 per cent in France and 13.9 per cent in Germany.

The Italian economy has very advanced and profitable sectors which use a technology second to none (Olivetti, Pirelli); its know-how is exported the world over (SNAM Projetti). It boasts the largest automated car plant in Europe (Fiat Mirafiori) yet its large state industries (Montedison, SIR, the State Steel concerns) are deeply in debt and notorious for their bureaucratic, inefficient management (mostly due to appointments made for political reasons), poor production statistics and even worse labour relations.

The most interesting, lively and profitable sector of the Italian economy is, however, the small business sector. This ranges from medium-sized privately-owned firms down to cottage industries. It is in these small businesses that the famous Italian initiative, imagination and entrepreneurial spirit have full play. Many of these enterprises are based on another fundamental Italian institution – the family – and it has been argued that they have done much to maintaining the prosperity of the Italian economy over recent years. This part of the economy has also been described as the *economia sommersa* (submerged economy) so called because it manages to avoid many of the government's laws and regulations regarding taxes, social security, wage rates and regulations of working conditions. The term covers a broad collection of micro firms whose performance is difficult to assess statistically for precisely the same reason that many of them exist, that is by avoiding a large part of government regulation and assessment.

The importance of small business to the Italian economy as a whole has no equivalent in other western-developed countries. Statistics which deal with this sector of the economy will for many reasons tend grossly to underestimate the real phenomenon – most of the really submerged sector will not be included. Notwithstanding this premise the following table clearly shows the numerical importance of small businesses within the Italian economy.

	NUMBER OF EMPLOYEES			
	1–9	10–99	100–999	over 1000
Italy (1971)	23.2	31.2	29.8	15.7
France (1962)	19.2	27.0	36.5	17.3
Belgium (1963)	7.4	26.7	41.1	24.8
West Germany (1961)	13.2	22.6	36.0	28.2
United States (1963)	3.3	22.9	43.3	30.5
United Kingdom (1968)	18.9		46.1	35.0
Japan (1963)	15.4	38.5	30.6	15.5

TABLE 1   Percentage employed according to Size of Firm in the Manufacturing Industries of some OECD Countries.[1]

The table clearly shows that, apart from Japan, in no other Western country are small businesses so highly represented. The very smallest category (1–9 employees) is very significant with respect to all the other countries. According to census data, in Italy during the twenty-year period from 1951 to 1971, the number of people employed in manufacturing industries was consistently above half the total number employed. However, when evaluating this data we must take into account that many of those employed in small firms escape being counted in official statistics altogether because their contribution to the production process is made up of 'lavoro nero' (black labour), the equivalent of cottage industry and the putting out system.

There have been various attempts at estimating the extent of this phenomenon. Numerous observers agree that 'black labour' employs at least 1,500,000 people in Italy – the equivalent of one-tenth of the working population. According to one survey of the female population of four small towns in the provinces of Bologna and Modena in 1972, 1,060 workers were using their own homes as their workplace compared to the 311 which the official census registered.[2]

In the textile and clothing industry the 1971 official census figures showed a total of 896,000 persons employed. At the same time a study[3] of 32 provinces alone unearthed at least another 500,000 'black' workers in the submerged part of this sector alone. Sometimes, however, these same unofficial workers are registered as agricultural workers in census data, since they work in both sectors at the same time. This is also true of some types of public employees whose working day often ends at 2.00pm, leaving them free to participate in the submerged economy for the rest of the day. Thus, we have nurses who are part-time carpenters or plumbers, and school janitors whose afternoon is spent in a micro firm assembling motors for refrigerators. A survey of the Marches region[4] which tries to estimate the real extent of 'black labour' shows that 27.5 per cent of the employed population is involved. 16.7 per cent have no social security coverage at all and women are more highly represented than men: 42.5 per cent to 16.0 per cent.

Why does Italy have so many small firms compared to other industrialised countries? What are the functions fulfilled by small business in the Italian economy? It may be supposed that small businesses fulfil the same functions in Italy as in other industrialised economies – experimenting with new models they operate in those areas which are technologically backward, and in productive processes which larger firms no longer find it profitable to undertake in rapidly changing market conditions; and they have a complementary function with regard to the large firm. This is certainly the case in Italy but it is only a partial explanation of why small business is of such notable relevance to the economy as a whole.

Economists have suggested as an explanation the existence of a dualistic development of the economy with a technologically advanced sector on the one hand and a more under-developed sector on the other. The modernisation of the economy has slowed down or even stopped, thus accounting for the large numbers of non-rationalised productive systems left over. This would explain in terms of 'backwardness' the presence of so many small firms fulfilling rearguard functions in out-of-date uneconomic productive processes.

Suzanne Berger[5] sees the survival of economically backward small firms as a consequence of the peculiarly Italian way of dealing with those problems connected with cyclical fluctuations of the economy. The small business sector in this explanation becomes the fundamental stabilising element of the system. The labour force is expanded or contracted according to the needs of the market. In times of expansion more workers are absorbed into the more modern technologically advanced sector (large industry), but when recession arrives the excess manpower is re-absorbed into the more backward sector (small firm). Thus, the small firm constitutes a reserve of manpower for the large firm.

This model is even more effective if applied to the agricultural sector; workers leave the industrial sector in times of recession to go back to their former agricultural activities (usually on their own smallholding). This is true not only of workers in large industrial firms but more often of those employed in medium-sized and small firms. In most areas of the Marches region we find the family at the centre of this osmosis between agricultural and industrial occupations. Some of the structures which exist in this region are very complex and economically can be put to many uses. A common case is that of the family in which grandparents and parents work on their smallholding while sons and daughters are employed in one of the manufacturing processes undertaken by small local firms. Another case is that in which the whole family is employed in manufacturing whilst in their free time they work their smallholding. The flexibility of both cases is evident: in a slack period agriculture provides a means of making a living to the whole extended family.

It is certainly true that explanations of the prevalence of small firms in the Italian economy emphasising their residual character with respect to the more technologically advanced sectors, can effectively be verified in some cases. However, this view has many limits, mainly because it only explains the backward, static, inefficient, non-rationalised aspects of the system. Many small firms cannot be fitted into this category. Their steady growth over the last ten years, the fact that a large percentage of their products are exported, together with the relatively high level of technology used in some production processes, show that in fact a large number of small firms are dynamic, efficient and rationalised. A demonstration of this is that many large firms have in recent years begun a process of decentralisation of production involving many small firms. When looking at small firms in the Bergamo area we shall see how even quite advanced technological types of production can be carried out in small workshops surrounding the parent factory. Although Fiat's factory in Turin, Mirafiori is the largest in Europe, its latest factories in the south of Italy are all relatively small.

The small firm has also been explained (mostly by sociologists) in terms of state intervention. The peculiarly Italian system of state intervention which is especially marked in the south of Italy but by no means unknown in other areas, in reality becomes a sort of political patronage, *largesse* in helping small firms in the constituency of a particular minister in order to gain votes and consensus. This interpretation of economic development serves to underline the backwardness of some parts of the country's political leadership and shows how political interests can block or distort economic growth.

The small firm is, to a much greater extent than the large firm, influenced by the international division of labour. The Italian economy is very much conditioned by being a latecomer to the industrial development of Western Europe. Development is seen as the ability to export and therefore is dependent on the international context. Italy's economy is characterised by high numbers of exported goods requiring a low level of technology in their production (leather goods, textiles, wood, derivates of non-ferrous minerals, steel, shoes) and a relatively low level of exported goods requiring high innovative levels of technology (aeroplanes, chemicals, precision instruments, electronic machinery). In the last few years there has been an increase in exports of those goods requiring an intermediate level of technology (inorganic chemicals, petroleum derivates, automobiles, buses and commercial vehicles, machinery). Amongst the thirteen most industrialised countries Italy accounts for 7.07 per cent of exports of goods with intermediate levels of technology and 8 per cent of goods with low levels of technology.[6] If we break this 8 per cent down we find that for some types of production the percentage is considerably higher: for example in the shoe sector Italian exports amount to 54.37 per cent, furniture 17.17 per cent and clothing 24.50 per cent.

We see clearly here the importance of the less advanced sector of the economy in relation to exports. Whilst the size of the firm which engages in this type of production is not specificallly mentioned in the statistics, it is easily demonstrable that it is in just these sectors that many small and micro firms have contributed to the growth of the last ten years. In the shoe industry, the five largest firms as far as total product is concerned account for only 9 per cent of the total production in this sector, 2.4 per cent of fixed investments and 4.3 per cent of its employees. The furniture industry's five largest firms account for 9.4 per cent of total production, 10 per cent of fixed investments and 6.6 per cent of all its employees. The statistics for other sectors with 'mature' technology mirror this tendency almost perfectly.

Sectors	up to 9	10–99	100–499	500 and over
Textiles	15.20	35.03	32.29	17.48
Clothing	34.77	30.84	23.53	10.85
Shoes	29.95	46.07	20.71	2.64
Leather and Pelts	29.12	51.14	17.08	1.94
Wood	58.05	32.66	8.18	0.96
Furniture and furnishings	37.13	49.03	11.85	1.72
Non-ferrous minerals	17.61	46.59	26.57	9.23
TOTAL (manufacturing industry)	23.34	31.16	22.24	23.25

TABLE 2   The Distribution of Employees in Sectors with Traditional Technology by Numbers of Employees (1971).[7]

The Table demonstrates once more how industries using traditional technology are extremely dispersed, in almost all cases well over half the employees in the industries working in firms of fewer than 100 employees.

Traditional production processes are often dispersed in small units and these find in their size their economic *raison d'être*. 'Mature' technology linked with reserves of labour and low labour costs, unstable demand and scarce control of markets, are a further encouragement to the small firm. But this type of industry is very much bound by two important restrictions; quick changes in fashion and consumption which are the cause of fluctuating demand; and the nature of the technology employed which is not liable to important labour-saving innovations. In other words, the greater part of Italian industry has to produce goods which are highly labour intensive with an extremely variable demand and unchanging technology. Under these circumstances it is hardly surprising that the small firm is much more important than in other countries. The small firm brings high degrees of flexibility to the system through the adaptability of the small entrepreneur, the use of the family as a productive unit the putting out system and 'black' labour in general. The hosiery industry, for example, has an average of 10 employees in Italy, 100 in France and Germany and 110 in the USA and these figures clearly demonstrate a net difference in the approach of these countries to industrial organisation.

The particular industrial structure of Italy, with a high number of small and micro firms, influences the social class composition of the country quite considerably.[8] As far as the middle class is concerned, Italy differs considerably from other Western countries in that it has a very low level of clerks and office workers in the private sector, out of the total working population, and a very high percentage of artisans and small entrepreneurs. Within the working class the diffusion of the micro firm and the putting out system gives rise to a class structure which is highly differentiated. The people forming the central core of the working class with more or less stable, regular jobs are proportionately fewer than in other Western countries, while the peripheral strata of the working class (those employed in the submerged economy) have no equivalent, in such numbers, in other advanced capitalist countries.

The analysis of the Italian economy as a dualistic system, large industry and small industry, advanced and mature technology, an official and an unofficial economy, has been inspired by the analysis of the American industrial system made by Averitt.[9] Averitt describes the industrial system of America as consisting of a central part with high capital intensity, large corporations, technologically advanced sectors, control over all productive processes and advanced marketing techniques. The other side of the coin is the peripheral part of the American economy which consists of small or medium-sized firms, traditional types of production, high labour intensity, interstitial production and highly specialised markets. The important difference between the Italian economy and that of the USA is that, proportionately, in the Italian economy the peripheral part assumes a fundamental importance, as we have seen in Table 1, whereas in the USA the large corporation overshadows the rest of the economy.

Italy has in recent years experienced a phenomenon which begins to blur the distinctions of dualism. Large firms have started to decentralise several phases of their production process, subcontracting substantial parts of it to satellite firms. Whilst this process has taken place for many years between the small and micro firms of Prato (as we shall see later) the adoption of this practice on the part of large firms is much more recent. We are beginning to witness a large-scale restructuring of industry at a national level. Observers tend to attribute this phenomenon to a reaction by large firms to the trade union activities of 1968-70 with their consequent legal and contractual concessions. It has been the large firm which has been called upon to pay the high cost of these concessions. Decentralisation of production can be seen as an answer on the part of the Italian industrial system to the sharp rise in labour costs and the general upheaval and disruption of work caused by both official and unofficial strikes.[10]

The relatively high labour costs and high levels of labour unrest depend (especially the former) on the particularly large share of employers' contributions to social security funds in total labour costs. The total bill for 'dependent' labour in 1970 was made up of 72 per cent gross pay and 28 per cent social security payments, compared with averages for Common Market countries of 81 per cent and 19 per cent (West Germany's bill was 87 per cent and 13 per cent, France's 78 per cent and 22 per cent). The resulting gap between Italy and other countries with respect to average pay received by workers compared to total labour costs (the former representing roughly 72 per cent of the Common Market average and the latter 81 per cent) was by no means commensurately filled by social security services of an equivalent level. In fact although Italian workers pay more, the standard of services they receives leaves much to be desired. The high labour costs have done much to weaken the financial position of firms in a recession – and particularly in conditions of slack demand but still rising costs – because social security contributions rise alongside wages paid. While in theory high labour costs apply to both small and large firms, the large firm cannot escape government vigilance and avoid paying its dues. The small firm, which has been also called the semi-submerged economy, declares less and therefore pays less tax, VAT and social security contributions. It can thus be seen that in a certain sense the large firm pays for the social services which small entrepreneurs and their dependent workers also use. As we have seen, social security payments are much higher for firms in Italy than in other European countries, but the number of self-employed persons in Italy is also higher (40 per cent of the total working population). In practice this means that large firms and dependent workers pay the bulk of the national social security bill leaving the small firm and self-employed worker to reap the eventual benefits while paying less than their share.

Trade union relations and the general well-being of the dependent worker are regulated in Italy by the 'Statuto dei Lavoratori'. This is the main concession resulting from the long series of strikes and political turmoil of 1968, '69 and '70. The working class, especially those employed in large firms, emerged from this period with greater protection and substantial gains. Wages were indexed to cost of living increases on a sliding scale; there was no longer a link between productivity and wages; wage differences between different types of workers were abolished; working hours were reduced; workers were entitled to some study leave during the year at full pay (150 hours); and finally working conditions and the environment were much improved.

The 'Statuto dei Lavoratori' fixes at 15 the number of employees in a firm below which article 35 is no longer applicable. Article 35 establishes extremely rigid and difficult conditions for the sacking of an employee making it difficult to get rid of any worker. Article 35 establishes compulsory membership of a trade union. Thus, we can see how the firm with less than 15 employees has much more flexible labour relations and can, in times of slack demand, get rid of excess labour. Labour relations in general in small firms are easier because the entrepreneur establishes a personal relationship with his employees, invoking their loyalty, making them feel involved personally in the progress of the firm.

Although the small firm is becoming increasingly important throughout the whole of Italy, there are certain regions in which it is particularly prevalent. These regions are in the centre and north-east of the country, the Marches, Emilia Romagna, Tuscany and the Veneto.[11] Those employed in firms with less than 290 employees are 86.3 per cent of the employed population in the Marches, 80.8 per cent in Emilia Romagna, 79.5 per cent in Tuscany and 75.5 per cent in the Veneto. The increase over the last 20 years has been considerable and has been accelerated since the 1971 census. From 1961 to 1971 the increase in firms with under 250 employees was 12.4 per cent in the Marches with the other regions following close behind.

What is the particular socio-economic structure of these central and north-eastern regions; what they have in common which enables the small firm to bloom and flourish here? Production in these regions tends to be organised in very specialised areas; for example, almost all the firms in the Prato area are involved in the textile industry; Carpi in Emilia Romagna and its surroundings specialises in knitwear; Modena and Reggio Emilia have important agglomerations of engineering firms. Often the reasons why one industry is attached to one town or district are cultural or historical in origin. Today's growth is linked to long artisan traditions or share-cropping agriculture. Artisans and peasants are capable of dealing with machinery and varied technologies, have developed sound business sense and entrepreneurial spirit while at the same time maintaining their local value systems. Recent economic developments have interesting historical precedents. Complex cultural elements are implicit in the process. Culture here does not mean just attitudes and ways of thinking but a whole complex of reciprocally accepted ways of behaviour, mutual expectations and customs.

One of the characteristics which these regions held in common was their agricultural organisation based on the share-cropping system (Mezzadria). It was common in other parts of Italy but in these regions it lasted longer, in some cases until after the last war. It can easily be demonstrated that the origins of the entrepreneurial spirit, propension towards hard work, a high degree of flexibility and a remarkable technical capacity are to be found in the share-cropping families of these regions. At the same time in the small towns spread throughout the area a thriving artisan class with strong traditions of craftsmanship catered for the needs of the landowners who stimulated a demand for all manner of goods and services.

Carpi is a good example of the continuity shown in the economic development of a town. Its historic manufacturing traditions and organisation are surprisingly similar to present-day ones. The system of production was based from the 16th century onwards on the merchant/entrepreneur figure who employed cottage labour, collecting the finished products (straw hats, and straw coverings for wine bottles) which he then sold in the markets and fairs in the surrounding districts. Today the product has changed (fashion knitwear), the market has become international but the entrepreneur still fulfils the same function and most of the work is done on a putting out basis.

The economic transformation which has taken place in these regions has been paralleled by a political and cultural transformation which, like the economic one, has at the same time retained important aspects of traditional social organisation. The type of development which the central and north-eastern regions have undergone has not radically changed pre-existing cultural and social forms but has in part conserved them by adapting them to new economic necessities. Voting behaviour tends to favour either a clear Christian-Democrat majority (the Veneto and some areas of the Marches) or a Communist majority (Tuscany and Emilia Romagna), atypical in Italy where the vote is usually spread over a wide range of parties. Figures for income, consumption, house ownership, number of hospital beds per inhabitant, provision of schools are all better than the national average. Society appears to be more integrated and development does not seem to have dismantled the basic structures of peasant society.

The historian Braudel has demonstrated how the evolution of Europe has depended on the birth and growth of 'everyday' structures, on the capacity of individuals, their creativity, inventiveness, on small businessmen and small merchants and their ability to react to the various changes in their society. Nowhere is this to be seen more clearly than in Prato. Even in the fourteenth century the Prato merchant described by Iris Origo – Francesco di Marco Datini – was doing business with the rest of Europe and Prato was already a centre of the wool trade. Today, almost 600 years later, Prato has a thriving textile industry whose products are exported internationally.

Much of this activity depends on structures and traditions which have been operating in Prato almost uninterrupted for centuries. The high degree of technical ability, professional skills and entrepreneurial spirit available permit the town to export in the face of competition from the newly industrialising countries. A large part of the organisation of production is done on a putting out basis, one entrepreneur organising the various phases of production and the marketing of the finished product. This system can only work within tight time schedules and with reciprocal faith, both on the ability of the outside worker to produce high quality goods at the agreed time and on the entrepreneur's ability to provide a constant stream of work and keep his designs and raw materials abreast of fashion. In Prato, textiles are sometimes carded, spun, woven and dyed with each operation completed in a different micro factory. Only the packing and shipping is carried by the entrepreneur.

Prato is looked upon with surprise and suspicion for the miracle it works daily. Many observers find it hard to understand how Prato expands and consolidates a productive sector which is generally considered too 'mature' for advanced industrialised countries. Prato manages to innovate incessantly the range of products it produces, keeping constantly in touch with the demands of the market as regards price, taste and quality. Its mode of production is flexible, often its phases are fragmented between firms and productive units (13,000 firms with 63,000 employees) compete between themselves. The organisation of the Prato model of production is based upon a diffused entrepreneurial spirit making use of highly qualified professional workers.

The working population of Prato in 1976 was 39.8 per cent of the total population. 70 per cent of these were engaged in industry. Italian Ministry of Labour estimates forecast an increase in the active working population in the 1981 census. Most of what is produced in Prato is exported. Germany is the best customer, 38 per cent of Prato's exports being sold there. Most of the working population is engaged in some activity connected either directly or indirectly with the textile industry. 40 per cent of employees work in firms with less than 10 employees and only 28 per cent in firms with more than 50 employees. The great majority of those employed in artisan workshops belong to the same nuclear family. The amount of women going out to work is more than 10 per cent above the national average but a true picture of the female working population would have to include workers in cottage industry. A sample taken in one zone of Prato showed that 18 per cent of women of working age engage in work in their own homes for at least three hours a day.

Prato, as an industrial area is characterised by its specialisation in one productive sector, in the growth of external economies which this specialisation induces. It manages to maintain high rates of production by keeping dependent workers to a minimum and offering them a form of participation in the firm's success. Increases in productivity bring about increased profits and consequently higher wages. Ironically, this happens in a town with a Communist Municipal government whilst nationally the Community Party has been instrumental in agitating for the abolition of production bonuses in the factory.

The 'Censis' survey of Prato[12] reports that among the population interviewed, the highest values were ascribed to 'hard work' (6.20 per cent) followed by 'spirit of initiative and enterprise' (52.2 per cent). Working hours were found to be from 220 to 234 hours per year (15 per cent) longer than the national average. Most of those interviewed who were engaged in some form of working activity linked to the textile industry, had a working day of 11 hours or longer. Incomes were also found to be higher than the national average although the interviewers suspected gross under-estimation on the part of the interviewees judging from their large, expensive houses, cars and consumer durables. In fact, the number of cars per 100 inhabitants is 31 per cent higher than the national average. Paradoxically, when asked questions relating to political opinions, 84 per cent replied that 'the majority of laws were made in the interests of those who had power and money'.

Before examining the small firm in the Marches and its relationship to family structure, it is interesting to look at the structure of the family in Italy as a whole. Paci[13] has suggested that the family plays a crucial role in the industrial development of modern Italy, thus spotlighting another of its distinguishing features. In the 18th and 19th centuries the percentage of households with relatives co-habiting is less than 30 per cent in north-west European countries (England, Scandinavia, Holland, France and Germany), whilst in Italy 58 per cent of households have co-habiting relatives. The same divergencies in the frequency of households composed of extended families is visible today; in England, 5 per cent of households are composed of extended families compared to 16.9 per cent in Italy. Paci also finds a high correlation between share-cropping and extended families. From the point of view of the small firm, the most relevant feature seems to be that the highest percentages of co-habiting extended families are to be found in those regions with traditions of share-cropping in agriculture and large numbers of small firms.

Unlike other industrial areas of Italy and many parts of Europe the Marches region is interesting because it is not suffering from stagnation. It has great flexibility both in its industrial structures and entrepreneurs which translates itself into capacity to change types of production, continuing sources of self-financing and renewal of the entrepreneurial class. Its labour structure is also flexible – its work-force is mobile, prepared to work long hours or go on short time as the demand arises and its degree of active participation in unions is low.

Like the other central and north-eastern regions, the Marches also tends to have towns given over to one specific type of industrial activity. In the valleys of the Rivers Esino and Misa the knitwear industry is widely dispersed in a myriad of micro factories and workshops. In the last twenty years, the industry has gone through a profound crisis and a consequent decentralisation of productive activity. Much of the labour force is female, the male population being occupied in agriculture, while the metallurgical industry is beginning to attract workers from the land. The small firm tends to be dependent on larger firms for the marketing of its final product, much of which is exported; thus, the vagaries of fashion and international demand are felt keenly. Small firms tend to be of two types: one consists of businesses attached to larger firms in northern Italy which prefer to have their products manufactured in small firms with lower labour costs and fewer union problems. The other type of firm exists because it succeeds in continually changing the final product to keep up with oscillations in fashion. Some completely autonomous firms manage to produce finished goods and market them independently. These firms usually farm work out to small workshops or female workers working at home and paid by the piece.

The shoe and footwear industry is concentrated in the provinces of Ascoli Piceno and Macerata. It has three characterising features: the low number of workers in each unit, the high level of artisans working in the sector and the increasing incidence of exports upon total production. In these districts the growth in numbers of artisan workshops is tied to the diffusion of work on commission. Both constant demand, which has been sustained for several years, and an effective sales network, which is indispensable in an industry like this where exports are paramount, have led many artisans and ex-workers to set up on their own account. Many larger firms have sub-contracted some of the processes of shoe-making to small workshops, so that cutting out, binding and sometimes even the final stitching together no longer take place in large firms.

The difference between small and medium-sized firms or artisan workshops are almost non-existent since the most relevant differences depend on the quantity produced. Therefore, in this sector there are no technological limits to the decentralisation of production. There are, however, barriers produced by the market, in other words small firms depend on having goods commissioned by larger firms or by import-export concerns. In some periods increases in demand are passed on to artisan workshops which may make the whole article or some part of it.

This is a picture of two typical small industries in the Marches. How has family structure and the share-cropping type of agricultural organisation influenced the extraordinary growth which this region has witnessed in the last twenty years? The head of the peasant family has for generations been used to organising the working life of his whole extended family which at times numbered forty heads. The link between working effort and economic return forced the entire share-cropping family into long working hours under the leadership of the head of the family. Thus, within the family itself a division of labour was created. Historians have recorded for generations the laboriousness of the Marches family and travellers marvelled at the resistance to fatigue and the speed at which the women of the household worked.

Towards the 1950s the share-cropper began to buy the piece of land which he had worked. To do this he had to enter into debt; thus, partly by choice and partly by necessity peasants began to work in the small industries which were beginning to set foot in the region. Increasingly, one or more members of the peasant family began to work in the small factories and artisan workshops or, in the case of the women, to take in work at home. The realisation of the economic benefits accruing from a combination of part-time farming and industrial employment accentuated even further the already existing division of labour in the family. The final step, which only a limited number of families ever arrive at, is that of the micro entrepreneur. Having quickly learned the trade and with his experience in directing the work of others and his experience in buying and selling, the peasant finds no difficulty in making the jump. The base of this activity remains the land; it is the kingpin upon which the entire system revolves and is of prime importance as a source of capital accumulation and labour, and it is used to help keep costs to a minimum.

Under the circumstances, the family remains the basis of micro industrial entrepreneurship. The ex-share-cropper gradually develops into worker and part-time farmer, then artisan and finally becomes a small businessman. In the transition period much of the industrial work is performed by various members of the family and later in the small firm stage by more distant members of the kinship group.

The research Brusco[14] undertook in Bergamo investigates two observations – that metallurgical firms were increasingly commissioning work outside the factory and that those workers in small firms who produced goods commissioned in this way enjoyed worse working conditions, lower wages and overtime pay than their fellows in large firms. The research tries to demonstrate whether, in fact, the level of technology used in the small firm was more backward than that of the large firm or if it was, as some observers have suggested, of an even higher technological level than that of the large firm.

In order to test the above hypothesis and evaluate the technological level of the production processes in small firms, it was necessary to look carefully at each type of production undertaken by the small firm on commission. From the complex data available it becomes clear that the metallurgical industry decentralises those parts of the production process for which economies of scale do not exist. In founding operations the complementary operations are decentralised. The situation in the carpentry sector is more differentiated; here, most firms decentralise all the work. Only in the very largest firms where the carpentry operation is of greater importance are the operations carried out within the factory with special machinery whilst the finishing touches are put by outside firms. Mechanical operations are almost all decentralised. The high percentage of decentralisation in the final assembly stage is to be explained by the fact that in almost all cases assembly is carried out in 'blocks' for which no special machinery is necessary.

The analysis carried out by Brusco confirms that within the complex set of operations necessary for the production of a particular article, there are a series of interstices within which economies of scale are of secondary importance. Some of the small firms in the survey operated within these interstices whilst others produced finished goods and were small only apparently; in reality they co-ordinated the work of a much greater number of workers than those on their official payroll.

Many factories decentralise the whole of their production, apart from the construction of prototypes and the final assemblage. This is the case, for example, of factories with less than thirty employees which produce scales, dishwashers or machinery for the paper industry and textile machinery.

As far as the types of machinery involved in the production of various goods are concerned there is a great deal of variation according to the size of the small firm. However, half of all the firms in the survey, even those with less than ten employees, attained a level of technological sophistication equivalent to semi-automatic machinery. The rest of the firms surveyed used techniques based on manually controlled machinery. Some processes, it must be remembered, cannot use automatic or semi-automatic machinery, whether they take place in large or small factories.

It can be seen that in Bergamo, technological requirements are less a determinant of the size of the firm than has usually been supposed. Technology imposes a minimum size on working units; for example, in the moulding of refrigerator bodies. This does not mean, however, that many working units of this type have all to work under the same roof. Each working unit can exist by itself in a whole network of small workshops and factories, each producing the same product or part of a finished product.

According to Brusco, the factors which favour the agglomeration of working units together in one large factory are fundamentally organisational whereas those leading in the opposite direction are political. Entrepreneurs find it easier to control workers in several small factories rather than in one large one, even though from an organisational point of view, the latter might be more efficient. As long as the control of the workforce is feasible, optimum technology only determines the scale of the working unit and the entrepreneur decides how many working units to group together in one factory. Only when the entrepreneur prefers to disperse the working units do the limits imposed on the optimum dimensions of the working units become operative.

The importance of the small business to the Italian economy is the result of many factors – technological, political, social, cultural and historical. All of these combine to give the sector its present-day dynamism and force. Although, as we have seen, some sectors depend on 'mature' technology (shoes, furniture, clothing) they also depend on good design and ability to change quickly to meet the demands of fashion. It is, above all, these latter qualities which qualify the Italian small business and help it to survive notwithstanding mounting competition from newly industrialising countries. Another new and important facet of the small business in Italy is the decentralisation of production operated by large firms. Although the decision to decentralise was initially political it also makes sound economic sense because even the large firms can in this way avoid paying at least some part of its crippling labour costs.

The development of the small business economy which we have seen principally in the central and north-eastern regions of the country is rapidly extending to other areas both in the north and south. Unlike many other European small businesses the Italian small firm is not a large firm in embryo but is born and destined to remain small. It is left very much to its own devices and receives precious little in the way of government help and assistance. Unfortunately, because of its size, the small firm cannot undertake research into possible technological innovations and it is here that its main weakness lies. Suitable government assistance and co-ordination in this field would do much to ensure the survival and development of small businesses in Italy.

ENDNOTES

1. Table adapted by A. Bagnasco, *Tre Italie – la problematica territoriale dello sviluppo italiano* (Mulino, Bologna, 1977).
2. See L. Bergonzini, 'Casalinghe o lavoranti a domicilio', in *Inchiesta*, 1973.
3. L. Frey, 'Le piccole e medie imprese industriali di fronte al mercato del lavoro in Italia', in *Inchiesta*, 1974.
4. F. Bugarini, 'Il lavoro irregolare e l'attività per l'auto consumo', in M. Paci, *Famiglia e Mercato del lavoro in un' Economia Periferica* (Franco Angeli, Milan, 1980).
5. S. Berger, 'Uso politico e sopravivenza dei ceti in declino', in *Il caso italiano*, ed. F. L. Cavazza and S. R. Granbard (Milan, 1974).
6. Statistics from A. Bagnasco, *op. cit.*
7. ISTAT.
8. See P. Sylos Labini, *Saggio sulle classi sociali* (Bari Laterza, 1974).
9. R. T. Averitt, *The Dual Economy* (Notton & Co., New York, 1968).
10. See G. Podbielski, *Italy's Development and Crisis in the Post-War Economy* (Clarendon Press, Oxford, 1974).
11. Regional distribution of the small firm has been discussed at length – see A. Bagnasco, *op. cit.*
12. See *Il caso Prato*, ricerca a cura del CENSIS ETAS libri (Milan, 1980).
13. *Famiglia e Mercato del favoro in un Economia Periferica*, ed. M. Paci (Franco Angeli, 1980).
14. S. Brusco, 'Economie di scala e livello tecnologico nelle piccole imprese', in *Crisi e Ristrutturazione nell' Economia Italiana*, ed. A. Graziani (Einaudi, Turin, 1975).

Thoughts on the present discontents in Britain

Krishan Kumar

'By far the greatest obstacle to the progress of science and to the new undertaking of new tasks . . . is found in this: that men think things impossible . . .'

Francis Bacon, *Novum Organum*, Bk.I, xcii.

It can hardly have escaped anyone's attention that what Carlyle called 'the condition of England' question is with us again. But what a difference. When commentators wrote about the condition of England in the early nineteenth century they were discussing the social consequences of England's pioneering leap into industrialism, her revolutionary turning of the course of world history. Growth, not stagnation, was the cause of the concern of moralists and sociologists. Now the situation is precisely the opposite. The country's problems seem to be the product of illness and senescence, rather than youth and vigour. An acute case of 'the British disease' is pronounced (lately re-termed 'Englanditis' by Her Majesty's Ambassador to Washington[1]). Its symptoms are economic inefficiency, antiquated attitudes and institutions, national complacency, a general and deep-seated inability to pull ourselves out of a growing pit of declining standards in all areas of the society. All in all, the situation is widely glossed as a 'crisis'.

The British themselves have taken the lead in breast-beating. Not surprisingly, much foreign opinion echoes this judgement, and gleefully propagates it. But there is a group which thinks quite differently. This includes such distinguished foreign observers and residents as John Kenneth Galbraith, Arthur Koestler, and Ralf Dahrendorf. These see in many of the symptoms of the 'disease' the signs of a national strength which other industrial countries might well come to envy and even to imitate.

'Your real problem', says Galbraith, 'is that you were the first of the great industrialised nations, and so things happen here first. You are living out the concern for some more leisurely relationship with industrial life that other people have been discussing for fifty years or more.'[2] Dahrendorf, commenting on a *New Society* opinion poll which seemed to confirm the charge of national complacency, proposes that 'the desire to "Live a pleasant life" rather than "work as much as one can for as much money as one can get" is a source of strength, not of weakness in Britain'.[3] The American physicist Robert Socolow is even more definite: 'It seems likely to this visitor that the world's developed countries will be emulating Britain within a decade or less. The limits of nature's resources and the limits to our own cleverness in protecting ourselves from our own mischief put severe constraints on the level of activity any developed society will freely choose. As these limits are faced more and more squarely, developed countries will acknowledge the vigour attained by a mature society that cherishes the past, cares for its physical surroundings, socializes in pubs, and changes houses reluctantly . . . When the next round of industrialization – which will emphasize durability, quality, and community level systems – arrives, you will more quickly recognize how well matched its demands are to your national strengths.'[4]

In the nineteenth century, eminent foreign observers such as Marx and Tocqueville came to Britain to see and study the marvels of the new industrial society. In this century, some at least seem to be watching with close interest the emergence of the first post-industrial society.

Is this mere flattery? Is it just a gracious sop to a nation in decline, Britain playing Athens to America's Rome? We should at least acknowledge the appeal of a view that recognizes the long-term, historical nature of the current predicament. Britain was the first industrial society in the history of the world. From having this head start over her competitors she reaped great rewards. But she has long been losing out in the race to stay among the leaders of the industrial nations. Parallels with past civilizations would suggest that it is difficult and dangerous for a society to strive to regain the leadership in the same race. Better by far to start a new one, with different rules. First in, first out.

I return to this theme later. First however it seems necessary to consider Britain's predicament within the context of the more general crisis of industrial societies as a whole.

I. Growth or No-Growth?

On this subject, no passage seems more frequently quoted than the following from John Stuart Mill's *Principles of Political Economy:*

> 'I cannot . . . regard the stationary state of capital and wealth with the unaffected aversion so generally manifested towards it by political economists of the old school. I am inclined to believe that it would be, on the whole, a very considerable improvement on our present condition. I confess I am not charmed with the ideal of life

held out by those who think that the normal state of human beings is that of struggling to get on; that the trampling, crushing, elbowing, and treading on each other's heels, which form the existing type of social life, are the most desirable lot of human kind, or anything but the disagreeable symptoms of one of the phases of industrial progress . . . the best state for human nature is that in which, while no one is poor, no one desires to be richer, nor has any reason to fear being thrust back, by the efforts of others to push themselves forward . . . the stationary state of capital and population implies no stationary state of human improvement.'

The argument between proponents of expansive material growth, on the one hand, and human improvement or the quality of life as the sufficient end, on the other, is one of the oldest in Western thought, as many writers have pointed out.[5] It is to be found, for instance, in the distinction Aristotle makes in the *Politics* between *oiconomike* (household management) which 'attends more to men than to the acquisition of material things', and *chrematistike* (the pursuit of wealth), which must be the always strictly delimited means to the end ('human excellence') set by the former. It continues throughout the medieval period, in the concept of the 'just price', where Aquinas distinguishes between *commutatio*, 'fair exchange' in the satisfaction of needs as the basis of economic relations, and *negotiatio,* which is exchange not for needs but for profit. And it is to be found in the writings of the Physiocrats, and of Rousseau, in the eighteenth century, with their idea of the essentially limited needs of individuals, and the necessity therefore of limiting economic activity to the satisfaction of these needs.

No one will deny, however, that the argument has been powerfully revived in recent years, fuelled by anxieties about environmental destruction, and the possible exhaustion of the physical resources of the earth on which economic growth depends. Indeed with the renewed concern with the 'stationary state' has gone a new view of world history, and especially of the industrial epoch, which bids fair to become a new orthodoxy in certain circles. The period of world history up till the end of the eighteenth century is seen as one of a 'steady state' economy and society. The Industrial Revolution of the nineteenth and twentieth centuries introduces a period of acute destabilization, an 'exponential era' marked by rapid and unbalanced growth, especially but not exclusively economic. Now, in the last quarter of the twentieth century, a second turning point is discerned, bringing about a renewed switch to a steady state system.[6]

There is much that is attractive in this view, both in its conception of the past and its proposals for the future. But there are profound ambiguities in the whole conception of a 'no-growth' society. What is meant by no-growth? It seems fairly clear that what most of its proponents mean by it is a slow-down in the production of *material goods*, which they associate with an increasingly prodigal expenditure of men, machines, and natural resources, as well as an increasingly intolerable level of environmental pollution and destruction. But of course we could switch production towards more *services* without in any way abandoning the goal of economic growth. Nor would this goal necessarily be affected by a radical change in the tastes and desires of the industrial populations. As Mancur Olson says, 'if the tastes of modern man were suddenly to change in such a way that he devoted most of the time and money he now devotes to cars and television, to cathedrals and art galleries, the change would not reduce economic output or growth: it could, like other changes in the composition of output, be perfectly consistent with an increase in the rate of economic growth.'[7] The link between welfare and economic activity, Olson goes on to assert, can be made far more inclusive than most people suppose: 'Because of the arbitrariness involved in any restrictive definition of what is economic, I have, like other economists of the more single-minded sort, often defined utility or welfare from any source or of any kind as part of income or welfare. With this definition, there is an economic problem whenever people have wants which cannot be entirely satisfied with existing resources, and economic growth whenever existing wants are satisfied to a greater degree than they were in a previous period. Reality, in this view, is not divided into departments, like a university; the economic dimension has no logical outer limit.'[8]

Accordingly, on this definition, there is no necessary link, say, between a pro-environment policy and a no-growth policy, and no necessary contradiction between environmentalism and growth-manship. All that would be involved, if one pursues the former, is a change of policies and regulations making it economically more attractive for firms to produce 'cleaner' or socially more useful goods, with cleaner processes of production (involving perhaps intensive re-cycling of waste materials), and economically punitive to do otherwise.[9]

It is obviously important for no-growth advocates to make precise, both to themsleves and to others, exactly what they are opposing or proposing, if only to prevent people arguing past each other. Nevertheless, as Olson himself admits, it is usually not difficult to see what current proponents of no-growth are getting at, and to allow the strength of the case. What they are saying is that the *present* conception of economic growth, as reflected in the national statistics which are used to calculate Gross National Product, emphasises the wrong priorities in the assessment of national wealth. It counts as wealth-creating, activities which are either actually harmful to human beings and their natural environment or are simply forms of 'defensive' and reparative expenditures caused by those activities. At the same time the statistics ignore activities – in the home, for instance, or in voluntary organizations – which are self-evidently valuable although currently don't involve market or state expenditure. Once we acknowledge the contribution of a whole realm of activities conventionally deemed 'unproductive', but which to some people may constitute the very basis of a creative and satisfying life, it certainly makes sense to oppose 'growth' as that is currently accounted and practised.

It may be true to say that, in principle, the composition of the GNP could be changed to suit the wishes of the no-growth advocates, in which case they would have no reason to oppose growth. But in practice the change of priorities involved may be so formidable, the vested political and economic interests so powerful, that the no-growth slogan may prove the most effective rallying-cry in trying to bring about a change of direction. For there is, as Hugh Stretton has stressed, a real conflict of values and interests involved in the debate about growth. 'Better social accounting which measured real net welfare might allow environmentalists to join in favouring growth as a general principle. But still not agree about it in detail – people with different interests and values would still want to count different things as "real welfare" and weight them differently according to who was to enjoy them. It is a mistake . . . to pin extravagant hopes to the development of better economic and social indexes. Indexes can't alter the fact that one citizen sees as goods what another sees as costs or wastes; what one wants to consume, another wants to leave in the ground. Indexes of net welfare have to be constructed by controversial judgements of good and bad . . . Better accounting can serve all sorts of good purposes, and reconcile some mistaken conflicts of opinion, but it can't reconcile real conflicts of interest and value.'[10] It is this that makes so disingenous the arguments of those who – like Wilfrid Beckerman and the late Antony Crosland in Britain[11] – are fervent advocates of growth. They meet all the objections smoothly at the level of abstract economic theory. We *can* have our cake and eat it – in fact we must, if we're to have any cake at all. But they ignore the political facts which are equally relevant to the argument, and which in present circumstances almost inevitably tend to impose a particular direction on growth, for the benefit of particular interests.

Much of the discussion about growth has centred on the physical limits, as exemplified in the Club of Rome report, *The Limits of Growth*. Recently in a powerfully argued book, *The Social Limits to Growth*,[12] Fred Hirsch has added a fresh dimension. The basic argument turns on the difficulties encountered once a society gets beyond a certain level of material production, and enters on a competitive struggle for goods within the 'positional economy' – such goods as satisfying and creative jobs, quietness, privacy. The old law of imitation – 'what the few have today, the many want tomorrow' – continues to operate at the level of aspiration but, unlike the case with material goods, cannot work at the level of achievement. It breaks down in that sector of the economy where the satisfactions deriving from the good turn entirely on its restricted and reserved nature, thus making it self-defeating for all to pursue it. The positional economy, unlike the material economy, is a zero-sum economy.

Hirsch's argument is not strictly speaking an argument against growth as such – indeed it presupposes a quite considerable level of material growth. Moreover to my mind it takes an excessively narrow and closed view of the character and potentialities of the positional economy. Hirsch's assumptions are evidently conservative ones – that the structure of work and organization will remain substantially as it is now, for instance, so that there will always be the same strictly limited number of creative and responsible jobs, or 'leadership roles'; or that we cannot use our imaginations to conceive of a better arrangement for the enjoyment of countryside, lakeland, and sea-shore, such that we can mix both privacy and sociability, thus enriching the satisfaction of the good as well as increasing the number able to enjoy it.[13]

Nevertheless, Hirsch is surely right to point to the enormous problems encountered when the growth mentality becomes lodged in societies.[4] His own solutions are offered without any great conviction. Mostly they imply policies of 'levelling-down' as well as 'levelling-up', to lessen the fierceness of the struggle for positional goods. The pay given for intrinsically interesting jobs, for instance, should be lowered; the tie between the attainment of educational qualifications and the gaining of financially lucrative jobs should be loosened. Here he is close to those many others who have also offered bleak scenarios for the future of no-growth societies. Mostly they emphasize the acute distributional struggles which will ensure with the slowing-down or stopping of growth, leading either to a breakdown of the political order or, more likely, to the rise of strongly authoritarian political regimes. Charles Taylor grimly looks out on a prospect 'of a Byzantine society in which production and consumption are held in a static pattern by a myriad of controls, and in which the pattern of consumption is marked by the drab uniformity of the utility good. The economics of Byzantium combine with the taste of wartime Britain . . .'[15]

These melancholy predictions no doubt might lead us to incline to the view of those who briskly dismiss no-growth altogether, as 'a disguised ideology of privilege, or a form of romantic reaction.'[16] The haves are trying to stop the have-nots getting in on the act, as so often in the past. The Hudson Report, *The United Kingdom in 1980*, roundly puts the matter thus: 'Britain is a country of 56 million people living on a crowded and poor island, in no sense self-sufficient in food or raw materials, and . . . decreasingly self-sufficient even in manufactured goods. There is no possibility of supporting Britain's population except through the mechanism of modern industrial society (i.e. growth); the options of retreat into a rural stable-state or zero growth economy are sentimentalities.'[17]

Sentiment can be a great thing, especially when there is a certain amount of necessity mixed in with the desire. Indeed, whose who, like Hirsch, Heilbroner, and Taylor, fear the consequences of the end to growth, pin their hopes to a remarkable extent on the development of strong collective feeling to take us through the difficult times ahead: a recurrence of 'the Dunkirk spirit', or a revival of religion.[18] Are they being too gloomy? Assuming that we have to look forward to something that is more like a steady state than a growth economy, need the transition be quite so much the vale of tears conjured up by these writers? Once more we need to see that the alternatives are being deployed on too restricted a plane. The accounting tends to leave out a good deal of the benefits that may be expected to come – and which in fact have already come – from the slowing down of material growth. Such things as a new concept of and attitude towards 'waste', a concern with the renovation, repair, and re-cycling of materials, a renewed respect for the whole realm of nature. Put more strongly, there is in most of these accounts a failure to ask what kind of society ultimately we may want – and to see whether the check to our automatic, routine growth mentality may not be as full of opportunities as it is of threats and fears. In Britain's case particularly there are good grounds for thinking that the society is peculiarly well-placed to come to terms with the new situation.

II. Manufacturing or Services?

Whether or not Britain opts for renewed economic growth, or maintains economic output at something like the current level, it is clear that she will have to make a choice about what kind of economic activities to support and promote. Here is a typical statement from the Department of Industry, blessed by no less than four Secretaries of State: 'The success of manufacturing is vital to the country's future. The Government, through its industrial strategy, is committed to giving it priority over other objectives . . . Society needs to recognise the contribution of manufacturing industry in creating wealth on which we depend to preserve and improve our social provisions and personal standards of living.'[20]

Nothing could be plainer than that, and nothing more likely to command heartfelt assent from all concerned with public affairs. Moreover the DOI's document is correct in noting that government policy has since the war consistently favoured manufacturing, and – though this is unspoken – been consistently hostile to service activities. As public policy the attitude seems to date back to Keynes,[21] with his incisive analysis of Britain's weak manufacturing sector in comparison with its world-wide financial operations. As a general view, however, the attitude clearly has deeper roots, and derives from the writings of Adam Smith, Say, and others, on the nature of 'productive' and 'unproductive activities'. In this classification, manufacturing (and agriculture) are productive, services largely unproductive. This view has taken an almost religious hold on educated opinion. Politicians, trade unionists, their advisers, all have accepted the apparently common sense view that if something doesn't hurt when you drop it on your foot, it can't become an export. To champion services as against manufacturing, to suggest that the future might lie more in the development of the former than of the latter, is to invite the charge of crankiness, if not actual treason.

There has been a public consensus, unprecedented in its weight of advocacy and narrowness of content, on the need to 'get manufacturing industry moving again', to put more people back into 'productive', that is, manufacturing industry, whether or not this would be a good thing for manufacturing anyway, and at whatever cost to the rest of the economy and society. Services have been persistently penalized – most notoriously with the Selective Employment Tax of 1966-73, a product of Lord Kaldor's advisory role, and under the influence of his strongly pro-manufacturing economic writing.[22] Symbolically the official antipathy to services is shown by the fact that right up till 1970 the Queen's Award for Export could not be given to the exporter of a service. At a different level it was shown in the reaction of the backwoodsmen who returned their M.B.E.s on the award of the same honours to the Beatles in 1965 for their contribution to Britain's overseas earnings.

For many people, the case against services was decisively put by the Oxford economists Robert Bacon and Walter Eltis, in their influential analysis of Britain's economic problems.[23] Carefully read, their book does not really back up the prescriptions popularly derived from it, but the authors' general emphasis – and the book's title – is such as easily to lead to misunderstanding. What seemed to follow from their account was that there has been an excessive movement of employees and investment funds from manufacturing to services. Manufacturing is seen as productive, 'wealth-creating', and is largely identified with the private, market, sector. Services are seen as mostly non-productive and are largely identified with the non-market, public, sector.[24] The fact that the State also manufactures and sells – e.g. steel and ships – is acknowledged but not, apparently, regarded as very significant. Similarly the existence of a highly successful services branch – e.g. retail and banking – in the private sector is recognized, but this too does not seem to carry much weight. Eltis and Bacon's analysis, popularized in an influential Sunday newspaper, led to a chorus of demands for cut-backs in services, and massive inducements to get more men and women back into manufacturing.

And yet the merest glance at some widely available figures tells a different story, for those with ears to hear. Consider this picture of manufacturing decline. For the first half of the nineteenth century, as was hardly to be wondered at in the world's first industrial nation, British manufacturing dominated the world. In 1870 British manufactured exports accounted for 40 per cent of all world trade in manufactures. By 1900 this was down to 30 per cent; by 1930, 20 per cent; by 1960 – following a period of temporary recovery largely owing to the smashed industrial economies of Japan and Continental Europe – it was 15 per cent; in 1976, less then 9 per cent.[25]

It could scarcely be clearer from these figures how long-term, basic, and structural Britain's manufacturing decline must be; and so it has been widely acknowledged.[26] From about 1870 onwards all the relevant economic indices – rates of growth, productivity, investment, technical innovation, and so on – take a downward turn. They have continued to plunge in this century, except for a few short periods. The reasons for this decline are complex and much discussed, but an obvious one was quite simply that other countries were now industrializing, and had many of the well-known advantages of latecomers. France, Belgium, Germany, Sweden, the United States, Japan, Russia, all grew at Britain's expense. They invaded not just her foreign but her home markets. Later came competition from Canada and Australia, later still the challenges from the intensely capitalist eastern enclaves: Taiwan, Hongkong, Singapore, South Korea. Now countries like Brazil and India are also threatening some of Britain's traditional markets, and other competitors are already in sight. As *The Times* put it in 1971 – before the position could be seen to have actually worsened – 'Britain is now little more than standby capacity for world manufactured exports; the complete elimination of Britain's industrial capacity could now be made up by the expansion in the rest of the world inside a few months.'[27]

This being so, on what grounds do its advocates urge the strategy of economic recovery through manufacturing? No one surely can expect a reversal of so secular a decline within the foreseeable future. Certainly it would go against any historical parallel that springs to mind. Britain's manufacturing base has now become so precarious that every attempt to strengthen and broaden it has invited punishment. Every impulse to growth in the last two decades has been halted by the inescapable and finally unacceptable rise in imports, leading to a severe balance of payments crisis. To put it in the economist's terms, the income elasticities of demand for British imports are high, those for British exports are low. In other words, the British need other people's goods; other people seem neither to need nor to want British goods.[28] The British government's policy has for long been geared to the idea of growth through the export of manufactured goods. But as the Hudson Report puts it, 'there is a basic question of just what Britain will export. Manufactures have been a stagnant component of exports but a rapidly rising component of imports. It seems much more likely therefore that an increase in investment and output will create an increase in imports, not the desired exports . . .'[29] The change in the structure of imports reveals the pattern of increasing dependency. Britain imports half her food, and up to 1960 this accounted for a third of all imports. During the following twelve years this proportion dropped to 18 per cent of total imports. By contrast imports of manufactured goods and machinery rose sharply – by some 16 per cent – so that at the end of the same period they accounted for 55 per cent of total imports. The position with regard to fuels and raw materials has, it is well known, deteriorated even more sharply in recent years, especially following the OPEC decision to quadruple the price of crude oil in 1973. Britain imports two-thirds of her raw material and half her fossil fuels (and North Sea oil and gas will be very short-lived). As a manufacturing nation she is, clearly, very dependent on overseas goods and resources. As these increase in price or scarcity her ability to compete with the rest of the world's industrial nations declines even further.[30]

But if British *manufacturing* glory seems over, the same thing cannot be said for British *services*. The contrast here with manufacturing could hardly be more striking. Britain is second only to the United States in the world trade in 'invisible', i.e. services, with 12 per cent of the total trade. She has a permanent and rising surplus on current account. Whereas the import content of manufacturing exports is already 19 per cent and going up, that of service exports is less than 9 per cent. Productivity in service industries, though notoriously difficult to measure, seems to be higher than manufacturing in many branches (compare Marks and Spencer's to British Steel). In 1975 the insurance and banking services of the City of London earned twice as much in exports as the motor car industry. Tourism, one of the most successful and fastest growing industries, contributed in 1977 £3000 million to the balance of payments, and has a surplus on account of £1000 million. It earns for Britain more than the total sales abroad of electrical machinery and appliances. In fact services already account for over 40 per cent of total overseas earnings, and on current trends bid fair to overtake manufacturing.[31]

One might have thought that these figures would be publicised and their implications seriously discussed. But they are not. A clear alternative to current official strategy presents itself – to promote and prosecute the service activities of the economy as vigorously as possible. And yet, as we have seen, strong suspicions and prejudices abound in this field. For instance, alarmed by the tourist invasion Sir Malby Crofton, leader of one of London's biggest boroughs, proposes the imposition of a tourist quota and special tourist taxes to discourage the trade. Moralists and economists, mindful of past manufacturing triumphs, denounce the wealth created by tourism as fleeting and insubstantial. There is an uneasy sense that Britain may turn into a nation of Benidorms, or of Arab bazaars selling cheap trinkets.

What is peculiarly misguided about these attitutes is that they think that they are reacting against some novel phenomenon, something more suited to foreigners and alien to the noble native manufacturing tradition. In fact tourism is simply one of the more recent[32] expressions of a field of economic activities – the tertiary or service sector – which of course long pre-dates the Industrial Revolution. But there is something more important about this, from the point of view of Britain's future. *Services are the thing that Britain has always been good at*, well before she launched the industrial revolution the turned her society – and the world – towards manufacturing. By the end of the eighteenth century Britain had already outdistanced her European competitors in the crucial services of banking, insurance, and shipping. Over two centuries she had established the pattern and practice of overseas investment. London had superseded Amsterdam as the centre of the world's money market. Long before she was an industrial community, then, Britain was an organized commercial and financial community. On the basis of her service economy she had made herself by the end of the eighteenth century the richest country in the world.

Financial and mercantile services, together with overseas investment, constitute the historic core of the nation's foreign trade in 'invisibles', traditionally centred on the City of London. The trade has swollen by every new addition of marketable services, whether in the form of tourism, technical expertise, clothes design, symphony orchestras, pop groups, television programmes, health and educational services. Now there is a fact about Britain's trade in invisibles which ought to be widely known, and reflected on. For most of this century politicians and economists have worried us, and the economic system, over deficits in the balance of payments. They have concentrated almost exclusively, as most people tend to when they talk about the balance of payments, on deficits in the trade in 'visible' goods, now mostly manufactures. But as W.A.P. Manser established in his book *Britain in Balance*, a deficit in the visible trade has been the normal thing in Britain ever since regular trading records began at the end of the seventeenth century. Taking just the more recent period, there was a surplus on the visible trading account only in 9 out of the last 177 years. The deficit moreover was at its largest in the nineteenth century, at the height of Britain's manufacturing prosperity.[33]

What has throughout made up the difference and – with the exception of a few years – bridged the gap between exports and imports of goods, has been the continuous and healthy surplus in invisibles. If Britain over the past couple of centuries has had a net surplus in its overall balance of payments, this has been entirely due to the earnings from the trade in invisibles. The service sector has bailed out the manufacturing sector.

But we may be able to go even further than this. Paradoxical as it may sound in the nation that created the world's first industrial society, there is actually something artificial, aberrant almost, in the rise to pre-eminence of British manufacturing industry in the nineteenth century. It went against the grain of the society's cultural values, as well as important parts of its social structure. 'Trade' in the form of the merchant banker or the West Indian planter was respectable. After an initial encounter with feudal values, the City became an accepted part of the Establishment. The sons and daughters of such 'tradesmen' married easily enough into the gentry and aristocracy, whose ample rural style of life continued to dominate the aspirations of all classes throughout the last century and well into this.

But manufacturing: that was a different matter. Manufacturers were provincial. They were often Dissenters (which meant, for one thing, not being able to go to Oxford or Cambridge). They were looked down upon not just by the aristocracy and gentry but by the merchants and bankers of the City. Faced with such social pressure who can be surprised if their children hurried to escape from this despised social category – indeed were pressed to do so by their own parents. The historians monotonously record the movement out of manufacturing of the great industrial families, the Arkwrights, Boultons, Strutts, Wilkinsons, Wedgwoods, Courtaulds. 'From shirt-sleeves to hunting-jacket in three generations', is how David Landes sums up the process.[34] D.C. Coleman sees it as the result of the persistent pressure to cross the only important divide in English society, that between 'Players' and 'Gentlemen'.[35] The ideal of the English gentleman, originally thought up to tame the turbulent knights of the Tudor period, was refurbished in the nineteenth century – with the help of the public schools – to tame the rough energetic industrialists and technologists of the Industrial Revolution.

Some of this was true of other European countries as well. But nowhere – for reasons much discussed[36] – was the persistence of gentry culture and life-style so deep and long-lasting as in Britain. The sheer energy and success of early industrialism carried it along for a time. But the weight of the stronger cultural tradition, always present alongside, eventually proved too much. The consequences were already apparent by the last quarter of the nineteenth century. British manufacturing then began its long downhill slide from its position of supremacy. From the 1870s we also begin to hear the litany of complaints, now so familiar, about Britain's backwardness in technical education, the lack of entrepreneurial ambition, the preference of the best brains for the professions and public service rather than for manufacturing industry.[37]

But there was a strong element of hypocrisy in the complaints. British society had *chosen* the values which it recognized and rewarded, and it was idle to expect ambitious individuals to ignore this fact. The structure of higher education which emerged at the end of the nineteenth century made this only too clear. It continued the divide between gentlemen and players, between commissioned and non-commissioned officers, between the two cultures of the cultivated amateur and the technical expert. For the governing class there were Oxford and Cambridge, to complete the work of the Public Schools. For the non-commissioned officers there were the new provincial universities with their strong utilitarian and technological bias. Matthew Arnold was driven to comment thus on the disturbing consequences: 'So we have amongst us the spectacle of a middle class cut in two and in a way unexampled anywhere else, of a professional class brought up on the first plane, with fine and governing qualities, but without the idea of science; while that immense business class, which is becoming so important a power in all countries, on which the future so depends, . . . is in England brought up on the second plane, cut off from the aristocracy and the professions, and without governing qualities.'[38] Who, given the opportunity to choose, would deliberately opt to join the second rank? Commenting on the educational developments of this period, Michael Fores has aptly observed that '"pecking orders" of occupational groups in society determine which educational courses can be set up successfully, not the other way round. Exhortations to teach more "science" in schools and universities missed the point. It is more important to note that the middle – and late – Victorians preferred not to send their sons to learn the useful arts because these did not fit in well with the new type of society which they wanted to create.'[39]

By the end of the nineteenth century the British, it seems, had already had their fill of manufacturing. They gratefully reverted to the older, culturally more comfortable pattern of getting their wealth through services. As Britain's share of world manufacturing trade declined, her trade in invisibles increased its share of world market. 'It could well be said', says Fores, 'that Britain changed from being the workshop of the world in about 1850 to being the service agency of the world about half a century later.'[40] Nothing much has changed in the course of the present century, either in the external environment or in the character of British society, to suggest that this direction could or should be reversed. At regular intervals the anguished national debates about Britain's poor manufacturing and technological performance have taken place, the last before the present round being the controversy over Sir Charles Snow's Rede Lecture, *The Two Cultures and the Scientific Revolution* (1959). These debates have nearly always simply recapitulated the nineteenth century discussion of the same problem. And, for the same reasons now as before, attitudes towards manufacturing industry remain stubbornly negative.

A recent discussion paper from the Department of Industry, *Industry, Education and Management*,[41] underlines the point forcibly (and depressingly, from the Department's point of view). It states the problem with great clarity. It sees the need to improve the quality of British industrial management. It realises that this will only happen if the society can improve the status and image of manufacturing industry, and of technology and science generally. Yet the document shows that the proportion of graduates going into manufacturing had dropped to an all time low of 26 per cent by 1975. The fall is in actual as well as proportionate numbers, and represents a more or less steady decline from the 35-40 per cent of a decade ago. Even more worrying must be the drop in the proportion of the science and technology graduates who go into manufacturing – from 42 per cent (technology) and 20 per cent (science) in 1961, to 26 per cent and 11 per cent respectively in 1975. Moreover the demand for science and technology places at universities continues to be static, while that for arts and social science subjects goes on rising. Add to this that the quality of students entering to read technological subjects is significantly lower than that for all other subjects, and the Department of Industry's disquiet is understandable. All this when both the quantity and quality of industrial management, backed by social esteem, continues to increase in most other industrial societies.

This section is not meant to be a tract against manufacturing. Manufacturing always has been and always will be a part of the nation's economy. The idea of a pure service economy is nonsense. But the important question is the balance of national endeavour; what we recognise and reward; what we see to be the strengths of the society in relation to what our industrial competitors can do. On that basis the prejudice against services, and the obstacles put in the way of their development, is extremely short-sighted. One suspects here a strong residual puritanism in economic matters: that there's only money where there's muck. In the framework of a capitalist economy this is the sheerest hypocrispy. Why should anyone object if the Beatles make more money for Britain than British Leyland? There are good grounds moreover for thinking that the growth of services will benefit the society not just economically, but socially and culturally. In certain of the service areas, at least, the nature of the work, the scale of organization, the nature of the product, and the social effects of the process of production, are all very much to be preferred than in the bulk of manufacturing industry.[42]

The country has in any case, because of the prevailing prejudices, so far only scratched the surface of its service potential. It has relied very much on the historic services of the City of London. Much imagination and enterprise must lie dormant or undeveloped for lack of encouragement. But there are some indications. The boom in English language schools suggests one additional line of development. So, too, does the success of the broadcasting organizations in selling their television programmes abroad, and of the Open University in selling its educational services. Tourism, for all its spectacular development, is still very much restricted to a few well-known English cities, and is clearly capable of much greater growth. Most far-reaching of all might be the opening up of the health and educational services. Passions are bound to be aroused by this. But properly handled there is no reason why these highly developed national resources should not pay handsomely without loss of quality or service to the native population. It is quite clear, from the demand for places in private health clinics in British schools and universities, that these services are highly regarded and widely sought after by people overseas. Yet both Labour and Tory governments in the Seventies have been hostile to university expansion, and the present Conservative administration under Mrs Thatcher seems bent on undermining British universities altogether. It seems foolish that with such obviously marketable services to hand, the government should cut back on these in the interests of a decaying manufacturing industry.

Britain launched the first industrial revolution on the world. For nearly a century she reaped the rewards of being a pioneer. Now she is suffering, inevitably and naturally, from industrial senility. To attempt to rejuvenate British society by propping up its creaking manufacturing industries is like trying to restore the looks of an ageing beauty with quantities of cream and rouge: pathetic and impossible. The world no longer seems to want or need British textiles, British steel, British ships, British cars, British electrical goods. It does however want a whole host of British services and will pay well for them. To encourage these with as much political will as can be harnessed seems to promise not simply a sounder economic future but the possibility of a more lively, humane, and satisfying society.

III. The Longer-Term – a Household Economy?

The strategy of going for services is conventional on most criteria. It is contained within the framework of a capitalist market economy. It assumes the goal of continuing economic growth, although accepting that such growth is likely to be slower for all industrial countries than has been the case in recent decades. It assumes that Britain remains heavily dependent on imports of food, fuel, and manufactured goods, and therefore has to have something to sell in the overseas markets of the world. Although it provides a breathing-space, it may be short-term.

On the other hand it may provide the bridge to a future that is radically different. It does at least break the psychological tie with the past, and is firm in its rejection of the nostalgic hope for a revival of old industrial glories. It may lead to a search for activities which, besides being commercially viable, call upon resources of enterprise, creativity, and imagination that are rewarding in themselves. It may, in short, seriously raise the question of quality versus quantity, of a way of life satisfying by virtue of the values which it cultivates as against the goal of material growth for its own sake.

What, therefore, are the prospects for a move towards a society of welfare or well-being – something akin to Illich's 'convivial society'? A society in which considerations of continuing material growth are displaced by considerations of continuous personal growth? We are, doubtless, all for this in theory, but most people would regard such a goal as utopian in present circumstances. I want to suggest that it may be utopian in the sense that one cannot easily specify the mechanisms which will take us from here to there; but that it is properly utopian in confronting us with choices and values which we must decide upon in the pursuit of any long-term future goal. Moreover it goes to a considerable extent with, not against, many current developments.

Such a strategy would question, first, the current forms of social accounting, and the reality of the measurement of welfare contained within their terms. It inquires of the present order: by the criteria of genuine welfare, how efficient, productive, and satisfying is it? It questions in particular current conceptions of 'wealth' and 'productive work'. We have already had reason to note the narrowness as well as the possible illusoriness of the concept of 'wealth creation' contained in the statistics of national income. James Robertson thus challenges the idea that it is only industry and commerce which creates wealth: 'We question the idea of 'wealth' as something created by manufacturers of cigarettes and sweets, but not by doctors and dentists; created by bankers and commercial lawyers, but not by housewives and social workers; created by agri-business, but not by people working their smallholdings, allotments, and gardens; created by advertising agencies but not by schools; created by the arms trade, but not by the peacepeople. Is it a law of nature that compels us to make more and more *things*, including many that are harmful or useless, before we can attend to the needs of *people*? . . . The idea of wealth as something that has to be created by the 'economic' activities of industry and commerce, so that it can then be spent on something quite different called 'social' wellbeing, is part of the metaphysic of the industrial age . . .'[43]

Once accept this broader, and patently saner, concept of wealth, and the goods, services, and activities that go to make it undergo a change of character that may be very far-reaching. Tom Burke gives the following account of what it might mean to be truly accounted wealthy:

'The new wealth might count as affluent the person who possessed the necessary equipment to make the best use of natural energy flows to heat a home or warm water – the use which accounts for the bulk of an individual's energy demand. The symbols of this kind of wealth would not be new cars, T.V.s, or whatever, although they would be just as tangible and just as visible. They would be solar panels, insulated walls, or a heat pump. The poor would be those who remained dependent on centralised energy distribution services, vulnerable to interruption by strike, malfunction, or sabotage, and even more vulnerable to rising tariffs set by inaccessible technocrats themselves the victims of market forces beyond their control. The new rich would boast not of how new their television set was but of how long it was expected to last and how easy it would be to repair. Wealth might take the form of ownership of, or at least access to, enough land to grow a proportion of one's food. This would reduce the need to earn an even larger income in order to pay for increasingly expensive food. Wealth might consist in having access to most goods and services within easy walking or cycling distance of home thus reducing the need to spend more time earning more money to pay for more expensive transport services. A high income could be less a sign of wealth than of poverty since it would indicate dependence on the provision by someone else of a job and a workplace in order to earn the income to rent services. Wealth would consist in having more control over the decisions that affected well being, and in having the time to exercise that control.'[44]

The important point about re-conceptualizing wealth is that it changes the constraints normally supposed to exist on the amount of 'free' or 'leisure' time, and potentially expands this sphere greatly. More accurately, perhaps, it changes the very definition of 'work' and 'leisure', and suggests the possibility of a working life lived equally 'productively' in both spheres. At the moment most of us accept the utilitarian 'felicific calculus' of work being the necessary pain for the pleasure of leisure. Work is painful, and by virtue of that, necessary and productive; leisure is pleasure, and by virtue of that, contingent and passive. Commenting on this 'vision of inertia' C. B. Macpherson rightly says: 'It is almost incredible, until you come to think of it, that a society whose keyword is *enterprise*, which certainly sounds active, is in fact based on the assumption that human beings are so inert, so averse to activity, that is, to expenditure of energy, that every expenditure of energy is considered to be painful, to be, in the economist's term, a disutility. This assumption, which is a travesty of the human condition, is built right into the justifying theory of the market society . . . The market society is commonly justified on the grounds that is maximizes utilities, i.e., that it is the arrangement by which people can get the satisfaction they want with the least effort. The notion that activity itself is pleasurable, is a utility, has sunk almost without trace under this utilitarian vision of life.'[45]

What are the practical possibilities of revising and reversing this utilitarian assessment? Can we move towards a society in which work done at home or in the community, normally thought of as spare-time activity, can become the central focus of an individual's life, the chief source of his identity? The interesting thing is the extent to which this has already been happening. Hugh Stretton has given us the most perceptive account of this development. 'The first industrial revolution', he says, 'had moved production out of the family into the factory; the second industrial revolution moved a lot of it back again.' Mass-produced household goods, network water and gas and electricity, ubiquitous transport, all produced another great shift of productive resources. 'By 1970 the British housewife was using the horsepower the British factory worker had used in 1910. Households could *make* and *do* things: a steadily increasing number and variety of things. With materials and equipment supplied by the commercial economy, they were soon producing a good deal of the twentieth century standard of living for themselves.'[46]

In similar fashion, Jay Gershuny has shown that there is already under way a movement to what he calls 'the self-service economy'. Contrary to the views of some 'post-industrial' theorists such as Daniel Bell, people are consuming more, not less, goods, and less, not more, services supplied by the formal money economy. A process of substitution of goods for services has been going on steadily for some considerable time. 'This change', comments Gershuny, 'runs deeper than it sounds; it is more than just a simple modification of buying habits. Goods are not consumed in the way services are – goods consumption is much more akin to investment. What the evidence shows is a real transformation in investment patterns, from investment in the money economy to investment in the household, from investment in laundries and theatres and railways to investment in washing machines and televisions and motor cars. This pattern of change results from two ongoing economic trends. On the one hand rising costs – particularly labour costs – and on the other technical change enabling the substitution of labour by capital, reducing both the necessary time and the necessary skill levels. These together enable more and more final production by the final consumer himself – by 'direct labour'. This is the self-service economy'.[47]

The implication of this shift from market to home, from the 'formal' to the 'informal' economy, is, as Stretton points out, that 'the flow of consumer goods has been overrated as the characteristic product of industrialization. The most profound achievement of modern industry – of the forty-hour week of organized alienated labour – has been to give people at home energy, equipment, materials and communications, and time and space and freedom, to produce for themselves: to make and do what they want, when and where and how they want, working together or apart as they feel inclined, and enriching their time and social experience in all sorts of ways freely chosen by themselves'. Already, as he further shows, in present-day industrial societies much more than a half of all working time is spent at home or near it. More than a third of all capital is invested there, more than a third of work is done there. Depending on what we choose to count as goods, some high proportion of all goods are produced there, and even more are enjoyed there. 'More than three-quarters of all subsistence, social life, leisure and recreation happen there. Above all, people are produced there, and endowed there with the values and capacities which will determine most of the quality of their social life and government away from home.'[48]

It would, clearly, be going too far to say that the desirable transformation is already more or less accomplished. Indeed aspects of the current development could lead to a society of a highly undesirable kind: privatized, passive, consumerist, characterised by an educated elite doing all the interesting work and running the society, and a majority employed in unrewarding tasks at work and undemanding consumption at home (something, in fact, like the scenario sketched in Michael Young's *The Rise of the Meritocracy*). The materials for the change exist. But they have to be given a definite shape and direction. The assumption underlying the design of current household tools and appliances, for instance, is that they should be time-saving and undemanding of skill and effort. Household work is regarded as a marginal activity, to be undertaken with the minimum effort and in the minimum time. 'Real' work takes place outside the home – in the money economy. The ideal home is a place of leisure and inactivity. It refreshes and re-creates the worker for the serious and productive work elsewhere.

The aim, then, should be to re-define the place and the function of the household. Here, only the briefest indications can be given of how we might achieve this.

First, make production in the formal, institutional, economy as efficient as possible. This may mean pushing capital intensity, specialization, and mechanization as far and as fast as possible. The price may well be abandoning the hope of humanizing work in this sphere. It is a price we should not be afraid to pay. The extent to which work in a complex industrial economy can be humanized will always be limited. Alienation is its hallmark. The gain will be correspondingly great, however: cheapness of goods and, above all, increase in free time. Most of us will need to spend no more than two or three days at work in the formal economy. Some people, probably, with particular drives and aptitudes will want to spend most of their time on activities in the formal economy. The rest of us will be freed for activities in the household and the community.

Next, much of the technology of the household will need to be re-designed. The capital goods produced in the formal economy for use in the household must be of the kind that will enhance the skill and productivity of the individual user or small group (by household, of course, I mean anything from the nuclear family to a small village, urban or rural). A domestic cooker (or typewriter) is an ideal model:

it aids, does not substitute for, time-intensive, skill-intensive, non-alienating, non-polluting, eminently productive activity. Many of the tools that have accompanied the 'Black and Decker do-it-yourself revolution' have these characteristics. One can, for instance, now purchase domestic lathes for turning metal, wood, or clay, which can be installed in very small workshops. Similarly the miniaturization and simplification of print technology makes it perfectly feasible for small household units to print and publish newspapers, magazines, and books. On this count, generally, many technological developments are going in the direction of scaled-down, household size units.[49]

The goods made in the formal economy should be those which emphasise durability and reparability. They should be capable of being repaired and serviced by people with modest technical skills and relatively simple tools. They should as far as possible be components which can be assembled in small workshops.

Lastly there is the need to cut as far as possible reliance on imports of food, fuels, and raw materials. This means going in for the familiar strategy of low-energy technologies, use of 'alternative' sources of energy (wind, water, sun), production of long-life durables, and processes involving re-cycling, re-use, renovation, and repair. For instance the British electricity generating system is prodigiously wasteful, wasting three out of every four tons of coal consumed. The importance of this is seen in the fact that about one-third of all primary energy is consumed in the generation of electricity. Similarly one-quarter of all energy consumed in Britain is for domestic space heating in homes with very poor insulation standards. Consumption can be cut by about one-third at a cost to each house of about £200 spent on insulation.[50] Most far-reaching of all might be the savings possible in food imports (Britain imports half her food). Michael Allaby has shown how, by certain not very spectacular and often very desirable changes in the national diet, Britain could become well-nigh self-sufficient in food. The changes involve mainly cutting back by about half on the consumption of beef, veal, pig and poultry products (though leaving lamb and mutton consumption much as it is now), and making up the additional protein through increased grain consumption. There would also have to be less sugar consumed.[51]

We might, finally, note the relation of an overall strategy of this kind to two dominant anxieties of the present time: unemployment, and the power of the multinationals. As to the first, it must be clear how little 'unemployment' has to do with the lack of *work*. There are over three million unemployed in Britain at the moment. They are not, that is, 'in work', employed for wages in the formal economy. But are they all not working? How many unemployed husbands and wives now spend more time doing jobs around the home, renovating and extending domestic facilities ('building' and 'construction'), taking more time with their children ('education' and 'child-rearing'), growing more of their own food in gardens and allotments ('agriculture')? How many services and goods are being exchanged not involving cash transactions, or undeclared cash transactions – car repairs in return for examination tuition, tomatoes and lettuces in return for baby-sitting? How many of the young unemployed have used or developed skills to run small trades or businesses in the informal economy – small-scale construction and maintenance, gardening, window-cleaning, carpentry and furniture making – for all of which there is unfilled demand both in large cities and in small country towns? How many of those who don't, who are demoralized and made apathetic by unemployment, are so because of the excessive valuation placed on employment in the formal economy?

There are many of those in employment who are already aware of a dissatisfaction, an uncertainty, about where the line between work and non-work should be drawn. Much of what they do at work strikes them as unproductive even if time-consuming. Much else that they do in their 'leisure time' seems worthwhile and rewarding. It is pointless to entice industry to create jobs which are often useless to the industry and degrading to the worker. There is no shortage of work to be done. It is mainly a matter of acknowledging this, of conferring legitimacy on particular activities. In an instructive Canadian example, the Canada Council 'creates' jobs by conferring legitimacy on tasks proposed by people in local communities. Worthwhile activities are not identified and organized from the top down, but from the bottom up – by people proposing and carrying out particular tasks. It is interesting that this process started through a conventional 'job creation' scheme, initiated by government agencies with traditional assumptions about work and employment. It was the local community workers and their 'clients' who re-defined the tasks to suit the actual needs of the local community.[52] It hardly needs pointing out how much a move to a household-based economy would further obliterate orthodox distinctions between work done in the formal money economy and work done outside it. Once the latter sphere is acknowledged as legitimate and productive, the opportunities for creative work are boundless. A high level of official 'unemployment' could come to be a sign of a society that had changed its priorities from continuing material growth to personally satisfying work.

The multinational problem isn't so easily dealt with. There may be features of a move to a household economy that the multinationals view with alarm – specifically, the fact that there may be a declining demand for some of their goods and services. But in a number of ways there may be no great incompatibility, in the short term at least, between the interests of the multinationals and the growth of locality-based economies. Many commentators have in fact envisaged a future world division of labour in which the multinationals act basically as servicing agencies, supplying the products which cannot be produced locally, especially those requiring high-science, high-technology, and high-energy inputs. Both the large and the small units may gain from this arrangement. This is the dual economy on the international plane.[53]

No doubt there is reason to suspect so neat a resolution. But assuming a conflict of interests in the long run, is there not more hope for small-scale communities from the rivalry between great powers, leaving the other elements as the *tertium gaudens*? Was it not the rivalry between Papacy and Empire which allowed the Italian city-states to revive and thrive after the fall of the Roman Empire? Was it not the rivalry between King and Parliament after 1688 which created the conditions for the intense social and economic developments in England in the subsequent century and a half? The spectre of omnipotent multinationals crushing the autonomy of small communities may be the stuff of demonology rather than of sociology. In the competition between nation state and international agencies, between national corporations and the multinationals, the small may still find the space to manoeuvre, and the means to retain their freedom.

*   *   *

'If you had to constitute new societies, you might on moral and social grounds, prefer corn fields to cotton factories; an agricultural to a manufacturing population. But our lot is cast; we cannot change it and we cannot recede.'[54] Thus spoke Sir Robert Peel in 1846 as, reluctantly but stoically, he forced upon the Conservative Party the repeal of the Corn Laws, and inaugurated the 'Golden Age' of manufacturing prosperity in Britain. He was right, of course, for the time and place. But might not a change of similar magnitude be upon us in Britain now? A century after Peel the certainties, the accomplished fact, of industrialism are breaking up. A definite new direction has not yet emerged. Our lot is not yet cast. Various options seem open to us, and we may, indeed must, on 'moral and social grounds' choose which to follow. The suggestion of this piece is that there is much in Britain's tradition that, perhaps more than any other industrial society, prepares her for a social order going beyond the confines of classic industrialism. She has retained attitudes and values that may allow her to pioneer a post-industrial revolution. And if this involves recovering aspects of the past before industrialism, if it may include more people working once more in corn fields than in cotton factories, who can now say that this is either impossible or regrettable?

ENDNOTES

Parts of this paper were first given at two conferences organized by the Acton Society Trust: the first at Cumberland Lodge, Windsor Great Park, in July 1977; the second at the Certosa di Pontignano, Siena, in September 1977. I should particularly like to acknowledge the help I received from the papers and comments of Jay Gershuny, Peter Harper, and James Robertson. Thanks, too, to Ray Pahl for the continuing stimulus of conversation.

1. Peter Jay, 'Englanditis', in R. Emmett Tyrrell, Jr. (ed.), *The Future That Doesn't Work: Social Democracy's Failure in Britain* (Doubleday, New York, 1977), pp. 167-85.
2. J. K. Galbraith, interviewed in the *Sunday Times*, 21 January 1977. See also the similarly expressed sentiments of Arthur Koestler, interviewed in *The Times*, 21 February 1977.
3. Ralf Dahrendorf, 'A Reply to the Britain-Bashers', *The Sunday Times*, 1 May 1977. For the report of the *New Society* survey, see T. Forester, 'Do the British Sincerely Want to be Rich?' *New Society*, 28 April 1977.
4. R. Socolow, letter to *The Times*, 14 October 1976.
5. I have drawn here on the historical discussion in J. Gershuny, *After Industrial Society* (Macmillan, London, 1978), Ch. 1.
6. For such a sketch see Maurice Lamontagne, 'The Loss of the Steady State', in A. Rotstein (ed.), *Beyond Industial Growth* (Toronto University Press, Toronto, 1976), pp. 1-21.
7. Mancur Olson, 'Introduction', to Mancur Olson and Hans Landsberg (eds.). *The No-Growth Society* (The Woburn Press, London, 1975), p. 4.
8. Mancur Olson and Hans Landsberg (eds), *op cit.* (1975), p. 4.
9. Cf. the following proposal by Roland McKean: 'The preferable course would be to attack directly conventional forms of pollution (making use of effluent charges and price mechanisms wherever they appear to be economical), and to tax the use of non-renewable resources. This direct and more finely tuned approach would, of course, reduce growth and final output, as conventionally measured, thereby generating some of the costs and benefits attributed to no-growth. Whether it reduced the growth of the GNP to 1 per cent, to zero, or to a negative 2 per cent would not be highly relevent as long as its impact on pollution and the exhaustion of resources was one in which gains exceeded sacrifices. The parts of the GNP that this policy would reduce are those that produce more social cost than gain, and the parts it would preserve are those that yield more social gain than cost.' 'Growth vs. No-Growth: An Evaluation', in Olson and Lansberg (eds.), *op cit.*, (1975), p. 225.
10. Hugh Stretton, *Capitalism, Socialism, and the Environment* (Cambridge University Press, Cambridge, 1976), p. 314, n. 1.
11. See W. Beckerman, 'Why We Need Economic Growth', *Lloyds Bank Review*, No. 102, October, 1971, pp. 1-15; 'What No-Growth Society?', *New Statesman* 18 March 1977. For Crosland's view, see C. A. R. Crosland, *Socialism Now, and Other Essays* (Cape, London, 1974). It should perhaps be said here that, for all their gestures in an environmentalist direction, Beckerman and Crosland clearly stand for old-fashioned material growth, and have so been understood by both supporters and critics.
12. Fred Hirsch, *The Social Limits to Growth* (Routledge and Kegan Paul, London, 1977). This is a more radical statement than the earlier one by E. J. Mishan, *The Costs of Economic Growth* (Penguin Books, Harmondsworth,

1969), in that it cannot really be dealt with by proposed changes in the composition of Gross National Product, whereas Mishan makes clear proposals of that kind. For a lucid summary of the main physical and social objections to continued economic growth, see H. V. Hodson, *The Diseconomics of Growth* (Earth Island, London, 1972).

13. See the review of Hirsch by J. Gershuny, 'We Cannot All Stand on Each Others Shoulders . . .?' *Futures*, Vol. 10, No. 1 (February 1978).

14. In the bleak, Depression-like, conservationist no-growth scenario sketched by Stretton, he observes that things will be worse for the population of that society than for those in past societies living at comparable economic levels. For the new masses can remember that things were very different not so long ago: 'The generations since the environmental revolution are spoiled by the folk memory of that short glorious century when it was different: when it was for each generation better, warmer, growing more, knowing more, discovering and inventing, doing and making more, travelling far, living longer. When men have once tasted that wonderful apple of growth and lived through that springtime, nothing can be as good again.' Hugh Stretton, *op cit.*, (1976), p. 26.

15. Charles Taylor, 'The Politics of the Steady State', in Rotstein (ed.), *op cit.*, (1976), p. 60. For a similar prediction, see Jeremy Bugler, 'Towards the No-Growth Society', *New Statesman*, 11 March 1977; R. Heilbroner, *Business Civilization in Decline* (Penguin Books, Harmondsworth, 1977).

16. The Hudson Report, *The United Kingdom in 1980*, (Associated Business Programmes, London, 1974), p. 58.

17. The Hudson Report, *op. cit.*, (1976), p. 61.

18. Since historical analogies abound in the literature of the kind we're considering, we should here add the decline of Rome to Venice, Spain, Turkey. In Heilbroner's formulation: 'A crucial element in the transformation of the Roman system into the wholly different medieval period was the influence of the new religion of Christianity, which at first undermined the old order and later provided the spirit and shaped the institutional forms of the new order. So, too, in our future, I suspect that a major force for the transformation of business civilization will be a new religious orientation, directed against the canons and precepts of our time, and oriented towards a wholly different conception of the meaning of life and a mode of social organization congenial to the encouragement of that life.' He goes on to see the content of that religion as most likely to be a 'deification of the state', a kind of 'religious politicism' already foreshadowed in Mao's China. R. Heilbroner, *op. cit.*, (1977), pp. 94-5.

19. In parts of this section I have drawn upon my article, 'A Future in the Past?', *New Society*, 24 November 1977.

20. 'Foreword' by the Secretaries of State for Industry, Education, Scotland, and Wales, to the Department of Industry's Discussion Paper, *Industry, Education, and Management* (Department of Industry, London, July 1977).

21. See Marcello de Cecco 'Keynes's Analysis of the British Disease', *The Spectator*, 19 June 1976.

22. See especially Nicholas Kaldor, *Causes of the Slow Rate of Economic Growth of the United Kingdom* (Cambridge University Press, Cambridge, 1966). A similar hostility to services is shared by many left-wing writers: see A. Glyn and B. Sutcliffe, *British Capitalism, Workers, and the Profits Squeeze* (Penguin Books, Harmondsworth, 1972) p. 121; Stuart Holland, *The Socialist Challenge*, (Quartet Books, London, 1975), P. 394.

23. R. Bacon and W. Eltis, *Britain's Economic Problems: Too Few Producers* (Macmillan, London, 1976).

24. In their book Bacon and Eltis settle on the terms 'marketable' and 'non-marketable' output sectors to indicate the distinction which they wish to make between 'productive' and 'non-productive' economic activities. Thirlwall com-

ments: 'The distinction between marketable and non-marketable output is not to be confused with the distinction between privately produced and publicly produced output or with the distinction between goods and services. Having said that, however, substantial overlaps may exist. Marketable output tends to be privately produced and a large part of publicly produced output tends to be of the service variety not sold in the market place.' A. P. Thirlwall, 'Britain's Economic Problem: Too Few Producers or a Fundamental Balance of Payments Constraint?' *National Westminster Bank Review*, February 1978.

25. For these figures, see Phyllis Deane and W. A. Cole, *British Economic Growth 1688-1959*, 2nd ed., (Cambridge University Press, Cambridge, 1967), pp. 30-33; Ajit Singh, 'UK Industry and the World Economy: A Case of De-Industrialisation?' *Cambridge Journal of Economics*, Vol. 1, 1977, pp. 113-36. There is a parallel story to be told in the decline in manufacturing output. In 1850 British manufacturing output amounted to 40 per cent of the world's total; in 1870 it was still 32 per cent. By 1900 it was 20 per cent, by 1914, 14 per cent and – to cut the story short – by 1963 it had dropped to 4 per cent. See Glyn and Sutcliffe, *op. cit.*, (1972), pp. 16-17.

26. See especially John Knapp, 'Pragmatism and the British Malaise', *Lloyds Bank Review*, No. 90, October 1968, pp. 1-21; Michael Fores, 'Britain's Economic Growth and the 1870 Watershed', *Lloyds Bank Review*, No. 99, January 1971, pp. 27-41; Corelli Barnett, 'The Hundred Year Sickness'. *Management of Human Resources*, Vol 8, No. 6 (June 1977).

27. *The Times, The Prospect of Britain*, A collection of leading articles (Times Newspapers Ltd., London, 1971), p. 21.

28. See A. Singh, *op. cit.*, (1977); and A. P. Thirlwall, *op. cit.*, (1978). Singh comments (p. 132): 'The evidence suggests that the main reason for the UK's high income elasticity of demand for imports (as well as the unfavourable export elasticity) is to be found in the lower quality, design and general performance of its products relative to other countries . . . The faster growing, more dynamic economies are in a position to achieve greater technical progress and make product improvements in all the above mentioned directions, and are therefore able to respond more effectively to changing patterns of demand as consumer incomes rise.'

29. The Hudson Report, *op. cit.*, (1974) p. 43. As they further comment: 'Much post war policy for growth has been firmly tied to 'export-led' stimulation with a resulting emphasis on traditional manufacturing industries. For this reason, the motto 'Export or Die' may contain the wrong conjunction: for it has guaranteed that Britain has maintained those manufacturing sectors often of greatest age or the most inefficient construction.'

30. The Hudson Report, *op. cit.*, (1974), p. 53, Table 13. For the later – and worse – position regarding imports, see V. Woodward, 'No Cause for Optimism over Imports', *The Times*, 23 June 1976.

31. For these figures, and a general discussion of the contribution of services to the British economy, see *Britain's Invisible Earnings*, Report of the Committee on Invisible Exports (National Export Council, London, 1967); W. M. Clarke, *The City in the World Economy* (Institute of Economic Affairs, London, 1965); Russell Lewis, *The New Service Society* (Longman, London, 1973); Ian Bradley, 'Made in Britain', *Sunday Times Magazine,* 27 March 1977; S. Medlik, *Britain – Workshop or Service Centre to the World?*', (University of Surrey, England, 1977).

32. More recent only is its scale and organised nature, perhaps. I live in a city, Canterbury, which has lived off tourism ever since the martyrdom of Thomas a Becket in 1170, and which for long prospered mightily by it.

33. W. A. P. Manser, *Britain in Balance: The Myth of Failure*, (Longman, London, 1971), especially pp. 5-14.

34. D. Landes, *The Unbound Prometheus: Technological Change and Industrial*

Development in Western Europe from 1750 to the Present (Cambridge University Press, Cambridge, 1969), p. 336. For the general discussion, emphasizing cultural and institutional factors, see pp. 326 ff.

35. See D. C. Coleman, 'Gentlemen and Players', *Economic History Review*, Vol 26, No. 1, (1973), pp. 92-116. The whole article is a splendid historical discussion of the culture of British economic life. The persistence of this set of cultural preferences in contemporary economic life is argued by J. P. Nettl: 'Consensus or Elite Domination: The Case of Business', *Political Studies*, Vol 13, No. 1, pp. 22-44.

36. Especially the original 'classic' statement of the New Left view of English history, see Perry Anderson, 'Origins of the Present Crisis', in P. Anderson and R. Blackburn (eds), *Towards Socialism*, (Fontana, London, 1965), pp. 11-52.

37. For a good selection of the anxieties expressed by the parliamentary commissions, educational committees, and the like, see Corelli Barnett, *op. cit.*, (1977), and G. C. Allen, *The British Disease: A Short Essay on the Nature and Causes of the Nation's Lagging Wealth*, (Institute of Economic Affairs, London, 1976).

38. Quoted Fores, *op. cit.*, (1971), p. 37.

39. Fores, *op. cit.*, (1971), p. 28. And cf. Coleman, *op. cit.*, (1973), p. 115: 'How, historically, were the successful businessmen of Victorian or Edwardian England suddenly to learn to renounce the long traditions by which their predecessors had abandoned their counting houses and climbed into the gentry? And if, by some unlikely magic, they had turned themselves into single-minded, constantly profit-maximising entrepreneurs, what sort of world might have resulted? If it is true that one of the costs of the Public Schools producing 'first-class administrators' was some lag in industrial advance, how can we know that the price was not worth paying?'.

40. Fores, *op. cit.*, (1971), p. 35.

41. See note 20, above.

42. For these characteristics of the service sector see especially V. Fuchs, *The Service Economy*, (Columbia University Press, New York, 1968). One must at the same time see that this is by no means true of all service activities, many of which are as routine and alienating – and worse paid – as in manufacturing. The direction given to the service economy is clearly of great importance in enhancing the social as opposed to the purely economic benefits.

43. James Robertson, letter to *The Times* 16 February 1977. One is reminded here of Ruskin's distinction: 'Possession is in use only, which for each man is sternly limited; so that such things and so much of them as he can use, are indeed well for him, or wealth; and more of them, and any other things, are ill for him, or Illth.' *Munera Pulveris*.

44. Tom Burke, *The New Wealth*, (Friends of the Earth, London, 1977).

45. C. B. Macpherson, *The Real World of Democracy*, (Clarendon Press, Oxford, 1966).

46. Stretton, *op. cit.*, (1976), p. 186. A number of other writers have picked out this trend and drawn similar inferences. See J. Goldthorpe, D. Lockwood, F. Bechhofer, J. Platt, *The Affluent Worker in the Class Structure* (Cambridge University Press, Cambridge, 1969); M. Young and P. Willmott, *The Symmetrical Family*, (Routledge and Kegan Paul, London, 1973); James Robertson, 'Towards Post-Industrial Liberation and Reconstruction', *New Universities Quarterly*, Vol 32, No. 1 (Winter 1977/8), pp. 6-24; Hazel Henderson, 'The Coming Economic Transition', *Technological Forecasting and Social Change*, Vol 8, (1976), pp. 337-351.

47. J. I. Gershuny, 'The Self-Service Economy', *New Universities Quarterly*, Vol 32, No. 1 (Winter 1977/78), pp. 54-5.

48. Stretton, *op. cit.*, (1976), pp. 183, 186-7.

49. See Peter Harper and Godfrey Boyle (eds), *Radical Technology*, (Wildwood House, London, 1977), for detailed sketches of some possible combinations of household technology and workshop/garden-allotment units of production.
50. For a detailed specification of technologies relevant to Britain's condition, see J. D. Davis, 'Appropriate Technology for a Crowded World', *New Universities Quarterly*, Vol 32, No. 1 (winter 1977/78), pp. 25-36.
51. Michael Allaby, *Inventing Tomorrow*, (Sphere Books, London, 1977), Ch. 8 'Will We Eat?'.
52. For an account of this episode, and an enlightening general discussion, see Gail Stewart and Cathy Starrs, *Re-Working the World: A Report on Changing Concepts of Work*, (The Public Policy Concern, Ottawa, 1973).
53. See, for instance, Edward Goodman, 'How the Economies of Scale might Benefit Small Units of Spontaneous Co-operation', (Acton Society Occasional Paper, Siena Series 1977/79, No. 18).
54. Quoted W. A. P. Manser, *op. cit.*, (1971), P. 40.

Open letter to Edward Goodman (Système Technicien et Représentation du Monde)

Alain Birou

You have asked me to show how, viewed over a long period, the techniques, tools and forms of organisation in a society can be seen to have their origins in its culture, values and systems of belief. The subject is so formidable in its breadth and complexity that I prefer to reply in an open letter: a letter is a reply to *somebody*. I do not claim that I can reply fully to the question, nevertheless.

1) But first, *why do you ask me such a question?*
Behind the statement of your problem is a concern that present-day socio-technical and socio-cultural phenomena are pulling us towards changes we can no longer control. Still more deeply I sense a questioning of techno-scientific reasoning and the validity of the kinds of progress it brings about. Like many other thinkers you have fears and apprehensions about the nature and the scale of the crisis we are going through. Beyond the employment crisis, the energy crisis, the crisis of the Third World, the crisis of both capitalism and socialism, you sense a crisis of mankind and of civilisation. Everything we have considered for the last four centuries as providing the cultural and social foundations of our life is collapsing beneath our feet.

Whilst the present-future forms the horizon of the problems humanity must resolve, it is the past-present of our knowledge and skills that provides the firm ground of well-tried methods to carry us securely into the future; and in order not to fear that future, we must have faith in the past which sustains us. If we become aware that in acquiring power and mastery we are being dragged towards impotence and enslavement, the whole future becomes insecurity, fear and anguish. A few thinkers and a large number of young people may be wondering anxiously where we are going, but the rest of us are still hurtling along in the vehicle we call "progress", even though the road we take is becoming increasingly confused.

2) *What is the scale of the problem?*
Different dimensions, or more exactly different levels of analysis would be needed to examine such a hypothesis fully. A unified history

of science, technology, economic and political power, of cultures, beliefs and morals would have to be formed for us to understand what it was that started those processes in the Middle Ages and in the Renaissance which have given rise to the modern age.

The transformations in the reasoning and the will of men of science and action are due, according to some historians to the success of scientific power and method which have undermined earlier accounts of Man and his world. Others stress that Man's relationship with Nature and cosmic forces had to be overturned before he would dare to apply radical technical methods in fields hitherto regarded as sacred. In order to call himself "master and possessor of Nature" (Descartes), Man must place himself outside and above her.

With an open mind and using a multi-disciplinary method without any of our present day categorisations, I should like to be able to carry out a new survey of the end of the Middle Ages and of the Renaissance, taking into account the analyses of the following historians: G. Lagarde (*La naissance de l'esprit laïque au declin du Moyen Age*), Maurice Daumas (*Histoire Générale des techniques*), Paul Hazard (*La crise de la conscience europeéne*), Georges Gusdorf (*Les sciences humaines et la pensée occidentale*), and Jean Gimpel (*Les bâtisseurs de cathédrales* and *Contre l'art et les artistes ou la naissance d'une religion*). These men have considered the advance signs, the ideological signals and the different material and spiritual forces which have brought about the commotion of the modern age and have projected it as irreversible human history.

But beside this predominantly socio-historic approach, it is quite evident that another approach, not only anthropological and philosophical but also religious and theological is imperative. In other words, in order to understand what has happened we must raise our consciousness to the level of the great thinkers, to their visions of the universe which have shaped our modern age and which have given birth to a totally new epistemology. It would be very presumptuous of me to venture alone in any one of these fields, let alone to claim to unite them in one superior vision.

3) *What teaches us the experience of the present?*

Minds that consider themselves pragmatic and for whom only concrete facts matter will be aware first of the immediate problems facing society and the practical means of solving them. Concerned only with the play of material forces, they recoil from any discussion of the purpose of Man and the meaning of life in a technological society. The "positivistic" way of asking questions is a philosophical method for avoiding other questions. Refusal to ask questions about the historical, anthropological and ethical causes of our problems implies a particular image of Man and his place in the world. Certainly, genuine philosophical questioning is always the result of experience but this is surely an enlightenment which comes from beyond a purely material perception of the facts.

It is worth noting that problems which today seem absolutely crucial to a reasonable human life and even to the survival of mankind, former generations would have considered blasphemous: the possible meaninglessness of scientific and technical progress, human contradictions in the economic development of the world, the enslavement of men to their instruments and their work, the extreme power of material things resulting in human impotence. The major problem of our time is to understand why men in society have let themselves be progressively subjugated, enslaved externally and alienated internally by the knowledge, the power, the techniques and the systems that they themselves have set up. Why has Man let himself be moulded by the logic of his own creations so that he has become the instrument of a system which functions without him?

4) *Some dimensions of the phenomenon of technology*

Rather than wasting time on a definition of technique, which has already been done 100 times, I would prefer to make some brief observations on the meaning and range of the phenomenon of technology. The first important observation to make is that technique is not a thing in itself, a reality which can be isolated and analysed independently of scientific, economic, political and cultural contexts. Every concrete technical phenomenon is at the same time an economic or social phenomenon, inseparable from social structures and institutions.

The second observation is that the increasing complexity of technological systems and the social and technical structures required to put them into practice must change the very nature of the entire social structure.[1] It is in this sense, for example, that the machine is no longer an extension of the tool but is turning progressively into its opposite. As Hegel had already seen, 'Man deceives Nature into making her work for him.' But we must note that human work is not reduced by this fact, but becomes part of the functioning of the machine. Man no longer works in direct contact with crude nature. Instead, he serves the machine. As machines become more complicated and industry more automated, it is not the tool which serves men, but on the contrary work is modified in order to adapt to technological operations.

Informatics and computers, used as much for the organisation and control of the firm as for production, are transforming organisational and productive systems so that social relationships are also radically altered.

Is there an irreversible logic in these structural changes which compels us to take ever larger and more complex steps? The system seems to be already structured to obey this logic and to perpetuate it. Why do people always speak of the human and social consequences of technical and industrial progress, and never of the need to control and limit technology and industry in order to improve the quality of human life? This is a very important and much neglected field for enquiry.

5) *Culture and representation of the world*

From a phenomenological point of view it is usual to say that techniques determine social structures, which in their turn mould institutions and morals, thereby giving new priorities in values. Culture in the final analysis would be no more than the human results of this process. However, this definition of culture shows only the necessary expression of a material civilisation in which nobody can see where it has come from nor what it is looking for.

In fact there can only be genuine culture when all the aspects of life in a society have a positive meaning for all its members. Culture is the common and shared expression a human group gives to its existence, through complementary activities acknowledged by everybody, and not admiration of works done by others. It is both a system of representations and a context for action. The former gives an image of the universe which can be understood by all the members of the group. The context for action provides a series of organised practical means for living and for giving meaning to life, so that everyone feels that his activities are part of the social life of the whole group.

But every age has its own modes of expression, according to the beliefs, ideologies, techniques and methods of the time. In the modern age a new way of conceiving the world and Man's place in it has been adopted first by the intellectual élite, then in the customs of the ruling class and finally by the people themselves. The human mind has been taken as the unique centre and as the exclusive principle of action. Man no longer revolves around God, he revolves solely around himself. This predominant mentality has only gradually become apparent during the course of five centuries. It is only expressed openly by the enlightened and it has only recently been generally accepted in modern and industrial society. But in this time, from the vision of a few men it has spread first throughout the Western world and now throughout the entire world.

The reader refer here to my other work: *La volonté de l'Homme prend le pouvoir absolu.*

6) *At the roots of the modern age*

Man no longer acknowledges the limits of his intelligence but describes the world according to the self-image reflected in his own consciousness, thereby dismissing all metaphysical obstacles. In this new ideological context the human will is the radical controller of Man's individual and collective destiny, and it is this conception which is at the root of the experience of the modern age. We already have some idea of the extreme power it gives when served by scientific knowledge.

From this founding principle other aspects follow: the first is the increasing priority given to applied science and technique, the unimpeachable instruments with which Man can make himself master of nature. Other dimensions come from these: the division of labour, production for the market instead of for individual needs, industrialisation and mechanisation, mass production, concentration in large industrial units, proletarisation, salaried work, high levels of differentiation and specialisation, the class struggle, the spread of 'education', the emergence of new intellectual and economic powers, the growth of a particular kind of State Reason, secularisation of social life, etc. The new vision of the world based on progress where the desire for change is the driving force of Man's activity, means that there is a continual necessity for adaptations in all areas to these changes, and a corresponding increase in the need for information to keep up with current trends. With science and techniques Man has given himself the means to act on the world and so to transform himself. Furthermore, men have declared that this is the sole meaning of humanity, which humanity itself accomplishes.

If Man's only vocation in time is to master the world for his own satisfaction and for his own self-accomplishment then it is obvious that withdrawal from the world and an understanding of it through reflection (theoria) must from now on give way to that extraordinary form of acquisition made possible by scientific knowledge and technical ability (praxis). Basically there is no longer an objective universe, respected by men of limits who are conditioned by this world and eventually called to another world. There are only 'education', the emergence of new intellectual and economic powers, the growth oexterior conditions which the will of power must confront. One can see, then, why all the techno-industrial systems exalt production and the absolute primacy of the economy, of work, of the continual increasing of needs and consumption. An essential consequence of the will of power is the total subservience of men to their mastery of the world.

'Is it Man's *destiny*,' asks Beaufret, 'to be today the servant of technique? For essentially it has none of the instrumental neutrality to which one would wish to see it reduced. Its true nature and logic lead it to reveal its essential imperialism.'[2]

7) *Towards the imperialism of the techno-industrial system*

In order to understand our present day situation in anthropological and epistemological terms, we must show how in the course of the last two centuries particularly, science and technique have progressively become the masters of the future of societies by adapting themselves to new situations which they have created and by bending their methods to preserve their empire: at first mechanics were predominant, an atomistic view of phenomena, an individualistic view of Man, then the position was taken by thermodynamics, an entropic vision of the world giving way to the famous matter/energy equation. Systemic thought, a product of informatics and electronics, is the latest phase of science to maintain its grip on the world. But what I am saying in a few sentences requires entire books to cover fully and to show how novelists, thinkers, philosophers and even theologians have reflected this climate of opinion in their work.[3]

A techno-industrial and organisational milieu has developed which has gradually become the control system of society, particularly in the last fifty years. I use the term 'techno-industrial system' to refer to the complex of objective realities which men have set up but which now have their own coherence, their own logic, their own global structure and their own social requirements. But this is also a system in the sense that it is the concrete manifestation of organised principles of applied knowledge which constitute a rational whole. Applied knowledge and techniques which were still considered as social instruments until the eighteenth century gradually became social objectives and were organised by industry into a continuous and autonomous environment, eventually becoming the sustaining force of the whole of society. This objective reality, which is both outside of and within human societies, has an internal need for historical credence, for rationality, for integrated technology and for organisation. It is a global technostructure, not in Galbraith's terms, but as a system as a whole which comprises technical, industrial and administrative structures as well as the knowledge necessary to control and maintain them. Some people even speak of a technetronic universe after the electronic.

The paradox is that idealism and its opposite, theoretical and practical materialism, were necessary, so that this abstraction which is the techno-industrial system becomes the dominant reality, more real in its way than the men who serve it and only exist through it.

8) *The indisputable and the controvertible*

There is a process there which is in some ways irreversible. From the great colonial age up to our time the history of the world has taken a radically new direction. Whether one likes it or not, western civilisation has become a world phenomenon. It has produced a historical change, the consequences of which are only now beginning to be felt; something more radical and infinitely more sudden than the transition from the Paleolithic to the Neolithic ages.

The political, social, cultural and religious consequences of this state of affairs are enormous. Sociologically speaking law and morality are in a process of disappearing from collective behaviour. There are no longer fixed objective nheiorms to regulate society ethically and morally. Morality and behaviour are becoming the means, the instruments for achieving objectives made necessary by the logic of the system.

What is going to happen? Some people imagine that the techno-industrial system and its operational rationale will end up by digesting and reabsorbing all malfunctions and rebellions. But, very likely, as the techno-industrial system becomes more systematic and more absorbing, so the disorder and the chaos will grow. This can be verified by noting the monstrous increase over the last thirty years in military expenditure, the permanence of the 'hawk' lobby, the development of violence and terrorism, the growth of injustices and inequalities between nations and all the so-called economic and social crises of the present day.

Does all this mean anything? If Man is not attached to any absolute, no meaning can be given to what happens, and perhaps there is not even the means to have any clear idea of what has happened to our humanity. The techno-industrial system asserts that only by means of its own presuppositions can it be understood, and that any desire for reorientation must accept such presuppositions as an unavoidable reality. It is almost impossible to imagine a world without this system and it is equally impossible to imagine the survival of humanity operating according to the logic of the present day.

Perhaps we must again question the nature of Man's will and ask if he is capable by himself of reorienting it according to a 'superior Good'. It is totally against the 'nature' of the modern world to restrict itself and not to use all the power it has at its disposal. We always prefer to respond to human evils caused by the development of technostructures by adding further techniques and making the system more complex.

The myth of Prometheus applies to the whole of modern socio-cultural life. Prometheus is a Titan, an ancient earth god, a holder of force, and an image of Man wholly assured of his power. He steals fire from heaven (the energy which gives life to everything) in order to increase his temporal power infinitely. According to Aeschylus, he was nailed to a rock by Zeus's servants who are none other than Kratos and Bia, violence and coercion. Brute force, domination, violence and need are the most visible characteristics of our techno-industrial and politico-military world. Should the fire not have been stolen from heaven, or once it had been stolen, should it have been returned as a gift to Zeus who would then have told us how to use it? Can Man relearn measure and a sense of limits? But God alone is the measure of Man and He alone can measure him. Hubris can only be cured by love.

9) *Culture, madness and measure*

Culture assures the cohesion of a society by giving it meaning and by opening up the way to collective projects. It is at the same time moderation, the stability of the different parts of society, the quality of ordinary life and the manifestation of the meaning and beauty of the world.

But 'modern life has given in to excess. Madness spreads everywhere, in actions and thoughts, in public and private life.' (Simone Weil). Immoderation is an act of violence which overturns the order of the world and brings punishment. But this is often a *nemesis*, a further madness which takes hold of the arrogant and leads to further disorder. Culture, in that case, is a continuous struggle against the many forces of excess on every front. 'It is more important to extinguish excess than fire.' (Heraclitus).

We have arrived, therefore, at a point where effectively a common culture in which everyone can participate is impossible. The whole techno-industrial system unifies us materially but dissociates and divides us humanly. Culture has become an interstitial residue which escapes the system but only offers up marginal crises of revolt and leisure-time protests. Our pseudo-culture is the product of a commercialised art which is itself no more than an anaesthetic, a narcotic or a safety-valve. We must not let our time become one of cultural darkness.

As I was saying at the beginning, we are in an age when the solid ground of the ideology of progress which sustained us until now, is collapsing. Scientific methods which claimed to offer solutions are themselves becoming problematic and their logic increases the human problems which they maintained they could solve. Modern Man has ceased to let his life revolve around God under the pretext that his God was an illusion and that his life ought to revolve from now on around himself. He suddenly realises that he is spinning giddily over a void which is sucking him in like a giant maelstrom. Nietzsche had proudly declared that God was dead. Some philosophers in our panic-stricken century declare shamefacedly that Man in his turn is dead.

10) *Only we ourselves can save ourselves from drowning*
As with every time that someone indulges in a radical critique of the rationale of our society, 'sensible people' are going to call me a prophet of doom, a gloomy Cassandra who has no confidence in the humanity of today. You know that I do not wish for a return to the past, nor do I wish to disparage reasoned knowledge and the ordered capabilities of Man.

However, no ideology nor any social pressure will prevent me from stating in what I judge to be clear terms the problems of our time, on which you have imprudently questioned me. We are aware of being dragged towards the eye of the storm and, fearing catastrophe, we are tempted to seek refuge from our own shipwreck on a larger and even more powerful vessel. Instead, we should get away from the vessel which is dragging us to the bottom, and stay afloat by ourselves. It is only this response in defiance of defeat which is worthy of the name culture. This response should also be a raising of hands towards heaven, an appeal and a prayer. But who now thinks to call on God for help? Our 'teachers', who do not wish to understand the conversion that such an appeal represents, would say that this was a recourse to 'magic'.

There, my friend, is where my thoughts have led me: to try to bring to light the snare which has made Man the slave of his own creations. 'How has *lack of principle* infiltrated thought and methodical action?'[4] It is when vain hopes founder that hope resumes its radical meaning. To end, let me quote Heraclmeitus once more: "If Man does not hope, he will not find the unhoped-for, for that is unexplorable and inaccessible." However, only something unhoped-for can bring back the life and freedom we have lost.
Translated by Simon Carter.

ENDNOTES

1. The reader could refer here to G. Simondon's masterwork: *Du mode d'existence de l'objet technique.*
2. J. Beaufret, *Dialogue avec Heidegger II*, ed. de Minuit, p. 178.
3. See for example Michel Serres, *Feux et signaux de brumes – Zola*, (Ed. Grasset).
4. Simone Weil, *La pesanteur et la grâce*, p. 176.

ACTON SOCIETY OCCASIONAL PAPERS, SIENA SERIES
(Available from the Acton Society, 9 Poland Street, London W1.
Price £3.00 each.)

1. What Size should Organisations be: a Viewpoint *Professor Peter Abell and Kerry Thomas*

2. Some Reflections on Information Economics *Professor J. Stiglitz* (transcript by Dr. Rosemary Brown)

3. Information and Economic Organisation *Professor J. Stiglitz* (transcript by Dr. Rosemary Brown)

4. Some Relative Efficiency and Comparative Institutional Properties of Markets *Professor David Teece*

5. The Organisation and Diversification of the Modern Business Enterprise *Professor David Teece*

6. The Economic Efficiency and the Internal Structure of the Business Enterprise: Theory and Evidence *Professor David Teece and Henry O. Armour*

7. New Model of the Process of Business Concentration with Special Reference to Public Policy towards Small Firms *Professor Robin Marris*

8. Contract and the Economics of Organisation *Dr. Felix FitzRoy and Professor Dennis C. Mueller*

9. The Economies of Scale in Agriculture *Professor G. Coda Nunziante*

10. Alienation, Freedom and Economic Organisation *Dr. Felix FitzRoy*

11. Information Technology and the Size of Firms *Ronald Stamper*

12. Thoughts on the Present Discontents in Britain: a Review and a Proposal (Original full-length version) *Dr. Krishan Kumar*

13. The Contribution of Small Units of Enterprise to the German Economic Miracle *Willibrord Sauer*

14. Hierarchy and Democratic Authority *Professor Peter Abell*

15. The Concept of Property, An Historical and Conceptual Outline *Iain Hampsher-Monk*

16. Casualties of Ignorance: The Dilemma of Small Businesses in the USA *G. T. Solomon and B. G. Whiting*